10TH EDITION

WASHINGTON REAL ESTATE PRACTICES

KATHRYN HAUPT

MEGAN DORSEY

DAVID JARMAN

JENNIFER GOTANDA

ROCKWELL PUBLISHING COMPANY

Copyright 2019 Rockwell Publishing, Inc.
13218 N.E. 20th
Bellevue, WA 98005
(425)747-7272 / 1-800-221-9347

Tenth Edition

ISBN: 978-1-939259-95-0

PRINTED IN THE UNITED STATES OF AMERICA

TABLE OF CONTENTS

1

REAL ESTATE AGENCY

BEFORE ACTING AS A REAL ESTATE AGENT

- Affiliation with a firm
- Planning and budgeting

REAL ESTATE AGENCY LAW

- Licensee's duties to all parties
- Agent's duties to the principal
- Legal effects of agency relationships

CREATING AGENCY RELATIONSHIPS

TERMINATING AGENCY RELATIONSHIPS

AGENCY DISCLOSURE REQUIREMENTS

- When disclosures must be made
- Acting in accordance with the disclosures
- Licensee acting as a principal

TYPES OF REAL ESTATE AGENCY RELATIONSHIPS

- Seller agency
- Buyer agency
- Dual agency
- Non-agency

INTRODUCTION

You've gotten your first listing, and you're eager to help your client and a buyer close a sale and then collect your commission. But what services can you provide to the buyer without violating your duties to the seller? And what obligations do you have to the buyer even though the seller is your client? Making a mistake along these lines can cause a deal to fall apart, and might even lead to liability for you and your firm.

This chapter begins with a brief look at steps you can take to get your career off the ground. It then covers a licensee's duties under Washington's real estate agency law, the ways in which agency relationships can be formed and ended, agency disclosure requirements, and the different types of agency relationships.

BEFORE ACTING AS A REAL ESTATE AGENT

As you know, before you can act as a real estate agent, you must first be licensed. In Washington, there are two types of individual real estate licenses: broker and managing broker.

- A **broker** is licensed to perform brokerage services on behalf of a real estate firm, under the supervision of the firm's designated broker. No previous real estate experience is needed to get a real estate broker license. Brokers who have been licensed for less than two years are subject to heightened supervision by their firm.

- A **managing broker** is also licensed to perform brokerage services on behalf of a real estate firm under the supervision of the firm's designated broker. In addition, if authorized by the designated broker, a managing broker may supervise other licensees. To become a managing broker, a person generally must have worked as a licensed broker for at least three of the previous five years. (The Director of the Department of Licensing may approve equivalent work experience instead.) The license applicant must also complete additional real estate coursework and pass the managing broker's license examination.

Each real estate firm must also be licensed. Each firm is managed by its **designated broker**, who must have a managing broker's license and is ultimately responsible for all of the firm's activities.

A firm can establish one or more branch offices under the firm's name. Each branch is required to have a branch manager who—under the supervision of the firm's designated broker—will oversee the branch's activities. A branch manager needs a managing broker's license.

AFFILIATION WITH A FIRM

A licensee cannot perform any real estate services until she is affiliated with a real estate firm. When choosing which firm to work for, there are many factors to consider; there's a lot of variety among real estate firms, and it's important for an agent to find a good fit. Agents must decide whether they would thrive in a high-pressure office or do better in a low-key atmosphere.

When comparing firms, here are some of the elements a new agent should examine:

- **Size.** A firm may be a small independent office run as a sole proprietorship, or part of a national franchise that has thousands of agents and hundreds of offices.

- **Specialty.** Some firms work with all types of property and offer both traditional and nontraditional real estate services, including sales, property management, escrow, investment counseling, and mortgage brokerage services. Other firms are very specialized, handling only certain types of properties or certain types of transactions. For example, a particular commercial real estate firm might do nothing but tax-deferred exchanges, or a residential brokerage might focus strictly on subdivision sales.

- **Support services.** Some firms offer training and supervision far beyond the minimum required by law. For example, some firms have mentoring programs or in-house instructors, while others send new licensees to classes that help them get off to a good start. A firm may offer only basic office support, such as telephones, shared workspace, and membership in the local multiple listing service; or it might provide more amenities, including conference rooms, centralized advertising services, and extensive training programs.

- **Commission structure.** Many firms pay their agents with commission splits; for instance, an agent might receive 60% of the firm's share of the commission from a sale. Other firms charge their agents a substantial monthly desk fee, but let them keep 100% of the commissions they earn. Some firms use a combination of a desk fee and commission splits.

EXAMPLE: The Mitchells list their home with ABC Realty through an ABC broker named Sarah. They agree to pay ABC a commission equal to 6% of the sales price if a buyer is found. They eventually accept a $400,000 offer presented by Luis, a broker working for Lakeside Realty. So Sarah is the listing agent with ABC Realty, and Luis is the selling agent with Lakeside Realty. The listing and selling offices are splitting the commission 50/50. ABC pays its agents on a 60/40 commission split. Lakeside Realty charges each of its agents a monthly desk fee, but pays them 90% of the commission on the sales they close. Here's how the commission splits on the sale of the Mitchells' home would be calculated:

$24,000	Total commission paid by the Mitchells
× .50	ABC's percentage of the commission
$12,000	ABC's share of the commission
× .60	Sarah's percentage of ABC's commission share
$7,200	Sarah's share of the commission
$24,000	Total commission paid by the Mitchells
× .50	Lakeside's percentage of the commission
$12,000	Lakeside's share of the commission
× .90	Luis's percentage of Lakeside's commission share
$10,800	Luis's share of the commission

Note that a few firms treat their agents as employees and pay them salaries. However, most real estate agents are independent contractors, not employees. Generally, under IRS rules, a person is an **independent contractor** if she sets her own work hours and is compensated on a commission basis. In contrast, a person who is paid a fixed salary and has a defined work schedule is classified as an employee.

In a real estate firm, licensees are usually independent contractors and non-licensed staff are usually employees. While independent contractors typically aren't eligible for most employee benefits, like health insurance or retirement plans, the state of Washington does require real estate firms to pay workers' compensation insurance for all licensees. (Of course, being an independent contractor doesn't mean that a real estate licensee is his own boss. By law, every real estate broker must work for a firm under the supervision of the designated broker or a branch manager.)

PLANNING AND BUDGETING

New licensees should approach their real estate careers as if they're starting a new business, because that's exactly what they're doing. A licensee who works as an independent contractor, paid on a commission basis, is essentially operating his own business under the umbrella of his real estate firm. Like any new business owner, a licensee should create a business plan, develop and follow a realistic operating budget, set up an accounting system (or hire an accountant), purchase all the necessary business equipment, and put aside enough cash reserves to pay business expenses for at least six months.

Before even thinking about making that first cold call or listing presentation, every new licensee should prepare the following:

- a business plan that addresses both short-term and long-term goals and performance expectations;
- a budget that takes into account cash flow, gross income, business expenses, and personal expenses (mortgage payment, living expenses, health insurance, retirement savings, etc.);
- a plan for building up financial reserves that will see the licensee through economic downturns;
- a list of start-up expenses, such as a computer, a phone, business or accounting software, marketing materials (such as business cards and yard signs), association membership fees, insurance premiums, and professional fees (such as accounting or legal fees).

Licensees should monitor their finances and adjust their budgets as needed. For instance, a lower-than-expected monthly income makes it necessary to reduce expenses and/or find ways to increase revenues.

REAL ESTATE AGENCY LAW

Now let's turn our attention to agency law. Agency law forms the basis for the real estate agent's relationship with her client. An **agent** is a person who has been authorized by a **client** (also called a **principal**) to represent that client in dealings with **third parties**. A client may be a real estate seller, buyer, landlord, or tenant. In transactions where the agent is representing a seller or a landlord, third parties are sometimes called **customers**. A customer may be a buyer or a tenant.

EXAMPLE: Sullivan lists his house with North Realty through Broker Harris, a licensee who works for the firm. Harris shows Sullivan's house to Brown, who makes an offer to purchase the house. Sullivan is the client, or principal, of North Realty and Broker Harris; North Realty and Harris are Sullivan's agents; and Brown is the customer, or third party.

Would it make a difference if Harris were considered the buyer's agent instead of the seller's agent? It would make a great deal of difference, because an agent owes a different set of duties to his principal than he owes to third parties.

Until 1997, real estate agency relationships in Washington were governed by general agency law. Under general agency law, the duties owed by agents to their principals are called **fiduciary** duties. A fiduciary is a person who occupies a position of special trust in relation to another person. Fiduciary duties include the duties of reasonable care and skill, obedience and utmost good faith, accounting, loyalty, and disclosure of material facts.

In 1997, the Real Estate Brokerage Relationships Act went into effect in Washington. In real estate transactions, this law replaced fiduciary duties with statutory duties. These statutory duties are divided into two types: the general duties that a real estate licensee owes to any party, and the agency duties that a real estate licensee owes only to his client (principal).

LICENSEE'S DUTIES TO ALL PARTIES

Traditionally, a real estate agent owed fiduciary duties to his principal, but owed third parties only the duty of honesty and fair dealing. It was not always clear what the duty of honesty and fair dealing required of the agent. In many situations, the duty of honesty and fair dealing owed to a third party appeared to conflict with the agent's duties to his principal.

EXAMPLE: A real estate agent is representing a seller who explained to the agent why he is moving: "I really hate this house. Even though there are a lot of windows, they all face north. It's so dark that I'm depressed all winter. Plus, there's no storage space and the neighbors are really loud."

Now the agent is showing the house to a buyer who has confided to the agent that she suffers from seasonal affective disorder and wants a house with lots of windows and light. Should the agent be loyal to the seller and remain silent, or does his duty of honesty and fair dealing require him to disclose the seller's complaints about the lack of light?

Under Washington's real estate agency law (the Brokerage Relationships Act), the general duty of honesty and fair dealing has been replaced by a statutory list of duties. A real estate licensee owes these duties to any party she renders services to, regardless of which party she is representing. In fact, the licensee owes these duties even if she is not representing any of the parties.

> **EXAMPLE:** Licensee Powell is helping a buyer and a seller complete a real estate transaction. She is not acting as either party's agent in the transaction; instead, she is acting as a facilitator. She has fully disclosed her non-agency status to both parties and is acting in accordance with that disclosure. Even though Powell is not acting as an agent, she still owes several statutory duties to both parties. (We discuss non-agency at the end of this chapter.)

The statutory duties that a real estate licensee owes to any party involved in a transaction are:

- reasonable care and skill,
- honesty and good faith,
- presenting all written communications,
- disclosure of material facts,
- accounting,
- providing a pamphlet on agency law, and
- disclosing any existing agency relationship.

REASONABLE CARE AND SKILL. A real estate licensee is required to use the same degree of care and skill that would be expected of a reasonably competent real estate licensee. If a licensee harms a party because of carelessness or incompetence, he may be held liable for the harm caused by his negligence.

HONESTY AND GOOD FAITH. A licensee must act toward every party with honesty and good faith. Making inaccurate statements or misrepresentations to prospective buyers or sellers breaches this duty. The party to whom the misrepresentation was made could rescind the transaction and/or sue the licensee and her brokerage firm for damages.

PRESENT WRITTEN COMMUNICATIONS. All types of written communications—including all written offers—to or from either party must be presented to the other party in a timely manner. This duty to present all offers continues even after the property is subject to an existing contract or the buyer is already a party to an existing contract.

> **EXAMPLE:** Seller Sanders has just accepted an offer from Buyer Barton. Garcia, a real estate licensee, receives another written offer for the same property from Buyer Bell. Garcia has a duty to present Bell's offer to Sanders, even though Sanders has already accepted Barton's offer.

DISCLOSURE OF MATERIAL FACTS. A licensee must disclose a material fact to a party if:

1. the licensee knows about it, and
2. it is not apparent or readily ascertainable by the party.

Washington's real estate agency law defines a **material fact** as information that has a substantial negative impact on the value of the property, on a party's ability to perform, or on the purpose of the transaction. The law excludes certain types of information from this definition, however. It is not considered material if the property (or a neighboring property) was or may have been the site of a violent crime, a suicide or other death, drug- or gang-related activity, political or religious activity, or any other occurrence that doesn't adversely affect the physical condition of or title to the property.

> **EXAMPLE:** Agent Kipling is showing Buyer Green a home. Green has three children and wants a safe family home to live in. The home Kipling is showing Green was the site of a murder-suicide three years ago. This information is not considered a material fact and need not be disclosed to Green.

However, if (in the example above) Green asked Kipling whether he was aware of any crimes that had occurred on the property, Kipling would have to answer honestly. Regardless of whether the information requested is a material fact, a licensee is obligated to answer questions honestly and in good faith.

Also, criminal activity is considered to be a material fact if it affects the physical condition of the property. For example, an illegal drug lab may leave behind dangerous chemical residues that substantially affect the condition of the property. So if a house has been used as a drug lab, that would have to be disclosed to prospective buyers.

Note that neither a licensee nor a seller has a legal duty to disclose the presence of a sex offender in the neighborhood. Prospective buyers can readily obtain that information on the internet.

In some situations, a licensee may be required to make a disclosure concerning criminal activities because of a particular buyer's circumstances. But this type of disclosure is usually based on the duty of honesty and good faith rather than on the duty to disclose material facts.

> **EXAMPLE:** In the past year, there have been several muggings in the neighborhood where the listed home is located. The victims were all frail, elderly women who were walking alone.
>
> Potential buyers, a married couple with teenage children, tell the real estate agent that they plan on moving the wife's elderly mother into the home's spare bedroom. In this situation, the agent should disclose the muggings in the neighborhood. While it may not be a material fact according to the statutory definition, the licensee's duty of honesty and good faith requires her to disclose this information to these buyers.

In most cases, a material fact requiring disclosure would be a latent defect in the property. A **latent defect** is a problem that a prospective buyer would not discover by ordinary inspection. Common examples of latent defects in real property include cracks in the foundation, plumbing issues, or a leaky roof.

Some states require real estate licensees to physically inspect the property and report their findings to the buyer. In Washington, however, the real estate agency law states that licensees do not have the duty to investigate any matters they have not specifically agreed to investigate. A licensee has no duty to inspect the property, investigate either party's financial position, or independently verify statements made by either party or any reasonable source.

ACCOUNTING. Real estate licensees must be able to account for all funds (or other valuables) entrusted to their care. These are referred to as **trust funds**. Licensees are required to report the status of all trust funds to their clients on a regular basis. They must also avoid mixing, or **commingling**, trust funds with their own business or personal funds.

REAL ESTATE AGENCY LAW PAMPHLET. A licensee must give each party that she renders services to a pamphlet that sets forth the provisions of Washington's real

```
┌─────────────────────────────────────────────────────────────┐
│  FIG. 1.1    REAL ESTATE LICENSEE'S DUTIES                    │
│  ┌──────────────────────────────────────────────────────┐   │
│  │  GENERAL DUTIES OWED TO ANY PARTY (INCLUDING THE       │   │
│  │  PRINCIPAL)                                            │   │
│  │    • REASONABLE CARE AND SKILL                         │   │
│  │    • HONESTY AND GOOD FAITH                            │   │
│  │    • PRESENT ALL WRITTEN COMMUNICATIONS                │   │
│  │    • DISCLOSE MATERIAL FACTS                           │   │
│  │    • ACCOUNTING                                        │   │
│  │    • AGENCY PAMPHLET                                   │   │
│  │    • AGENCY DISCLOSURE                                 │   │
│  │                                                        │   │
│  │  AGENCY DUTIES OWED ONLY TO THE PRINCIPAL              │   │
│  │    • LOYALTY                                           │   │
│  │    • DISCLOSE CONFLICTS OF INTEREST                    │   │
│  │    • CONFIDENTIALITY                                   │   │
│  │    • ADVISE PRINCIPAL TO SEEK EXPERT ADVICE            │   │
│  │    • GOOD FAITH AND CONTINUOUS EFFORT                  │   │
│  └──────────────────────────────────────────────────────┘   │
└─────────────────────────────────────────────────────────────┘
```

estate agency law, the Real Estate Brokerage Relationships Act. A party must receive the agency pamphlet before signing an agency agreement with the licensee, before signing an offer in a transaction handled by the licensee, before consenting to a dual agency, or before waiving any agency rights, whichever comes first.

AGENCY DISCLOSURE. In a real estate transaction handled by a licensee, before a party signs an offer, the licensee must disclose in writing to that party whether the licensee represents the buyer, the seller, both, or neither. Agency disclosure is discussed in more detail later in this chapter.

AGENT'S DUTIES TO THE PRINCIPAL

In addition to the general duties owed to every party, there is a set of duties that licensees owe only to the parties that they represent. If a licensee represents the seller, these agency duties are owed to the seller. If she represents the buyer, they are owed to the buyer. And if she's acting as a dual agent—representing the seller and the buyer in the same transaction—she owes these duties to both of them.

The additional duties that an agent in a real estate transaction owes to the principal are:

- loyalty,
- disclosing conflicts of interest,

- confidentiality,
- advising the principal to seek expert advice, and
- a good faith and continuous effort to fulfill the goals of the agency.

LOYALTY. Real estate licensees must put the interests of their clients above their own interests and above the interests of any other party. Loyalty means that an agent must not make any **secret profits** from the agency. For example, it is a breach of agency duty for a licensee to list a property for less than it is worth, secretly buy it through an intermediary, and then sell it for a profit.

If a licensee is acting as a dual agent, this duty of loyalty is modified. It is not really possible to be loyal to two different principals with opposing interests, so a dual agent simply owes her principals the duty to take no action that is detrimental to either party's interests, such as disclosing one party's negotiating position to the other party.

CONFLICTS OF INTEREST. Any conflicts of interest must be disclosed to the principal. For instance, the seller's agent must inform the seller if there is any relationship between the agent and a prospective buyer. If the buyer is a friend, relative, or business associate of the agent, or a company in which the agent has an interest, there may be a conflict of interest. The principal has the right to have this information when making his decision. This disclosure must be made before the principal decides whether to accept the buyer's offer.

CONFIDENTIALITY. An agent may not disclose any confidential information about the principal, even after the agency relationship terminates. The Brokerage Relationships Act defines **confidential information** as information from or concerning a principal that:

1. was acquired by the licensee during the course of an agency relationship with the principal;
2. the principal reasonably expects to be kept confidential;
3. the principal has not disclosed or authorized to be disclosed to third parties;
4. would, if disclosed, operate to the detriment of the principal; and
5. the principal isn't obligated to disclose to the other party.

Information about latent defects must never be concealed on the grounds that the information is confidential. Because the principal is legally obligated to disclose a latent defect to buyers, such information is by definition not confidential information. Agents should advise their clients that they (the agents) may be legally obligated to disclose certain types of information that the principal may have believed to be confidential.

EXPERT ADVICE. A real estate agent must advise the principal to seek expert advice on any matters relating to the transaction that are beyond the agent's expertise. For instance, if the principal has questions about the property's structural soundness, the agent should advise the principal to contact a home inspector.

GOOD FAITH AND CONTINUOUS EFFORT. A real estate agent has a duty to make a good faith effort to fulfill the terms of the agency agreement. This means an agent representing a seller must make a good faith and continuous effort to find a buyer for the property. An agent representing a buyer must make a good faith and continuous effort to find a suitable property for the buyer to purchase.

There are some limits on this duty. A seller's agent doesn't have to seek additional offers to purchase the property while the property is already subject to a sales contract (although she still must present any additional offers that come in). A buyer's agent doesn't have to seek additional properties for the buyer to purchase while the buyer is a party to a sales contract.

LEGAL EFFECTS OF AGENCY RELATIONSHIPS

An agency relationship has other significant legal implications beyond the issue of agency duties. For a third party, dealing with an agent can be the legal equivalent of dealing with the principal. When an agent who is authorized to do so signs a document or makes a promise, it's as if the principal signed or promised.

Further, under certain circumstances, if an agent does something wrong, the principal may be held liable to third parties for harm resulting from the agent's actions. This is called **vicarious liability**.

Under the Brokerage Relationships Act, however, a seller or a buyer isn't liable for harm caused by his real estate agent. The two exceptions are: 1) when the principal participated in or authorized the act, error, or omission; or 2) when the principal benefited from the act, error, or omission and a court determines that it is highly probable that the agent can't cover the cost of the injured party's losses.

CREATING AGENCY RELATIONSHIPS

Under common law, agency relationships can be formed in one of four ways:

1. **Express agreement.** The principal appoints someone to act as an agent, and the agent accepts the appointment.

2. **Ratification.** The principal gives approval after the fact to acts performed by a person who was without authority to act for the principal.
3. **Estoppel.** It would be unfair to a third party to deny an agent's authority because the principal allowed the third party to believe there was an agency relationship.
4. **Implication.** If one person behaves toward another in a way that implies that she is acting as that person's agent, an agency may be created by implication.

The Brokerage Relationships Act made some changes to how real estate agency relationships are created in Washington. A written listing agreement (express agreement) is still the most common way to create an agency relationship between a firm and a property seller. But the statute has had a major impact on the creation of buyer agency relationships. Now a licensee who performs real estate brokerage services for a buyer automatically becomes the buyer's agent, unless there is a written agreement to the contrary.

EXAMPLE: Brenner, a prospective buyer, walks into Taylor Realty, where she begins talking to Agent Daley. Brenner tells Daley that she is looking for her first home. She tells him her general price range and the kind of house she wants. Daley goes to his computer, enters in some information, and gets a printout of homes that Brenner might be interested in. After making some phone calls, Daley takes Brenner to look at three of the homes.

Under Washington's real estate agency law, Daley (acting for Taylor Realty) is Brenner's agent. This buyer agency relationship was created automatically when Daley began performing brokerage services for Brenner.

Note that a buyer agency relationship is not created automatically if there is a written agreement to the contrary, such as a listing agreement with a seller.

EXAMPLE: Agent Daley is holding an open house for one of his listings. Brenner, a first-time buyer who doesn't have an agent of her own, comes to the open house. As Daley shows Brenner the property, he talks to her about what kind of home she's looking for, the home buying process, and the current market. This doesn't automatically create an agency relationship between Daley and Brenner, because Daley already has a written listing agreement with the seller.

Generally, however, a buyer automatically has an agency relationship with the licensee who's working with her. Because of this rule, most home buyers in Washington are now represented by their own agent.

TERMINATING AGENCY RELATIONSHIPS

An agency relationship may be terminated either by the actions of the parties or through operation of law. Once an agency has been terminated, the agent no longer represents the principal.

TERMINATION BY THE PARTIES

Since agency requires the consent of both the principal and the agent, they can end the agency relationship at any time. This may occur by mutual agreement, revocation, or renunciation.

MUTUAL AGREEMENT. In some cases, the principal and the agent simply agree to end the agency. If the agency was originally established with a written document, it's advisable to formally terminate it in writing, too.

REVOCATION. A principal may revoke an agent's authority at any time. Under some circumstances, however, the revocation may be a breach of contract. In that case, the principal may be liable to the agent for damages resulting from the breach of contract.

> **EXAMPLE:** Davidson decides she distrusts and dislikes the firm she listed her house with, but their exclusive listing won't expire for another two months. Even though Davidson could terminate the listing unilaterally, revoking the firm's authority to represent her, it would be much better if she could get the firm to agree to the termination instead. A unilateral revocation would be a breach of the listing agreement, and the firm could sue Davidson for the commission.

RENUNCIATION. An agent also has the right to terminate the agency relationship unilaterally, without the principal's consent. This is called renouncing the agency. Like revocation, renunciation may be a breach of contract, and the agent could end up owing the principal damages for the breach. But damages are usually not an issue when a real estate agent renounces an agency.

TERMINATION BY OPERATION OF LAW

An agency relationship can terminate by operation of law, without any action on the part of the principal or agent. This can happen as a result of the expiration of the agency, fulfillment of purpose, death or incapacity, or the extinction of the subject matter.

EXPIRATION. If an agency agreement has a termination date, the agent's authority to represent the principal terminates automatically when the expiration date arrives. If there is no termination date, the agency will be deemed to expire within a reasonable time (which would vary, depending on the type of agency in question).

Note that an agency agreement without a termination date can usually be ended by either party without liability for damages; unilateral termination does not represent a breach of the agreement. In some situations, however, the other party could ask for reimbursement of expenses incurred in the course of the agency.

FULFILLMENT OF PURPOSE. An agency relationship terminates automatically (before its expiration date) when its purpose has been fulfilled. A listing agreement, for example, is fulfilled when the sale of the listed property closes. The real estate agent's services are no longer needed.

DEATH OR INCAPACITY. An agency relationship terminates if the principal dies or becomes legally incapacitated (mentally incompetent). As a general rule, the agent's authority to act on behalf of the principal ends at the moment the principal dies or is declared incompetent by a court, even if the agent is not informed of the event until later on.

The death or incapacity of the agent can also terminate an agency, but in Washington that isn't true in the real estate context. A listing or buyer representation agreement is a contract with the real estate firm, not with the individual licensee, so the agency relationship continues even if something happens to that licensee.

EXTINCTION OF SUBJECT MATTER. If the subject matter of an agency is destroyed or otherwise ceases to exist, the agency terminates. For example, the subject matter of a property management agreement is the principal's property. If the principal sells the property, the agent's authority terminates.

AGENCY DISCLOSURE REQUIREMENTS

When there is confusion about agency relationships, it can result in lost commissions, lawsuits, and disciplinary action. The best way to prevent confusion is with proper agency disclosure. Agency disclosure makes it clear to all parties who is representing whom, and it is required by state law.

WHEN DISCLOSURES MUST BE MADE

A licensee must inform the parties in a transaction whether the licensee is representing the seller, the buyer, both parties, or neither party. This disclosure must be made in writing, and it must be made to each party before that party signs a purchase and sale agreement form to make or accept an offer. Generally, licensees make an initial agency disclosure to their client in the agency agreement, and then make another disclosure to both parties in the purchase and sale agreement.

While standard MLS agency and purchase and sale agreement forms contain the required disclosures, sometimes you have to use a nonstandard form. For example, when your sale involves a bank-owned property, the bank's required contract form might not include an agency disclosure provision. In that case, you should use a separate agency disclosure form such as the one shown in Figure 1.2. The disclosure form has a blank where the agent fills in which party or parties (buyer, seller, both, or neither) he is representing, as well as blanks for the signatures of the buyer and the seller.

ACTING IN ACCORDANCE WITH DISCLOSURES

The disclosures mandated by state law are fairly straightforward. However, once the disclosures have been made, the licensee also must act in accordance with those disclosures. This may be more difficult than it sounds.

EXAMPLE: Carville is the listing agent for Sharp's house. Carville discloses this fact, in writing, to Blaine, a potential buyer. But over the course of a few days, Carville begins acting more and more like Blaine's agent. He gives Blaine a lot of advice about making an offer and negotiating the best terms. Blaine begins to rely on Carville's advice, and by the time Blaine is ready to make an offer on Sharp's house, he feels confident that Carville is working in his (Blaine's) best interests.

In this case, even though Carville properly disclosed his status as the seller's agent, his actions may imply an agency relationship with Blaine. This could create what is known as an inadvertent dual agency. In other words, Carville would be unintentionally representing the buyer as well as the seller in this transaction. If Blaine or Sharp later became dissatisfied with the transaction, either of them could accuse Carville of breaching his agency duties.

FIG. 1.2   AGENCY DISCLOSURE FORM

Form 42
Agency Disclosure
Rev. 7/10
Page 1 of 1

©Copyright 2010
Northwest Multiple Listing Service
ALL RIGHTS RESERVED

AGENCY DISCLOSURE

Washington State law requires real estate brokers to disclose to all parties to whom the broker renders real estate brokerage services whether the broker represents the seller (or lessor), the buyer (or lessee), both the seller/lessor and buyer/lessee, or neither.   1 2 3

This form is for use when the transaction forms **do not** otherwise contain an agency disclosure provision.   4

THE UNDERSIGNED BROKER REPRESENTS: _____   5

**THE UNDERSIGNED BUYER / LESSEE OR SELLER / LESSOR ACKNOWLEDGES RECEIPT   6
OF A COPY OF THE PAMPHLET ENTITLED "THE LAW OF REAL ESTATE AGENCY"   7**

_____ DATE _____   8
Signature

_____ DATE _____   9
Signature

_____ DATE _____   10
Signature

_____ DATE _____   11
Signature

BROKER _____   12
Print/Type

BROKER'S SIGNATURE _____   13

FIRM NAME AS LICENSED _____   14
Print/Type

FIRM'S ASSUMED NAME (if applicable) _____   15
Print/Type

If a licensee's conduct is not consistent with his agency disclosure, he may be subject to disciplinary action by the Department of Licensing. Possible DOL sanctions against the licensee include:

- suspension or revocation of his real estate license;
- restriction and/or monitoring of his real estate activities;
- a fine of up to $5,000 per violation;
- probation;
- the required completion of a relevant real estate course; and/or
- censure or reprimand.

LICENSEE ACTING AS A PRINCIPAL

If you are a licensee and are also a principal in a transaction—as either the seller or the buyer—you must disclose that you are a real estate licensee, that you are purchasing or selling the property for your own benefit, and that you intend to make a profit.

When you are a principal in a transaction, you should only represent yourself; do not try to act as an agent for the other party. Have your designated broker or branch manager review any contracts involved before you make or accept an offer. It is also a good idea to recommend that any unrepresented party get representation.

Your brokerage firm may have office policies about buying or selling your own property. If so, you should become familiar with them and follow them.

TYPES OF AGENCY RELATIONSHIPS

Real estate transactions routinely involve more than one real estate agent. Here's a typical example. A prospective buyer contacts or visits a real estate office in the area of the city that he is interested in. A licensee who works for that firm interviews the buyer to find out what kind of a home he wants and can afford, and then starts showing him suitable properties. Nearly all firms belong to a multiple listing service, so the licensee will show the buyer not only homes that are listed directly with her own firm, but also homes that are listed with other MLS members.

When the buyer becomes interested in a particular home, negotiations for the purchase of the home will involve the listing agent as well as the licensee who has been showing properties to this buyer. In addition, other licensees have been showing this home to other buyers, and they also may be submitting offers and negotiating with the listing agent. (Once the seller accepts a buyer's offer, the agent of that buyer is referred to as the selling agent.) To understand the role that each licensee is playing in this situation, you need to understand the different types of agency relationships.

There are four basic types of real estate agency relationships in Washington:

- seller agency,
- buyer agency,
- dual agency, and
- non-agency.

SELLER AGENCY

In a seller agency, the agent represents only the seller.

EXAMPLE: Sterling, a property owner, has listed her home with Jenson, an agent at Bellvale Realty. A buyer, Chang, makes an offer on the home. Sterling accepts the offer. The sale closes, and Sterling pays a commission to Bellvale Realty. Sterling (the seller) is the principal, Jenson is the seller's agent, and Chang (the buyer) is a third party.

Before the Real Estate Brokerage Relationships Act, real estate agents in Washington almost always represented the seller, even when they were helping the buyer. Buyer agency was rare.

EXAMPLE: Suppose Jenson listed Sterling's home, but a licensee working for a different real estate firm found the buyer for Sterling's home. Traditionally, not only Jenson and his firm (Bellvale Realty) but also the other licensee and her firm would have been considered Sterling's agents.

Now, however, a licensee generally represents the seller only if she has entered into a listing agreement with the seller on behalf of her firm. (In a listing agreement, the seller hires an agent to find a buyer who is ready, willing, and able to purchase the property on the seller's terms.)

SELLER'S AGENT'S DUTIES TO SELLER. As we discussed earlier, a real estate agent owes additional duties to his principal, above and beyond the duties that he owes to any party. In general, a seller's agent must use his best efforts to promote the interests of the seller.

SELLER'S AGENT'S DUTIES TO BUYER. A seller's agent must always treat a prospective buyer with honesty and good faith, and must use reasonable care and skill in the transaction. But the seller's agent must not act as if she is representing the buyer. While the agent must fully disclose all the material facts and answer the buyer's questions honestly, the agent should not give the buyer advice, such as suggesting how much to offer for the listed property.

The seller's agent has the duty of confidentiality in regard to the seller; the agent must not disclose any confidential information obtained from the seller. However, the duty of loyalty to the seller requires the seller's agent to pass on to the seller any important information obtained from the buyer.

> **EXAMPLE:** Suppose that as Jenson shows Sterling's house to Buyer Chang, Chang says to Jenson, "I really love this house, but there's no way I'm going to offer full price right off the bat. How about if I offer $15,000 below the listing price?"
>
> Or suppose Chang says, "This house is great! I'm going to offer full price. I declared bankruptcy about a year and a half ago, so I don't know if I'll qualify for a loan. But it's worth a shot, right?"
>
> Or Chang might say to Jenson, "Wow! This house is really underpriced! I'm going to buy it for the full listing price, then turn around and sell it for $40,000 more than the owner is asking!"
>
> In each of these cases, Jenson would be obligated to pass Chang's comments on to the seller. Remember, Jenson must act in the best interests of his client, Sterling.

When a listing agent works closely with a buyer, the buyer may mistakenly assume that the agent is working on his behalf. Such a buyer might freely disclose vital information to the agent, expecting it to be kept confidential, as in the example above. The buyer is likely to feel betrayed when the agent passes this information on to the seller, as the agent is obligated to do. Thus, it is imperative to make sure that the buyer understands that the listing agent is, in fact, the seller's agent. Again, the agent must fully disclose his status as the seller's agent and act in accordance with that disclosure. Otherwise, the situation could give rise to an inadvertent dual agency.

SERVICES TO BUYERS. There are many services that a seller's agent can provide to a buyer, however, without creating a dual agency. In fact, many of these services actually promote the interests of the seller, because they increase the chances of a sale and may help the sales transaction close smoothly. These services include:

- discussing the buyer's housing needs;
- showing the property to the buyer;
- disclosing all pertinent information about the property (including material facts that adversely affect the property's value);
- answering questions about the property and the neighborhood;
- discussing financing alternatives;
- furnishing copies of documents that affect the property (such as CC&Rs and easements);
- explaining the process of presenting the offer, negotiation, and closing the transaction; and
- referring the buyer to other professionals, if necessary.

PRE-EXISTING RELATIONSHIPS. Sometimes the seller's agent has previously represented the buyer. If so, this calls for extra emphasis by the agent on his agency status.

EXAMPLE: Sterling was so pleased with how quickly Jenson found a buyer for her old home, she wants Jenson to help her find a new home. Jenson selects a suitable home that he has listed and shows it to Sterling.

Under the circumstances, it would be easy for Sterling to assume that Jenson is acting as her agent. But unless otherwise agreed, Jenson is the seller's agent, and he should emphasize this fact to Sterling. Jenson should disclose his agency relationship with the seller to Sterling, remind Sterling that he is obligated to tell the seller any material information Sterling reveals to him, and emphasize to Sterling that he will be representing the seller in all negotiations.

An agent's allegiance to the new principal rather than to the old one does have a limit, however. Under the Brokerage Relationships Act, an agent cannot disclose confidential information about a principal even after the termination of the agency relationship.

EXAMPLE: During Jenson's earlier agency relationship with Sterling, he learned that Sterling has a substantial trust fund. As a result, when Jenson shows Sterling one of his own listings, he knows that Sterling can afford to pay full price for it. But this is confidential information that Jenson learned during their agency relationship. Therefore, Jenson cannot reveal it to the seller in the new transaction.

BUYER AGENCY

As explained earlier, under Washington law a real estate licensee generally becomes a buyer's agent just by providing services to the buyer. (The exception is when there's a written agreement to the contrary, such as a non-agency agreement or a listing agreement.) As a result of this rule, the majority of home buyers in Washington are represented by their own agent. This means that they can relax and divulge key information about their housing needs and financial situation, knowing that their agent must keep these matters confidential.

EXPLAINING BUYER AGENCY TO BUYERS. When you disclose your agency status to a buyer you're representing, you can explain the benefits of the relationship by breaking them down into three categories:

- agency duties,
- objective advice, and
- help with negotiations.

AGENCY DUTIES. A buyer's agent owes agency duties to the buyer rather than to the seller. For many buyers, the loyalty and confidentiality owed to them by their agent is the most important benefit of a buyer agency relationship. Because of the duties of loyalty and confidentiality, a buyer's agent must put the buyer's interests ahead of her own interests, and any information the buyer discloses to the agent must be kept confidential.

EXAMPLE: Ashworth is a first-time home buyer. Donnelly is helping him find a home. Donnelly shows Ashworth a condo he is very interested in. Its listing price is $359,000 and Ashworth could afford a place that costs $60,000 more. Donnelly must put Ashworth's interests before her own, so she encourages him to make an offer, even though she would receive a larger commission if he purchased a more expensive property.

Ashworth is eager to buy the condo and suggests making a full price offer. Donnelly suspects he could get the property for about $5,000 less than the listing price, so she advises him to offer $353,900. Even though Donnelly knows Ashworth is willing to pay the full listing price, she is obligated to keep this information confidential. If she had been the seller's agent, she would have been required to disclose this information to the seller.

OBJECTIVE ADVICE. Seller's agents develop expert sales techniques that are designed to convince the buyer to sign on the dotted line. Buyer's agents, on the other hand, are free to advise the buyer on the pros and cons of purchasing any given home.

> **EXAMPLE:** The Whittiers looked very seriously at two homes before they bought a third one. Their agent, Smith, gave them invaluable advice throughout the house-hunting process.
>
> The Whittiers responded to the beautiful grounds and elegant interior of the first home, and they were immediately ready to make a full price offer. At Smith's urging, though, they looked into the property taxes, heating costs, and upkeep and realized immediately that the house would be too costly to maintain.
>
> The second home they were interested in was much more affordable. But Smith, who was very familiar with the neighborhood, knew that the city was planning to change the zoning and allow high-rises on the arterial two blocks away. He pointed out that the taller buildings would increase traffic and noise. The neighborhood's peaceful quality was what had attracted the Whittiers in the first place. They decided against making an offer.
>
> The third home seemed ideal, even after Smith helped them evaluate all the information about it. Smith prepared a competitive market analysis (CMA) for the property and advised the Whittiers to offer $12,000 less than the listing price. Their offer was accepted and the transaction closed without a hitch. If it weren't for Smith's objective advice, they might have ended up with a property that wasn't right for them.

HELP WITH NEGOTIATIONS. While some buyers are happiest when they're dickering over a sales price, many buyers are decidedly uncomfortable negotiating for a home they want. They are afraid to offer full price, because they don't want to pay too much for the home. On the other hand, they are afraid to make an offer that's too low, for fear of offending the seller and ruining any chance of reaching an agreement. A buyer's agent is extremely useful during the negotiation phase. The agent can use her knowledge of the real estate market to help the buyer get the property on the best possible terms.

> **EXAMPLE:** The Browns are first-time buyers. They have decided to make an offer on a starter home, but they are unsure about how much to offer. Their

agent, Cohen, suggests an amount for an opening offer based on a CMA and her experience with sellers in this price range. She also discusses other important terms of the offer, such as the amount of the earnest money deposit, the closing date, and how the parties will divide the closing costs.

BUYER REPRESENTATION AGREEMENTS. As we discussed previously, buyer agency relationships are created automatically under the Brokerage Relationships Act. Even so, a real estate firm may choose to direct its agents to enter into a written agreement with the buyers they represent. A buyer representation agreement describes the rights and duties of both parties, including the agent's duty to search for suitable properties and negotiate the terms of a purchase, and the circumstances in which the buyer will be obligated to pay the agent's compensation.

As an example, a buyer representation agreement form published by the Northwest Multiple Listing Service (NWMLS) is shown in Figure 1.3. The top section of the form establishes that this is a contract between the buyer and the real estate firm. Paragraph 1 explains that the selling broker—the agent working with this buyer—and the managing broker(s) who supervise the selling broker's work with this buyer are the buyer's agents. It goes on to state that none of the firm's other affiliated licensees represent the buyer unless specifically appointed to do so.

In Paragraph 4 in the NWMLS form, the buyer consents to dual agency in connection with properties listed with the selling broker's firm. If the buyer is shown a property listed by another licensee at the firm, any managing brokers who supervise both the listing broker and the selling broker will become dual agents. If the selling broker shows the buyer one of her own listings, the selling broker herself will become a dual agent, along with her supervising broker(s). (For more about this, see the discussion of in-house transactions later in this chapter.)

The provisions in a buyer representation agreement typically establish whether the agreement is exclusive or not, when it will terminate, and in which neighborhoods the agent should look for properties. These agreements also usually include a provision regarding warranties and representations. Generally, the buyer agrees to be responsible for investigating and inspecting the property. The buyer's agent does not make any warranties or representations regarding the value of any property or its suitability for the buyer's purposes. Additionally, most forms provide that the buyer's agent will not assist in a transaction that is a distressed home conveyance unless that is agreed to in writing.

FIG. 1.3   BUYER REPRESENTATION AGREEMENT

Form 41A
Buyer's Agency Agreement
Rev. 7/10
Page 1 of 2

©Copyright 2010
Northwest Multiple Listing Service
ALL RIGHTS RESERVED

BUYER'S AGENCY AGREEMENT

This Buyer's Agency Agreement is made this _____ between 1

_____ ("Real Estate Firm" or "Firm") 2

and _____ ("Buyer"). 3

1. **AGENCY.** Firm appoints _____ ("Selling Broker") 4
    to represent Buyer. This Agreement creates an agency relationship with Selling Broker and any of Firm's brokers 5
    who supervise Selling Broker's performance as Buyer's agent ("Supervising Broker"). No other brokers affiliated 6
    with Firm are agents of Buyer, except to the extent that Firm, in its discretion, appoints other brokers to act on 7
    Buyer's behalf as and when needed. Buyer acknowledges receipt of the pamphlet entitled "The Law of Real 8
    Estate Agency." 9

2. **EXCLUSIVE OR NON-EXCLUSIVE.** This Agreement creates a ☐ sole and exclusive; ☐ non-exclusive (non- 10
    exclusive if not checked) agency relationship. 11

3. **AREA.** Selling Broker will search for real property for Buyer located in the following geographical areas: 12
    _____ 13
    _____ (unlimited if not filled in) ("Area"). 14

4. **FIRM'S LISTINGS/SELLING BROKER'S OWN LISTINGS/DUAL AGENCY.** If Selling Broker locates a property 15
    listed by one of Firm's brokers other than Selling Broker ("Listing Broker"), Buyer consents to any Supervising 16
    Broker, who also supervises Listing Broker, acting as a dual agent. Further, if Selling Broker locates a property 17
    listed by Selling Broker, Buyer consents to Selling Broker and Supervising Broker acting as dual agents. 18

5. **TERM OF AGREEMENT.** This Agreement will expire _____ (120 days from signing if not filled in) or by 19
    prior written notice by either party. Buyer shall be under no obligation to Firm except for those obligations existing 20
    at the time of termination. 21

6. **NO WARRANTIES OR REPRESENTATIONS.** Firm makes no warranties or representations regarding the value 22
    of or the suitability of any property for Buyer's purposes. Buyer agrees to be responsible for making all inspections 23
    and investigations necessary to satisfy Buyer as to the property's suitability and value. 24

7. **INSPECTIONS RECOMMENDED.** Firm recommends that any offer to purchase a property be conditioned on 25
    Buyer's inspection of the property and its improvements. Firm and Selling Broker have no expertise on these 26
    matters and Buyer is solely responsible for interviewing and selecting all inspectors. 27

8. **COMPENSATION.** Buyer shall pay Firm compensation as follows: 28
    _____ 29
    _____ 30
    _____ 31

    a. **Exclusive.** If the parties agree to an exclusive relationship in Paragraph 2 above and if Buyer shall, during the 32
        course of this Agreement, purchase a property located in the Area, then Buyer shall pay to Firm the 33
        compensation provided for herein. If Buyer shall, within six (6) months after the expiration or termination of 34
        this Agreement, purchase a property located in the Area that was first brought to the attention of Buyer by the 35
        efforts or actions of Firm, or through information secured directly or indirectly from or through Firm, then Buyer 36
        shall pay to Firm the compensation provided for herein. 37

    b. **Non-Exclusive.** If the parties agree to non-exclusive relationship in Paragraph 2 above and if Buyer shall, 38
        during the course of or within six (6) months after the expiration or termination of this Agreement, purchase a 39
        property that was first brought to the attention of Buyer by the efforts or actions of Firm, or through information 40
        secured directly or indirectly from or through Firm, then Buyer shall pay to Firm the compensation provided for 41
        herein. 42

BUYER: _____   BUYER: _____

Reprinted courtesy of Northwest Multiple Listing Service. All rights reserved.

Form 41A
Buyer's Agency Agreement
Rev. 7/10
Page 2 of 2

BUYER'S AGENCY AGREEMENT

Continued

    c. MLS. Firm will utilize a multiple listing service ("MLS") to locate properties and MLS rules may require the 43
seller to compensate Firm by apportioning a commission between the Listing Firm and Firm. Firm will disclose 44
any such commission or bonuses offered by the seller prior to preparing any offer. Buyer will be credited with 45
any commission or bonus so payable to Firm. In the event that said commission and any bonus is less than 46
the compensation provided in this Agreement, Buyer will pay the difference to Firm at the time of closing. In 47
the event that said commission and any bonus is equal to or greater than the compensation provided for by 48
this Agreement, no compensation is due to Firm herein. If any of Firm's brokers act as a dual agent, Firm 49
shall receive the listing and selling commission paid by the seller plus any additional compensation Firm may 50
have negotiated with the seller. All such compensation shall be credited toward the fee specified above. 51

9. V.A. TRANSACTIONS. Due to VA regulations, VA financed transactions shall be conditioned upon the full 52
commission being paid by the seller. 53

10. NO DISTRESSED HOME CONVEYANCE. Firm will not represent or assist Buyer in a transaction that is a 54
"Distressed Home Conveyance" as defined by Chapter 61.34 RCW unless otherwise agreed in writing. A 55
"Distressed Home Conveyance" is a transaction where a buyer purchases property from a "Distressed 56
Homeowner" (defined by Chapter 61.34 RCW), allows the Distressed Homeowner to continue to occupy the 57
property, and promises to convey the property back to the Distressed Homeowner or promises the Distressed 58
Homeowner an interest in, or portion of the proceeds from a resale of the property. 59

11. ATTORNEYS' FEES. In the event of suit concerning this Agreement, including claims pursuant to the Washington 60
Consumer Protection Act, the prevailing party is entitled to court costs and a reasonable attorney's fee. The 61
venue of any suit shall be the county in which the property is located. 62

12. OTHER AGREEMENTS (none if not filled in). 63

_____ 64

_____ 65

_____ 66

Buyer has read and approves this Agreement and hereby acknowledges receipt of a copy. 67

_____	_____	_____	68
Buyer	Date	Firm (Company)	
_____	_____	_____	69
Buyer	Date	By: (Selling Broker)	
_____			70
Address			
_____			71
City, State, Zip			
_____			72
Phone	Fax		
_____			73
E-mail Address			

BUYER'S AGENT'S COMPENSATION. Naturally, real estate agents are concerned about how they will be compensated for their time and effort. The way a seller's agent is compensated is well-established: the seller agrees to pay the listing agent a percentage of the sales price when the property is sold. If another firm is involved in effecting the sale, the listing firm and the selling firm will split the commission.

The arrangements for paying a buyer's agent's fee are not so clear-cut. There are three common methods of compensating a buyer's agent:

- a seller-paid fee,
- a buyer-paid fee, and/or
- a retainer.

The buyer and the buyer's agent may agree to one of these methods, or a combination of two or more methods.

SELLER-PAID FEE. Under the terms of most listing agreements, the buyer's agent will be paid by the seller, as a result of a commission split. The seller pays the commission to the listing agent, and the listing agent then splits the commission with the buyer's agent. This arrangement is based on a provision found in most listing agreements that entitles any cooperating agent who procures a buyer to receive the selling agent's portion of the commission, regardless of who that cooperating agent represents. (The source of the commission does not determine the identity of the agent's principal.)

EXAMPLE: Seller Forbes lists his property with Agent Webster. He agrees to pay Webster a commission of 7% of the sales price. The listing agreement includes a clause that entitles any cooperating licensee who procures a buyer to be paid the selling agent's portion of the commission.

Agent Lopez is representing Buyer Brown. Brown offers $400,000 for Forbes's house and Forbes accepts the offer. When the transaction closes, the $28,000 commission paid by Forbes is split between Webster and Lopez. Accepting a share of the commission paid by the seller does not affect Lopez's agency relationship with the buyer.

The commission split arrangement does not change the amount of the commission the seller is obligated to pay, making the arrangement fairly painless for sellers. Most buyer representation agreements provide that the buyer's agent will be paid by a commission split when the buyer purchases a home that is listed through a multiple listing service.

BUYER-PAID FEE. Buyer representation agreements may also provide for a buyer-paid fee. The fee may be based on an hourly rate, an arrangement that turns the agent into a consultant. Alternatively, a buyer's agent may charge a percentage fee, requiring the buyer to pay the agent a percentage of the purchase price of the property as a commission. A third possibility is a flat fee—a specified sum that is payable if the buyer purchases a property found by the agent.

Many buyer representation agreements provide that the buyer's agent will accept a commission split if one is available, but that the buyer will pay the fee if the purchased property was unlisted (for example, if the property was for sale by owner).

RETAINER. Some agents insist on a retainer—a fee paid upfront—before agreeing to a buyer agency relationship. The retainer is usually non-refundable, but will be credited against any hourly fee or commission that the buyer's agent becomes entitled to.

DUAL AGENCY

A dual agency relationship exists when an agent represents both the seller and the buyer in the same transaction. A **dual agent** owes agency duties to both principals. However, because the interests of the buyer and the seller nearly always conflict, it is difficult to represent them both without being disloyal to one or the other.

> **EXAMPLE:** Woodman represents both the buyer and the seller in a real estate transaction. The seller informs Woodman that she is in a big hurry to sell and will accept any reasonable offer. The buyer tells Woodman that he is very interested in the house and is willing to pay the full listing price. Should Woodman tell the buyer about the seller's eagerness to sell? Should Woodman tell the seller about the buyer's willingness to pay full price?

In fact, it is really impossible for a dual agent to fully represent both parties. Thus, instead of the duty of loyalty, Washington law imposes on a dual agent the duty to refrain from acting to the detriment of either party.

Because of this, a dual agent should explain to both of her principals that neither of them will receive full representation. Certain facts must necessarily be withheld from each party; the dual agent cannot divulge confidential information about one party to the other party. For instance, the dual agent will not tell the buyer the seller's bottom line, nor will the dual agent tell the seller how much the buyer is willing to pay.

IN-HOUSE TRANSACTIONS. The context in which a dual agency is most likely to occur is in an in-house transaction. It's called an in-house transaction when the listing agent and the selling agent both work for the same brokerage firm. In this situation, the listing agent represents only the seller and the selling agent represents only the buyer, but their firm's designated broker is a dual agent, representing both parties. Any other managing brokers at the firm who supervise both the listing agent and the selling agent are also dual agents.

> **EXAMPLE:** Werner, who works for Black Realty, has shown Miller several houses. Finally, Werner shows Miller a house listed by Nagano, who also works for Black Realty. Miller decides to make an offer on the house. Werner will continue to represent Miller, and Nagano will continue to represent the seller; but Black Realty's designated broker will be a dual agent, and so will any other managing brokers who supervise both Werner and Nagano.

Note that this kind of dual agency arrangement is sometimes referred to as a **split agency**. It may also be called a **designated**, **assigned**, or **appointed agency**, referring to the fact that one agent in the brokerage is assigned or appointed to represent one party, while another agent with the same firm represents the other party.

CONSENT TO DUAL AGENCY. Before acting as a dual agent, a licensee must obtain the parties' written consent. Listing agreements and buyer representation agreements typically include a consent to dual agency, which applies if the buyer's agent ends up showing a property listed by his brokerage. (The license law requires a dual agent to sign an agency agreement with each party.) Most purchase and sale agreement forms also contain a consent to dual agency.

A dual agency where an individual licensee (as opposed to a firm's designated broker) represents both the buyer and the seller is relatively uncommon. This practice is called "double-ending," since the agent gets both the listing agent's and the selling agent's commission share. While legal, many agents consider the practice ethically questionable (because full agency representation during negotiations is impossible) and recommend that both parties have their own agent.

On the other hand, sometimes parties who share a single agent can benefit. Since one agent is getting the entire commission, the parties may be able to negotiate a lower rate.

NON-AGENCY

Sometimes a buyer and a seller don't want agency representation, they just want a real estate licensee to facilitate their transaction. The Brokerage Relationships Act allows a licensee to assist in a transaction without representing either of the parties. This is called **non-agency**, and it's most common in commercial transactions.

In a non-agency transaction, the licensee involved is usually referred to either as a **facilitator** or as an **intermediary**. The licensee does not owe agency duties to either party, but still owes each of them the general duties that a licensee owes to any party, such as disclosure of material facts, reasonable care and skill, and honesty and good faith. (There is no way for a licensee to avoid those general duties.) The licensee must also provide the parties with the real estate agency law pamphlet. Naturally, the licensee's status as a non-agent and her responsibilities must be fully disclosed to both parties.

There are various forms available that can be used when a licensee wants to act as a non-agent in a transaction. These forms typically spell out the licensee's status as a non-agent and include blanks for filling in the termination date of the relationship and the method of compensation.

CHAPTER SUMMARY

1. Whether or not there is an agency relationship, a real estate licensee owes these general duties to every party to the transaction: reasonable care and skill, honesty and good faith, presenting all written communications, disclosure of material facts, accounting, providing a pamphlet on agency law, and disclosing any agency relationship.

2. When a real estate licensee enters into an agency relationship, he owes his principal not only the general duties owed to any party, but also agency duties. These agency duties are loyalty, disclosure of conflicts of interest, confidentiality, advising the principal to seek expert advice, and a good faith and continuous effort to fulfill the terms of the agency agreement.

3. A seller agency relationship is usually created with a listing agreement. A buyer agency relationship is created by written agreement or by law. Under Washington's real estate agency law, the Real Estate Brokerage Relationships Act, a licensee automatically represents the buyer she is working with, unless there is a written agreement (usually a listing agreement) to the contrary.

4. Washington law requires agents to disclose to all parties which party they represent in the transaction. A disclosure must be made to each party before that party signs an offer to purchase. The disclosure must be in writing, and it may be a separate document or simply a provision that's included in the purchase and sale agreement.

5. A real estate licensee can represent the buyer, the seller, or both parties to a real estate transaction. Alternatively, the licensee may choose to act as a non-agent and represent no one.

CHAPTER QUIZ

1. A house has been the site of gang activity in the past. A buyer asks the agent if any gangs have been known to operate in the neighborhood. The agent says nothing about the gang activity in the house. What duty has the agent breached?

   a. The duty to disclose material facts

   b. The duty of reasonable care and skill

   c. The duty of honesty and good faith

   d. None; the agent acted properly

2. A real estate agent must do which of the following in order to disclose all material facts?

   a. Physically inspect the property

   b. Disclose latent defects the licensee knows about

   c. Investigate the financial position of both parties

   d. Actively search for material facts

3. The duty of accounting does not include which of the following responsibilities?

   a. To disclose the terms of the listing agent's compensation

   b. To be able to account for all funds or valuables entrusted to the brokerage

   c. To avoid commingling trust funds with the firm's business funds

   d. To report to clients on the status of all trust funds regularly

4. A real estate agent is required to give a buyer or a seller a pamphlet on Washington real estate agency law before any of the following events occur, except when the:

   a. buyer or seller waives any agency rights

   b. agent shows the buyer her listed property during an open house

   c. buyer or seller consents to a dual agency

   d. buyer or seller signs an agency agreement

5. In which of the following situations should the agent advise the principal to seek expert advice?

   a. A buyer asks her agent to help her look into properties that aren't listed with the MLS

   b. A buyer asks his agent for advice about whether a house is structurally sound

   c. A seller asks her agent for advice on whether she should accept an offer below the listing price

   d. A seller asks his agent for advice on what improvements to make so his house will sell for a better price

6. Which of the following is a limit on the duty to make a good faith and continuous effort to fulfill the goals of the agency?

    a. The buyer's agent doesn't have to seek additional properties for the buyer when the buyer has made an offer on a property

    b. The seller's agent doesn't have to present an offer if the seller already has a higher offer for the same property

    c. The seller's agent doesn't have to seek additional offers when the property is subject to an existing sales contract

    d. The seller's agent doesn't have to disclose material facts she learns after the sales contract has been signed

7. Whether or not you have an agency relationship with a party to a transaction does not affect:

    a. whether that party may be held liable for your actions

    b. the extent of the duties you owe to that party

    c. whether your actions will be binding on that party

    d. whether you have a duty to investigate the financial condition of the other party

8. Proper agency disclosure may be made:

    a. anywhere in the purchase and sale agreement

    b. in a separate document

    c. in a separate paragraph in the purchase and sale agreement

    d. Both b and c

9. Which of the following is not one of the four basic types of real estate agency relationships in Washington?

    a. Net agency

    b. Non-agency

    c. Dual agency

    d. Buyer agency

10. Which of the following situations involves a change from one type of agency relationship to another?

    a. A non-agent explains to the seller and the buyer that she is acting only as a facilitator in the transaction

    b. The buyer's agent receives the selling agent's share of the commission, even though the commission was paid by the seller

    c. After showing a buyer a number of other houses, the real estate agent shows the buyer one of her own listings

    d. A buyer representation agreement provides that the buyer's agent will accept a commission split if available, but otherwise the buyer will pay a commission

ANSWER KEY

1. c. The agent is not required to disclose the gang activity as a material fact, but by not responding truthfully to a specific question, the agent has breached the duty of honesty and good faith.

2. b. An agent is required to disclose any material facts of which she is aware, but she is not required to independently investigate the parties or the property.

3. a. The duty of accounting requires a licensee to account for all trust funds he holds. The licensee must keep the parties updated as to the status of the trust funds and avoid commingling them with his personal or general business funds. (The listing agent's share of the brokerage commission does not have to be disclosed to the parties.)

4. b. A real estate agent is not required to give a buyer a pamphlet on Washington real estate agency law before simply showing a listed house to a buyer.

5. b. The structural soundness of a house is a question that exceeds the expertise expected of a real estate agent. The agent should advise the client to consult with an expert on the subject.

6. c. The duty to make a good faith and continuous effort to fulfill the goals of the agency does not require the agent to seek additional offers or alternative properties once the client has entered into a purchase and sale agreement.

7. d. An agency relationship with one of the parties to a transaction doesn't create a duty to investigate the other party's financial condition.

8. d. The required agency disclosure may be made in the purchase and sale agreement or in a separate document. If it is incorporated into the purchase and sale agreement, it must be in a separate paragraph.

9. a. The basic types of real estate agency relationships in Washington are seller agency, buyer agency, dual agency, and non-agency.

10. c. The licensee and her firm are representing only the buyer until the licensee shows the buyer one of her own listings. As the listing agent, she's already representing the seller in connection with that property. In this situation, the licensee's firm's status changes: it becomes a dual agent. The licensee usually also becomes a dual agent, unless another licensee from the firm is assigned to represent one of the parties.

CHAPTER

2

LISTING AGREEMENTS

TYPES OF LISTING AGREEMENTS

- Open listings
- Exclusive agency listings
- Exclusive right to sell listings

ELEMENTS OF A LISTING AGREEMENT

- Basic legal requirements
- Provisions of a typical listing agreement form
- Modifying a listing agreement

SELLER DISCLOSURE STATEMENT

- Disclosure requirements
- Timing and effect of disclosure
- When circumstances change
- Limitations on liability under the disclosure law

LISTING VACANT LAND

INTRODUCTION

When you begin your real estate career, your designated broker or branch manager will encourage you to obtain listings as soon as possible. Listing agreements can generate a lot of business activity, both for you and your brokerage firm.

• When a new "For Sale" sign shows up in a neighborhood, potential buyers start calling the office for more information. Even if they are ultimately not interested in that particular property, they may be interested in another listed property.
• When you hold an open house for the listed property, you meet potential buyers and sellers with whom you may be able to do business in the future.
• And when the listed property sells, you get a portion of the commission, no matter who finds the buyer. Plus, a "Sold!" banner across your yard sign is good advertising for both you and your brokerage firm.

Obtaining your first listing is a positive and financially rewarding experience. You will learn a variety of techniques to help you get listings; these methods are thoroughly explained in courses and books on sales techniques. However, using a listing agreement properly and fulfilling the legal obligations imposed on you by that agreement are just as important as obtaining listings.

This chapter describes three different types of listing agreements, the elements of a valid listing agreement, and the provisions that are found in most listing agreement forms. It also discusses the seller disclosure statement form, which you will typically ask the sellers to fill out when you take their listing. The chapter ends with a section on listing vacant land.

TYPES OF LISTING AGREEMENTS

A **listing agreement** is a written employment contract between a property owner and a real estate firm. The owner hires the firm to find a buyer (or a tenant) who is **ready, willing, and able** to buy (or lease) the property on the owner's terms.

There are three different types of listing agreements:

• the open listing,
• the exclusive agency listing, and
• the exclusive right to sell listing.

OPEN LISTING AGREEMENTS

Open listings are rarely used in residential transactions (in fact, many multiple listing services don't allow them), but you still need to understand how they work. Under an open listing, the seller is obligated to pay your brokerage a commission only if you are the **procuring cause** of the sale. The procuring cause is the person who is primarily responsible for bringing about the agreement between the seller and a buyer. To be the procuring cause, you usually must have personally negotiated the offer from the ready, willing, and able buyer. Open listings can lead to disputes between agents as to who was actually the procuring cause, which is one reason that many MLSs prohibit them.

EXCLUSIVE AGENCY LISTING AGREEMENTS

In an exclusive agency listing, the seller agrees to list with only one brokerage, but retains the right to sell the property herself without being obligated to pay the firm a commission. The firm is entitled to a commission if anyone other than the seller finds a buyer for the property, but not if the seller finds the buyer without the help of an agent.

Exclusive agency listings are uncommon in residential transactions because they increase the chance of a commission dispute between the seller and the firm as to who was the procuring cause of the sale.

EXCLUSIVE RIGHT TO SELL LISTING AGREEMENTS

In an exclusive right to sell listing, the seller agrees to list with only one brokerage firm, and that firm is entitled to a commission if the property sells during the listing term, regardless of who finds the buyer. Even if the seller makes the sale directly, without the help of an agent, the brokerage is still entitled to the commission.

Not surprisingly, most firms prefer an exclusive right to sell listing. It gives the listing firm the best chance of getting paid, and the potential for conflict with the seller over who was the procuring cause is eliminated. The licensees involved in the transaction might disagree about who's entitled to the selling agent's share of the commission, but the seller will have to pay the listing firm in any event.

The great majority of residential listing agreements are exclusive right to sell listings.

FIG. 2.1   TYPES OF LISTING AGREEMENTS

OPEN LISTING
- SELLER MAY GIVE OPEN LISTINGS TO SEVERAL BROKERAGE FIRMS
- LISTING FIRM COMPENSATED ONLY IF PROCURING CAUSE

EXCLUSIVE AGENCY LISTING
- SELLER GIVES LISTING TO ONLY ONE BROKERAGE
- LISTING FIRM COMPENSATED IF ANY AGENT FINDS A BUYER
- NO COMPENSATION IF SELLER FINDS A BUYER

EXCLUSIVE RIGHT TO SELL LISTING
- SELLER GIVES LISTING TO ONLY ONE BROKERAGE
- LISTING FIRM COMPENSATED IF ANYONE FINDS A BUYER

ELEMENTS OF A LISTING AGREEMENT

Now that we've discussed the types of listing agreements, we can explore various provisions that are typically found in a listing agreement form. But first, let's start with the three elements that a listing agreement must contain in order to be enforceable.

BASIC LEGAL REQUIREMENTS

Under Washington law, for a brokerage to enforce a listing agreement, the agreement must:

- identify the property to be sold,
- authorize the brokerage to sell the property in exchange for compensation, and
- be in writing and signed by the seller.

IDENTIFY THE PROPERTY. The property must be clearly identified in the agreement. The best practice is to use a legal description. A street address is useful, but not adequate by itself. The listing form shown in Figure 2.2 calls for the property's legal description to be attached as Exhibit A.

AUTHORIZATION TO SELL THE PROPERTY. A listing agreement must give the brokerage the authority to list the property and seek a buyer on the seller's behalf, in exchange for a commission or other compensation. Authority to "sell" doesn't enable the listing agent to sign a purchase and sale agreement on a seller's behalf or otherwise bind a seller to a sale without the seller's approval (unless the seller has given him a power of attorney). It simply enables the agent to market the property and try to find a buyer.

The listing agreement should specify how the brokerage will be compensated. The commission is usually stated as a percentage of the sales price, but it may be a fixed dollar amount instead.

The commission can be based on the seller's net requirements, although this is frowned upon. In a **net listing**, the seller stipulates a certain net amount that she wants from the sale of the property. If the sales price exceeds that net figure, the firm is entitled to keep the excess as its compensation.

> **EXAMPLE:** Warshaw wants you to sell her home. She wants to get $135,000 from the sale. She says you can have anything over that. In other words, if you can sell the property for $140,000, you get a $5,000 commission. If you sell the property for $150,000, you get a $15,000 commission.

Net listings are discouraged because they give unscrupulous agents an opportunity to take advantage of clients who don't know the true value of their property. They are illegal in some states.

The listing agreement should also clearly state the conditions under which the brokerage firm will be entitled to the agreed compensation. For example, the seller could promise to pay the brokerage when a ready, willing, and able buyer has been found (as in the form shown in Figure 2.2). An agreement more heavily favoring the seller might state instead that the commission isn't due until a contract is signed, or unless a sale actually closes.

IN WRITING. Washington's statute of frauds requires all listing agreements to be in writing and signed by the seller. Without a written, signed listing agreement, the firm can't sue for the commission. Note, however, that the writing requirement doesn't mean that you must have a formal listing agreement. Some notes jotted on a piece of paper could be sufficient.

> **EXAMPLE:** George runs into his old friend Brad. Brad wants to put his property up for sale, and he's delighted to discover that George is now a real

estate agent working for Hanson Realty. He'd like to list his property with George right away.

George doesn't have easy access to his brokerage's online form, so he writes the following on a piece of paper: "I will pay Hanson Realty 6% of the selling price if George Stanwick finds a ready, willing, and able buyer for the only piece of property I own—Hillshire Orchards—in Yakima County." George has Brad sign the paper. This would be an enforceable listing agreement in Washington, assuming that Brad is legally competent.

PROVISIONS OF A TYPICAL LISTING AGREEMENT FORM

Now let's take a look at the many provisions found in a typical listing form. In Washington and most other states, there is no single standard listing agreement form. Typically, your multiple listing service or brokerage specifies a listing agreement form for you to use.

The following is a general discussion of provisions likely to be encountered in a typical form, but any given form might omit some of these provisions and include others not discussed here. As an example, an exclusive right to sell listing form published by the Northwest Multiple Listing Service is shown in Figure 2.2.

PROPERTY DESCRIPTION. As we discussed earlier, a listing agreement must include a full and accurate description of the property—preferably a legal description. The software that agents use to complete a listing form can usually acquire the legal description directly from the MLS. If not, the legal description can be obtained from a title company or from the county recorder's website. You should photocopy or print the description on a separate piece of paper and attach it to the listing agreement as Exhibit A.

BROKERAGE AUTHORITY AND LISTING PERIOD. The first lines in a listing agreement form usually identify the brokerage firm, establish the firm's agency authority, and specify the date on which the listing period will expire.

BROKERAGE NAME. Even though the listing agreement form is filled out and signed by an affiliated licensee, the listing agreement is actually a contract between the seller and the brokerage. Remember, only a brokerage may directly provide brokerage services to the public.

AGENCY AUTHORITY. The listing agreement gives the brokerage the authority to "submit offers to purchase." The firm is not given authority to sell the property. It is up to the seller to accept an offer and transfer the property to the buyer.

FIG. 2.2   EXCLUSIVE RIGHT TO SELL LISTING AGREEMENT FORM

Form 1A
Exclusive Sale
Rev. 7/15
Page 1 of 2

EXCLUSIVE SALE AND LISTING AGREEMENT

©Copyright 2015
Northwest Multiple Listing Service
ALL RIGHTS RESERVED

_____ ("Seller") hereby grants to,   1

_____ ("Firm") from date hereof until midnight of   2
Seller   Seller

_____ ("Listing Term"), the exclusive right to sell the real property ("the Property")   3

commonly known as _____, City _____ ,   4

County _____, WA, Zip _____; and legally described on Exhibit A.   5

1. **DEFINITIONS.** For purposes of this Agreement: (a) "MLS" means the Northwest Multiple Listing Service; and (b) "sell"   6
includes a contract to sell; an exchange or contract to exchange; an option to purchase; and/or a lease with option to   7
purchase.   8

2. **AGENCY/DUAL AGENCY.** Seller authorizes Firm to appoint _____   9
as Seller's Listing Broker. This Agreement creates an agency relationship with Listing Broker and any of Firm's brokers   10
who supervise Listing Broker's performance as Seller's agent ("Supervising Broker"). No other brokers affiliated with   11
Firm are agents of Seller, except to the extent that Firm, in its discretion, appoints other brokers to act on Seller's behalf   12
as and when needed. If the Property is sold to a buyer represented by one of Firm's brokers other than Listing Broker   13
("Buyer's Broker"), Seller consents to any Supervising Broker, who also supervises Buyer's Broker, acting as a dual   14
agent. If the Property is sold to a buyer who Listing Broker also represents, Seller consents to Listing Broker and   15
Supervising Broker acting as dual agents. If any of Firm's brokers act as a dual agent, Firm shall be entitled to the entire   16
commission payable under this Agreement plus any additional compensation Firm may have negotiated with the buyer.   17
Seller acknowledges receipt of the pamphlet entitled "The Law of Real Estate Agency."   18

3. **LIST DATE.** Firm shall submit this listing, including the Property information on the attached pages and photographs of   19
the Property (collectively, "Listing Data"), to be published by MLS by 5:00 p.m. on _____ ("List Date"),   20
which date shall not be more than 30 days from the effective date of the Agreement. Seller acknowledges that exposure   21
of the Property to the open market through MLS will increase the likelihood that Seller will receive fair market value for   22
the Property. Accordingly, prior to the List Date, Firm and Seller shall not promote or advertise the Property in any   23
manner whatsoever, including, but not limited to yard or other signs, flyers, websites, e-mails, texts, mailers, magazines,   24
newspapers, open houses, previews, showings, or tours.   25

4. **COMMISSION.** If during the Listing Term (a) Seller sells the Property and the buyer does not terminate the agreement   26
prior to closing; or (b) after reasonable exposure of the Property to the market, Firm procures a buyer who is ready,   27
willing, and able to purchase the Property on the terms in this Agreement, Seller will pay Firm a commission of (fill in   28
one and strike the other) _____% of the sales price, or $ _____ ("Total Commission"). From the   29
Total Commission, Firm will offer a cooperating member of MLS representing a buyer ("Selling Firm") a commission of   30
(fill in one and strike the other) _____% of the sales price, or $ _____. Further, if Seller shall, within   31
six months after the expiration of the Listing Term, sell the Property to any person to whose attention it was brought   32
through the signs, advertising or other action of Firm, or on information secured directly or indirectly from or through   33
Firm, during the Listing Term, Seller will pay Firm the above commission. Provided, that if Seller pays a commission to a   34
member of MLS or a cooperating MLS in conjunction with a sale, the amount of commission payable to Firm shall be   35
reduced by the amount paid to such other member(s). Provided further, that if Seller cancels this Agreement without   36
legal cause, Seller may be liable for damages incurred by Firm as a result of such cancellation, regardless of whether   37
Seller pays a commission to another MLS member. Selling Firm is an intended third party beneficiary of this Agreement.   38

5. **SHORT SALE / NO DISTRESSED HOME CONVEYANCE.** If the proceeds from the sale of the Property are insufficient   39
to cover the Seller's costs at closing, Seller acknowledges that the decision by any beneficiary or mortgagee, or its   40
assignees, to release its interest in the Property, for less than the amount owed, does not automatically relieve Seller of   41
the obligation to pay any debt or costs remaining at closing, including fees such as Firm's commission. Firm will not   42
represent or assist Seller in a transaction that is a "Distressed Home Conveyance" as defined by Chapter 61.34 RCW   43
unless otherwise agreed in writing. A "Distressed Home Conveyance" is a transaction where a buyer purchases   44
property from a "Distressed Homeowner" (defined by Chapter 61.34 RCW), allows the Distressed Homeowner to   45
continue to occupy the property, and promises to convey the property back to the Distressed Homeowner or promises   46
the Distressed Homeowner an interest in, or portion of, the proceeds from a resale of the property.   47

6. **KEYBOX.** Firm is authorized to install a keybox on the Property. Such keybox may be opened by a master key held by   48
members of MLS and their brokers. A master key also may be held by affiliated third parties such as inspectors and   49
appraisers who cannot have access to the Property without Firm's prior approval which will not be given without Firm   50
first making reasonable efforts to obtain Seller's approval.   51

_____   _____   _____   _____
Seller's Initials   Date   Seller's Initials   Date

Form 1A
Exclusive Sale
Rev. 7/15
Page 2 of 2

EXCLUSIVE SALE AND LISTING AGREEMENT
Continued

7. **SELLER'S WARRANTIES AND REPRESENTATIONS.** Seller warrants that Seller has the right to sell the Property on 52
the terms herein and that the Property information on the attached pages to this Agreement is correct. Further, Seller 53
represents that to the best of Seller's knowledge, there are no structures or boundary indicators that either encroach on 54
adjacent property or on the Property. Seller authorizes Firm to provide the information in this Agreement and the 55
attached pages to prospective buyers and to other cooperating members of MLS who do not represent the Seller and, 56
in some instances, may represent the buyer. If Seller provides Firm with any photographs of the Property, Seller 57
warrants that Seller has the necessary rights in the photographs to allow Firm to use them as contemplated by this 58
Agreement. Seller agrees to indemnify and hold Firm and other members of MLS harmless in the event the foregoing 59
warranties and representations are incorrect. 60

8. **CLOSING.** Seller shall furnish and pay for a buyer's policy of title insurance showing marketable title to the Property. 61
Seller shall pay real estate excise tax and one-half of any escrow fees or such portion of escrow fees and any other 62
fees or charges as provided by law in the case of a FHA or VA financed sale. Rent, taxes, interest, reserves, assumed 63
encumbrances, homeowner fees and insurance are to be prorated between Seller and the buyer as of the date of 64
closing. Seller shall prepare and execute a certification (NWMLS Form 22E or equivalent) under the Foreign Investment 65
in Real Property Tax Act ("FIRPTA") at closing. If Seller is a foreign person or entity, and the sale is not otherwise 66
exempt from FIRPTA, Seller acknowledges that a percentage of the amount realized from the sale will be withheld for 67
payment to the Internal Revenue Service. 68

9. **MULTIPLE LISTING SERVICE.** Seller authorizes Firm and MLS to publish the Listing Data and distribute it to other 69
members of MLS and their affiliates and third parties for public display and other purposes. This authorization shall 70
survive the termination of this Agreement. Firm is authorized to report the sale of the Property (including price and all 71
terms) to MLS and to its members, financial institutions, appraisers, and others related to the sale. Firm may refer this 72
listing to any other cooperating multiple listing service at Firm's discretion. Firm shall cooperate with all other members 73
of MLS, or of a multiple listing service to which this listing is referred, in working toward the sale of the Property. 74
Regardless of whether a cooperating MLS member is the agent of the buyer, Seller, neither or both, such member shall 75
be entitled to receive the selling firm's share of the commission. MLS is an intended third party beneficiary of this 76
agreement and will provide the Listing Data to its members and their affiliates and third parties, without verification and 77
without assuming any responsibility with respect to this agreement. 78

10. **PROPERTY CONDITION AND INSURANCE.** Neither Firm, MLS, nor any members of MLS or of any multiple listing 79
service to which this listing is referred shall be responsible for loss, theft, or damage of any nature or kind whatsoever to the 80
Property, any personal property therein, or any personal injury resulting from the condition of the Property, including entry by 81
the master key to the keybox and/or at open houses. Seller is advised to notify Seller's insurance company that the Property is 82
listed for sale and ascertain that the Seller has adequate insurance coverage. If the Property is to be vacant during all or part of 83
the Listing Term, Seller should request that a "vacancy clause" be added to Seller's insurance policy. Seller acknowledges that 84
intercepting or recording conversations of persons in the Property without first obtaining their consent violates RCW 9.73.030. 85

11. **FIRM'S RIGHT TO MARKET THE PROPERTY.** Seller shall not commit any act which materially impairs 86
Firm's ability to market and sell the Property under the terms of this Agreement. In the event of breach of the foregoing, 87
Seller shall pay Firm a commission in the above amount, or at the above rate applied to the listing price herein, 88
whichever is applicable. Unless otherwise agreed in writing, Firm and other members of MLS shall be entitled to show 89
the Property at all reasonable times. Firm need not submit to Seller any offers to lease, rent, execute an option to 90
purchase, or enter into any agreement other than for immediate sale of the Property. 91

12. **SELLER DISCLOSURE STATEMENT.** Unless Seller is exempt under RCW 64.06, Seller shall provide to Firm 92
as soon as reasonably practicable a completed and signed "Seller Disclosure Statement" (Form 17 (Residential), Form 17C 93
(Unimproved Residential), or Form 17 Commercial). Seller agrees to indemnify, defend and hold Firm harmless from and 94
against any and all claims that the information Seller provides on Form 17, Form 17C, or Form 17 Commercial is inaccurate. 95

13. **DAMAGES IN THE EVENT OF BUYER'S BREACH.** In the event Seller retains earnest money as liquidated 96
damages on a buyer's breach, any costs advanced or committed by Firm on Seller's behalf shall be paid therefrom and 97
the balance divided equally between Seller and Firm. 98

14. **ATTORNEYS' FEES.** In the event either party employs an attorney to enforce any terms of this Agreement and 99
is successful, the other party agrees to pay reasonable attorneys' fees. In the event of trial, the successful party shall be 100
entitled to an award of attorneys' fees and expenses; the amount of the attorneys' fees and expenses shall be fixed by 101
the court. The venue of any suit shall be the county in which the Property is located. 102

Are the undersigned the sole owner(s)? ❏ YES ❏ NO   103

_____   _____ 104
Seller's Signature   Date   Real Estate Firm

_____   _____ 105
Seller's Signature   Date   Broker's Signature   Date

EXAMPLE: You take a listing on Sorenson's house. Wilson is very interested in purchasing the house. She makes an offer that meets all of Sorenson's criteria. You do not have the authority to accept this offer; you only have the authority to present the offer to Sorenson. Sorenson can choose whether or not to accept the offer.

Typically, the listing agreement also gives the brokerage firm the authority to accept earnest money deposits from prospective buyers on behalf of the seller.

AGENCY RELATIONSHIPS. The listing form shown in Figure 2.2 allows the designated broker to appoint a particular agent as the listing agent. Both parties agree that the listing agreement creates an agency relationship between the seller, the firm, and the named agent (and only the named agent). There is no agency relationship between the seller and any other affiliated licensees of the brokerage (except to the extent that the firm may appoint another broker to represent the seller as needed). Any licensee working for a cooperating firm who finds a buyer for the property will not be the seller's agent, and may be the buyer's agent.

The form then goes on to describe the circumstances under which a dual agency may arise: when the property is sold to a buyer represented by the same firm and/or the same listing agent. The seller gives her consent to a dual agency under these circumstances. (Dual agency is discussed in Chapter 1.)

LISTING PERIOD. The term of the listing is virtually always included in the agreement. A termination date is especially important in an exclusive listing agreement, since an exclusive listing essentially prevents the seller from hiring other agents. However, unlike many other states, Washington does not require an exclusive listing agreement to include a termination date. In Washington, a listing agreement with no termination date will end after a reasonable time.

Of course, a listing agreement—like any other agency agreement—can end before its termination date for the reasons we discussed in Chapter 1, such as revocation by the client or renunciation by the agent.

LIST DATE. A form should specify that the brokerage that takes the listing will submit information about the property to the multiple listing service within a specified number of days after the listing agreement is signed. (There would be no reason for a brokerage not to do so; publishing information about a property with the MLS is the main way that a brokerage brings a listed property to the attention of agents working for other firms.) The NWMLS version of this provision prohibits promoting the property through newspaper advertising, open houses, or any other method before the information is published by the MLS.

COMMISSION. A listing agreement form usually includes a blank in which to fill in the percentage or amount of the commission. Commissions must be negotiable between the seller and the brokerage firm; it is a violation of antitrust laws for firms to set uniform commission rates. (See Chapter 3 for a discussion of antitrust laws and how they affect real estate licensees.)

A listing agreement should also explain how and when the commission is earned. An exclusive right to sell listing form commonly provides that the listing agent will earn a commission if any of these events occur:

1. during the listing period, the listing agent (or another agent in the MLS) secures a buyer who is ready, willing, and able to buy on the terms specified by the seller in the listing agreement or on other terms acceptable to the seller;
2. during the listing period, the seller sells, exchanges, or enters into a contract to sell or exchange the property; or
3. within a certain period (often six months) after the listing expires, the seller sells the property to anyone who first became aware of it through any advertising or other marketing activities of the listing agent (or other agents in the MLS).

EXTENDER CLAUSE. Number three on the list above is an example of an extender clause (also called a safety clause, protection clause, or carryover clause). Occasionally, behind the listing agent's back, a buyer and a seller agree to postpone entering into a contract until after the listing expires, to save the cost of the brokerage commission. An extender clause makes it clear the commission is still owed in this situation (unless the buyer and seller are willing to wait a long time).

Extender clauses differ from one listing agreement form to another. Sometimes the obligation to pay a commission after the listing has expired is triggered only when the property is sold to a buyer that the agent actually negotiated with during the listing period.

> **EXAMPLE:** You have listed Baker's property. The extender clause in your listing agreement applies only to buyers you've negotiated with.
> One buyer, Abrams, is very interested in Baker's property. You present her offer to Baker and spend a few days trying to negotiate the terms of the

sale. Finally, Abrams decides that she is not willing to raise her final offer by the extra $1,000 that Baker wants, and she walks away from the property. Another buyer, Thornwood, sees your "For Sale" sign posted on the property and calls you on the phone to ask some questions about the property. You have no further contact with Thornwood, who does not sound very interested in the property after all.

Suppose Abrams buys the property after your listing agreement with Baker expires. Since you actually negotiated with Abrams, your extender clause applies and Baker owes you a commission. On the other hand, if Thornwood were to purchase the property during the extension period, Baker would not owe you a commission. Since you never actually negotiated with Thornwood, the extender clause does not apply.

Some extender clauses are more broadly worded and require the seller to pay a commission if the property is sold within the extension period to anyone who learned about it in any way that could be traced to the listing firm or the MLS.

EXAMPLE: Under this type of extender clause, if Thornwood were to buy Baker's property during the extension period, Baker would still owe you a commission. Even though you never actually negotiated with Thornwood, he learned the property was for sale because of your "For Sale" sign and then contacted you to find out more about the property.

Some extender clauses provide safeguards for the seller. For example, you may be required to give the seller a list of all the potential buyers you negotiated with during the listing period. Or the extender clause might state that a commission will not be due if the property is listed with another real estate firm during the extension period. This protects the seller from becoming liable for two commissions. Some extender clauses state that, in these circumstances, if the commission owed to the second listing agent is less than that owed to the first listing agent, the first listing agent is entitled to the excess amount.

EXAMPLE: Your listing agreement with Baker expires and Baker immediately lists the property with a new agent. Your listing agreement specified a 6% commission; the new listing agreement calls for a 5% commission. Shortly afterwards, Abrams (the buyer you negotiated with before your listing expired) purchases the property. Under the extender clause in your listing agreement, Baker owes a 5% commission to the new listing agent, but he also owes you a 1% commission.

SHORT SALES AND DISTRESSED HOME CONVEYANCES. In a short sale, the proceeds from a property's sale aren't enough to repay the debt secured by the property; nevertheless, the lender agrees to accept the sale proceeds and release the borrower from the debt. When a potential short sale is being listed, Washington law requires the listing agent to give the seller a written disclosure explaining that the lender's approval of a short sale won't necessarily relieve the seller of liability for costs owed at closing, including the brokerage commission. This disclosure may be included in the listing form itself.

To help protect the agent from liability under Washington's Distressed Property Conveyances statute (discussed in Chapter 3), the listing agreement may provide that the firm will not represent the seller in a distressed home conveyance unless agreed to in writing.

ACCESS AND KEYBOXES. Listing forms typically give you the right to enter the property at reasonable times, so you can show it to prospective buyers. And since MLS members will be acting as cooperating agents—helping to find a buyer— they need a way to gain access to the property as well. Thus, MLS listing forms usually include a provision authorizing the installation of a keybox on the property and permitting MLS agents to enter and show the home.

It's common to include a disclaimer of liability for any loss of or damage to the seller's property that may occur because of misuse of a keybox. The form will also usually encourage the seller to notify his insurance company that the property is for sale and to make sure that coverage is adequate.

BROKERAGE'S RIGHT TO MARKET PROPERTY. Under the terms of many listing agreement forms, the seller agrees not to interfere with the firm's right to market the property. For example, if the seller leases the property, grants an option on the property, or enters into any other agreement that might interfere with selling the property, she will be liable for the full commission. At the same time, the firm is not obligated to pass along offers to rent the property, requests for an option, or any other proposals that would not result in the immediate sale of the property.

CLOSING COSTS. The listing form is also likely to provide that the seller will pay for the buyer's title insurance policy and certain other closing costs, such as the excise tax and part of the escrow fees. Keep in mind that these provisions in the listing agreement do not create any obligation to potential buyers. These are promises the seller makes to the brokerage, and failure to fulfill them can lead to liability only for the commission, not to any liability toward a buyer.

SELLER'S WARRANTIES. Most listing agreement forms include some warranties by the seller, including those stating that:

- the seller has the right to sell the property on the terms stated in the listing agreement;
- the information about the property included in the listing is accurate; and
- there are no encroachments against the property, and/or the property complies with zoning regulations.

There is usually also a "hold harmless" clause to protect the brokerage. This clause states that the seller takes responsibility for the information given and will indemnify the firm against any losses caused by errors or omissions.

> **EXAMPLE:** You have listed Carr's property. Carr knows that his garage encroaches on the neighboring lot, but he doesn't disclose that to you or to buyers. The Bolts purchase the property, and when they later discover the encroachment, they sue Carr and also you and your firm. Since you relied on the information in the listing agreement and had no reason to doubt it, Carr must pay for any losses you and the firm may suffer because of his omission.

MULTIPLE LISTING SERVICE PROVISION. Most listing agreements include a provision in which the seller authorizes you to submit the listing to your local multiple listing service. It also reminds the seller that the information in the listing is not confidential—it will be circulated among the members of the MLS. In addition, the provision states that the MLS assumes no responsibility for the accuracy of the information.

The MLS provision usually explains the relationship of the MLS members to the seller. Typically, listing agreements state that MLS members are considered "cooperating agents" and may act as the agent of the buyer, as the agent of the seller, or in some other capacity as agreed to by the parties. No matter who the selling agent represents, she will be entitled to the selling office's share of the commission.

DEPOSIT AS DAMAGES. Most purchase and sale agreements provide that if the buyer breaches the contract, the seller can keep the earnest money deposit as liquidated damages. Listing agreements commonly provide that under those circumstances the seller will first use the deposit to reimburse the listing firm for any costs incurred; then the seller and the firm will split the remainder of the deposit, with half going to the firm as compensation for the services rendered.

ATTORNEYS' FEES. Most listing forms provide that if either the brokerage or the seller has to resort to a lawsuit to enforce the contract, the winner's attorneys' fees must be paid by the other party.

LISTING INFORMATION. Listing forms used by multiple listing services include one or more pages for information about the property, such as the listing input sheet shown in Figure 2.3. The purpose of a listing input sheet is to generate detailed information about the property and the listing that will be distributed by the MLS. The form is completed online and submitted to the MLS.

All of the following basic information is typically required on a residential listing input sheet:

- property address,
- location of the property (according to a coded MLS map),
- listing price,
- expiration date of the listing,
- county tax ID number,
- identification of the listing agent,
- selling firm's share of the commission,
- age of the home,
- square footage of the home and the lot,
- architectural style of the home,
- number of bedrooms and bathrooms,
- school district information,
- name of the occupant, and
- name and phone number of the owner.

The rest of the input sheet has spaces to fill in or boxes to check off to describe a wide variety of property features and amenities. There is also a place for information about any existing encumbrances and the annual property taxes.

SIGNATURES. A listing agreement should be signed by both parties: the listing firm and the seller. (The firm can't enforce the agreement unless the seller signs.) When you prepare a listing agreement form, you will sign on behalf of your firm.

FIG. 2.3 LISTING INPUT SHEET

NWMLS Form 1 Rev. 11/18
Copyright 2018
Northwest Multiple Listing Service
All Rights Reserved

RESIDENTIAL Exclusive Listing Agreement (page 1 of 5)
LISTING INPUT SHEET

PROPERTY TYPE 1

ADDRESS   • Indicates Required information   ( ) Indicates Maximum Choice   *Indicates "Yes" By Default   **LISTING #**

• **County**

• **City**

• **ZIP** Code   + 4

• **Area**

• **Community/District**

Direction
❑ N ❑ S ❑ E ❑ W
❑ NE ❑ NW ❑ SE ❑ SW

• **Street # (HSN)**   **Modifier**

• **Street Name**

Suffix
❑ Ave ❑ Blvd ❑ Ct Av ❑ Drive Ct ❑ Lane ❑ Pkwy ❑ Street ❑ St Pl ❑ Way
❑ Ave Ct ❑ Cir ❑ Ct St ❑ Hwy ❑ Loop ❑ Place ❑ St Ct ❑ Terr
❑ Ave Pl ❑ Court ❑ Drive ❑ Junction ❑ Park ❑ Road ❑ St Dr ❑ Trail

Post Direction
❑ N ❑ S ❑ E ❑ W
❑ NE ❑ NW ❑ SE ❑ SW
❑ KPN ❑ KPS

Unit #

LISTING

$

• **Listing Price**   • **Listing Date**   • **Expiration Date**   • **Tax ID#**

• **Preliminary Title Ordered**
❑ Yes ❑ No

• **Offers** (1)
❑ Seller intends to review offers upon receipt
❑ Seller to review offers on Offer Review Date
   (may review/accept sooner)

Offer Review Date
(required if 2nd "Offers" option is selected)

FIRPTA withholding required?
❑ Yes ❑ No

LOCATION

Lot Number

Block

Plat/Subdivision/Building Name

MAP BOOK
❑ Thomas ❑ RR-Mason ❑ RR-Clallam ❑ P-Grant ❑ Yellow Pgs
❑ RR-Kitsap ❑ RR-Thurs ❑ RR-Grays ❑ P-Kittitas ❑ R'A-Clark
❑ RR-Jeff ❑ RR-Lewis ❑ Totem ❑ P-Yakima ❑ Unknown

Map Page   **Top Map** Coord.   **Side Map** Coord.

PROPERTY INFORMATION

• **Prohibit Blogging**   • **Allow Automated Valuation**   • **Show Map Link**   • **Internet Advertising**   • **Show Address to Public**
❑ *Yes ❑ No   ❑ *Yes ❑ No   ❑ *Yes ❑ No   ❑ *Yes ❑ No   ❑ *Yes ❑ No

• **SOC** (Selling Office Com.)   **Selling Office Commission Comments** (40 characters maximum)

Effective Year Built Source
❑ Public Records ❑ See Remarks

• **Year Built**   **Effective Year Built**

• **ASF - Total** (Square Feet)   • **Lot Size** (Square Feet)   • **Lot Size Source**

Virtual Tour URL (Please include http:// or https://)

BROKER INFORMATION

• **LAG** Listing Broker ID#   **Broker Name and Phone**   **Listing Firm** - ID# **Firm Name and Phone**

Co Broker - ID# **Co Broker Name and Phone**   **Co Firm** - ID# **Co Firm Name and Phone**

INITIALS: _____ _____   _____ _____   _____ _____
Seller   Date   Seller   Date   Broker   Date

NWMLS Form 1 Rev. 11/18
Copyright 2018
Northwest Multiple Listing Service
All Rights Reserved

RESIDENTIAL Exclusive Listing Agreement (page 2 of 5)
LISTING INPUT SHEET

PROPERTY TYPE **1**

LISTING INFORMATION

Listing Address: _____   LAG # _____

- **Possession** (3)
  - ❑ Closing
  - ❑ Negotiable
  - ❑ See Remarks
  - ❑ Sub. Tenant's Rights

- **Showing Information** (10)
  - ❑ Appointment
  - ❑ Call Listing Office
  - ❑ Day Sleeper
  - ❑ Gate Code Needed
  - ❑ MLS Keybox
  - ❑ Other Keybox
  - ❑ Owner-Call First
  - ❑ Pet in House
  - ❑ Power Off
  - ❑ Renter-Call First
  - ❑ Security System
  - ❑ See Remarks
  - ❑ Vacant

- **Potential Terms** (10)
  - ❑ Assumable
  - ❑ Cash Out
  - ❑ Conventional
  - ❑ Farm Home Loan
  - ❑ FHA
  - ❑ Lease/Purchase
  - ❑ Owner Financing
  - ❑ Rehab Loan
  - ❑ See Remarks
  - ❑ State Bond
  - ❑ USDA
  - ❑ VA

- **Tax Year** _____
- **Annual Taxes** $_____
- **Senior Exemption** ❑ Yes ❑ No
- **Right of First Refusal** ❑ Yes ❑ No

- **Monthly H.O. Dues** $_____
- **Monthly Rent** $_____
- **Form 17** (1)
  - ❑ Exempt
  - ❑ Not Provided
  - ❑ Provided
- **Common Interest Cmty** (RCW 64.90) ❑ Yes ❑ No

SCHOOL & OWNER INFO.

- **School District** _____
- Elementary School _____
- Junior High/Middle School _____
- Senior High School _____

- **Owner Name** _____
- Owner Name 2 _____
- **Owner's Phone** _____
- **Occupant Type** (Owner/Presale/Tenant/Vacant) _____

- **Phone to Show** _____
- **Owner's City and State** _____
- **Occupant's Name** _____

- **Bank Owned/REO** ❑ Yes ❑ No
- **3rd Party Aprvl Req.** (2)
  - ❑ None
  - ❑ Short Sale
  - ❑ Other - See Remarks
- **Auction** ❑ Yes ❑ No

SITE INFORMATION

- **Lot Dimensions** _____
- Waterfront Footage (Feet) _____
- **Pool** (1)
  - ❑ Above Ground
  - ❑ Community
  - ❑ Indoor
  - ❑ In-Ground
- **Zoning Code** _____

Zoning Jurisdiction (1)
- ❑ City
- ❑ County
- ❑ Unknown

Lot Topog./Veg. (7)
- ❑ Brush
- ❑ Dune
- ❑ Equestrian
- ❑ Fruit Trees
- ❑ Garden Sp.
- ❑ Level
- ❑ Partial Slope
- ❑ Pasture
- ❑ Rolling
- ❑ Sloped
- ❑ Steep Slope
- ❑ Terraces
- ❑ Wooded

View (6)
- ❑ Bay
- ❑ Canal
- ❑ City
- ❑ Golf Course
- ❑ Jetty
- ❑ Lake
- ❑ Mountain
- ❑ Ocean
- ❑ Partial
- ❑ River
- ❑ See Remarks
- ❑ Sound
- ❑ Strait
- ❑ Territorial

Waterfront (5)
- ❑ Bank-High
- ❑ Bank-Low
- ❑ Bank-Medium
- ❑ Bay
- ❑ Bulkhead
- ❑ Canal
- ❑ Creek
- ❑ Jetty
- ❑ Lake
- ❑ No Bank
- ❑ Ocean
- ❑ River
- ❑ Saltwater
- ❑ Sound
- ❑ Strait
- ❑ Tideland Rights

Site Features (14)
- ❑ Arena-Indoor
- ❑ Arena-Outdoor
- ❑ Athletic Court
- ❑ Barn
- ❑ Boat House
- ❑ Cabana/Gazebo
- ❑ Cable TV
- ❑ Deck
- ❑ Dock
- ❑ Dog Run
- ❑ Fenced-Fully
- ❑ Fenced-Partially
- ❑ Gas Available
- ❑ Gated Entry
- ❑ Green House
- ❑ High Speed Internet
- ❑ Hot Tub/Spa
- ❑ Moorage
- ❑ Outbuildings
- ❑ Patio
- ❑ Propane
- ❑ RV Parking
- ❑ Shop
- ❑ Sprinkler System
- ❑ Stable

Lot Details (7)
- ❑ Alley
- ❑ Corner Lot
- ❑ Cul-de-sac
- ❑ Curbs
- ❑ Dead End St.
- ❑ Drought Res Landscape
- ❑ High Voltage Line
- ❑ Open Space
- ❑ Paved Street
- ❑ Secluded
- ❑ Sidewalk
- ❑ Value in Land

INITIALS: _____ Seller _____ Date _____ Seller _____ Date _____ Broker _____ Date

NWMLS Form 1 Rev. 11/18
Copyright 2018
Northwest Multiple Listing Service
All Rights Reserved

RESIDENTIAL Exclusive Listing Agreement (page 3 of 5)
LISTING INPUT SHEET

PROPERTY TYPE **1**

Listing Address: _____ LAG # _____

BUILDING INFORMATION

• Sewer (2)
- ❑ Available
- ❑ None
- ❑ Septic
- ❑ Sewer Connected

Basement (3)
- ❑ Daylight
- ❑ Fully Finished
- ❑ None
- ❑ Partially Finished
- ❑ Roughed In
- ❑ Unfinished

• Parking Type (4)
- ❑ Carport-Attached
- ❑ Carport-Detached
- ❑ Garage-Attached
- ❑ Garage-Detached
- ❑ None
- ❑ Off Street

Aprvd # of Bedrooms (septic) _____

• Total Covered Parking _____

Builder _____

• New Construction
- ❑ Yes ❑ No

New Construction State (1)
- ❑ Completed
- ❑ Presale
- ❑ Under Construction

• Building Information (3)
- ❑ Built on Lot
- ❑ Manufactured Home
- ❑ Detached
- ❑ Modular
- ❑ Planned Unit Dev
- ❑ Attached/Zero Lot Line

• Style Code _____

• Roof (3)
- ❑ Built-up
- ❑ Cedar Shake
- ❑ Composition
- ❑ Flat
- ❑ Green (Living)
- ❑ Metal
- ❑ See Remarks
- ❑ Tile
- ❑ Torch Down

Manufactured Home Serial No. _____

Manufactured Home Model Number _____

• Exterior (4)
- ❑ Brick
- ❑ Cement Planked
- ❑ Cement/Concrete
- ❑ Log
- ❑ Metal/Vinyl
- ❑ See Remarks
- ❑ Stone
- ❑ Stucco
- ❑ Wood
- ❑ Wood Products

Foundation (3)
- ❑ Concrete Block
- ❑ Concrete Ribbon
- ❑ Post & Block
- ❑ Post & Pillar
- ❑ Poured Concrete
- ❑ See Remarks
- ❑ Slab
- ❑ Tie down

Building Condition (1)
- ❑ Average
- ❑ Fair
- ❑ Fixer
- ❑ Good
- ❑ Remodeled
- ❑ Restored
- ❑ Under Construction
- ❑ Very Good

Architecture (1)
- ❑ A-Frame/Dome
- ❑ Cabin
- ❑ Cape Cod
- ❑ Colonial
- ❑ Contemporary
- ❑ Craftsman
- ❑ Modern
- ❑ NW Contemporary
- ❑ See Remarks
- ❑ Spanish/SW
- ❑ Traditional
- ❑ Tudor
- ❑ Victorian

Manufactured Home Manufacturer _____

Accessibility Features (12)
- ❑ Accessible Approach
- ❑ Accessible Entrance
- ❑ Accessible Central Living/Common Area
- ❑ Accessible Bedroom
- ❑ Accessible Bath
- ❑ Accessible Kitchen
- ❑ Accessible Utility
- ❑ Modifications for Hearing/Vision
- ❑ Accessible Elevator or Lift Installed
- ❑ Ceiling Track
- ❑ Smart Technology
- ❑ Other

ACCESSORY DWELLING UNIT INFO.

Accessory Dwelling Unit (1)
- ❑ Attached Dwelling
- ❑ Detached Dwelling

Detached Dwelling
(Finished Square Feet) _____

ADU Bedrooms _____

ADU Baths _____

GREEN BUILDING INFO.

Green Certification (4)
- ❑ Built Green™
- ❑ LEED™
- ❑ Northwest ENERGY STAR®
- ❑ Other - See Remarks

Built Green™ (1)
- ❑ 1 Star
- ❑ 2 Stars
- ❑ 3 Stars
- ❑ 4 Stars
- ❑ 5 Stars

LEED™ (1)
- ❑ Platinum
- ❑ Gold
- ❑ Silver
- ❑ Certified

Northwest ENERGY STAR® (1)
- ❑ NWESH Certified
- ❑ NWESH Presale
- ❑ NWESH Under Construction

Construction Methods (2)
- ❑ Advanced Wall
- ❑ Double Wall
- ❑ Ins. Concrete Form (ICF)
- ❑ Post & Beam
- ❑ Standard Frame
- ❑ Steel & Concrete
- ❑ Strawbale
- ❑ Structural Ins. Panel (SIPs)
- ❑ Tilt-up

EPS Energy Score (0-99,999kWh) _____

HERS Index Score (0-150) _____

INITIALS: _____

Seller _____ Date _____ Seller _____ Date _____ Broker _____ Date _____

NWMLS Form 1 Rev. 11/18
Copyright 2018
Northwest Multiple Listing Service
All Rights Reserved

RESIDENTIAL Exclusive Listing Agreement (page 4 of 5)
LISTING INPUT SHEET

PROPERTY TYPE **1**

Listing Address: _____   **LAG #** _____

INTERIOR FEATURES

(Approximate Square Footage Excluding Garage)

Finished _____   **Unfinished** _____   • **Square Footage Source** _____

Type of Fireplace (1)
- ❑ Both
- ❑ Gas
- ❑ Wood

Lower Fireplaces _____   **Upper Fireplaces** _____   **Main Fireplaces** _____

Leased Equipment _____   **Water Heater Type** _____   **Water Heater Location** _____

• Energy Source (6)
- ❑ Electric
- ❑ Geothermal
- ❑ Ground Source
- ❑ Natural Gas
- ❑ Oil
- ❑ Pellet
- ❑ Propane
- ❑ See Remarks
- ❑ Solar (Unspecified)
- ❑ Solar Hot Water
- ❑ Solar PV
- ❑ Wood

• Heating/Cooling (8)
- ❑ 90%+ High Efficiency
- ❑ Baseboard
- ❑ Central A/C
- ❑ Ductless HP-Mini Split
- ❑ Forced Air
- ❑ Heat Pump
- ❑ HEPA Air Filtration
- ❑ High Efficiency (Unspecified)
- ❑ Hot Water Recirc Pump
- ❑ HRV/ERV System
- ❑ Insert
- ❑ None
- ❑ Other - See Remarks
- ❑ Radiant
- ❑ Radiator
- ❑ Stove/Free Standing
- ❑ Tankless Water Heater
- ❑ Wall

Floor Covering (5)
- ❑ Bamboo/Cork
- ❑ Ceramic Tile
- ❑ Concrete
- ❑ Fir/Softwood
- ❑ Hardwood
- ❑ Laminate
- ❑ Other Renewable
- ❑ See Remarks
- ❑ Slate
- ❑ Vinyl
- ❑ Wall to Wall Carpet

Interior Features (16)
- ❑ 2nd Kitchen
- ❑ 2nd Mstr BR
- ❑ Bath Off Master
- ❑ Built-in Vacuum
- ❑ Ceiling Fan(s)
- ❑ Dbl Pane/Strm Windw
- ❑ Dining Room
- ❑ FP in Mstr BR
- ❑ French Doors
- ❑ High Tech Cabling
- ❑ Hot Tub/Spa
- ❑ Jetted Tub
- ❑ Loft
- ❑ Sauna
- ❑ Security System
- ❑ Skylights
- ❑ Solarium/Atrium
- ❑ Vaulted Ceilings
- ❑ Walk-in Pantry
- ❑ Walk-in Closet
- ❑ Wet Bar
- ❑ Wine Cellar
- ❑ Wired for Generator

Appliances That Stay (10)
- ❑ Dishwasher
- ❑ Double Oven
- ❑ Dryer
- ❑ Garbage Disposal
- ❑ Microwave
- ❑ Range/Oven
- ❑ Refrigerator
- ❑ See Remarks
- ❑ Trash Compactor
- ❑ Washer

UTILITY/COMMUNITY

Community Features (8)
- ❑ Age Restriction
- ❑ Airfield
- ❑ Boat Launch
- ❑ CCRs
- ❑ Clubhouse
- ❑ Community Waterfront / Pvt Beach Access
- ❑ Golf Course
- ❑ Tennis Courts

• Water Source (3)
- ❑ Community
- ❑ Individual Well
- ❑ Lake
- ❑ Private
- ❑ Public
- ❑ See Remarks
- ❑ Shared Well
- ❑ Shares
- ❑ Well Needed

Water Company _____   **Power Company** _____   **Sewer Company** _____

Bus Line Nearby
- ❑ Yes ❑ No   **Bus Route Number** _____

INITIALS: _____ _____ _____
Seller Date Seller Date Broker Date

NWMLS Form 1 Rev. 11/18
Copyright 2018
Northwest Multiple Listing Service
All Rights Reserved

RESIDENTIAL Exclusive Listing Agreement   (page 5 of 5)
LISTING INPUT SHEET

PROPERTY
TYPE **1**

Listing Address: **LAG #**

ROOM LOCATION

• **Level** (1)   U for Upper   M for Main   L for Lower   S for Split   G for Garage

Entry	U M L S	**Kit w/o Eating Space**	U M L	**Extra Fin. Room**	U M L G
Living Room	U M L	**Master Bedroom**	U M L	**Rec Room**	U M L
Dining Room	U M L	**Bonus Room**	U M L	**Family Room**	U M L
Kit with Eating Space	U M L	**Den/Office**	U M L	**Great Room**	U M L

No. of Bedrooms   U_____ M_____ L_____   **Utility Room**   U_____ M_____ L_____ G_____

No. of Full Baths   U____ M____ L____ G____   **Approved Accessory**   U_____ M____ L_____
                                                     Dwelling Unit

No. of ¼ Baths   U____ M____ L____ G____

No. of ½ Baths   U____ M____ L____ G____

REMARKS

Marketing Remarks. CAUTION! The comments you make in the following lines are limited to descriptions of the land and improvements only. These remarks will appear in the client handouts and websites. (500)

_____
_____
_____
_____
_____
_____
_____
_____

Confidential Broker-Only Remarks. Comments in this category are for broker's use only. (250)

_____
_____
_____
_____

• **Driving Directions to Property** (200)

_____
_____
_____
_____

INITIALS: _____ _____ _____ _____ _____ _____
          Seller   Date   Seller   Date   Broker   Date

Write your firm's name (as licensed) on the line labeled "Firm" and sign your own name on the "Broker's signature" line underneath.

If more than one person owns the property, make sure all of them sign the form.

EXAMPLE: You are preparing a listing agreement for property owned by the Mastersons, a married couple. Unless both the husband and the wife sign the listing agreement form, the contract might not be unenforceable.

In some cases, the sellers are unsure of the names of all the owners. For example, this might happen if the property was inherited by several people, or if it is owned by a partnership. If the sellers seem at all uncertain, or if you simply want to double-check the ownership, your options include obtaining a copy of the deed or other title instrument from the seller or online, checking with a title company, or checking the county tax records.

RECEIPT OF COPY. You are required by state law to give a copy of any document you prepare to the parties at the time of signature. So a listing agreement form often includes the seller's acknowledgment of receipt of a copy of the agreement.

MODIFYING A LISTING AGREEMENT

Once a listing agreement (or any contract) has been signed, it can be modified only with the written consent of all of the parties.

EXAMPLE: You and the Mastersons signed a listing agreement. Two days later, all of you decide to change the listing's expiration date. You've agreed that a 90-day listing would be more appropriate than a 60-day listing. So you cross out the old expiration date on the form and write in a new expiration date. To make this change legally effective, you must write your initials and the date beside the change, and both of the Mastersons must do the same.

With simple changes, it's acceptable to modify terms in a listing agreement by crossing out what was filled in and replacing it with new information (as long as both parties initial and date the change, as in the example above). However, it's a better practice to use an amendment form specifically designed for changing the terms of a listing agreement, such as the form shown in Figure 2.4. Of course, the amendment form must also be signed and dated by all parties to the original agreement.

FIG. 2.4   LISTING AMENDMENT FORM

Form 18
Amendment to Exclusive Listing Agreement
Rev. 5/13
Page 1 of 1

©Copyright 2013
Northwest Multiple Listing Service
ALL RIGHTS RESERVED

AMENDMENT TO EXCLUSIVE LISTING AGREEMENT

This amends the Exclusive Listing Agreement ("Agreement") dated _____ , 1

between _____ ("Seller") 2
             Seller   Seller

and, _____ ("Firm") 3

concerning the property, listing no. _____, commonly known as _____ , 4

in the City of _____, County of _____, WA, Zip _____ . 5

SELLER AND FIRM AGREE AS FOLLOWS: 6

☐ **Price Change.** The listing price is changed to $ _____ . 7

☐ **Agreement Extended.** The Agreement is extended until midnight of _____ . 8
    If the Agreement expired prior to the parties' execution of this Amendment, the Agreement (and any prior 9
    Amendments thereto) are incorporated herein by this reference and this Amendment shall constitute a new 10
    Exclusive Listing Agreement. 11

☐ **Other:** 12

    13
    14
    15
    16
    17
    18
    19
    20
    21
    22
    23
    24

ALL OTHER TERMS AND CONDITIONS of the Agreement remain unchanged. 25

_____ _____ 26
Seller's Signature   Date   Real Estate Firm

_____ _____ 27
Seller's Signature   Date   Broker's Signature   Date

SELLER DISCLOSURE STATEMENT

Some listing agreements include a clause that describes the seller's obligation to fill out a seller disclosure statement. Although the seller does not have to give the disclosure statement to the buyer until a purchase and sale agreement has been signed, it's customary to have the seller fill it out and give it to the listing agent as soon as possible.

DISCLOSURE REQUIREMENTS

Washington law requires a real property seller to give the buyer a disclosure statement when a purchase and sale agreement is signed. This requirement applies to all types of real property except agricultural or timber land.

A seller disclosure statement is generally only required in standard sales transactions. For example, it isn't necessary to provide one in a foreclosure sale or when property is being gifted to a family member. And if a sale requires a public offering statement or another type of disclosure statement to comply with the Common Interest Ownership Act or the Timeshare Act, then it isn't necessary to also provide a seller disclosure statement.

The seller disclosure statement is a statutory form, which means that the contents are dictated by statute. There are different versions for unimproved residential property, improved residential property, and commercial property.

In the disclosure statement, the seller is required to share her knowledge about the property, including the condition of any buildings, the availability of utilities, the existence of easements or other encumbrances, and other material information. A copy of the seller disclosure statement form for improved residential property is shown in Figure 2.5.

As a real estate agent, you are not responsible for filling out the disclosure form; the seller is, and you should not do it for the seller. However, you must be familiar with the legal requirements so that you can explain them to the seller.

The disclosure statement form begins with instructions to the seller, along with a notice to the buyer explaining the form and the buyer's legal rights (which we'll discuss shortly). On the version for improved residential property, the part of the form that presents questions about the property is broken down into the following sections:

1. **Title.** This section asks questions about the seller's authority to sell the property; encumbrances that affect the title; easements, rights-of-way,

boundary disputes, encroachments, CC&Rs, or other restrictions that affect use of the property; and any other elements (such as a written maintenance agreement, survey project, or zoning violation) that might affect title or use.

2. **Water.** The seller must disclose the source and condition of the household water supply, any water rights that go along with the property, and the condition of the sprinkler system.

3. **Sewer/on-site sewage system.** The form asks for information about the property's sewer or septic tank system, including what type of sewage disposal system is used. If it's an on-site system, there are questions to answer about its construction and upkeep, such as when the system was last inspected and pumped.

4. **Structural components.** This section of the form asks for information about the various structural components of the property, such as the roof and the foundation. The seller must also answer questions about any additions or remodeling; the settling or sliding of the structures; and various types of inspections, including pest inspections.

5. **Systems and fixtures.** This section lists several types of systems, fixtures, or appliances—such as the electrical system, the plumbing system, the hot water tank, the heating and cooling system, wood-burning appliances, and the security system—and asks if they have any defects. (Note: If the property is new construction that has never been occupied, sections 4 and 5 do not need to be completed.)

6. **Homeowners association/common interests.** Here the seller lists information about the homeowners association (if any), assessments by the homeowners association, and any commonly owned areas.

7. **Environmental.** This section asks about soil or water problems, fill materials, damage caused by natural disasters, flooding, environmental hazards, the presence of shorelines or other critical areas, utility equipment, and radio tower interference with telephone reception.

8. **Lead-based paint.** This section requires disclosures concerning the possible presence of lead-based paint on the property if the house was built before 1978. (The federal lead-based paint disclosure law is discussed in Chapter 7.)

FIG. 2.5   SELLER DISCLOSURE STATEMENT

Form 17 Seller Disclosure Statement Rev. 7/15 Page 1 of 6	**SELLER DISCLOSURE STATEMENT** **IMPROVED PROPERTY**	©Copyright 2015 Northwest Multiple Listing Service ALL RIGHTS RESERVED

SELLER: _____   1
          Seller   Seller

To be used in transfers of improved residential real property, including residential dwellings up to four units, new construction,   2
condominiums not subject to a public offering statement, certain timeshares, and manufactured and mobile homes. See RCW   3
Chapter 64.06 for further information.   4

INSTRUCTIONS TO THE SELLER   5
Please complete the following form. Do not leave any spaces blank. If the question clearly does not apply to the property check   6
"NA." If the answer is "yes" to any asterisked (*) item(s), please explain on attached sheets. Please refer to the line number(s) of   7
the question(s) when you provide your explanation(s). For your protection you must date and initial each page of this disclosure   8
statement and each attachment. Delivery of the disclosure statement must occur not later than five (5) business days, unless   9
otherwise agreed, after mutual acceptance of a written purchase and sale agreement between Buyer and Seller.   10

NOTICE TO THE BUYER   11
THE FOLLOWING DISCLOSURES ARE MADE BY THE SELLER ABOUT THE CONDITION OF THE PROPERTY LOCATED AT   12
_____ , CITY _____ ,   13
STATE _____ , ZIP _____, COUNTY_____ ("THE PROPERTY") OR AS   14
LEGALLY DESCRIBED ON THE ATTACHED EXHIBIT A.   15

SELLER MAKES THE FOLLOWING DISCLOSURES OF EXISTING MATERIAL FACTS OR MATERIAL DEFECTS TO BUYER BASED   16
ON SELLER'S ACTUAL KNOWLEDGE OF THE PROPERTY AT THE TIME SELLER COMPLETES THIS DISCLOSURE   17
STATEMENT. UNLESS YOU AND SELLER OTHERWISE AGREE IN WRITING, YOU HAVE THREE (3) BUSINESS DAYS FROM   18
THE DAY SELLER OR SELLER'S AGENT DELIVERS THIS DISCLOSURE STATEMENT TO YOU TO RESCIND THE AGREEMENT   19
BY DELIVERING A SEPARATELY SIGNED WRITTEN STATEMENT OF RESCISSION TO SELLER OR SELLER'S AGENT. IF THE   20
SELLER DOES NOT GIVE YOU A COMPLETED DISCLOSURE STATEMENT, THEN YOU MAY WAIVE THE RIGHT TO RESCIND   21
PRIOR TO OR AFTER THE TIME YOU ENTER INTO A PURCHASE AND SALE AGREEMENT.   22

THE FOLLOWING ARE DISCLOSURES MADE BY SELLER AND ARE NOT THE REPRESENTATIONS OF ANY REAL ESTATE   23
LICENSEE OR OTHER PARTY. THIS INFORMATION IS FOR DISCLOSURE ONLY AND IS NOT INTENDED TO BE A PART OF   24
ANY WRITTEN AGREEMENT BETWEEN BUYER AND SELLER.   25

FOR A MORE COMPREHENSIVE EXAMINATION OF THE SPECIFIC CONDITION OF THIS PROPERTY YOU ARE ADVISED   26
TO OBTAIN AND PAY FOR THE SERVICES OF QUALIFIED EXPERTS TO INSPECT THE PROPERTY, WHICH MAY INCLUDE,   27
WITHOUT LIMITATION, ARCHITECTS, ENGINEERS, LAND SURVEYORS, PLUMBERS, ELECTRICIANS, ROOFERS,   28
BUILDING INSPECTORS, ON-SITE WASTEWATER TREATMENT INSPECTORS, OR STRUCTURAL PEST INSPECTORS.   29
THE PROSPECTIVE BUYER AND SELLER MAY WISH TO OBTAIN PROFESSIONAL ADVICE OR INSPECTIONS OF THE   30
PROPERTY OR TO PROVIDE APPROPRIATE PROVISIONS IN A CONTRACT BETWEEN THEM WITH RESPECT TO ANY   31
ADVICE, INSPECTION, DEFECTS OR WARRANTIES.   32

SELLER ❑ IS/ ❑ IS NOT OCCUPYING THE PROPERTY.   33

I. SELLER'S DISCLOSURES: 34
*If you answer "Yes" to a question with an asterisk (*), please explain your answer and attach documents, if available and not   35
otherwise publicly recorded. If necessary, use an attached sheet.   36

		YES	NO	DON'T KNOW	N/A	
						37
1. TITLE						38
A.	Do you have legal authority to sell the property? If no, please explain.	❑	❑	❑	❑	39
*B.	Is title to the property subject to any of the following?					40
	(1) First right of refusal	❑	❑	❑	❑	41
	(2) Option	❑	❑	❑	❑	42
	(3) Lease or rental agreement	❑	❑	❑	❑	43
	(4) Life estate?	❑	❑	❑	❑	44
*C.	Are there any encroachments, boundary agreements, or boundary disputes?	❑	❑	❑	❑	45
*D.	Is there a private road or easement agreement for access to the property?	❑	❑	❑	❑	46
*E.	Are there any rights-of-way, easements, or access limitations that may affect the Buyer's use of					47
	the property?	❑	❑	❑	❑	48
*F.	Are there any written agreements for joint maintenance of an easement or right-of-way?..............	❑	❑	❑	❑	49
*G.	Is there any study, survey project, or notice that would adversely affect the property?	❑	❑	❑	❑	50
*H.	Are there any pending or existing assessments against the property?	❑	❑	❑	❑	51

_____   _____   _____   _____
SELLER'S INITIALS   Date   SELLER'S INITIALS   Date

Reprinted courtesy of Northwest Multiple Listing Service. All rights reserved.

Form 17
Seller Disclosure Statement
Rev. 7/15
Page 2 of 6

**SELLER DISCLOSURE STATEMENT
IMPROVED PROPERTY**
(Continued)

	YES	NO	DON'T KNOW	N/A	
					52 53
*I. Are there any zoning violations, nonconforming uses, or any unusual restrictions on the property that would affect future construction or remodeling?	❑	❑	❑	❑	54 55
*J. Is there a boundary survey for the property?	❑	❑	❑	❑	56
*K. Are there any covenants, conditions, or restrictions recorded against the property?	❑	❑	❑	❑	57

PLEASE NOTE: Covenants, conditions, and restrictions which purport to forbid or restrict the conveyance, encumbrance, occupancy, or lease of real property to individuals based on race, creed, color, sex, national origin, familial status, or disability are void, unenforceable, and illegal. RCW 49.60.224. — 58 59 60 61

2. WATER — 62

A. Household Water — 63

(1) The source of water for the property is: ❑ Private or publicly owned water system — 64
❑ Private well serving only the subject property *❑ Other water system — 65

	YES	NO	DON'T KNOW	N/A	
*If shared, are there any written agreements?	❑	❑	❑	❑	66
*(2) Is there an easement (recorded or unrecorded) for access to and/or maintenance of the water source?	❑	❑	❑	❑	67 68
*(3) Are there any problems or repairs needed?	❑	❑	❑	❑	69
(4) During your ownership, has the source provided an adequate year-round supply of potable water?	❑	❑	❑	❑	70
If no, please explain: _____					71
*(5) Are there any water treatment systems for the property?	❑	❑	❑	❑	72
If yes, are they: ❑ Leased ❑ Owned					73
*(6) Are there any water rights for the property associated with its domestic water supply, such as a water right permit, certificate, or claim?	❑	❑	❑	❑	74 75
(a) If yes, has the water right permit, certificate, or claim been assigned, transferred, or changed?	❑	❑	❑	❑	76
*(b) If yes, has all or any portion of the water right not been used for five or more successive years?	❑	❑	❑	❑	77
*(7) Are there any defects in the operation of the water system (e.g. pipes, tank, pump, etc.)?	❑	❑	❑	❑	78

B. Irrigation Water — 79

	YES	NO	DON'T KNOW	N/A	
(1) Are there any irrigation water rights for the property, such as a water right permit, certificate, or claim?	❑	❑	❑	❑	80 81
*(a) If yes, has all or any portion of the water right not been used for five or more successive years?	❑	❑	❑	❑	82 83
*(b) If so, is the certificate available? (If yes, please attach a copy.)	❑	❑	❑	❑	84
*(c) If so, has the water right permit, certificate, or claim been assigned, transferred, or changed?	❑	❑	❑	❑	85
*(2) Does the property receive irrigation water from a ditch company, irrigation district, or other entity?	❑	❑	❑	❑	86
If so, please identify the entity that supplies water to the property:					87 88

C. Outdoor Sprinkler System — 89

	YES	NO	DON'T KNOW	N/A	
(1) Is there an outdoor sprinkler system for the property?	❑	❑	❑	❑	90
*(2) If yes, are there any defects in the system?	❑	❑	❑	❑	91
*(3) If yes, is the sprinkler system connected to irrigation water?	❑	❑	❑	❑	92

3. SEWER/ON-SITE SEWAGE SYSTEM — 93

A. The property is served by: — 94
❑ Public sewer system ❑ On-site sewage system (including pipes, tanks, drainfields, and all other component parts) — 95
❑ Other disposal system — 96
Please describe:_____ — 97

_____ SELLER'S INITIALS ____ Date _____ SELLER'S INITIALS ____ Date

**SELLER DISCLOSURE STATEMENT
IMPROVED PROPERTY**

(Continued)

	YES	NO	DON'T KNOW	N/A	
B. If public sewer system service is available to the property, is the house connected to					98
					99
the sewer main?	❑	❑	❑	❑	100
If no, please explain: _____					101
*C. Is the property subject to any sewage system fees or charges in addition to those covered					102
in your regularly billed sewer or on-site sewage system maintenance service?..............	❑	❑	❑	❑	103
D. If the property is connected to an on-site sewage system:					104
*(1) Was a permit issued for its construction, and was it approved by the local health					105
department or district following its construction?	❑	❑	❑	❑	106
(2) When was it last pumped? _____					107
*(3) Are there any defects in the operation of the on-site sewage system?	❑	❑	❑	❑	108
(4) When was it last inspected? _____			❑	❑	109
By whom: _____					110
(5) For how many bedrooms was the on-site sewage system approved? _____ bedrooms			❑	❑	111
E. Are all plumbing fixtures, including laundry drain, connected to the sewer/on-site					112
sewage system?	❑	❑	❑	❑	113
If no, please explain: _____					114
*F. Have there been any changes or repairs to the on-site sewage system?	❑	❑	❑	❑	115
G. Is the on-site sewage system, including the drainfield, located entirely within the					116
boundaries of the property?	❑	❑	❑	❑	117
If no, please explain: _____					118
*H. Does the on-site sewage system require monitoring and maintenance services more frequently					119
than once a year?	❑	❑	❑	❑	120

NOTICE: IF THIS RESIDENTIAL REAL PROPERTY DISCLOSURE IS BEING COMPLETED FOR NEW CONSTRUCTION 121
WHICH HAS NEVER BEEN OCCUPIED, SELLER IS NOT REQUIRED TO COMPLETE THE QUESTIONS LISTED IN ITEM 4 122
(STRUCTURAL) OR ITEM 5 (SYSTEMS AND FIXTURES). 123

4. STRUCTURAL 124

	YES	NO	DON'T KNOW	N/A	
*A. Has the roof leaked within the last 5 years?	❑	❑	❑	❑	125
*B. Has the basement flooded or leaked?	❑	❑	❑	❑	126
*C. Have there been any conversions, additions or remodeling?	❑	❑	❑	❑	127
*(1) If yes, were all building permits obtained?	❑	❑	❑	❑	128
*(2) If yes, were all final inspections obtained?	❑	❑	❑	❑	129
D. Do you know the age of the house?	❑	❑	❑	❑	130
If yes, year of original construction: _____					131
*E. Has there been any settling, slippage, or sliding of the property or its improvements?	❑	❑	❑	❑	132
*F. Are there any defects with the following: (If yes, please check applicable items and explain)	❑	❑	❑	❑	133

❑ Foundations	❑ Decks	❑ Exterior Walls		134
❑ Chimneys	❑ Interior Walls	❑ Fire Alarms		135
❑ Doors	❑ Windows	❑ Patio		136
❑ Ceilings	❑ Slab Floors	❑ Driveways		137
❑ Pools	❑ Hot Tub	❑ Sauna		138
❑ Sidewalks	❑ Outbuildings	❑ Fireplaces		139
❑ Garage Floors	❑ Walkways	❑ Siding		140
❑ Wood Stoves	❑ Elevators	❑ Incline Elevators		141
❑ Stairway Chair Lifts	❑ Wheelchair Lifts	❑ Other _____		

	YES	NO	DON'T KNOW	N/A	
*G. Was a structural pest or "whole house" inspection done?	❑	❑	❑	❑	142
If yes, when and by whom was the inspection completed?					143
_____					144
H. During your ownership, has the property had any wood destroying organism or pest infestation?.........	❑	❑	❑	❑	145
I. Is the attic insulated?...	❑	❑	❑	❑	146
J. Is the basement insulated?	❑	❑	❑	❑	147

_____   _____
SELLER'S INITIALS   Date   SELLER'S INITIALS   Date

Form 17
Seller Disclosure Statement
Rev. 7/15
Page 4 of 6

**SELLER DISCLOSURE STATEMENT
IMPROVED PROPERTY**
(Continued)

©Copyright 2015
Northwest Multiple Listing Service
ALL RIGHTS RESERVED

	YES	NO	DON'T KNOW	N/A	
					148
					149

5. SYSTEMS AND FIXTURES

*A. If any of the following systems or fixtures are included with the transfer, are there any defects? — 150

If yes, please explain: _____ — 151

	YES	NO	DON'T KNOW	N/A	
Electrical system, including wiring, switches, outlets, and service	❑	❑	❑	❑	152
Plumbing system, including pipes, faucets, fixtures, and toilets	❑	❑	❑	❑	153
Hot water tank	❑	❑	❑	❑	154
Garbage disposal	❑	❑	❑	❑	155
Appliances	❑	❑	❑	❑	156
Sump pump	❑	❑	❑	❑	157
Heating and cooling systems	❑	❑	❑	❑	158
Security system: ❑ Owned ❑ Leased	❑	❑	❑	❑	159
Other _____	❑	❑	❑	❑	160

*B. If any of the following fixtures or property is included with the transfer, are they leased? — 101
(If yes, please attach copy of lease.) — 162

	YES	NO	DON'T KNOW	N/A	
Security System: _____	❑	❑	❑	❑	163
Tanks (type): _____	❑	❑	❑	❑	164
Satellite dish: _____	❑	❑	❑	❑	165
Other: _____	❑	❑	❑	❑	166

*C. Are any of the following kinds of wood burning appliances present at the property? — 167

	YES	NO	DON'T KNOW	N/A	
(1) Woodstove?	❑	❑	❑	❑	168
(2) Fireplace insert?	❑	❑	❑	❑	169
(3) Pellet stove?	❑	❑	❑	❑	170
(4) Fireplace?	❑	❑	❑	❑	171

If yes, are all of the (1) woodstoves or (2) fireplace inserts certified by the U.S. Environmental Protection Agency as clean burning appliances to improve air quality and public health? ❑ ❑ ❑ ❑ — 172 / 173

D. Is the property located within a city, county, or district or within a department of natural resources fire protection zone that provides fire protection services? ❑ ❑ — 174 / 175

E. Is the property equipped with carbon monoxide alarms? (Note: Pursuant to RCW 19.27.530, Seller must equip the residence with carbon monoxide alarms as required by the state building code.) ❑ ❑ ❑ ❑ — 176 / 177

F. Is the property equipped with smoke alarms? ❑ ❑ ❑ ❑ — 178

6. HOMEOWNERS' ASSOCIATION/COMMON INTERESTS — 179

A. Is there a Homeowners' Association? ❑ ❑ ❑ ❑ — 180
Name of Association and contact information for an officer, director, employee, or other authorized agent, if any, who may provide the association's financial statements, minutes, bylaws, fining policy, and other information that is not publicly available: _____ — 181 / 182 / 183

B. Are there regular periodic assessments? ❑ ❑ ❑ ❑ — 184
$ _____ per ❑ month ❑ year — 185
❑ Other: _____ — 186

*C. Are there any pending special assessments? ❑ ❑ ❑ ❑ — 187

*D. Are there any shared "common areas" or any joint maintenance agreements (facilities such as walls, fences, landscaping, pools, tennis courts, walkways, or other areas co-owned in undivided interest with others)? ❑ ❑ ❑ ❑ — 188 / 189 / 190

7. ENVIRONMENTAL — 191

*A. Have there been any flooding, standing water, or drainage problems on the property that affect the property or access to the property? ❑ ❑ ❑ ❑ — 192 / 193

*B. Does any part of the property contain fill dirt, waste, or other fill material? ❑ ❑ ❑ ❑ — 194

*C. Is there any material damage to the property from fire, wind, floods, beach movements, earthquake, expansive soils, or landslides? ❑ ❑ ❑ ❑ — 195 / 196

D. Are there any shorelines, wetlands, floodplains, or critical areas on the property? ❑ ❑ ❑ ❑ — 197

*E. Are there any substances, materials, or products in or on the property that may be environmental concerns, such as asbestos, formaldehyde, radon gas, lead-based paint, fuel or chemical storage tanks, or contaminated soil or water? ❑ ❑ ❑ ❑ — 198 / 199 / 200

*F. Has the property been used for commercial or industrial purposes? ❑ ❑ ❑ ❑ — 201

SELLER'S INITIALS _____ Date _____   SELLER'S INITIALS _____ Date _____

Form 17
Seller Disclosure Statement
Rev. 7/15
Page 5 of 6

SELLER DISCLOSURE STATEMENT
IMPROVED PROPERTY
(Continued)

	YES	NO	DON'T KNOW	N/A	
					202
					203
*G. Is there any soil or groundwater contamination?	❏	❏	❏	❏	204
*H. Are there transmission poles or other electrical utility equipment installed, maintained, or					205
buried on the property that do not provide utility service to the structures on the property?	❏	❏	❏	❏	206
*I. Has the property been used as a legal or illegal dumping site?	❏	❏	❏	❏	207
*J. Has the property been used as an illegal drug manufacturing site?	❏	❏	❏	❏	208
*K. Are there any radio towers in the area that cause interference with cellular telephone reception?	❏	❏	❏	❏	209

8. **LEAD BASED PAINT** (Applicable if the house was built before 1978).   210

   A. Presence of lead-based paint and/or lead-based paint hazards (check one below):   211

    ❏ Known lead-based paint and/or lead-based paint hazards are present in the housing   212
    (explain). _____   213

    ❏ Seller has no knowledge of lead-based paint and/or lead-based paint hazards in the housing.   214

   B. Records and reports available to the Seller (check one below):   215

    ❏ Seller has provided the purchaser with all available records and reports pertaining to   216
    lead-based paint and/or lead-based paint hazards in the housing (list documents below).   217

    _____   218

    ❏ Seller has no reports or records pertaining to lead-based paint and/or lead-based paint hazards in the housing.   219

9. **MANUFACTURED AND MOBILE HOMES**   220

   If the property includes a manufactured or mobile home,   221

*A. Did you make any alterations to the home?	❏	❏	❏	❏	222
If yes, please describe the alterations: _____					223
*B. Did any previous owner make any alterations to the home?	❏	❏	❏	❏	224
*C. If alterations were made, were permits or variances for these alterations obtained?	❏	❏	❏	❏	225

10. **FULL DISCLOSURE BY SELLERS**   226

   A. Other conditions or defects: 227
    *Are there any other existing material defects affecting the property that a prospective   228

buyer should know about?	❏	❏	❏	❏	229

   B. Verification   230
    The foregoing answers and attached explanations (if any) are complete and correct to the best of Seller's knowledge and   231
    Seller has received a copy hereof. Seller agrees to defend, indemnify and hold real estate licensees harmless from and   232
    against any and all claims that the above information is inaccurate. Seller authorizes real estate licensees, if any, to deliver a   233
    copy of this disclosure statement to other real estate licensees and all prospective buyers of the property.   234

235

_____   _____   236
Seller   Date   Seller   Date

If the answer is "Yes" to any asterisked (*) items, please explain below (use additional sheets if necessary). Please refer to the line   237
number(s) of the question(s).   238

239
240
241
242
243
244
245
246
247
248
249
250
251

Form 17
Seller Disclosure Statement
Rev. 7/15
Page 6 of 6

SELLER DISCLOSURE STATEMENT
IMPROVED PROPERTY
(Continued)

II. NOTICES TO THE BUYER   252

1. SEX OFFENDER REGISTRATION   253

INFORMATION REGARDING REGISTERED SEX OFFENDERS MAY BE OBTAINED FROM LOCAL LAW ENFORCEMENT   254
AGENCIES. THIS NOTICE IS INTENDED ONLY TO INFORM YOU OF WHERE TO OBTAIN THIS INFORMATION AND IS NOT   255
AN INDICATION OF THE PRESENCE OF REGISTERED SEX OFFENDERS.   256

2. PROXIMITY TO FARMING   257

THIS NOTICE IS TO INFORM YOU THAT THE REAL PROPERTY YOU ARE CONSIDERING FOR PURCHASE MAY LIE IN   258
CLOSE PROXIMITY TO A FARM. THE OPERATION OF A FARM INVOLVES USUAL AND CUSTOMARY AGRICULTURAL   259
PRACTICES, WHICH ARE PROTECTED UNDER RCW 7.48.305, THE WASHINGTON RIGHT TO FARM ACT.   260

III. BUYER'S ACKNOWLEDGEMENT   261

1. BUYER HEREBY ACKNOWLEDGES THAT: 262

A.   Buyer has a duty to pay diligent attention to any material defects that are known to Buyer or can be known to Buyer by   263
utilizing diligent attention and observation.   264

B.   The disclosures set forth in this statement and in any amendments to this statement are made only by the Seller and   265
not by any real estate licensee or other party.   266

C.   Buyer acknowledges that, pursuant to RCW 64.06.050(2), real estate licensees are not liable for inaccurate information   267
provided by Seller, except to the extent that real estate licensees know of such inaccurate information.   268

D.   This information is for disclosure only and is not intended to be a part of the written agreement between the Buyer and Seller.   269

E.   Buyer (which term includes all persons signing the "Buyer's acceptance" portion of this disclosure statement below) has   270
received a copy of this Disclosure Statement (including attachments, if any) bearing Seller's signature(s).   271

F.   If the house was built prior to 1978, Buyer acknowledges receipt of the pamphlet *Protect Your Family From Lead in Your*   272
Home.   273

DISCLOSURES CONTAINED IN THIS DISCLOSURE STATEMENT ARE PROVIDED BY SELLER BASED ON SELLER'S   274
ACTUAL KNOWLEDGE OF THE PROPERTY AT THE TIME SELLER COMPLETES THIS DISCLOSURE. UNLESS BUYER   275
AND SELLER OTHERWISE AGREE IN WRITING, BUYER SHALL HAVE THREE (3) BUSINESS DAYS FROM THE DAY   276
SELLER OR SELLER'S AGENT DELIVERS THIS DISCLOSURE STATEMENT TO RESCIND THE AGREEMENT BY   277
DELIVERING A SEPARATELY SIGNED WRITTEN STATEMENT OF RESCISSION TO SELLER OR SELLER'S AGENT. YOU   278
MAY WAIVE THE RIGHT TO RESCIND PRIOR TO OR AFTER THE TIME YOU ENTER INTO A SALE AGREEMENT.   279

BUYER HEREBY ACKNOWLEDGES RECEIPT OF A COPY OF THIS DISCLOSURE STATEMENT AND ACKNOWLEDGES   280
THAT THE DISCLOSURES MADE HEREIN ARE THOSE OF THE SELLER ONLY, AND NOT OF ANY REAL ESTATE   281
LICENSEE OR OTHER PARTY.   282

                                                                                                                283
_____   _____   _____   _____   284
Buyer   Date   Buyer   Date

2. BUYER'S WAIVER OF RIGHT TO REVOKE OFFER   285
Buyer has read and reviewed the Seller's responses to this Seller Disclosure Statement. Buyer approves this statement and   286
waives Buyer's right to revoke Buyer's offer based on this disclosure.   287

                                                                                                                288
_____   _____   _____   _____   289
Buyer   Date   Buyer   Date

3. BUYER'S WAIVER OF RIGHT TO RECEIVE COMPLETED SELLER DISCLOSURE STATEMENT   290
Buyer has been advised of Buyer's right to receive a completed Seller Disclosure Statement. Buyer waives that right.   291
However, if the answer to any of the questions in the section entitled "Environmental" would be "yes," Buyer may not waive   292
the receipt of the "Environmental" section of the Seller Disclosure Statement.   293

                                                                                                                294
_____   _____   _____   _____   295
Buyer   Date   Buyer   Date

_____   _____   _____   _____
SELLER'S INITIALS   Date   SELLER'S INITIALS   Date

9. **Manufactured and mobile homes.** This section applies when the property being sold includes a manufactured or mobile home. The seller is asked about any alterations to the manufactured or mobile home.

10. **Full disclosure.** Finally, the form asks whether there are any other material defects affecting the property or its value that a buyer should be aware of.

Many of the questions in the disclosure form are marked with an asterisk. If the seller answers "Yes" to any of those questions, she is required to provide additional information at the end of the form or on additional sheets.

After answering the questions about the property, the seller must sign a verification provision. It states that the information provided is complete and correct to the best of the seller's knowledge. It also states that if the information is challenged as inaccurate, the seller will indemnify the real estate licensees and hold them harmless from claims based on the inaccuracy. The seller acknowledges receipt of a copy of the form and authorizes the real estate agent to distribute copies to other licensees and to prospective buyers.

The next section of the form is the buyer's acknowledgment. By signing this section, the buyer acknowledges that he has received the disclosure form and understands his rights and responsibilities—including the duty to look for problems with the property on his own behalf. The buyer also acknowledges that the disclosures were made by the seller, not by any of the real estate licensees.

At the end of the form are two waiver provisions. By signing one of these, the buyer can waive rights provided by the seller disclosure law. (Waiver is discussed below.) Note that if any answer to a question in the form's "Environmental" section is "yes," the buyer cannot waive receipt of that portion of the statement.

TIMING AND EFFECT OF DISCLOSURE

The seller must ordinarily give the buyer the disclosure statement within five days after the purchase and sale agreement is signed. (Note that the statement is for disclosure purposes only; it does not become part of the purchase and sale agreement.) The parties may agree in writing to a different deadline for delivery of the disclosure statement or, by signing the waiver provision at the end of the form, the buyer may waive the right to receive a completed statement (again, he can't waive the right to receive negative environmental information).

Within three business days after receiving a completed disclosure statement, the buyer can either "approve and accept" the disclosure statement or **rescind** the purchase and sale agreement. The choice between acceptance and rescission is completely up to the buyer. If he does not like the information in the disclosure statement for any reason, however trivial, he can rescind the agreement.

If the buyer decides to rescind the agreement, he must notify the seller or the seller's real estate agent in writing within the three-day period. The buyer will then be entitled to a full refund of the earnest money deposit.

If the seller fails to give the buyer a disclosure statement, the buyer can rescind the purchase and sale agreement at any time until closing.

WHEN CIRCUMSTANCES CHANGE

After the buyer accepts a disclosure statement, information may come to light that makes the disclosure statement inaccurate.

EXAMPLE: Stein and O'Neil signed a purchase and sale agreement. Stein filled out the seller disclosure statement and gave it to O'Neil within five days. O'Neil examined the statement, was satisfied with it, and decided to go ahead with the purchase. Two weeks later, Stein realizes that the roof leaks. The disclosure statement given to O'Neil is no longer accurate.

When newly discovered information makes the disclosure statement inaccurate, the seller may either give the buyer an amended disclosure statement, or else fix the problem so that the disclosure statement is made accurate once again. Note that if the new property information is discovered by the buyer or someone acting on the buyer's behalf (such as the buyer's home inspector), the seller does not have a duty to amend the disclosure report.

If the seller amends the disclosure statement, the buyer again has three days to either accept the amended disclosure statement or rescind the purchase and sale agreement.

EXAMPLE: Stein gives O'Neil an amended disclosure statement, this time listing the true condition of the roof. O'Neil, who has had second thoughts about buying the property anyway, decides to rescind the purchase and sale agreement.

If the seller chooses to fix the problem, the corrective action must be completed at least three days before closing, or else the closing date may be extended to allow for a three-day rescission period. Once the sale has closed, the buyer can no longer rescind, even if new information is discovered.

LIMITATIONS ON LIABILITY UNDER THE SELLER DISCLOSURE LAW

Washington's seller disclosure law states that the information in the disclosure statement is based on the seller's actual knowledge of the property. The seller's answers to the questions are not representations made by the real estate agent. Furthermore, the statement is not a warranty from either the seller or the real estate agent. Neither the seller nor the real estate agent will be liable to the buyer for inaccuracies in the statement, unless they had personal knowledge of the inaccuracies.

On the other hand, the seller disclosure statement does not limit the responsibility of the seller and the real estate agent to disclose latent defects and other material facts to the buyer. Even if there is no question on the disclosure statement about a particular problem, the seller and the agent must disclose it if they are aware of it.

LISTING VACANT LAND

Some real estate transactions involve vacant land. In many cases, you will use the same listing agreement for vacant land as you do for single-family homes. However, the listing input sheet is likely to be quite different. (A sample vacant land input sheet is shown in Figure 2.6.) Also, a different form must be used for the seller's disclosures to the buyer when the property is vacant land.

Vacant land is usually bought for development purposes. This means that the availability of utilities is particularly important to the buyer. Zoning restrictions and drainage issues are also of special interest. In addition, the dimensions of the property itself often take on more importance with a vacant lot than with improved property. All of these items and more must be noted on the vacant land listing input sheet.

As a general rule, a seller can't offer a portion of a larger property for sale unless it has been platted and the plat has been recorded in the county where the property is located. However, some counties allow lots to be offered for sale after the preliminary plat is approved.

FIG. 2.6   VACANT LAND LISTING INPUT SHEET

NWMLS Form 5 Rev. 7/18
Copyright 2018
Northwest Multiple Listing Service
All Rights Reservedd

VACANT LAND LISTING INPUT SHEET   (page 1 of 3)

PROPERTY TYPE **4**

• Indicates Required information   ( ) Indicates Maximum Choice   *Indicates "Yes" By Default   **LISTING #**

ADDRESS

• **County**

• **City**

• **ZIP** Code   + 4

• **Area**

• **Community/District**

• **Street #** (HSN)   **Modifier**

Direction
☐ N ☐ S ☐ E ☐ W
☐ NE ☐ NW ☐ SE ☐ SW

• **Street Name**

Suffix

☐ Ave	☐ Blvd	☐ Ct Av	☐ Drive Ct	☐ Lane	☐ Pkwy	☐ St Ct	☐ Street	☐ Way
☐ Ave Ct	☐ Cir	☐ Ct St	☐ Hwy	☐ Loop	☐ Place	☐ St Dr	☐ Terr	
☐ Ave Pl	☐ Court	☐ Drive	☐ Junction	☐ Park	☐ Road	☐ St Pl	☐ Trail	

Post Direction
☐ N ☐ S ☐ E ☐ W
☐ NE ☐ NW ☐ SE ☐ SW
☐ KPN ☐ KPS

Unit #

LISTING

$

• **Listing Price**   • **Listing Date**   • **Expiration Date**   • **Tax ID#**

• **Preliminary Title Ordered**
☐ Yes ☐ No

• **Offers** (1)
☐ Seller intends to review offers upon receipt
☐ Seller to review offers on Offer Review Date (may review/accept sooner)

Offer Review Date
(required if 2nd "Offers" option is selected)

FIRPTA withholding required?
☐ Yes ☐ No

LOCATION

Lot Number   .   **Block**   **Plat/Subdivision/Building Name**

• **3rd Party Approval Required** (2)
☐ None ☐ Other - See Remarks ☐ Short Sale

• **Bank Owned/REO**
☐ Yes ☐ No

• **Auction**
☐ Yes ☐ No

MAP BOOK
| ☐ Thomas | ☐ RR-Jeff | ☐ RR-Thurs | ☐ RR-Clallam | ☐ Totem | ☐ P-Kittitas | ☐ Yellow Pgs | |
| ☐ RR-Kitsap | ☐ RR-Mason | ☐ RR-Lewis | ☐ RR Grays | ☐ P-Grant | ☐ P-Yakima | ☐ R A-Clark Unknown | |

Map Page   **Top Map** Coord.   **Side Map** Coord.

PROPERTY INFORMATION

• **Owner Name**   **Owner Name 2**   • **Owner's Phone**   • **Owner's City and State**

• **Lot Size** (Square Feet)   • **Lot Size Source**

• **Prohibit Blogging**
☐ *Yes ☐ No

• **Allow Automated Valuation**
☐ *Yes ☐ No

• **Show Map Link**
☐ *Yes ☐ No

• **Internet Advertising**
☐ *Yes ☐ No

• **Show Address to Public**
☐ *Yes ☐ No

• **SOC** (Selling Office Com.)   **Selling Office Commission Comments** (40 characters maximum)   **Virtual Tour URL** (Please include http:// or https://)

BROKER INFORMATION

• **LAG** Listing Broker ID#   **Broker Name and Phone**   **Listing Firm** - ID# **Firm Name and Phone**

Co Broker - ID#   **Co Broker Name and Phone**   **Co Firm** - ID# **Co Firm Name and Phone**

INITIALS:

Seller   Date   Seller   Date   Broker   Date

NWMLS Form 5 Rev. 7/18
Copyright 2018
Northwest Multiple Listing Service
All Rights Reservedd

VACANT LAND LISTING INPUT SHEET (page 2 of 3)

PROPERTY TYPE **4**

LISTING INFORMATION Listing Address: _____ LAG # _____

General Zoning Classification (6)
- ❏ Agricultural
- ❏ Business
- ❏ Commercial
- ❏ Farm & Ranch
- ❏ Forestry
- ❏ Industrial
- ❏ Industrial-Light
- ❏ Multi-Family
- ❏ Office
- ❏ Residential
- ❏ Retail
- ❏ See Remarks

• **Style Code** _____

• Zoning Jurisdiction (1)
- ❏ City
- ❏ County
- ❏ See Remarks

Zoning Code _____

Restrictions (4)
- ❏ CC&R
- ❏ NO Manufactured Homes
- ❏ Manufactured Homes OK
- ❏ No Restrictions
- ❏ Timber Clause
- ❏ Unknown
- ❏ See Remarks

• Possession (3)
- ❏ Closing
- ❏ Negotiable
- ❏ See Remarks
- ❏ Sub. Tenant's Rights

• Form 17 (1)
- ❏ Exempt
- ❏ Not Provided
- ❏ Provided

• Sketch Submitted
- ❏ Yes ❏ No

_____ $ _____
Tax Year   Annual Taxes

Assessment Fees (6)
- ❏ Electric
- ❏ Gas
- ❏ Parks
- ❏ Road
- ❏ School
- ❏ Sewer
- ❏ Water
- ❏ See Remarks

• Potential Terms (10)
- ❏ Assumable
- ❏ Cash Out
- ❏ Conventional
- ❏ Farm Home Loan
- ❏ FHA
- ❏ Lease/Purchase
- ❏ Owner Financing
- ❏ Rehab Loan
- ❏ See Remarks
- ❏ State Bond
- ❏ VA

Senior Exemption
❏ Yes ❏ No

Right of First Refusal
❏ Yes ❏ No

• Common Interest Cmty (RCW 64.90)
❏ Yes ❏ No

Term Remarks (40 characters maximum) _____

SITE INFORMATION

Quarter (Sec/Twn/Rng) _____

Lot Dimensions (Feet) _____

Waterfront Footage (Feet) _____

Reports/Documents Completed (9)
- ❏ CCRs
- ❏ Drainage
- ❏ Geotech
- ❏ Road Agreement
- ❏ Septic "As Built"
- ❏ Topographical
- ❏ Well Agreement
- ❏ Wetland Delineation
- ❏ See Remarks

Waterfront (5)
- ❏ Bank-High
- ❏ Bank-Low
- ❏ Bank-Medium
- ❏ Bay
- ❏ Bulkhead
- ❏ Canal
- ❏ Creek
- ❏ Jetty
- ❏ Lake
- ❏ No Bank
- ❏ Ocean
- ❏ River
- ❏ Saltwater
- ❏ Sound
- ❏ Strait
- ❏ Tideland Rights

View (5)
- ❏ Bay
- ❏ Canal
- ❏ City
- ❏ Golf Course
- ❏ Jetty
- ❏ Lake
- ❏ Mountain
- ❏ Ocean
- ❏ Partial
- ❏ River
- ❏ See Remarks
- ❏ Sound
- ❏ Strait
- ❏ Territorial

Lot Details (7)
- ❏ Alley
- ❏ Corner Lot
- ❏ Cul-de-sac
- ❏ Curbs
- ❏ Dead End Street
- ❏ High Voltage Line
- ❏ Open Space
- ❏ Paved Street
- ❏ Secluded
- ❏ Sidewalk

Improvements (10)
- ❏ Barn
- ❏ Boat House
- ❏ Cabana/Gazebo
- ❏ Cable TV Avail
- ❏ Dock
- ❏ Dwelling
- ❏ Fenced-Fully
- ❏ Fenced-Partially
- ❏ Garage
- ❏ Outbuilding(s)
- ❏ Shop
- ❏ Stable

Property Features (12)
- ❏ Brush
- ❏ Comm. Grade Timber
- ❏ Corners Flagged
- ❏ Dune Grasses
- ❏ Evergreens
- ❏ Garden/Fruit Trees
- ❏ Heavily Forested
- ❏ Irrigation
- ❏ Lightly Treed
- ❏ ORV Trails
- ❏ Partially Cleared
- ❏ Pasture Land
- ❏ Pond
- ❏ Recreational
- ❏ Riding Trails
- ❏ Stream/Creek

Topography (5)
- ❏ Cliffs
- ❏ Fill Needed
- ❏ Gullies
- ❏ Level
- ❏ Rolling
- ❏ See Remarks
- ❏ Sloped
- ❏ Swale

• Road Information (5)
- ❏ Access Easement
- ❏ County Maintained
- ❏ County Right of Way
- ❏ Gravel
- ❏ Paved
- ❏ Privately Maintained
- ❏ Recorded Maint. Agrm
- ❏ Trail Permit
- ❏ See Remarks

Road on Which Side of Property _____

Slopes Down to The (40 characters maximum) _____

Level (40 characters maximum) _____

UTILITY

Community Features (9)
- ❏ Age Restriction
- ❏ Airfield
- ❏ Boat Launch
- ❏ CCRs
- ❏ Clubhouse
- ❏ Community Waterfront/Pvt Beach Access
- ❏ Gated Entry
- ❏ Golf Course
- ❏ Tennis Courts

• Water (5)
- ❏ Available
- ❏ Community Well
- ❏ Drilled Well
- ❏ In Street
- ❏ Lake
- ❏ Not Available
- ❏ On Property
- ❏ Private Well
- ❏ Share Available
- ❏ Shared Well
- ❏ Unknown
- ❏ Water Rights
- ❏ Well Needed
- ❏ Well Site Approved

Water Jurisdiction _____

• Gas (1)
- ❏ On Property
- ❏ In Street
- ❏ Available
- ❏ Not Available

• Electricity (1)
- ❏ On Property
- ❏ In Street
- ❏ Available
- ❏ Not Available

• Sewer (2)
- ❏ Available
- ❏ In Street
- ❏ Not Available
- ❏ On Property

INITIALS: _____

_____ _____ _____ _____ _____ _____
Seller   Date   Seller   Date   Broker   Date

NWMLS Form 5 Rev. 7/18
Copyright 2018
Northwest Multiple Listing Service
All Rights Reservedd

VACANT LAND LISTING INPUT SHEET   (page 3 of 3)   PROPERTY TYPE **4**

Listing Address: **LAG #**

Septic System Installed
☐ Yes ☐ No

Septic Approved for # of Bedrooms

Soil Feasibility Test Available
☐ Yes ☐ No

Soil Test Date

Septic Design Applied For
☐ Yes ☐ No

Septic Design Apprv. Date

Septic Design Exp. Date

Septic System Type

Survey Information

Homeowner Dues Include
☐ Common Area Maintenance
☐ Concierge
☐ Lawn Service
☐ Road Maintenance
☐ Security Services
☐ See Remarks
☐ Snow Removal

$
Monthly Homeowners Dues

Easements

SCHOOL & COMMUNITY

• **School District**   **Elementary School**   **Junior High/Middle School**   **Senior High School**

REMARKS

Marketing Remarks. CAUTION! The comments you make in the following lines are limited to descriptions of the land and improvements only. These remarks will appear in the client handouts and websites. (500)

Confidential Broker-Only Remarks. Comments in this category are for broker's use only. (250)

• **Driving Directions to Property** (200)

INITIALS: _____ _____ _____ _____ _____ _____
Seller   Date   Seller   Date   Broker   Date

CHAPTER SUMMARY

1. The listing agreement is a contract between the seller and the real estate brokerage. The seller agrees to pay the firm a stated commission if a ready, willing, and able buyer is found during the listing period.

2. The three types of listing agreements are the open listing, the exclusive agency listing, and the exclusive right to sell listing. The type of listing determines the circumstances under which the firm is entitled to a commission.

3. A brokerage firm can enforce a listing agreement if it is in writing, adequately identifies the property to be sold, authorizes the brokerage to sell the property in exchange for compensation, and is signed by the seller.

4. The listing agreement should also state the terms of sale the seller will accept, the conditions under which the commission will be paid, the duration of the contract, and the seller's warranties regarding the accuracy of the information provided about the property.

5. A multiple listing service is a cooperative association of licensed firms and licensees who exchange information about their exclusive listings and help sell properties listed by other members.

6. An extender clause provides that the seller will be liable for the commission if the property is sold during a certain period after the listing expires to a buyer the listing agent dealt with during the listing period.

7. When entering into a purchase and sale agreement, the seller is usually required to give the buyer a seller disclosure statement, disclosing any problems that could affect the title or use of the property. After receiving the disclosure statement, the buyer may choose to rescind the purchase and sale agreement.

8. There are special listing input sheets and disclosure forms for vacant land listings. The listing agent must be aware of how development issues and regulations may affect the sale of vacant land.

CHAPTER QUIZ

1. One disadvantage of an open listing agreement is that it:

   a. does not state the compensation as a fixed amount

   b. requires the listing agent to put more effort into marketing the property

   c. may lead to a dispute over which agent was the procuring cause, if the seller gives the listing to more than one brokerage

   d. prevents sellers from listing their property with as many real estate firms as they want

2. Of the following, which is not a requirement for a valid listing agreement under Washington law?

   a. In writing

   b. Identifies the property

   c. Authorizes the brokerage to sell the property in exchange for compensation

   d. Termination date

3. A typical listing agreement form does not authorize the brokerage to:

   a. act as the agent of the seller

   b. accept earnest money deposits from prospective buyers on behalf of the seller

   c. accept an offer to purchase the property

   d. submit offers to purchase to the seller

4. In Washington, if an exclusive listing agreement does not include a termination date, when does the agreement end?

   a. After a reasonable time

   b. After 90 days

   c. After 60 days

   d. The agreement goes on indefinitely

5. If a firm renounces a listing agreement, the:

   a. seller will be liable for any damages suffered by the firm

   b. seller will be required to pay the commission

   c. senior managing broker in the firm's office can take over the listing

   d. firm could be liable for the seller's damages caused by the breach of contract

6. An extender clause (safety clause) might provide that:
   a. the seller must pay a commission if the property is sold within the extension period to a buyer you negotiated with during the listing period
   b. the seller may not owe you a commission if the property is listed with another firm during the extension period
   c. the provision may not be enforceable unless you give the seller a list of all potential buyers you negotiated with during the listing period
   d. All of the above

7. In a listing agreement, the seller typically makes a number of warranties. Which warranty is not usually included?
   a. Seller has the right to sell the property on the terms stated in the agreement
   b. There are no latent property defects
   c. Information about the property stated in the listing is accurate
   d. No structures encroach on the property

8. The purpose of a listing input sheet is to:
   a. explain the agency relationships of MLS members to the seller
   b. allow the MLS to verify the accuracy of information about the listing
   c. gather information about the property for distribution by the MLS
   d. disclose information the seller is required to give to the buyer

9. With respect to the seller disclosure statement, which of the following statements concerning the buyer's rights is not true?
   a. If the buyer rescinds the purchase and sale agreement based on the disclosure statement, she gives up her earnest money deposit
   b. The buyer can rescind the purchase and sale agreement if she does not like something in the disclosure statement, no matter how trivial
   c. The buyer can only waive her rights in writing
   d. If the seller fails to provide a disclosure statement, the buyer can rescind the purchase and sale agreement at any time until closing

10. If the seller discovers new information that makes the seller disclosure statement inaccurate:
    a. the seller is required to take corrective action to fix the problem so that the disclosure statement is accurate again
    b. the seller does not have to give the buyer an amended disclosure statement if he can correct the problem so that the original statement is accurate again
    c. the buyer must accept any amended disclosure statement if she accepted the original disclosure statement
    d. the buyer may rescind the purchase and sale agreement after the sale closes

ANSWER KEY

1. c. Because a seller can give open listings to more than one brokerage, open listings can lead to disputes over which agent was the procuring cause of a sale.

2. d. Unlike many other states, Washington does not require a listing agreement to state a termination date. It's generally a good idea to include one, however.

3. c. Under the terms of nearly any listing agreement, an agent may submit offers to the seller, but only the seller can accept an offer. An agent cannot ordinarily accept an offer and create a contract that will be binding on the seller, unless the seller has also given the agent a power of attorney.

4. a. In Washington, a listing agreement that does not specify a termination date ends after a reasonable time.

5. d. Either party to a listing agreement, the firm or the seller, can unilaterally terminate the contract. This is called a renunciation if the firm terminates the contract, or a revocation if the principal terminates it. In either case, the termination may be a breach of contract, and the breaching party could be required to pay damages to the other party.

6. d. In addition to protecting the firm's commission for a specified period after the listing expires, an extender clause may also contain protections for the seller, such as the ones described in options b) and c).

7. b. A seller does not ordinarily warrant that there are no latent defects. (However, if there are any known latent defects, the seller must disclose them in the seller disclosure statement.)

8. c. The listing input sheet is filled in with information for the MLS to distribute to its members and use in listing the property. The MLS does not verify the information or take legal responsibility for it.

9. a. Within three days after receiving the seller disclosure statement, the buyer may rescind the purchase and sale agreement for any reason without penalty. If a disclosure statement is not provided, the buyer can rescind the agreement at any time until closing, but not after closing.

10. b. The seller has two choices. He can either give the buyer an amended disclosure statement, or else he can correct the problem to make the original disclosure statement accurate again.

CHAPTER 3

LISTING REGULATIONS

REAL ESTATE LICENSE LAW

- Commissions
- Ownership of a listing

DISTRESSED PROPERTY LAW

ANTIDISCRIMINATION LAWS

- Federal Fair Housing Act
- Washington antidiscrimination laws
- Complying with fair housing laws
- Americans with Disabilities Act

ANTITRUST LAWS AND LISTING PRACTICES

WASHINGTON UNFAIR BUSINESS PRACTICES AND CONSUMER PROTECTION ACT

ENVIRONMENTAL ISSUES

- Environmental laws
- Environmental hazards

INTRODUCTION

After a considerable amount of work, you now have a valid listing agreement signed by a seller. But do you know what would happen if the seller refused to pay your commission? Could you sue her? What should you do if the seller states that she doesn't want you to show the property to non-white buyers? Or what if you suspect there may be an environmental problem with the property?

A variety of laws affect real estate listing and marketing practices, and you'll need to be familiar with them if you're going to avoid some of the pitfalls of selling real estate. They include the real estate license law, antidiscrimination laws, antitrust laws, consumer protection laws, and environmental laws. In this chapter, we'll discuss the provisions of these laws that pertain to listing and marketing properties and to brokerage commissions.

REAL ESTATE LICENSE LAW

Washington's real estate license law includes rules concerning payment of brokerage commissions and the ownership and control of listings.

COMMISSIONS

As you know, a seller ordinarily pays the brokerage commission to the listing brokerage firm. In most cases, if two different brokerages are involved, the listing firm then pays a share of the commission to its own affiliated licensee (the listing agent) and another share to the selling brokerage. The selling brokerage, in turn, pays a share of what it received to its own agent (the selling agent).

These steps are necessary because the license law allows a firm to share a commission only with another licensed brokerage or with one of its own affiliated sales agents. A firm may not pay any compensation directly to an agent who is affiliated with another brokerage. Payment must be made to that agent's firm, which then pays the agent.

EXAMPLE: You work for Winston Realty. You found a buyer for a property that was listed by an agent working for Juarez Homes, Inc. When the sale closes, the seller pays Juarez Homes a $20,000 commission.

Of that $20,000, Juarez Homes keeps $10,000 as its share. From that, it will pay its own affiliated agent (the one who listed the property) $5,000. It pays the other $10,000 to your firm, Winston Realty, because Winston

Realty is the selling firm. Winston Realty pays you $5,000, because you found the buyer. It would be unlawful for Juarez Homes to pay your $5,000 directly to you. Your compensation must come from your own firm.

Note that affiliated licensees aren't allowed to share their compensation with other licensees, whether they work for different firms or the same firm. If two licensees are going to split a commission, the split must be handled by their firm or firms.

A valid written agency agreement (either a listing agreement or a buyer representation agreement) is required before a firm can sue for a commission. Only the firm can sue the seller (or buyer, if appropriate) for the commission. The affiliated licensee doesn't have a contract with the client—only the firm does—and therefore she has no right to sue the client. However, if the firm fails to pay the licensee's share of the commission, the licensee can sue the firm for it.

OWNERSHIP OF A LISTING

Under the license law, only a brokerage can deal directly with the principal. Even though a listing agreement is usually prepared and signed by a sales agent, the listing is in the name of the firm and belongs to the firm.

EXAMPLE: You work for Yamaguchi Realty now. You are making a listing presentation to Piper. He decides to list his property with you, and you and he both sign the listing agreement form. However, the listing is actually a contract between Yamaguchi Realty and Piper. When you sign the listing, you are signing it as an agent of Yamaguchi Realty.

Because the listing agreement is between the firm and the seller, if the sales agent goes to work for another firm, the listing stays with the original firm. (The same rule applies to all brokerage services contracts.)

EXAMPLE: You don't want to work for Yamaguchi Realty anymore, so you start working for Wilder Properties instead. Piper's listing agreement was with Yamaguchi Realty, not with you, so Yamaguchi Realty keeps the listing.

If a brokerage firm loses its license, all listing agreements with that brokerage are terminated. However, if the designated broker loses his license (or dies, or leaves the firm for other reasons), the firm may appoint a new designated broker.

DISTRESSED PROPERTY LAW

In 2008, Washington passed the Distressed Property Law to protect home-owners in financial distress from exploitative foreclosure rescue scams. This is a fairly complex law, but the good news is that it exempts real estate agents in many cases.

DEFINITIONS

Generally, the law imposes special duties on distressed home consultants, with the goal of preventing **equity skimming**. In this practice, buyers buy homes from financially troubled sellers, promising to help the sellers get back on their feet and then sell the home back to them. In reality, though, the buyer often pockets all or most of the equity in the property, leaving the sellers even worse off than before.

A **distressed home** is defined as a personal residence that is in danger of foreclosure because the homeowner is delinquent on mortgage or tax payments. A **distressed home consultant** is anyone who offers to help a homeowner stop or postpone the foreclosure sale, or arranges for the homeowner to lease or rent the home so he can retain possession of it.

A distressed home consultant must enter into a formal contract with the home-owner known as a **distressed home consultant agreement**. This agreement must disclose the services that will be provided and the compensation the consultant will receive, and makes it clear that the consultant owes fiduciary duties to the homeowner (the duty to disclose material facts, use reasonable care, provide a full accounting, and act loyally). Your MLS probably does not provide a distressed home consultant agreement form. An attorney should draft this agreement for the parties, and it should be attached as an addendum to the listing agreement.

MOST TRANSACTIONS EXEMPT

Generally, real estate licensees are not considered to be distressed home consultants when they are providing routine real estate brokerage services. However, this exemption from the law does not apply if a licensee actually participates in a distressed home conveyance. In a **distressed home conveyance**, a buyer purchases property from a distressed homeowner (one who's facing foreclosure), allows the homeowner to continue to occupy the property for more than 20 days past the closing date, and promises to convey the property back to the homeowner or promises the homeowner an interest in or a portion of the proceeds from a resale of the property.

Many standard listing agreement forms now include a clause stating that the licensee will not assist in a distressed home sale without a separate written agreement. You can see an example of this language in paragraph five of the NWMLS listing agreement shown in Chapter 2 (Figure 2.2), entitled "Short Sale/No Distressed Home Conveyance."

Because of the 20-day occupancy rule, a typical transaction won't be considered a distressed home conveyance, even if the homeowner is behind on his mortgage payment. However, it's important to keep this time frame in mind. If a seller is allowed to stay on the property for longer than 20 days after closing, the transaction may become a distressed home conveyance, and the provisions of the distressed property law will then apply.

ANTIDISCRIMINATION LAWS

Fair housing laws and other antidiscrimination laws affect both how you obtain listings and how you market properties once they are listed. Before we discuss the impact of these laws on listing and marketing practices, let's review the basic provisions of the main federal and state antidiscrimination laws that apply in real estate transactions.

FEDERAL FAIR HOUSING ACT

The federal Fair Housing Act, part of the Civil Rights Act of 1968, makes it illegal to discriminate on the basis of **race**, **color**, **religion**, **sex**, **national origin**, **disability**, or **familial status** in the sale or lease of residential property, or in the sale or lease of vacant land for the construction of residential buildings. The law also prohibits discrimination in advertising, lending, real estate brokerage, and other services in connection with residential real estate transactions.

PROHIBITED ACTS. The Fair Housing Act prohibits the following actions if based on discrimination against any of the protected classes listed above:

- refusing to rent or sell residential property after receiving a bona fide offer;
- refusing to negotiate for the sale or rental of residential property, or otherwise making it unavailable;
- changing the terms of sale or lease for different potential buyers or tenants;

- using advertising that indicates a preference or intent to discriminate;
- representing that property is not available for inspection, sale, or rent when it is in fact available;
- discrimination by an institutional lender in making a housing loan;
- limiting participation in a multiple listing service or similar service;
- coercing, intimidating, threatening, or interfering with anyone on account of her enjoyment, attempt to enjoy, or encouragement or assistance to others in enjoying the rights granted by the Fair Housing Act.

The discriminatory practices known as blockbusting, steering, and redlining are also prohibited.

1. **Blockbusting.** This occurs when someone tries to induce homeowners to list or sell their properties by predicting that people of another race (or, for example, disabled people or people of a particular national origin) will be moving into the neighborhood, and that this will have undesirable consequences, such as lower property values. The blockbuster then profits by purchasing the homes at reduced prices, or (in the case of a real estate agent) by collecting commissions on the induced sales. Blockbusting is also known as **panic selling**.
2. **Steering.** This refers to channeling prospective buyers or tenants toward or away from specific neighborhoods based on their race (or religion, national origin, etc.) in order to maintain or change the character of those neighborhoods.
3. **Redlining.** This is a refusal to make a loan because of the racial or ethnic composition of the neighborhood in which the proposed security property is located. Rejection of a loan application must be based on objective financial considerations concerning the buyer or the property.

EXEMPTIONS. There are some exemptions from the Fair Housing Act. However, these exemptions are very limited and apply only rarely. They *never* apply when a real estate agent is involved in a transaction.

ENFORCEMENT. The Fair Housing Act is enforced by the Department of Housing and Urban Development (HUD), through its Office of Fair Housing and Equal Opportunity. In a state such as Washington, where the state fair housing laws are very similar to the federal laws, HUD may refer complaints to the equivalent state agency (in Washington, the state Human Rights Commission).

When someone is held to have violated the Fair Housing Act, an administrative law judge or a court may issue an injunction ordering the violator to stop the discriminatory conduct. The violator may also be ordered to pay compensatory damages and attorney's fees to the injured party. In addition, in a court case, the violator may be required to pay punitive damages to the injured party. In an administrative hearing, the violator may be required to pay a civil penalty to the government.

WASHINGTON STATE ANTIDISCRIMINATION LAWS

Real estate agents must also comply with the state laws that prohibit discrimination. The Washington Law Against Discrimination and the real estate license law both include provisions designed to promote fair housing in this state.

WASHINGTON LAW AGAINST DISCRIMINATION. The Washington Law Against Discrimination is stricter than the federal Fair Housing Act. It covers a broader range of activities and protects more classes of people from discrimination.

The Washington law prohibits discrimination in real estate transactions based on **race**, **creed**, **color**, **national origin**, **sex**, **sexual orientation and gender identity, marital status**, or **familial status; sensory**, **physical**, **or mental disability**; the **use of a trained guide dog or service animal**; or **honorably discharged veteran or military status**. Note that those infected or perceived to be infected with **HIV** are protected from discrimination to the same extent that those with any other disability are.

UNLAWFUL DISCRIMINATORY PRACTICES. The Washington Law Against Discrimination is not just a fair housing law. It prohibits a wide range of discriminatory practices in employment, insurance, and credit transactions, places of public accommodation and amusement (such as movie theaters, restaurants, hotels, beauty shops, and most other commercial enterprises), and in regard to all types of real property—not just residential property.

The state law prohibits discrimination in any real estate transaction, including the sale, appraisal, exchange, purchase, rental, or lease of real property; transacting or applying for a real estate loan; and the provision of brokerage services.

If based on discrimination against a protected class, it is against the law to:

- refuse to engage in a real estate transaction;
- discriminate in the terms or conditions of a real estate transaction;
- discriminate in providing services or facilities in connection with a real estate transaction;

FIG. 3.1   COMPARISON OF ANTIDISCRIMINATION LAWS

FEDERAL FAIR HOUSING ACT

- APPLIES ONLY TO RESIDENTIAL TRANSACTIONS

- PROTECTED CLASSES: RACE, COLOR, RELIGION, SEX, NATIONAL ORIGIN, DISABILITY, OR FAMILIAL STATUS

- NO EXEMPTIONS FOR TRANSACTIONS INVOLVING REAL ESTATE AGENTS

WASHINGTON LAW AGAINST DISCRIMINATION

- APPLIES TO ANY REAL ESTATE TRANSACTION

- PROTECTED CLASSES: RACE, CREED, COLOR, NATIONAL ORIGIN, SEX, SEXUAL ORIENTATION AND GENDER IDENTITY, MARITAL STATUS, FAMILIAL STATUS, DISABILITY, USE OF A GUIDE DOG OR SERVICE ANIMAL, OR HONORABLY DISCHARGED VETERAN OR MILITARY STATUS

- NO EXEMPTIONS FOR TRANSACTIONS INVOLVING REAL ESTATE AGENTS

- refuse to receive or fail to transmit a bona fide offer;
- refuse to negotiate;
- represent that property is not available for inspection, sale, rental, or lease when it is in fact available;
- fail to advise a prospect about a property listing, or refuse to allow her to inspect the property;
- discriminate in the sale or rental of a dwelling, or otherwise make unavailable or deny a dwelling to anyone;
- make, print, circulate, or publish any advertisement, notice, or sign which indicates, directly or indirectly, an intent to discriminate;
- use any application form or make any record or inquiry which indicates, directly or indirectly, an intent to discriminate;
- offer, solicit, accept, or retain a listing with the understanding that a person may be discriminated against;
- expel a person from occupancy;
- discriminate in negotiating, executing, or financing a real estate transaction;
- discriminate in negotiating or executing any service or item in connection with a real estate transaction (such as title insurance or mortgage insurance);

- refuse to allow a disabled person to make reasonable modifications to a dwelling;
- refuse to make reasonable accommodations in rules or policies that would enable a disabled person to use a dwelling;
- fail to construct new multi-family dwellings in compliance with accessibility requirements imposed by the federal Fair Housing Act;
- induce or attempt to induce, for profit, anyone to sell or rent by making representations regarding entry into the neighborhood of a person of a protected class (blockbusting);
- insert in a written instrument relating to real property, or honor or attempt to honor, any condition, restriction, or prohibition based on a protected class (any such provision in a deed or any other conveyance or instrument relating to real property is void); or
- discriminate in any credit transaction (whether or not it is related to real estate) in denying credit, increasing fees, requiring collateral, or in any other terms or conditions.

In short, just about every form of discrimination in real estate transactions or any services associated with real estate transactions is unlawful if it is based on someone's membership in any of the protected classes.

EXEMPTIONS. The Washington law has very few exemptions and, like the federal Fair Housing Act, it has none that apply to a real estate agent engaged in professional activity.

ENFORCEMENT. Washington's antidiscrimination laws are enforced by the Washington Human Rights Commission. A person who feels his rights have been violated in a real estate transaction may file a complaint with the Human Rights Commission within one year of the discriminatory action. The commission will investigate and, if it feels the complaint has merit, will try to resolve the problem by conference, conciliation, and persuasion. If the problem remains unresolved, the commission can schedule a hearing before an administrative law judge. If the judge finds that there was unlawful discrimination, she may provide relief in the form of a cease and desist order, affirmative relief (such as requiring an apartment owner to give the next available apartment to the victim), compensatory damages, and/or a civil penalty.

Instead of pursuing an administrative remedy, the injured party may choose to have the attorney general bring a civil action against the alleged discriminator.

WASHINGTON REAL ESTATE LICENSE LAW. In addition to the federal and state laws already discussed, real estate licensees must comply with the antidiscrimination provisions of the license law and regulations.

Under the license law, a licensee's violation of any fair housing or civil rights law is grounds for disciplinary action. The Department of Licensing can suspend or revoke the license of a broker or managing broker who discriminates in sales or hiring activity against a member of a protected class, as well as impose a fine of up to $5,000 for each offense. The licensee could also be required to complete an educational course in civil rights laws and nondiscriminatory real estate practices. Violations of the license law are also punishable as gross misdemeanors.

COMPLYING WITH FAIR HOUSING LAWS

As you can see, these antidiscrimination laws cover a lot of territory. You must become familiar with their provisions and know what activities are prohibited. And you must remember that violating an antidiscrimination law does not require intent; if you do something that is considered discriminatory, you may be found guilty of violating the law even if you had good intentions.

EXAMPLE: You're giving a listing presentation at the seller's home. The sellers are from Central America and speak only limited English. You do not speak Spanish. During the listing presentation, you feel increasingly uncomfortable because of the communication barrier. When you finish your presentation, the sellers tell you they want to list their property with you right away. Somewhat sheepishly, you suggest that they may want to list their property with an agent who speaks Spanish. You explain tactfully that you have a very difficult time understanding them and believe that they would be happier with a Spanish-speaking agent.

They insist that they want to list with you. You tell them, in all honesty, that you think another agent would be able to give them better service and simply aren't comfortable taking them on. Your refusal to list their property, however well-intentioned, could be regarded as discrimination on the basis of national origin, and you could be found guilty of violating federal or state antidiscrimination laws.

To help you avoid unintentional discriminatory acts, we will discuss some basic guidelines to follow when you list property and when you advertise the properties you list.

COMPLIANCE WHEN LISTING PROPERTY. When you are listing property, you should remember the following general rules.

Never say or imply that the presence of persons of a particular protected class (race, national origin, etc.) in a neighborhood could or will result in:

- lower property values,
- a change in the composition of the neighborhood,
- a more dangerous neighborhood, or
- a decline in the quality of the schools in the neighborhood.

> **EXAMPLE:** Chadwick is making a listing presentation to Thompson, a home owner who is considering selling her property but isn't sure this is the right time. During the presentation, Chadwick says to Thompson, "I hear your neighbor, Bowen, has accepted an offer on his house from a minority couple. I'm sure they're good people, but it's a signal that the neighborhood is changing. I've seen it before. You know, it might be a good idea to get your house listed and an offer nailed down. Prices are likely to fall once word gets around." This is an example of blockbusting. Chadwick has violated the antidiscrimination laws.

Remember that you can't refuse to list property in a market area served by your office because of the presence or absence of particular protected groups. Nor can you state or imply that a home will be more difficult (or easier) to sell based on the presence or absence of a particular group of people.

> **EXAMPLE:** Norquist is discussing the listing price with the sellers. She tells them with enthusiasm, "Your house is in a great neighborhood! There aren't very many safe, white, middle-class neighborhoods left these days. Your home's really going to sell fast!" Norquist has just violated antidiscrimination laws.

Most agents would not act in an overtly discriminatory way; for example, they wouldn't raise the listing price because of the race of the prospective buyer. Yet some of these same agents might tell racist or homophobic jokes or make derogatory remarks about a particular group of people. Although these jokes or remarks don't necessarily indicate a willingness to actually discriminate in a transaction, a listener might assume that they do. And if an agent listens and says nothing while a seller, a buyer, or another agent makes discriminatory remarks or jokes, it can give the impression that the agent agrees with these discriminatory attitudes.

Avoid participating in or going along with slurs against a protected class, no matter what the source.

When you are taking a listing, if the seller makes remarks that suggest that she might act in a discriminatory manner, then you should discuss the fair housing laws with her, and state that you will strictly abide by them. Ask the seller to make a firm commitment to comply with fair housing laws. If she refuses, you should refuse to take the listing.

> **EXAMPLE:** You're making a listing presentation to the Boyds, a white couple who live in a predominantly white neighborhood. While you are discussing the listing terms, Mr. Boyd says, "You know, we certainly want the best price for our house. But we want you to be pretty careful who you show it to. We spent a lot of time fixing up this house. Hey, we raised our kids here. We don't really want to change the neighborhood. Our neighbors are good, traditional, hard-working folks. We don't want a buyer who would lower everybody else's property values. You know what we mean."
>
> Even though the Boyds don't come out and say so, they could easily be implying that they would not accept an offer from a buyer with a different racial or ethnic background. Their comments are red flags. You should discuss fair housing principles with them, emphasizing that equal opportunity is the law. If the Boyds seem uncomfortable with what you are saying, you would be wise to refuse to take the listing.

If you refuse a listing because you think the sellers would discriminate against potential buyers, you should immediately report it to your designated broker or branch manager.

In your relationships with potential sellers, be sure to provide equal service without regard to the seller's race, creed, color, religion, national origin, sex, sexual orientation, marital status, familial status, or disability. You should always follow the same listing procedures no matter who your client is.

COMPLIANCE WHEN ADVERTISING PROPERTIES. After you list a property, your next step is usually to advertise it. Keep in mind that you need to avoid discrimination in the way you market the property.

Sometimes apparently innocent statements or actions may be interpreted as discriminatory. Suppose that you're preparing and mailing out a flyer about your listing. You could be accused of discrimination if:

- you send flyers only to neighborhoods where the residents are all predominantly of the same race or ethnic background as the seller;

- you send them to all of the neighboring properties except those owned by members of a protected class; or
- the wording of the flyer suggests that the recipient can influence what type of person will buy the property.

EXAMPLE: Your flyer says that a neighbor can, by referring potential buyers, "uphold the standards of the community." But you fail to specify what community standards you're referring to. Unless you clearly describe these standards in nondiscriminatory language, a reader could infer that she can control the race or ethnic background of the buyer. Your flyer might be found to violate antidiscrimination laws.

As a real estate agent, you're likely to place many ads online or in newspapers and other print media, and you must be sure that your advertising strategies avoid even inadvertent discrimination.

- Your choice of newspapers, for example, could constitute racial steering.

EXAMPLE: You have listed a home in a predominantly minority neighborhood. Your sellers are members of the minority group. You decide to advertise the property in the neighborhood weekly newspaper rather than the city newspaper or any other neighborhood weeklies. You feel this is the best choice, because you think other minority residents from the same neighborhood would be more interested in the home than residents of other neighborhoods. This is discriminatory.

- The choice of models you use in display advertising could also lead to charges of discrimination.

EXAMPLE: A licensee is the listing agent for a large, exclusive housing development. She advertises the homes in the development online. In every ad, the buyers and sellers are depicted only by white models, even though 38% of the city's population is non-white. The use of only white models could be grounds for a discrimination suit.

When pictures of people are used in advertising, you should take all reasonable steps to make sure that the pictures give the impression that the housing is open to everyone.

- All your residential advertising should contain the Equal Housing Opportunity logo or slogan. Your brochures, circulars, business cards, direct mail

FIG. 3.2   FAIR HOUSING LOGO

EQUAL HOUSING
OPPORTUNITY

advertising, and all other forms of advertising should also include the Equal Housing Opportunity logo or slogan. In addition, a fair housing poster containing the logo must be displayed at any place of business involving the sale, rental, or financing of residential property.

ACTIONS THAT DO NOT VIOLATE FAIR HOUSING LAWS. Certain actions may initially appear to violate antidiscrimination laws, but in fact are not considered to be violations. Here are some examples.

- You may provide information required by a federal, state, or local agency for data collection or civil rights enforcement purposes.
- You may ask questions and provide information on forms in regard to marital status, in an effort to comply with the state's community property laws concerning the purchase, sale, or financing of real estate.
- You may ask questions or make statements as necessary to best serve the needs of a disabled person. This may include calling the attention of disabled clients or customers to particular buildings built or modified to meet their needs.
- You may use an affirmative marketing plan that tries to attract members of a particular group to an area or property that they might not otherwise be aware of. A brokerage or real estate board may also take affirmative steps to recruit minority employees or members.

  EXAMPLE: The developer of a large, moderately priced subdivision located on the fringes of the metropolitan area contacts you to assist in the sale of properties in the subdivision. The developer encourages you to target your marketing efforts toward recent immigrants who might be looking for affordable entry-level housing. In your area, most of the recent immigrants are non-white and live in a few older urban neighborhoods. You could devote extra effort to advertising in immigrant community newspapers or leafletting these neighborhoods, as long as you also advertise more widely.

- You may truthfully answer questions about the racial composition of neighborhoods, even if this results in unintentional racial steering. If a buyer expresses a desire not to be shown homes in a particular neighborhood, even if the buyer makes that decision because of the race or other characteristics of the residents, you are not obligated to show him homes in that neighborhood. Agents should not disparage a neighborhood or discourage buyers from looking there, however. It may be preferable (and your firm may require you) to tell buyers where to look for more information about neighborhoods (such as the Census Bureau or the local Chamber of Commerce), rather than saying anything that might create the impression of steering.

EXAMPLE: You are representing the Duvalls, who have only a limited amount of money to spend on their first home. You suggest a variety of neighborhoods where there are listings that fit their price range and other preferences, including the Greengate neighborhood. When Mr. Duvall asks about the people who live in Greengate, you truthfully respond that most of the residents belong to a particular immigrant group. Mr. Duvall says, "I'm not sure we'd feel comfortable there; we'd rather look in other areas." So long as you do not discourage the Duvalls from looking at properties in this neighborhood, you are not required to show the Duvalls houses in this area against their wishes.

AMERICANS WITH DISABILITIES ACT

To avoid discrimination and promote equal treatment, real estate licensees need to be familiar not only with the fair housing laws but also with the Americans with Disabilities Act. This federal law helps guarantee people with disabilities equal access to employment, goods, and services.

As we discussed, housing discrimination on the basis of disability is prohibited under the federal Fair Housing Act. The ADA has a different application. Under this law, no one may be discriminated against on the basis of disability in places of public accommodation or other commercial facilities.

The ADA defines a **disability** as any physical or mental impairment that substantially limits one or more major life activities. (This is the same definition of disability that's used in the Fair Housing Act.) The definition of **public accommodation** in the ADA covers any nonresidential place that is owned, operated, or leased by a private entity and that is open to the public, if operation of the facility affects commerce.

Most significantly, this means places of public accommodation or other commercial facilities must be accessible to the disabled. Physical barriers to access must be removed, wheelchair ramps must be added, and restrooms and other facilities must be modified.

PLACES OF PUBLIC ACCOMMODATION AND COMMERCIAL FACILITIES. A wide variety of facilities open to the public, both publicly and privately owned, meet the ADA's definition of places of public accommodation. Hotels, restaurants, retail stores, schools, theaters, and professional offices are all covered. For instance, the office of a real estate brokerage is open to the public and therefore must be accessible to people with disabilities. Even offices and workplaces that aren't ordinarily visited by the public need to be accessible if they fall within the broader category of commercial facilities.

ADA REQUIREMENTS. If you deal with commercial or retail property often, it is particularly important to be familiar with ADA requirements. The person who owns, leases, or operates a place of public accommodation is legally responsible for the removal of barriers to accessibility, so you may need to advise clients about modifications that may be necessary on properties that they might purchase or lease.

Changes that the owner or tenant of a commercial property might need to make so that the building complies with the ADA include:

- creating an accessible entrance, by installing ramps, adding parking spaces, or widening doorways;
- providing access to goods and services within a building, by installing elevators, widening aisles, or adding Braille or raised-lettering signage;
- improving restrooms, by adding larger stalls, grab bars, or more easily-operated faucets and door handles; or
- relocating other features, such as drinking fountains, so they are more easily reached.

Note that barrier removal is required only in public areas, and is not required where it is not "readily achievable." For example, the owner of a small, independently owned two-story retail business would not necessarily be required to install an elevator to the second story. However, the business would be required to make other accommodations to serve a disabled customer, such as having a salesperson bring items down to the customer on the first floor.

NEW CONSTRUCTION. If you are representing someone who plans to build a new building, you should be aware that all new construction of places of public accommodation or other commercial facilities must comply with ADA requirements.

Model homes are not ordinarily required to meet ADA requirements. However, if a model home is also serving as a sales office for a subdivision or complex, then the area used as a sales office would be considered a place of public accommodation.

ANTITRUST LAWS AND LISTING PRACTICES

As you go about the business of obtaining listings and negotiating listing terms, you must be aware of the restrictions imposed by federal antitrust laws. The purpose of antitrust laws is to foster fair business practices among competitors. These laws are based on the belief that free enterprise and healthy competition are good both for individual consumers and for the economy as a whole.

The most important federal antitrust law is the **Sherman Antitrust Act**, which was passed in 1890. The Sherman Act prohibits any agreement (or unilateral conduct) that has the effect of unreasonably restraining trade. This includes a **conspiracy**, defined in the law as two or more business entities participating in a common scheme, the effect of which is the unreasonable restraint of trade.

The Sherman Act doesn't apply only to big businesses, like large telecommunications companies and oil companies. Since 1950, antitrust laws have also applied to the real estate industry. In a landmark case, the United States Supreme Court held that mandatory fee schedules established and enforced by a real estate board violated the Sherman Act (*United States v. National Association of Real Estate Boards*).

The penalties for violating antitrust laws are severe:

- if an individual is found guilty of violating the Sherman Act, he can be fined up to one million dollars and/or sentenced to ten years' imprisonment; and
- if a corporation is found guilty of violating the Sherman Act, it can be fined up to one hundred million dollars.

To avoid violating antitrust regulations, you need to be aware of four types of prohibited activities. These are:

- price fixing,
- group boycotts,
- tie-in arrangements, and
- market allocation.

PRICE FIXING

Price fixing is defined as the cooperative setting of prices or price ranges by competing firms. Real estate firms can run afoul of the law against price fixing by setting, or appearing to set, uniform commission rates.

EXAMPLE: Members of a local organization of real estate agents decide that they should all insist on 7% commissions. They arrange for 7% to be pre-printed in all their listing forms, and when potential sellers question the commission rate, the real estate agents say, "It's the same rate everybody charges." This would be considered a blatant case of illegal price fixing.

One of the best ways to avoid the appearance of price fixing is to scrupulously avoid discussing commission rates with competing agents. (Note that it's a discussion between *competing* agents that is dangerous—it's all right for a designated broker to discuss commission rates with her own sales agents.) The only exception to this general rule is that two competing designated brokers may discuss a commission split in a cooperative sale. In other words, designated brokers who represent the buyer and the seller may discuss how they will split the sales commission.

Even casually mentioning that you're changing your commission rate could lead to antitrust problems.

EXAMPLE: A prominent designated broker attends a meeting of the local real estate agents' organization. He's asked to give a brief speech about his firm's sales goals. In the middle of his comments, he mentions that he's going to raise his firm's commission rate, even if nobody else raises theirs. The profitability of his firm depends on it.

These statements could be interpreted as an invitation to conspire to fix prices. If any other members of the agents' organization follow his lead and raise their rates, they might be accused of accepting his invitation to fix prices.

As this example illustrates, an agent doesn't have to actually consult with other agents to be accused of conspiring to fix commission rates. Merely mentioning, among competing agents, an intent to increase rates could be enough to lead to an antitrust lawsuit.

When you are taking a listing, it is important to emphasize to the seller that the commission rate is freely negotiable. You should never imply that commission rates are set by law or by your local MLS or Board of Realtors®. Don't mention the rates of competing agents, either.

> **EXAMPLE:** Harris is making a listing presentation to Bell. When Bell asks Harris about the commission, Harris casually says, "Oh, the commission rate is 7%." When Bell asks if she has to pay a 7% commission, Harris replies, "All the agents around here insist on a 7% commission. In fact, if you decided to pay a smaller commission, I'm not even sure that the MLS would accept the listing." Harris has violated the antitrust laws.

GROUP BOYCOTTS

Antitrust laws also prohibit group boycotts. A **group boycott** is an agreement between business competitors to exclude another competitor from fair participation in business activities. For example, an agreement between two or more real estate agents to exclude another agent from fair participation in real estate activities would be a group boycott. The purpose of a group boycott is to hurt or destroy a competitor, and this is automatically unlawful under the antitrust laws.

A group boycott doesn't have to be based on a formal arrangement or carried out by a large group of people.

> **EXAMPLE:** Barker and Jaffrey, two real estate agents, meet to discuss an offer on a house. After discussing the offer, they begin talking about the business practices of a third agent, Hutton. Barker, angry with Hutton because of a past business transaction, claims that Hutton is dishonest. Barker says, "That sleazy jerk! I'll never do business with him again!" Jaffrey laughs. Barker then says, "You know, I've stopped returning Hutton's calls when he's asking about my listings. You should do the same thing. With any luck, the guy will be out of business in a few months." Jaffrey, who also disapproves of Hutton, agrees. Barker and Jaffrey could be found guilty of a conspiracy to boycott Hutton.

It's one thing to think another agent is dishonest or unethical and to choose to avoid her. It's another matter entirely to encourage other agents to do the same. You should never tell clients or other agents not to work with a competing agent because (for example) you have doubts about that agent's competence or integrity. (If you have evidence of an agent's incompetence or dishonesty, you should report this to the licensing authority.)

It would also be considered a group boycott if a multiple listing service refused to allow an agent to become a member because he had a different kind of fee schedule. For example, an MLS can't refuse membership to a brokerage firm just because it charges a small flat fee for a listing, rather than a percentage of the sales price.

TIE-IN ARRANGEMENTS

Another type of business practice that antitrust laws prohibit is a tie-in arrangement. A **tie-in arrangement** (also known as a tying arrangement) is defined as an agreement to sell one product only on the condition that the buyer also purchases a different (or "tied") product.

> **EXAMPLE:** Fisher is a subdivision developer. Tyler, a builder, wants to buy a lot. Fisher tells Tyler that he will sell him a lot only if Tyler agrees that after Tyler builds a house on the lot, he will list the improved property with Fisher.

The type of agreement described in this example is known as a **list-back agreement**. List-back agreements are not unlawful. But requiring a lot buyer to enter into one as a condition of the sale is a tie-in arrangement and violates the antitrust laws.

Another danger area for real estate agents is agreeing to manage property only if the owner agrees to list that property with you.

> **EXAMPLE:** Dahl, a licensee, is negotiating a property management agreement with Heinz, a property owner. Dahl wants to include a clause in the agreement that provides that if Heinz ever decides to sell the managed property, he will list the property with Dahl. If Dahl tells Heinz that she'll enter into a management agreement only if it includes this listing clause, Dahl is violating the antitrust laws.

MARKET ALLOCATION

Market allocation occurs when competing agents divide up the market by agreeing not to sell certain products or services in certain areas, or agreeing not to sell to certain customers in particular areas. Market allocation between competing agents is illegal, as it limits competition.

As with group boycotts, it's the collective action that makes market allocation illegal. An individual agent is free to determine the market areas in which she wants her brokerage to specialize; similarly, she can allocate territory to particular affiliated licensees within her brokerage. It's allocation of territory between competing firms that is considered group action and therefore a violation of antitrust law.

> **EXAMPLE:** Cecilia of ABC Realty assigns Ava to handle all incoming customers in the luxury home market, and assigns Paxton to all incoming customers in the vacant land market. This practice does not violate antitrust law.
>
> However, if Cecilia of ABC Realty and Carson of XYZ Realty agree to allocate customers so that ABC Realty will handle all luxury homes and XYZ Realty will handle all vacant land, this would violate antitrust law.

WASHINGTON UNFAIR BUSINESS PRACTICES AND CONSUMER PROTECTION ACT

The Washington Unfair Business Practices and Consumer Protection Act (commonly called the Consumer Protection Act) prohibits the same anticompetitive practices as the federal antitrust laws, including price fixing, group boycotts, tie-in arrangements, and market allocation. Beyond this, the Consumer Protection Act is a comprehensive law that bans "unfair or deceptive acts or practices in the conduct of any trade or commerce." Although the real estate industry is primarily regulated through the license law, it is also covered by the Consumer Protection Act.

So a real estate agent's failure to disclose material facts to a customer (or a conflict of interest to a client) would violate both the real estate license law and the Consumer Protection Act. For example, if you know that a commercial property that you have listed lacks commercial potential, but you fail to inform potential buyers, you might be liable to the buyer for damages under the Consumer Protection Act. (Despite the name, the Consumer Protection Act covers both consumer and commercial transactions.)

The Consumer Protection Act also prohibits misleading and deceptive advertising. For instance, an ad for a property that misrepresents its features violates this law, and so does an ad for brokerage services containing false information about the firm. This has particularly been an issue where advertisements for land development promotions have misled consumers about the acceptability of the lots for sale.

EXAMPLE: Cunningham publishes an ad in a newspaper, offering inexpensive mountain-view lots in a new subdivision in eastern Washington. He neglects to mention that no utilities are available at the home sites, and that the ground is too dry to grow anything without installation of an irrigation system. Even if consumers bought the lots sight unseen, Cunningham could be required to give refunds to dissatisfied purchasers, or to pay for installation of utilities and other site improvements.

The Consumer Protection Act also applies to the sale of new homes. Under the act, the builder/seller of a new home gives the buyer an implied warranty of habitability. Latent defects that affect the safety and livability of the house violate the implied warranty, and the buyer could sue the builder/seller because of the defects.

EXAMPLE: The Vaughn family purchases a house in a large new subdivision, Carlisle Ridge. After winter rains, it becomes clear that the foundation is unstable and rapidly settling, causing large cracks in the interior walls of the house. This is a fundamental defect affecting the safety of the house, and the Vaughns have grounds for a suit against the developer of Carlisle Ridge. The developer may be required to pay for the cost of repairs, or the Vaughns may be allowed to rescind the purchase.

In a situation like the one in the example, if a real estate agent was involved in the sale of the property and knew of the latent defects, the buyers might be able to sue the agent as well as the developer under the Consumer Protection Act.

A private party suing under the Consumer Protection Act may recover damages, court costs, and attorney's fees, and the court is allowed to triple the damages award. The state may also bring suit against a company or individual under this law.

ENVIRONMENTAL ISSUES

As we mentioned in Chapter 2, the seller disclosure statement calls for the disclosure of environmental hazards. Because of the growing concern about environmental hazards related to real estate—even residential real estate—it's worthwhile to discuss some of those hazards and the laws related to them. While you aren't expected to be an environmental expert, you should have a basic understanding of the environmental issues affecting property owners and buyers.

ENVIRONMENTAL LAWS

A number of federal and state environmental laws affect real estate agents and property buyers and sellers. We will just highlight a few of the most important laws.

NATIONAL ENVIRONMENTAL POLICY ACT. The National Environmental Policy Act (NEPA) requires federal agencies to provide an **environmental impact statement** (EIS) for any action that would have a significant effect on the environment. NEPA applies to all types of federal development, such as construction projects, the building of highways, and waste control. NEPA also applies to private uses or developments that require the approval of a federal agency in the form of a license, a permit, or even a federal loan. In these cases, federal agencies may require submission of an EIS before approving the use or development.

An EIS should disclose the impact of the development on energy consumption, sewage systems, school population, drainage, water facilities, and other environmental, economic, and social factors.

STATE ENVIRONMENTAL POLICY ACT. Washington has its own version of NEPA, the State Environmental Policy Act (SEPA). SEPA requires an environmental impact statement for all acts of state and local government agencies that may have a significant effect on the quality of the environment.

SEPA applies not only to developments by state and local agencies, but also to private developments that require the approval of state, city, or county government agencies. For instance, SEPA requirements must be met before a city or county can approve rezones, variances, conditional use permits, or building permits.

SHORELINE MANAGEMENT ACT. The purpose of Washington's Shoreline Management Act is to protect shorelines by regulating development within 200 feet of a high water mark. The act applies to coastal shorelines, to the shores of lakes larger than 20 acres, and to streams that flow at a rate in excess of 20 cubic feet per second.

Developers of shoreline property are required to obtain a **substantial development permit** from the local city or county government before beginning any work. A development is considered "substantial" if its value exceeds a certain threshold (currently $6,416), or if it would materially interfere with the normal public use of the water or shoreline.

Someone who violates the Shoreline Management Act may be fined up to $1,000 per day while the violation continues. A court may also order that the shoreline be restored to its original condition—even if this means the complete removal of any buildings or improvements.

Since there is so much shoreline in Washington, the Shoreline Management Act affects a large amount of property. Anyone purchasing shoreline property needs to consider what impact this law may have on their plans for the property.

CERCLA. One of the most important environmental laws is the federal Comprehensive Environmental Response, Compensation, and Liability Act (CERCLA). CERCLA concerns liability for environmental cleanup costs and has dramatically changed the way property buyers view potential environmental liability.

CERCLA is best known for its creation of a multibillion-dollar fund called **Superfund**. The purpose of Superfund is to clean up hazardous waste sites. CERCLA also created a process for identifying the parties who are responsible for cleanup costs. Cleanup costs may include the cost of cleaning up the site where the waste was released, as well as any neighboring properties that were contaminated.

The parties responsible for the cleanup may include both present and previous landowners. In some cases, the current owners of contaminated property may be required to pay for the cleanup even if they did not cause the contamination. A buyer who is considering purchasing property that may have been contaminated should consult an environmental engineer and/or an attorney specializing in environmental law.

CLEAN WATER ACT. Of particular concern to land developers is the federal law protecting **wetlands**—swamps, marshes, ponds, and similar areas where the soil is saturated for part of the year. Section 404 of the Clean Water Act makes it illegal for a private landowner to fill or drain wetlands on his property without obtaining a permit from the Army Corps of Engineers. Violations may be punished with an order to restore the wetlands, civil penalties, and even criminal sanctions.

The presence of a wetland is not necessarily a complete barrier to the development of a property, though. A landowner may fill a wetland for development if she creates or restores new wetlands elsewhere, so that there is no net loss of wetland area. Alternatively, the landowner may purchase the right to develop in wetland areas by paying into a government fund that is used to develop new wetlands elsewhere.

ENDANGERED SPECIES ACT. The purpose of the Endangered Species Act is to conserve habitats that shelter endangered or threatened species. There are dozens of listed species within Washington, many of which make their habitat primarily on private lands.

As with wetlands, however, the presence of an endangered species on a property does not completely bar development; private landowners may develop land supporting listed species if they agree to a Habitat Conservation Plan and undertake conservation measures. Landowners who agree to a plan and carry it out won't be required to take additional steps later on, even if the environmental circumstances change.

While you should be familiar with the basic requirements of these environmental laws, if prospective buyers of developable land have questions about the impact of these laws, you should refer them to the U.S. Environmental Protection Agency, the U.S. Fish and Wildlife Service, or the Washington Department of Ecology.

ENVIRONMENTAL HAZARDS

Now let's take a look at some of the more common environmental hazards that real estate agents need to know about.

ASBESTOS. Asbestos was used for many years in insulation on plumbing pipes and heating ducts, and as general insulation material. It can also be found in floor tile and roofing material. In its original condition, asbestos is considered relatively harmless; but when asbestos dust filters into the air, it can cause lung cancer. Asbestos becomes a hazard in two ways: when it gets old and starts to disintegrate into a fine dust, and when it is damaged or removed during remodeling projects.

There are three methods of dealing with the presence of asbestos:

1. enclosure (this involves placing an airtight barrier between the asbestos and the rest of the space);
2. encapsulation (this involves covering the asbestos with an adhesive that will permanently seal in the asbestos fibers); or
3. removal.

Each of these three methods should only be undertaken by an experienced professional.

UREA FORMALDEHYDE. Urea formaldehyde may be found in the adhesives used in pressed wood building materials, which are widely used in furniture, kitchen cabinets, and some types of paneling.

Urea formaldehyde may release formaldehyde gas, which may cause cancer, skin rashes, and breathing problems. However, it emits significant amounts of dangerous gas only in the first few years. Older urea formaldehyde materials are not considered dangerous.

RADON. Radon, a colorless, odorless gas, is actually present almost everywhere. It is found wherever uranium is deposited in the earth's crust. As uranium decays, radon gas is formed and seeps from the earth, usually into the atmosphere. However, radon sometimes collects in buildings. For example, radon may enter a house through cracks in the foundation or through floor drains. Exposure to dangerous levels of radon gas may cause lung cancer.

There are three ways to lower radon levels in a home:

1. sealing the holes and cracks that allow the gas to enter the home;
2. increasing ventilation to dilute the gas, especially in the areas where radon enters, such as the basement or crawl spaces; and
3. pressurizing the home to keep the gas out.

LEAD-BASED PAINT. Lead, though useful for many things, is extremely toxic to human beings. Children are especially susceptible to lead poisoning because they absorb it more quickly and have a more adverse reaction to its toxicity. Lead damages the brain, the kidneys, and the central nervous system.

The most common source of lead in the home is lead-based paint. Many homes built before 1978 contain some lead-based paint. (Lead is now banned in consumer paint.) As lead-based paint deteriorates, or if it is sanded or scraped, it forms a lead dust that accumulates inside and outside the home. This dust can be breathed in or ingested, increasing the risk of toxic lead exposure.

If there is lead-based paint in a home, it can be either eliminated or covered with non-lead-based paint. This requires special equipment and training; homeowners should not try to handle lead-based paint on their own.

Under some circumstances, a seller or landlord is required by law to make disclosures concerning lead-based paint to prospective buyers or tenants. This disclosure law is discussed in Chapter 7.

FIG. 3.3 ENVIRONMENTAL HAZARDS

ENVIRONMENTAL HAZARDS THAT MAY AFFECT HOMES

- ASBESTOS
- UREA FORMALDEHYDE
- RADON GAS
- LEAD-BASED PAINT
- UNDERGROUND STORAGE TANKS
- WATER CONTAMINATION
- ILLEGAL DRUG MANUFACTURING
- MOLD
- GEOLOGIC HAZARDS: LANDSLIDES, FLOODING, SUBSIDENCE, AND EARTHQUAKES

UNDERGROUND STORAGE TANKS. Underground storage tanks are found not only on commercial and industrial properties, but also on residential properties. A storage tank is considered underground if 10% of its volume (including piping) is below the earth's surface. Probably the most common commercial use of underground storage tanks is for gas stations. Chemical plants, paint manufacturers, and other industries use underground storage tanks to store toxic liquids. In the residential setting, older homes used underground storage tanks to store fuel oil.

The principal danger from underground storage tanks is that they eventually grow old and begin to rust, leaking toxic products into the soil or, even more dangerously, into the groundwater.

Removing underground storage tanks and cleaning up the contaminated soil can be time-consuming and expensive. Both federal and state laws regulate the removal of storage tanks and the necessary cleanup.

WATER CONTAMINATION. Water can be contaminated by a variety of agents, including bacteria, viruses, nitrates, metals such as lead or mercury, fertilizers and pesticides, and radon. These contaminants may come from underground storage tanks, industrial discharge, urban area runoff, malfunctioning septic systems, and runoff from agricultural areas. Drinking contaminated water can cause physical symptoms that range from mild stomach upset to kidney and liver damage, cancer, and death.

If a homeowner uses a well as a water source, it should be tested by health authorities or private laboratories at least once a year. If well water becomes contaminated, the property owner may need to dig a new well.

ILLEGAL DRUG MANUFACTURING. If property has been the site of illegal drug manufacturing, there may be substantial health risks for the occupants. The chemicals used to manufacture certain illegal drugs are highly toxic, and the effects of the contamination can linger for a long time.

If property is currently being used to manufacture illegal drugs, it can be seized by the government. This can occur even if the owner has no knowledge of the illegal drug activity.

> **EXAMPLE:** Meyers owns a single-family home that has been used as a rental property for several years. Unknown to Meyers, the current tenants are manufacturing illegal drugs in the basement of the home. The property could be seized by the government, even though Meyers knows nothing about the drug activity.

Of course, a property should not be listed or sold until any hazardous conditions resulting from drug manufacturing have been eliminated.

MOLD. Mold is a commonplace problem, especially in damp parts of houses such as basements and bathrooms. For most people, the presence of mold does not cause any adverse effects. However, for people who are allergic to mold or who have respiratory problems, the presence of mold may render a house unlivable. You may hear references to "toxic mold," which is something of a misnomer; certain varieties of black mold can be particularly problematic for those who are sensitive to mold, but generally do not pose any more of a health hazard for most people than other types of mold.

Mold can never be completely eliminated, but it can be controlled by cutting off sources of moisture. Mold that is already growing can be removed by scrubbing with a water and bleach solution. Carpet or tile that is affected by mold may need to be removed and thrown out.

Mold problems that you're aware of should be treated as a latent defect and disclosed to prospective buyers. You should also disclose any knowledge of previous incidents of flooding or water damage, since that can start the growth of mold. Bear in mind that mold may grow out of sight, inside walls or heating ducts, and will not necessarily be discovered in the buyer's inspection, so your disclosure is particularly important.

"Mold contingencies," where sale of a property is contingent upon not finding mold during the inspection process, are sometimes written into purchase and sale agreements.

GEOLOGIC HAZARDS. Geologic hazards are a significant concern for many property owners in Washington, especially in the western part of the state.

LANDSLIDES. Probably the most costly geologic problem affecting homeowners is landslides. It's quite common for a house to be built close to the top of a cliff overlooking a body of water, in order to take advantage of the view. However, the weight of the house on unstable soil, particularly after heavy rainfall, can cause ground movement downhill, damaging the foundation or even tearing the house apart.

When you're dealing with a property located on or near a steep slope, you should always look for signs of ground movement. Active soil erosion, cracking, dipping, or slumping ground, and tilting trees are all indicators of slide activity. A property owner may take corrective steps, such as building retaining walls or rockeries, but they are expensive and unlikely to completely solve the problem.

If you see any evidence of landslide activity, it may be wise to consult with a geologist, in order to assess the magnitude of the problem. In addition, if you have listed a property where there is any evidence of ground movement, that should be considered a latent defect and disclosed to potential buyers.

FLOODING. Flooding can also be a serious problem for property owners. Whenever property is located in a flood plain—in the low-lying, flat areas immediately adjacent to a river—there is cause for concern. A prudent agent will check for signs of previous flood damage to structures, particularly in basements and foundations. An agent listing a flood-prone property should disclose frequent flooding as a latent defect.

SUBSIDENCE. Another potential geologic problem is subsidence, the collapse of ground into underground cavities. This can occur naturally, but only in areas of particularly porous bedrock. In most cases, subsidence is caused by man-made cavities. It may happen when forgotten underground storage tanks collapse, or when a water main breaks and washes away soil. It is most common where mining has occurred. Over 250 abandoned coal mines underlie parts of western

Washington, so before engaging in new construction in rural areas where coal mining once occurred, it may be advisable to obtain maps from state or local governments that depict old mines.

EARTHQUAKES. The most potentially destructive geologic problem is also the least predictable and least controllable: earthquakes. Because this is a regional problem, rather than one that affects one or a few properties, there is not much sense in disclosing general earthquake hazards to potential buyers.

However, steps can be taken to protect buildings against earthquakes. In fact, seismic retrofitting can make a property more desirable and increase its value. The most important step in this process involves bolting elements of a home's wood frame to the underlying foundation. Many contractors are able to perform this type of work, and information about seismic retrofitting is widely available from state and local government agencies.

CHAPTER SUMMARY

1. The real estate license law imposes certain restrictions on your listing activities. As a licensee, you can be paid your commission only by your own brokerage. You can't be paid by other firms or other licensees, or by the principal. And you may not sue the principal for a commission; only the firm may sue the principal.

2. A listing agreement belongs to the listing firm. It is a contract between the property seller and the firm; you sign the listing agreement only as an agent of your firm. Should you stop working for the listing firm, the listing remains with the firm. You can't take it with you to your new firm.

3. Under the state's distressed property law, if a licensee meets the definition of a distressed home consultant (which would be rare), she must have a distressed home consultant agreement with the distressed homeowner (seller). She will also owe fiduciary duties to the distressed homeowner.

4. The federal Fair Housing Act prohibits discrimination based on race, color, religion, sex, national origin, disability, or familial status. The Washington Law Against Discrimination prohibits discrimination based on race, creed, color, national origin, sex, sexual orientation and gender identity, marital status, familial status, veteran or military status, or sensory, physical, or mental disability, or the use of a trained guide dog or service animal. Both laws apply to real estate agents acting in their professional capacity *without exception*.

5. While dealing with potential clients and taking listings, you need to scrupulously follow all fair housing laws. Never imply that the presence of a particular group of residents will change property values or other characteristics of a neighborhood. Never refuse to list a property because of a protected characteristic (such as the race or ethnic background) of the home seller. Avoid making any kind of discriminatory slur, including telling racial or ethnic jokes or passively listening to them. You should also review fair housing laws with the seller before taking a listing. If you think the seller may discriminate against potential purchasers, you must refuse to take the listing.

6. When you advertise listed properties, make sure that all your advertising complies with fair housing laws. Never send flyers or choose advertising media based on discriminatory ideas, and make sure any models included in ads are not used in a discriminatory manner. Remember to include the fair housing logo or slogan in your ads.

7. Antitrust laws prohibit price fixing, group boycotts, tie-in arrangements, and market allocation. To avoid charges of price fixing, you should never discuss your commission rates with competing agents, and you must be sure to explain to the seller that the commission rate is fully negotiable. Never use a listing agreement form that has a commission amount or rate already filled in.

8. Federal and state environmental laws that may be relevant to a real estate transaction include the National Environmental Policy Act, the State Environmental Policy Act, the Shoreline Management Act, and the Comprehensive Environmental Response, Compensation, and Liability Act (CERCLA). CERCLA is particularly important, because it may impose liability on property owners for the cost of cleaning up hazardous substances, regardless of fault.

9. The environmental hazards you need to be aware of include asbestos, urea formaldehyde, radon, lead-based paint, underground storage tanks, water contamination, the effects of illegal drug manufacturing, and geologic hazards such as landslides. If you recognize signs of potential environmental hazards in a listed property, these must be disclosed to the buyer.

CHAPTER QUIZ

1. Agent Jackson and Agent Robinson work for the same real estate firm, Stellar Properties. They've both worked closely with a particular buyer. When that buyer finally purchases a house, Stellar Properties receives the selling agent's share of the commission and pays Jackson half of it. Jackson then gives half of her share of the commission to Robinson. This is:

    a. legal, because once a commission share has been paid to a licensee, she is entitled to do whatever she wants with it

    b. legal, because agents are allowed to share compensation if they work for the same firm

    c. illegal, because a firm can share a commission only with another licensed firm

    d. illegal, because a commission split must be handled by the firm or firms involved

2. Generally speaking, a real estate licensee will not be considered a distressed home consultant (and subject to the distressed property law requirements) unless:

    a. he helps a buyer purchase a home that will foreclose soon

    b. he helps a seller sell her home before a foreclosure sale

    c. he personally participates in a distressed property transaction

    d. the buyer delays taking possession until she sells her current home

3. Although the federal Fair Housing Act and the Washington Law Against Discrimination are similar, one significant difference between them is that:

    a. only the Washington law allows an award of damages

    b. the Washington law applies to a wider range of real estate transactions than the Fair Housing Act

    c. the Fair Housing Act covers all types of real property, while the Washington law covers only housing

    d. the Washington law allows an exemption for real estate agents engaged in professional activity

4. Which of the following is not an example of illegal steering?

    a. An agent working with a buyer who has a disability calls his attention to a property with modifications that meet his needs

    b. An agent avoids showing an unmarried buyer houses in neighborhoods where most residents are married couples with children

    c. An agent working with a white couple only shows them homes in predominantly white neighborhoods

    d. An agent working with a minority couple only shows them homes in predominantly minority neighborhoods

5. Your advertising for residential properties should always include:

   a. models from the same ethnic group as the residents of the neighborhood you are advertising in

   b. models of a different ethnic background than the residents of the neighborhood you are advertising in

   c. the Equal Housing Opportunity logo or slogan

   d. a specific explanation of the standards of the community

6. Which of the following actions is most likely to be considered discriminatory?

   a. When a white buyer asks about the racial composition of a neighborhood, an agent truthfully answers that it is predominantly minority

   b. The listing agent for a home in a predominantly minority neighborhood decides to advertise only in the neighborhood newspaper because he thinks other minorities are most likely to be interested in the home

   c. A brokerage uses a marketing plan to let minority buyers know about properties in predominantly white neighborhoods that they might not otherwise be aware of

   d. A white couple expresses a desire not to be shown homes in a minority neighborhood, and their agent complies with their request

7. Which of the following is an example of price fixing?

   a. A listing agent and a selling agent discuss a commission split in a cooperative sale

   b. An agent making a listing presentation tells the seller that she is asking for a 7% commission, but emphasizes that the commission is negotiable

   c. A designated broker holds a staff meeting with her sales agents to discuss commission rates for the office

   d. A designated broker is having lunch with two other designated brokers and mentions that he is raising his commission rate, but there is no further discussion of the matter

8. The Consumer Protection Act does not:

   a. make property owners responsible for the cost of cleaning up hazardous waste even if they did not cause the contamination

   b. prohibit misleading and deceptive advertising

   c. apply to the real estate industry

   d. prohibit the same anticompetitive practices as federal antitrust law

9. Which environmental law requires developers to obtain a substantial development permit before beginning work?

   a. Shoreline Management Act
   b. Endangered Species Act
   c. National Environmental Policy Act
   d. Clean Water Act

10. As a listing agent, what is your responsibility with respect to environmental issues?

    a. Informing your client if you observe any signs of environmental problems, and also disclosing them to buyers
    b. Making sure that buyers receive an environmental impact statement
    c. Deciding what corrective action needs to be taken to solve the problem
    d. All of the above

ANSWER KEY

1. d. Two agents working for the same firm may split a commission, but the commission split must be handled by their firm. A licensee can only receive a commission through her firm.

2. c. Most real estate licensees are exempt from the provisions of the distressed property law when they are providing routine real estate brokerage services. However, if a licensee actually participates in a distressed property transaction, he may be considered a distressed home consultant.

3. b. The Washington Law Against Discrimination covers all real estate transactions, not just residential transactions. It also specifically prohibits a broader range of activities and protects more classes of people than the Fair Housing Act.

4. a. An agent can legitimately bring properties that are specially suited to the needs of a disabled buyer to the buyer's attention.

5. c. Regardless of what type of advertising you use to market a home, it should always include the Equal Housing Opportunity logo or slogan.

6. b. Advertising can be considered discriminatory if it appears only in a publication directed toward the minority neighborhood where the property is located. The advertising should also appear where it will be seen by a broader section of the population.

7. d. Any communication between competing designated brokers about prices, even if they do not explicitly decide to cooperate in fixing prices, could be seen as an invitation to engage in price fixing.

8. a. The Consumer Protection Act overlaps significantly with federal antitrust law and the real estate license law. Liability for cleanup of hazardous waste is determined under CERCLA and other environmental laws.

9. a. Under the Shoreline Management Act, developers must obtain a substantial development permit before starting work on property within 200 feet of a high water mark.

10. a. If you observe signs of environmental issues on a property you've listed, this must be disclosed to your client (the seller) and also to prospective buyers. If they have questions, recommend that they seek expert advice from an environmental engineer or attorney.

4

EVALUATING AND PRICING PROPERTY

AGENT'S ROLE IN PRICING PROPERTY

VALUE

- Types of value
- Value vs. price or cost

EVALUATING RESIDENTIAL PROPERTY

- Neighborhood analysis
- Site analysis
- Building analysis
- Design and layout
- Design deficiencies

PREPARING A COMPETITIVE MARKET ANALYSIS

- CMA software
- Analyzing the seller's property
- Choosing comparable properties
- Price adjustment
- Presenting a CMA

THE PROBLEM OF A LOW APPRAISAL

INTRODUCTION

How quickly your listing sells, or whether it sells at all, depends largely on the listing price. How is a competitive listing price determined? If your seller insists on listing her home at a ridiculously inflated price, should you simply take the listing and hope for the best?

In this chapter, we discuss the listing agent's role in pricing a seller's home, the dangers of setting a listing price too high, the concept of value, factors that affect the value of homes, and the process of preparing a competitive market analysis. The chapter ends with a look at what can happen if the property's appraised value turns out to be lower than the price the parties agreed on.

THE AGENT'S ROLE IN PRICING PROPERTY

It is your seller's responsibility—not yours—to decide on a listing price for his home. However, the average seller does not have the expertise to arrive at a realistic price; he depends on you for information and advice about this important decision. Without your expertise, the seller could easily underprice or overprice his property. Either of these mistakes could have serious consequences for the seller and for you.

EXAMPLE: Jeffries is listing his home with you. He asks you for advice on setting a listing price, but you tell him that the price is up to him.

Jeffries has noticed a few houses in his neighborhood that have been for sale for many months. He believes the houses haven't sold because they are overpriced. He thinks his house is comparable to these other houses, but he wants a quick sale. So Jeffries sets his listing price by deducting $10,000 from the listing price of the other houses. He ends up listing his house for $320,000.

Jeffries's house is actually very appealing and sells quickly at that price. When his house is appraised, he discovers to his dismay that it was actually worth about $350,000. He's very angry—he just lost $30,000 and he considers it entirely your fault. If he decided to sue you, you could lose your commission and might even have to pay additional damages as well.

On the other hand, suppose that when Jeffries sets his listing price, he thinks his house is worth much more than it really is. With a listing price of $390,000, his house languishes on the market for several months. Finally, your listing agreement expires and Jeffries decides to list the property with another firm. Because of an inflated listing price, Jeffries waited in vain for a sale, you wasted a good deal of effort trying to sell an overpriced house, and your reputation in the neighborhood suffered as your "For Sale" sign faded and was then removed without a "SOLD!" banner.

Your ability to suggest a competitive listing price is one of the most important services you can provide a seller. Your advice on a listing price will generally take the form of a **competitive market analysis** or CMA (also called a comparative market analysis or a broker price opinion). A CMA compares your seller's house to similar nearby homes that are on the market or have recently sold. Your analysis of the listing or selling prices of those other houses helps the seller set a realistic listing price for her own house.

In a formal appraisal, a professional appraiser uses the sales comparison approach to estimate a property's value by comparing that property to similar properties that have recently sold. The sales comparison approach is considered the most reliable method for appraising single-unit residential properties, and the CMA process is a modified version of that approach; however, a CMA is not an appraisal. An appraiser uses professional training and experience to estimate a property's market value as of a specific date. A residential appraiser is usually hired to do this by a lender, to help the lender set a maximum loan amount for a loan applicant who wants to buy the property. The appraiser bases this estimate on a wide variety of data, including general social and economic data, so appraisals are generally more complex and based on more information than CMAs. By law, most residential appraisals must be prepared by licensed or certified appraisers in accordance with procedural and ethical guidelines called the Uniform Standards of Professional Appraisal Practice. Since CMAs don't fulfill those requirements, they should not be referred to or treated as appraisals.

As the listing agent, you have a different role than an appraiser. Your job is to provide a home seller with information about the pricing of similar homes in the local market and what those prices indicate about the value of the seller's home—how much it's likely to sell for. This is the information presented in your CMA. With your guidance, the seller can use this information to decide how much to ask for her property.

We'll examine the details of evaluating residential property and preparing a CMA shortly. But first, let's take a brief look at the concept of value.

VALUE

The value of a home has many consequences for the owner. The value largely determines not only how much it costs to buy the home, but also the financing, the property tax assessment, the insurance coverage, the potential rental rate, the eventual selling price, and the income tax consequences of its sale. To estimate a home's value, you need a general understanding of the concept of value.

TYPES OF VALUE

Appraisers distinguish between several different types of value. A property's value can vary depending on which type of value is in question in a given situation. For example, **value in use** is the subjective value placed on a property by someone who owns or uses it. By contrast, **value in exchange** (commonly referred to as **market value**) is the objective value of a property in the eyes of the average person. The difference between these two types of value is one reason the seller needs your help in setting a listing price.

> **EXAMPLE:** Darnell owns a large old house that has been in his family for generations. Because of the history of the house, it is very valuable to Darnell. In other words, its value in use is very high. Yet if an objective third party were considering buying the house, she would not be willing to pay very much for it. The plumbing is poor, the wiring is old, and the design is very outdated. The property's value in exchange is not nearly as high as its value in use.

Real estate agents are concerned with value in exchange, or market value. Here is the most widely accepted definition of market value, the one used by Fannie Mae and Freddie Mac:

> *The most probable price which a property should bring in a competitive and open market under all conditions requisite to a fair sale, the buyer and seller each acting prudently and knowledgeably, and assuming the price is not affected by undue stimulus.*

VALUE VS. PRICE OR COST

When you're estimating the value of property, always remember that there's an important distinction between market value and market price. Market value, under the definition above, is what should be paid if a property is purchased and sold under all the conditions of a fair sale. **Market price** is the price actually paid for a property, regardless of whether the parties to the transaction were informed and acting free of unusual pressure.

Another related concept is that of cost. **Cost** is the amount of money that was paid to acquire the property and build the structures on it. A property's cost, value, and price may all be different.

> **EXAMPLE:** A developer paid $135,000 for a parcel of vacant land and then spent $150,000 to build a house on the land. After the house was completed, the property was worth $350,000. But the developer needed some fast cash, so he sold the property at the "fire sale" price of $325,000. The cost of the house was $285,000, the value of the house was $350,000, and the price of the house was $325,000.

The basis for a good listing price for a home is its market value, not its original cost or purchase price. And the real estate agent's best tool for estimating market value is a competitive market analysis, which begins with an understanding of how to evaluate residential property.

EVALUATING RESIDENTIAL PROPERTY

As we said, competitive market analysis involves comparing the seller's home (often called the **subject property** in this context) to similar nearby homes that have recently sold or are for sale. (These are known as **comparable properties**, comparables, or sometimes just "comps"). CMAs are an effective way to predict a property's likely selling price because an informed buyer acting free of pressure will not pay more for a particular property than she would have to pay for an equally desirable substitute property. Thus, if the seller is objective, he will base his listing price on recent selling prices and listing prices for similar properties in the same area. To provide a reliable indication of the subject property's market value, the comparables should be as similar to the subject property as possible in terms of location, physical features, and other considerations that affect value.

So before we turn to the process of preparing a CMA, let's look at factors that may have an impact on the value of a home. These are things to notice when you're gathering information about the subject property, and also (to a lesser extent) when you're choosing the comparables for your CMA. The factors fall into three categories:

1. the property's neighborhood,
2. the property (or site) itself, and
3. the improvements on the property.

NEIGHBORHOOD ANALYSIS. Few factors have as great an impact on a property's value as its location, or neighborhood. A neighborhood is an area that contains similar types of properties. Its boundaries may be determined by physical obstacles (such as highways and bodies of water), land use patterns, the age and value of homes or other buildings, and the economic status of the residents.

Location may have an especially dramatic impact on the value of a house that is notably better or worse in quality than the rest of the neighborhood. A high-quality house in a neighborhood of low-quality houses loses value. And the value of a relatively weak property is enhanced by a desirable neighborhood.

Here are some factors to look at when evaluating a residential neighborhood:

1. **Percentage of homeownership.** Is there a high degree of owner-occupancy, or do rental properties predominate? Owner-occupied homes are generally better-maintained and less susceptible to deterioration.

2. **Vacant homes and lots.** An unusual number of vacant homes or lots suggests a low level of interest in the area, which has a negative effect on property values. On the other hand, significant construction activity indicates strong interest in the area.

3. **Conformity.** The homes in a neighborhood should be reasonably similar in style, age, size, and quality. Strictly enforced zoning and private restrictions promote conformity and protect property values.

4. **Changing land use.** Is the neighborhood in the middle of a transition from residential use to some other type of use? If so, the properties may be losing value or, in some cases, gaining value.

5. **Contour of the land.** Mildly rolling topography is preferable to terrain that is either monotonously flat or excessively hilly.

6. **Streets.** Wide, gently curving streets are more appealing than narrow or straight streets. Streets should be hard-surfaced and well maintained.

7. **Utilities.** Does the neighborhood have electricity, gas, water, sewers, and phone service? What about cable television and internet access?

8. **Nuisances.** Not surprisingly, nuisances (odors, eyesores, industrial noises or pollutants, or exposure to unusual winds, smog, or fog) in or near a neighborhood hurt property values.

9. **Reputation.** Is the neighborhood considered prestigious? If so, that will increase property values.

10. **Proximity.** How far is it to traffic arterials and to important points such as downtown, employment centers, and shopping centers?

11. **Schools.** What schools serve the neighborhood? Are they highly regarded? Are they within walking distance? The quality of a school or school district can make a major difference in property values in a residential neighborhood.

12. **Public services.** How well is the neighborhood served by public transportation, police, and firefighting units?

13. **Governmental influences.** Does zoning in and around the neighborhood promote residential use and insulate the property owner from nuisances?

Of course, as you gain experience, you'll become familiar with the neighborhoods in your area and their distinguishing characteristics. Before long, you'll be able to gauge the effect of the neighborhood on a property's value as soon as you hear where the property is located.

SITE ANALYSIS. Studying a property's site means collecting information about the following factors:

1. **Width.** This refers to the lot's measurements from one side boundary to the other. Width can vary from front to back, as in the case of a pie-shaped lot on a cul-de-sac.

2. **Frontage.** Frontage is the length of the front boundary of the lot, the boundary that abuts a street or a body of water. The amount of frontage can be an important consideration if it measures the property's access or exposure to something desirable, such as a lake or a river.

3. **Depth.** Depth is the distance between the site's front boundary and its rear boundary. Greater depth (more than the norm) can mean greater value, but it doesn't always. For example, suppose Lot 1 and Lot 2 are the same, except that Lot 2 is deeper; Lot 2 is not necessarily more valuable than Lot 1. Each situation must be analyzed individually to determine whether more depth translates into greater value.

4. **Area.** Area is the total size of the site. The area of a residential lot is commonly stated either in square feet or in acres.

5. **Shape.** Lots with uniform width and depth (such as rectangular lots) are almost always more useful than irregularly shaped lots; a standard shape is more versatile for building purposes.

6. **Topography.** A site is generally more valuable if it is aesthetically appealing. Rolling terrain is preferable to flat, monotonous land. On the other hand, if the site would be costly to develop because it sits well above or below the street or is excessively hilly, that lessens its value.

7. **Position and orientation.** How a lot is situated relative to the surrounding area influences its value. Consider whether the site has a view, and how much sunshine it gets during the day. And is it sheltered, or exposed to the elements and/or to traffic noise?

8. **Title.** Matters that affect a property's title can also affect its value. When you examine the site, look for signs of easements or encroachments. If a utility company has an easement across the rear portion of the property, for example, this would reduce the value of the property in comparison to a similar property with no easement.

BUILDING ANALYSIS. After evaluating the neighborhood and the site, the next step is to examine the improvements built on the property. For many residential properties, this means a house and garage, and perhaps a garden shed or workshop. Here are some of the primary factors to analyze.

1. **Size of house (square footage).** This includes the improved living area, excluding the garage, basement, and porches. For most buyers, the size of the house is one of the most important concerns, along with the number of bedrooms and bathrooms (see below). As a general rule, these three factors affect market value more than any others aside from location.

2. **Number of bedrooms.** The number of bedrooms has a major impact on value. For instance, if all else is equal, a two-bedroom home is worth considerably less than a three-bedroom home.

3. **Number of bathrooms.** A full bath is a wash basin, toilet, shower, and bathtub; a three-quarter bath is a wash basin, toilet, and either a shower or tub. A half bath is a wash basin and toilet only. The number of bathrooms can have a noticeable effect on value.

4. **Basement.** A functional basement, especially a finished basement, contributes to value. (However, the amount a finished basement contributes to value is almost never enough to recover the cost of the finish work.)

5. **Air conditioning.** The presence or absence of an air conditioning system is important in hot regions.

6. **Energy efficiency.** Energy-efficient features, such as double-paned windows, good insulation, and weather stripping, increase value.

7. **Garage or carport.** An enclosed garage is generally better than a carport. How many cars can it accommodate? Is there work or storage space in addition to space for parking? Is it possible to enter the home directly from the garage or carport, protected from the weather?

8. **Construction quality.** Is the quality of the materials and workmanship good, average, or poor?

9. **Age/condition.** How old is the home? Is its overall condition good, average, or poor? Depending on the condition, the "effective age" of the home may be more or less than its actual age.

10. **Design and layout.** Is the floor plan functional and convenient? Are the design and layout attractive and efficient, or are there obvious design deficiencies? (These issues are discussed below.)

11. **Curb appeal.** A house that impresses potential buyers as they drive up is halfway sold. What overall visual impression does the property make?

The last four factors on the list—quality, condition, layout, and curb appeal—involve more subjective judgment than the rest. Taken together, though, those four factors are nearly as important as the size of the house and the number of bedrooms and bathrooms. Further increasing their importance is that CMA software doesn't ordinarily take these more subjective factors into account. That means it's up to you to evaluate what impact they have on the value of the property in question, as we'll discuss later on.

While curb appeal and condition can be subjective, standard layout or design problems usually are not. Let's take a look at this particular factor in more detail.

DESIGN AND LAYOUT. A good layout adds real value to a house, while a poor one makes the property significantly less desirable. Here are some questions to ask yourself as you examine the design of a house.

GENERAL DESIGN. The number of bedrooms in a house usually determines which buyers will consider purchasing it. Keep in mind the family size of those potential buyers as you evaluate the house.

In relation to the number of bedrooms, is the house large enough overall? Are there enough bathrooms, and an adequate number of closets? Is there a separate family room, children's playroom, or other recreational space?

More generally, is there sufficient work space in the kitchen and laundry room, and is there storage space for cleaning and gardening tools? Are there enough windows and natural light, especially in the kitchen and other work or recreational spaces?

LIVING ROOM AND FAMILY ROOM. How large are the living room and the family or recreation room (if any)? Will the shape of each room and the available wall space accommodate the furniture that will probably be placed in it?

DINING ROOM OR DINING AREA. Is the dining area convenient to the kitchen and large enough for the number of people who will be eating there?

KITCHEN. Is the kitchen convenient to an outside entrance and to the garage or carport? Is there adequate counter and cabinet space?

BEDROOMS. How large are the bedrooms? Is there a master bedroom that's significantly larger than the other bedrooms? Are the bedroom closets big enough? Where are the bedrooms located in the house? It's better for the bedrooms to be located apart from the living room, family room, kitchen, and other work or recreational spaces.

BATHROOMS. There should be at least two bathrooms if the house has more than two bedrooms. In many areas, particularly in newer houses, a private bathroom off the master bedroom is standard. Are there windows or ceiling fans in the bathrooms to provide adequate ventilation?

DESIGN DEFICIENCIES. Here are some common design deficiencies to watch out for:

- No front hall closet.
- Back door hard to reach from kitchen, or from driveway or garage.
- No comfortable area in or near kitchen where family can eat informally.
- Kids' bedrooms on different floor than parents' bedroom (makes supervision harder).
- Dining room not easily accessible from kitchen.

- Stairway leading to the second story is off of a room rather than in a hallway or foyer.
- Bathroom or some bedrooms visible from living room or foyer.
- Family room or recreation room not visible from kitchen.
- No direct access to basement from outside the house.
- Bedrooms not separated by bathroom or closet wall (for soundproofing).
- It's necessary to pass through one of the bedrooms to reach another bedroom.
- Outdoor living areas (such as patio or deck) not accessible from kitchen.

As we said, a home's market value may be affected by any of the factors concerning the neighborhood, the site, and the building itself. Keep in mind, however, that the less important factors aren't ordinarily taken into account when you're preparing a competitive market analysis. Most CMAs focus only on the factors that have the greatest impact on market value.

PREPARING A COMPETITIVE MARKET ANALYSIS

Now that you understand how to evaluate residential property, let's take a closer look at preparing a CMA. Here are the main steps:

1. collecting and analyzing information about the seller's property,
2. choosing the comparable properties,
3. comparing the seller's property to each comparable and noting differences that may affect value, and
4. estimating an appropriate listing price or price range for the seller's property based on the comparables' prices.

Any CMA involves these basic steps, but the process may be more or less complicated—and more or less automated—depending on the type of property involved and how active the market has been. For example, if the seller's property is in a large subdivision of very similar, relatively new houses where there have been numerous sales in the past few months, there are likely to be plenty of excellent comparable properties available, and the result generated by the CMA software you use is likely to be a reliable estimate of the market value of the seller's home. On the other hand, if the seller's property is an unusual old house in a neighborhood of dissimilar homes where sales have been sluggish during most of the past year, really good comparables may not exist. In that situation, you'll need to do more analysis and use your judgment to arrive at a reliable result.

CMA SOFTWARE

Various computer programs are available to help real estate agents prepare CMAs. In many cases, a CMA function is included in the program agents use to access their multiple listing service database. In addition, there is commercially available (non-MLS) software that creates a somewhat more polished-looking CMA report and incorporates other features of use to agents. This type of commercial software is licensed by the MLS to search the MLS database to find comparable properties and use that information to generate price estimates. Many larger brokerage firms have similar programs.

Our discussion describes how agents use CMA software only in very general terms, avoiding the level of detail that varies from one program to another. In other words, this is an overview of the CMA process, not step-by-step instructions.

ANALYZING THE SELLER'S PROPERTY

The starting point for a competitive market analysis is gathering information about the seller's property. You import or type this data into your CMA program, and the program uses the location and key characteristics of the seller's property to suggest comparables from the MLS database.

The MLS database may already include useful information about the seller's home from previous sales of the property. Other online resources can also provide helpful information; for example, you might look up the seller's home on Trulia or similar property-listing websites. And since your seller is almost certain to have looked at Zillow, you want to be familiar with Zillow's price estimate for the property and be prepared to address weaknesses in the Zillow valuation if it's higher than your own.

You may find it worthwhile to generate a preliminary CMA using only information collected online. This is for your own use, to get a sense of how the seller's property fits into the current market. The software typically offers a "quick CMA" option to make that easy. However, to accurately evaluate the seller's property, there's no substitute for seeing it in person, inside and out. Before creating a final CMA report and presenting your conclusion to the seller, you'll need to visit the property and tour the interior (see Chapter 5). A drive-by visit to look only at the exterior of the seller's home risks missing something about the property—good or bad—that's important for your pricing recommendation.

CHOOSING COMPARABLE PROPERTIES

Once you've visited the seller's property and added information about it to your CMA program, the next step is to search for comparables. Comparables for a CMA can include completed sales, pending sales, current listings, and/or listings that have expired without a sale.

Based on key aspects of the subject property and other criteria you specify, the CMA software searches the MLS database and generates a list of potential comparables for you to choose from. We'll discuss CMA search criteria shortly. First, though, there are some basic requirements for comparables that you need to know.

BASIC REQUIREMENTS. A potential comparable that fails to meet the requirements described below doesn't reliably indicate market value, so you shouldn't use it in a CMA.

If a potential comparable is a current or recently expired listing, you'll be concerned with only two factors:

1. **Location of comparable.** Ideally, a comparable property should be in the same neighborhood as the seller's property. If you can't find enough comparables in the seller's neighborhood, you can choose comparables from similar-quality neighborhoods nearby.

   Even if your comparable is located in the same neighborhood as the seller's home, you may have to take into account differences in value due to location *within* the neighborhood.

   EXAMPLE: Two identical properties located one block apart in the same neighborhood may have very different values if one of the properties borders a lake and the other does not. The values of the properties could also differ substantially if one is located on a busy main avenue, while the other is on a quiet side street.

2. **Physical characteristics.** Of course, to qualify as a comparable, a property must have physical characteristics that are similar to the subject property. As discussed, square footage and number of bedrooms and bathrooms are the most important features; but it's also preferable for the comparables to resemble the subject property in style, layout, construction materials, and condition.

If the comparable is a completed or pending sale, you will also be concerned with these additional factors:

3. **Date of comparable sale.** The sale should be recent. The comparison is more reliable if the sale occurred within the last six months; within three months is even better. Sales older than six months should be considered only if there are no other alternatives. Older sales aren't reliable enough, since market conditions (such as sales prices, interest rates, and construction costs) change over time.

4. **Terms of sale.** Unless the buyer paid cash, how was the sale financed? If the financing terms did not affect the price paid for the property, the financing is called **cash equivalent**. For instance, if the buyer used a standard conventional loan to finance the purchase of the home, the financing is cash equivalent and the price paid accurately represents the market value of the property. On the other hand, if the seller helped the buyer qualify for institutional financing, the sales price does not indicate what a standard or cash equivalent buyer would have paid.

   EXAMPLE: The buyer's lender is charging $10,000 in discount points. The seller is going to pay the points to help the buyer qualify for the loan. The purchase price the buyer has agreed to pay is about $10,000 more than he would otherwise have paid, to compensate the seller for paying the points. Thus, the sales price is higher than what a cash or cash equivalent buyer would pay.

   Seller financing—when a seller provides all of the financing for the transaction, or secondary financing to supplement a standard loan—often is not cash equivalent. For example, the buyer might benefit from a below-market interest rate, a small downpayment, or no loan fees. The seller offers this advantageous financing as an inducement, in order to get a higher selling price than a cash equivalent buyer would pay. However (in contrast to the very simple example given above), it's often difficult to estimate how much the terms of the seller financing affected the price. The same is true for institutional financing with nonstandard terms or features.

   Because of these complexities, you should generally stick to standard lender-financed transactions or all-cash transactions when choosing comparables.

5. **Conditions of sale.** This factor concerns the motivations of the buyer and seller in a particular transaction. A sale can be used as a comparable only

if it took place under normal market conditions: it was an arm's length transaction (between unrelated parties), neither party was acting under unusual pressure, and both parties acted prudently and knowledgeably and in their own best interests.

EXAMPLE: Morgan has been transferred to another city, and she's due to begin her new job in four weeks. Her employer is paying for her moving expenses and has also offered to make up the difference between the market value of her house and any reasonable offer that is made in the first three weeks. Morgan can accept a low offer just to make a quick sale, since she won't personally lose any money on the transaction. This seller is not typically motivated, so this transaction should not be used as a comparable.

If a sale didn't take place under normal conditions, the price paid doesn't indicate market value. For example, homes that are in foreclosure (or on the verge of it) often sell for less than their market value because the sellers are under pressure to sell quickly. You can typically eliminate foreclosure properties from your CMA by limiting your search for comparables to standard transactions. The MLS database won't necessarily include information about other conditions of sale, such as whether a sale was an arm's length transaction; however, whenever you see a property that's similar to the other proposed comparables yet has an oddly high or low price, it's a good bet that the conditions of sale weren't normal. It's best to avoid properties with outlier prices whether you know the reason for the price differential or not.

SEARCH CRITERIA. With those basic requirements for comparables in mind, let's discuss the search criteria for your CMA. Search criteria determine which properties from the MLS database will appear in your search results. You'll typically specify the criteria for a few of the most important elements and use the software's default settings for the rest.

TRANSACTION STATUS. One of the criteria you'll specify is the types of transactions you want included in the search results. As we said, comparables used in CMAs can be a combination of completed sales, pending sales, current listings, and expired listings. Sales prices are generally the best indicators of market value; listing prices tend to be somewhat higher than the prices properties actually sell for, to provide room for negotiation. Even so, it's a good idea to include some current listings in a CMA, because those are homes the subject property will be competing against. Listings that recently expired without a sale are also useful, since their prices show what buyers were unwilling to pay for a comparable property, which indicates an upper limit for a suitable price range for the subject property.

DATE RANGE. As you've seen, only recent transactions are good indicators of current market value. CMA software typically limits searches to the past year by default, but in most cases a shorter time window, such as six months or three months, should be used. The appropriate time frame depends on how busy and how volatile the market has been. A shorter period is especially advisable if prices have been rising or falling rapidly. However, if your search generates too few matches, it may be necessary to specify a longer date range and try again.

SIZE, BEDROOMS, AND BATHROOMS. Of course, the physical characteristics that have the greatest impact on value (square footage, number of bedrooms, and number of bathrooms) are key search criteria. But your search doesn't have to be limited to properties that match the seller's property exactly; the software will generally allow you to specify a range of values instead of a single number. For example, if the seller's house is 2,200 square feet, you might ask for potential comparables that are between 2,000 and 2,500 square feet. Another example: if the seller's house has three bedrooms, you would almost always limit your search to comparables with three bedrooms; but with much larger homes, the exact number of bedrooms might be less critical and you could specify a range.

GEOGRAPHIC SCOPE. Since location affects value as much or more than any other factor, one of the most important parameters you'll set is the geographical scope of the search. You can do this by specifying the name of the seller's neighborhood or subdivision, but most software also offers a map tool for this purpose. It shows you the location of the seller's property on the map and allows you to draw a circle of any size around it; only potential comparables located within that circle (and matching your other search criteria) will show up in your search results.

OTHER FEATURES. In addition to transaction types, date range, square footage, bedrooms, bathrooms, and location, CMA software typically allows you to set many other criteria for your search, including various specific property features. For example, if the seller's property has a swimming pool and a three-car garage, you might limit your search to comparables with a swimming pool and either a two- or a three-car garage. Typically you can also specify features such as house style, air conditioning, and so on.

Whether it's worthwhile to add these kind of limits to your search depends on the circumstances. The essential consideration is whether a particular item is likely to have a significant effect on market value. Another consideration is how many matches your initial search turns up. If the software generates a long list of potential comparables, you might use additional features to narrow down your choices.

HOW MANY COMPARABLES? Three completed sales has traditionally been the minimum number of comparables for a residential appraisal, and that's a good rule of thumb for CMAs too. Before the advent of CMA software, it was customary to use three sales, three current listings, and three expired listings as comparables, and that's still a common practice. But with the number-crunching power of software, you may want to use quite a few more comparables, if available. Remember, though, that including more comparables in a CMA report isn't always better. You want to provide the seller with enough information to make a good pricing decision, but not so much that it's confusing.

PRICE ADJUSTMENT

Once you've selected the best comparables available, the CMA software generates a price range for the seller's property, such as "between $354,000 and $395,800." The software usually also pinpoints a particular price within this range as the price the property is most likely to sell for. (A sample CMA summary page is shown in Figure 4.1.)

Looking at the price range and price suggested by the software, you must make a judgment call. Are these figures ones that you can pass along directly to the seller, or do they need downward or upward adjustment?

WHEN ADJUSTMENT IS NECESSARY. Deciding whether an adjustment is needed requires evaluating the comparable properties again. Solid comparables (ones that strongly resemble the subject property) indicate that you should leave the price range and price alone; that's the most common situation in a market with a reasonable number of recently sold properties. In a sparse market, though, the comps may be weak and adjustment is probably necessary. Adjustment also is likely to be needed if the seller's property is unique in some way.

Keep in mind that you're only interested in significant differences between the comparables and the seller's property. No comparable will be an exact match (except perhaps in new housing developments), and small differences can safely be ignored.

FIG. 4.1   COMPETITIVE MARKET ANALYSIS SUMMARY PAGE

Executive Summary: 458 Maple St.   Jeffersville, ST

House Value	Rental Value
$322,500 Probable Value	**$2,800**
$238/sq. ft.	$2.07/sq. ft.
$297,000 - $347,000	$2,630 - $2,980
$220/sq. ft. - $257/sq. ft.	$1.94/sq. ft. - $2.20/sq. ft.

Subject Attributes

PROPERTY TYPE	OWNER OCCUPIED	BEDROOMS	BATHS	GLA	LOT SIZE	YEAR BUILT	CONDITION
Single Family Detached	No	3	2	1,350	12,000	2011	Excellent

COMMENTS: Centrally located, convenient to business center and public transportation. No basement. Market is very competitive.

Recent Similar Sales

	Similarity	Distance	Address	Sale Price	Sale Date	Age	Beds	Baths	GLA	Site
1.	High	0.12 mi.	291 Maple St.	$320,000	1 mo. ago	8 yrs	3	1	1,250	12,000
2.	High	0.96 mi.	175 Main St.	$318,000	2 mo. ago	12 yrs	3	2	1,350	11,000
3.	High	0.64 mi.	389 5th Ave. S	$323,000	2 mo. ago	10 yrs	3	2	1,420	12,000
4.	High	0.47 mi.	995 Merrit St.	$314,000	2 mo. ago	5 yrs	2	2	1,415	11,500
5.	High	0.66 mi.	453 9th Ave.	$295,000	3 mo. ago	13 yrs	3	2	1,300	13,000
6.	High	1.0 mi.	620 Broadwater	$351,000	3 mo. ago	8 yrs	4	2	1,550	11,000
7.	High	1.01 mi.	1208 Lunenberg	$333,500	3 mo. ago	15 yrs	3	1	1,450	12,000
8.	High	1.02 mi.	1113 11th Ave.	$340,000	4 mo. ago	18 yrs	4	2	1,500	13,500
9.	High	0.68 mi.	550 Sullivan St.	$311,000	4 mo. ago	11 yrs	3	2	1,200	12,500
10.	High	0.28 mi.	412 Cobb St.	$298,000	4 mo. ago	9 yrs	3	2	1,300	11,500

Active Listings

	Similarity	Distance	Address	List Price	List Date	Age	Beds	Baths	GLA	Site	Days on Market
1.	High	0.43 mi.	256 Oak St.	$315,400	0 mo. ago	10 yrs	3	2	1,270	11,200	10
2.	High	0.24 mi.	1156 Larch St.	$312,000	1 mo. ago	6 yrs	3	1	1,400	12,000	35
3.	High	0.25 mi.	1052 8th Ave.	$305,250	2 mo. ago	7 yrs	3	2	1,300	11,200	55
4.	High	0.37 mi.	721 Bingham St.	$345,000	3 mo. ago	13 yrs	3	2	1,200	12,000	80
5.	High	0.42 mi.	315 Union St.	$350,000	11 mo. ago	13 yrs	3	2	1,350	12,500	320
6.	Moderate	0.40 mi.	808 2nd Ave.	$339,500	3 mo. ago	12 yrs	3	1	1,400	13,000	80
7.	Moderate	1.03 mi.	1220 Harvey St.	$347,500	3 mo. ago	9 yrs	3	2	1,400	12,000	100
8.	Low	0.95 mi.	1503 Cottle St.	$389,000	2 mo. ago	11 yrs	4	2	1,500	14,500	45
9.	Low	1.26 mi.	111 View Pl.	$472,000	2 mo. ago	14 yrs	4	3	1,900	14,000	50
10.	Low	0.88 mi.	303 9th Ave.	$415,000	3 mo. ago	14 yrs	4	2	1,650	13,000	90

Expired Listings

	Similarity	Distance	Address	List Price	List Date	Age	Beds	Baths	GLA	Site	Days on Market
1.	High	0.5 mi.	2782 Cherry Ln.	$333,600	9 mo. ago	6 yrs	2	2	1,150	12,000	120
2.	High	0.66 mi.	10012 7th Ave.	$338,800	7 mo. ago	4 yrs	3	2	1,300	11,200	95

In most cases, the comparables will already match the seller's property in number of bedrooms and bathrooms, and be similar in size, so you usually won't need to worry about adjustments for these basic factors. Unusual features such as outstanding landscaping or extensive custom cabinetry might call for adjustment. Also, it's unlikely that the software accounts for differences between the subject property and the comparables that are more subjective, such as curb appeal, layout, and condition. If your seller's property is significantly better or worse than the comps in one or more of these ways, then some kind of adjustment is probably called for.

An adjustment may also be needed if the market is very active or prices are rapidly rising or falling. If the comps are more than a couple of months old in such a market, your recommendation to the seller should take that into account.

MAKING ADJUSTMENTS. Let's briefly discuss the "how-to" of price adjustment. It will help to first describe how this step is handled in the sales comparison approach to value, the appraisal method that competitive market analysis was originally based on.

In a sales comparison appraisal, as in a CMA, each comparable's price helps indicate the subject property's value. If there are significant differences between a particular comparable and the subject property, the appraiser takes each difference into account by adjusting the price of the comparable upward or downward. If done correctly, the result shows what the comparable would have sold for if it matched the subject property more closely.

> **EXAMPLE:** Suppose one of the comparables sold for $525,000. It's very similar to the subject property (the seller's house), except that the comparable has a three-car garage and the subject property has a two-car garage. For the valuation of the subject property to reflect this difference, it's necessary to adjust the comparable's price downward. Let's suppose that market analysis or experience suggests that the value of a third garage space is approximately $15,000 in this neighborhood. So the appraiser subtracts $15,000 from the comparable's price: $525,000 − $15,000 = $510,000. In theory, if the comparable had only two garage spaces (like the subject property has), it would have sold for $510,000, not $525,000.
>
> If the situation were reversed, and the comparable had one less garage space than the subject property, the appraiser would adjust the comparable's price upwards by the value of the extra space.

FIG. 4.2   STEPS IN PREPARING A CMA

- GATHER INFORMATION ABOUT THE NEIGHBORHOOD AND THE PROPERTY

- USE CMA SOFTWARE TO GENERATE A LIST OF POTENTIAL COMPARABLES

- COMPARE EACH COMPARABLE PROPERTY TO THE SELLER'S PROPERTY AND CHOOSE THE BEST COMPS

- GENERATE A PRICE RANGE ESTIMATE BASED ON THE MAIN FACTORS (SQUARE FOOTAGE, BEDROOMS, BATHROOMS, NEIGHBORHOOD)

- IF NECESSARY, ADJUST THE PRICE RANGE BASED ON OTHER FACTORS (PROPERTY CONDITION, CURB APPEAL, LAYOUT, MARKET CONDITIONS)

Using this technique, a comparable that varies in some particular way from the subject property (but is otherwise similar) can still provide a useful indication of the subject property's value.

Real estate agents preparing CMAs by hand used to go through this adjustment process, and agents can still make the same kinds of up or down adjustments to the price of each comparable using their CMA software. However, in a typical market agents often don't do that—if only because they lack the training to put accurate dollar values on particular features. Instead, if the seller's property is noticeably better or worse than the comps overall, they simply adjust the software's recommended listing price (or price range) up or down by a certain amount based on their feel for the market.

How does a less experienced agent know how much of a price adjustment is appropriate for a particular CMA? Talking to more seasoned brokers in your office is the basic resource. In some firms, developing a listing price recommendation is a joint effort.

PRESENTING A CMA

The final step in a CMA is presenting your results to the seller, your prospective client. CMA software lets you generate a detailed, professional-looking report for the seller that can be printed out or shared electronically. Photos of the comps are featured, the price range estimate is explained, and various charts and graphs give the seller a context for understanding the pricing recommendation. A map shows the proximity of the comparables to the seller's property. The agent can tailor the report's contents to meet a particular seller's needs. We'll examine the presentation in more detail in the next chapter.

THE PROBLEM OF A LOW APPRAISAL

In spite of your best efforts to help sellers choose a listing price based on the market value of their home, you're likely to run into the problem of a low appraisal from time to time.

A low appraisal is an appraiser's estimate of value that is significantly lower than the price a seller and a buyer have agreed on. They've entered into a purchase and sale agreement at a sales price that both parties are pleased with. But when the property is formally appraised for the buyer's lender, the appraiser concludes that the property is not worth as much as the buyer has agreed to pay.

A low appraisal puts most financed sales in jeopardy. If the transaction is contingent on financing, the contingency often states that the buyer doesn't have to complete the sale if the appraised value turns out to be less than the agreed price. Even when a buyer would like to go ahead with the purchase in spite of the low appraisal, she may not be able to afford to do so. The purchase loan is based on the sales price or the appraised value, whichever is less, so in many cases a low appraisal means a smaller loan—and a bigger downpayment.

EXAMPLE:

1. Buyer is prepared to make a 10% downpayment and obtain a 90% loan.

2. Sales price is $210,000.

3. Appraisal is issued at $200,000.

4. Maximum loan amount is 90% of $200,000.

$200,000	Appraised value
× 90%	Loan-to-value ratio
$180,000	Maximum loan amount

Because of the low appraisal ($10,000 less than the sales price), the loan amount is limited to $180,000. The buyer expected to make a $21,000 downpayment ($210,000 sales price × 90% = $189,000 loan). But the buyer would now have to make a $30,000 downpayment ($210,000 − $180,000 loan = $30,000) to pay the $210,000 price.

The easy solution to the problem of a low appraisal is for the seller to lower the sales price to the appraised value. But the seller may not be willing to do this; once a seller has become accustomed to a certain sales price, he'll usually be reluctant to give it up.

Sometimes the buyer and seller will agree to a compromise price between the appraised value and the original sales price. More often, this solution runs up against both the seller's reluctance to lower the price and the buyer's reluctance (or inability) to pay any more than the appraised value.

Because of these problems, when there's a significant gap between the sales price and the appraised value, the most likely result is termination of the sale. It's the real estate agent's job to help the parties avoid this outcome whenever possible.

In some cases, the agent should ask the lender to reconsider the appraised value in the hope that it will be increased to a figure more acceptable to the buyer and seller. This is called a request for reconsideration of value.

REQUEST FOR RECONSIDERATION OF VALUE

Although appraisers try to be objective, subjective considerations are a part of every appraisal. In the end the appraiser's conclusions are only an opinion of value. When you get a low appraisal and you genuinely believe the appraiser is mistaken, you can appeal the appraisal by submitting a request for reconsideration of value to the lender. It's rare, but the request may lead to a new, higher valuation, possibly to the figure the buyer and seller originally agreed on.

If the home has undergone remodeling or has features that the appraiser might have missed, these should be pointed out in the request.

EVALUATING A LOW APPRAISAL. The sooner you find out about a low appraisal, the better. After the appraiser has inspected the seller's property, ask a representative of the lender (for example, the loan officer) to call you with the results of the appraisal as soon as they are received. Don't try to get the results directly from the appraiser; she has a fiduciary relationship with the lender and is not allowed to divulge information about the appraisal to others without the lender's permission.

If the appraisal comes in low, ask the loan officer for the following information:

1. the final value estimate,
2. the value indicated by the sales comparison method, and
3. the addresses of the comparables the appraiser used.

This is the essential information, because the sales comparison analysis is the heart of a residential appraisal, the part that the appraiser really relies on when estimating market value.

Evaluate the appraiser's comparables and update your competitive market analysis. Then decide if a request for reconsideration of value is a realistic option. You will have to support your request with at least three comparable sales (not listings) that indicate a higher value estimate is in order. If you're going to convince the lender that your comparables are more reliable than the appraiser's, yours must be more like the subject property than the appraiser's are.

If you believe the lender may grant a request for reconsideration, your next step is to prepare the request and a cover letter.

PREPARING A RECONSIDERATION REQUEST. Some lenders have their own form for requests for reconsideration of value. If so, you should use their form (in fact, you may be required to). Otherwise, you can prepare your own; your brokerage likely has software for preparing these requests.

Write a cover letter making your request and attach your competitive market analysis to it. The cover letter should be simple and very polite; do not criticize the appraiser.

Keep in mind that federal and state law prohibits anyone with an interest in a real estate transaction from inappropriately influencing the appraiser. The law prohibits a licensee from (among other things) providing an appraiser with an anticipated value, conditioning the payment of the appraiser's fee on the appraisal result, or otherwise encouraging a specific outcome. Violation of this law is grounds for disciplinary action. However, the law specifically permits asking an appraiser to:

1. consider additional information about the property,
2. provide further detail or explanation for the appraiser's conclusion, or
3. correct any factual errors in the appraisal report.

RESPONSE TO REQUEST. Upon receiving a request for reconsideration of value, the lender usually relays the additional comparables to the appraiser and asks the appraiser whether this information affects the final value estimate. The appraiser isn't likely to find the new information persuasive, but if she does, she may issue a revised appraisal report.

CHAPTER SUMMARY

1. It is the seller's responsibility to establish a listing price. However, your sellers will rely on you for advice about listing prices. Your advice will usually take the form of a competitive market analysis, which presents information about similar properties that are currently for sale or that have sold recently in the seller's neighborhood.

2. While there are many different types of value, you will be most concerned with market value, which should be the basis for the seller's listing price. Market value is the most probable price that a property should bring in under normal market conditions. (Remember to distinguish value from price and cost. Price is what a buyer actually paid for a property, and cost is what was paid to purchase a property and build an improvement on it.)

3. When you estimate the value of a seller's property, your first step is to collect and study information about the property. As you study the house itself, you should pay particular attention to its design and layout. Once you have a clear picture of all the features, amenities, and drawbacks of the seller's property, you can choose your comparables.

4. Comparables are properties in the seller's neighborhood (or a similar neighborhood) that are similar to the seller's property and that are currently for sale or have sold recently. Your CMA software will present a list of possible comparables for you to choose from. Once you select these, the software generates a suggested price range that you can adjust if necessary. The software also generates a report to give the seller as part of your presentation.

5. A low appraisal is one that concludes the property is worth less than the buyer has agreed to pay for it. If the sale is contingent on financing, the buyer won't be required to complete it. If it's clear the appraiser did not choose the best comparables, appealing a low appraisal by submitting a request for reconsideration of value to the lender may be worthwhile.

CHAPTER QUIZ

1. An appraisal is:
   a. the same as a competitive market analysis
   b. the same as a broker price opinion
   c. a more casual estimate of value than a CMA
   d. a more rigorous estimate of value than a CMA

2. A competitive market analysis (CMA) is an effective way to estimate value because:
   a. an informed buyer acting free of pressure will not pay more for a property than she could pay for another property that is equally desirable
   b. a buyer will never pay more than market value for a property
   c. it takes more neighborhoods into account when evaluating the property
   d. the income method of appraisal is the most reliable way to value residential property

3. Which of the following is true about neighborhood characteristics?
   a. The boundaries are defined by the county planning board
   b. Neighborhood characteristics set the upper limit of value for the properties located there
   c. Neighborhood characteristics do not affect the value of vacant lots located there
   d. A neighborhood's effect on property values is determined by the most expensive properties located there

4. What kind of topography is considered most desirable for a residential neighborhood?
   a. Level
   b. Sloping
   c. Gently subsiding
   d. Mildly rolling

5. A bathroom with a wash basin and toilet, but no shower or tub, is a:
   a. half bath
   b. three-quarter bath
   c. full bath
   d. design deficiency

6. Which of the following is a common design deficiency?

   a. More bathrooms than bedrooms

   b. Bedrooms not separated by bathroom or closets

   c. Bedrooms not visible from living room

   d. Kitchen too close to garage

7. Which of the following is an example of "normal market conditions"?

   a. The seller of the property is the buyer's uncle, but both the buyer and the seller are being advised by attorneys

   b. The seller of the property is the buyer's aunt, but the buyer and the seller are represented by agents working for different firms

   c. The seller is relocating to take a new job, so she lets her employer take care of selling the house for her

   d. The seller finds a buyer after the property has been on the market for two months and the buyer has been looking in this area for some time

8. Which of the following elements might make it necessary to adjust the listing price recommended by the CMA software?

   a. Seller's property has poor layout

   b. Value in use

   c. Cost

   d. Calm market

9. Your CMA software suggests a listing price range with an expected sale price based on five comparables you viewed in person. The comparables were all in good condition. However, your seller has lived in his house for more than 30 years and has not kept the property maintained at all. Which statement concerning the CMA price recommendation makes the best sense when discussing the CMA during a listing presentation?

   a. Computer analysis is very accurate and takes into account all relevant factors, so we should use the suggested price range as is

   b. The MLS prohibits changing the price range recommended by CMA software

   c. The CMA software can't look inside your house and doesn't evaluate factors like condition, layout, and views; given the condition of your house, it might be wise to shift the asking price downward

   d. We need to bring this house up to tip-top condition before putting it on the market or it won't sell at all

10. To have the best chance of succeeding with a request for reconsideration of value, you should use:

   a. exactly the same comparables as the appraiser

   b. the income approach to value

   c. only currently listed properties as comparables

   d. comparable sales that are more like the subject property than the appraiser's comparables

ANSWER KEY

1. **d.** A CMA is less detailed than an appraisal; an appraisal is used by a lender to determine how much security a property offers in the event of default. An appraiser is more likely to make fine adjustments of the comparables' sales prices in order to arrive at what is, in theory, a more exact valuation.

2. **a.** A CMA is a modified form of the sales comparison method of appraisal. It is based on the assumption that a buyer will not pay more for a property than she could pay for a similar comparable property.

3. **b.** Neighborhood characteristics set both the upper and lower limits of a property's value.

4. **d.** Mildly rolling terrain is usually considered preferable, both as a neighborhood characteristic and for the property site itself.

5. **a.** A bathroom with only a wash basin and a toilet is a half bath.

6. **b.** It's considered a design deficiency when two bedrooms share a wall without a bathroom or closets between them to provide soundproofing.

7. **d.** A sale under normal market conditions is one in which the parties were unrelated, neither party was acting under unusual pressure, both parties acted prudently and knowledgeably and in their own best interests, and the property was exposed on the open market for a reasonable length of time.

8. **a.** CMA software isn't likely to account for a poor layout and so adjustment might be needed.

9. **c.** Most buyers expect a discount for poor condition. Generally, CMA software has no way of evaluating the condition of the subject property. If the subject property is rundown, the listing agent should recommend a downward adjustment of the software's suggested asking price. Repairing the house might be a good idea, but it isn't necessary to sell the house.

10. **d.** To persuade the lender to accept your estimate of value over the appraiser's, you need to select comparable sales that are at least as similar to the subject property as the appraiser's comparables.

SALES TECHNIQUES AND PRACTICES

LISTING PRACTICES

- Prospecting for listings
  - Farming
  - Cold calls
  - Expired listings
  - For sale by owners
  - Referrals
  - Social media
- Listing presentations
- Servicing the listing

SELLING PRACTICES

- Finding a buyer
- Showing properties
- Making an offer

SAFETY ISSUES

REAL ESTATE ASSISTANTS

INTRODUCTION

To be successful, a real estate agent must list properties, find buyers for properties, or both. Finding a seller or finding a buyer is the main way to earn a commission. Therefore, listing and selling practices are the lifeblood of a real estate career. This chapter reviews the basic steps of listing a property, and the basic steps of finding a buyer for a property. It also covers the ways in which an assistant, licensed or unlicensed, can help an agent with listing and selling practices.

LISTING PRACTICES

A listing agent's job involves more than just completing a listing agreement and waiting for a buyer to come along. Once you have entered into a listing agreement with the seller, you'll need to continue to service the listing. This includes preparing the property, marketing the property, and communicating with the sellers about the work you're doing and the progress you're making.

PROSPECTING FOR LISTINGS

Agents should be familiar with a number of listing sources and activities that can generate listings. These include:

- farming,
- cold calling,
- expired listings,
- for sale by owners,
- referrals, and
- social media.

FARMING. Farming is a technique that involves choosing a neighborhood to concentrate your marketing activities in order to become well known in that area.

EXAMPLE: Marty Thompson is a new real estate agent. He needs to generate some listings, so he decides to "farm" an area. He decides that the area he knows best is his own neighborhood—a development containing about 150 homes. He starts out by joining a local neighborhood social network, making regular contributions to discussions of interest to the community. He sends an introductory letter to every home, introducing himself and describing the services he offers. He follows up the letter with a personal visit, leaving a refrigerator magnet or office accessory with his name, website, email address, and phone number at each home. Periodically, Marty sends a newsletter to every home in the neighborhood; it contains neighborhood news as well as information on local property values and market trends. He holds a barbecue in the summer and delivers cards to each home during the winter holidays. Soon, whenever neighborhood residents think about listing their homes, they immediately think of their neighbor, Marty Thompson.

By farming an area effectively and consistently, an agent can reasonably expect a constant supply of listings.

Traditionally, many agents chose their "farm" based on three factors. The first is **diversity**—diversity of floor plans, square footage, exteriors, amenities, and values. Diversity guarantees that a variety of buyers will be attracted to the area. The second factor is **affinity**. An agent will be more successful if she chooses an area that feels comfortable. An agent should be enthusiastic about her "farm." The third factor is **turnover**. A neighborhood that is too stable will not offer many opportunities for listings. On the other hand, an area with a lot of recent turnover may be ready for a dry spell. An area with a steady stream of new listings is ideal.

Licensees now have a sophisticated array of online tools to help them choose an area to farm. These tools let you compare proposed farm areas based on factors such as average sales price, competition, turnover rate, and estimated farming costs.

Farming works well for many agents. Other agents, however, are not comfortable farming and prefer to use other methods to generate listings.

COLD CALLS. Many agents use cold calling—contacting people with whom the agent does not have an established business relationship—as part of their business generation strategy. The agent contacts homeowners and asks if they are interested in selling their homes or if they know someone who is. The homeowners may be chosen randomly, or may be part of a systematic plan (such as contacting all of the homeowners in a particular area).

Cold calling works only if the agent is willing to make a great many calls. It's a "numbers game." One hundred calls may generate only one listing appointment. As with farming, many agents feel that cold calls are a waste of time, or they feel uncomfortable with the process. Other agents, however, do quite well with cold calls. Many brokerages designate certain licensees (often entry-level agents) to make initial contact and pass along successful lead information to a managing broker or team leader. Customer relationship management (CRM) software can assist in identifying leads and keeping track of attempts, responses, and follow-up.

In addition to direct voice calls, some agents use texting to contact potential sellers. Marketers often say texting garners a higher response rate than calling because the recipient can respond at her convenience.

An agent making cold calls or sending texts may not think of himself as a telemarketer, but he is bound by some of the same laws as other telemarketers. The Telephone Consumer Protection Act prohibits cold calls or texts to a mobile number using an auto-dialer; any cold calling or texting must be done individually. Cold calls to residential land lines may not use pre-recorded messages.

In addition, an agent may not contact individuals who have registered with the Do Not Call registry maintained by the Federal Trade Commission. It is the agent's responsibility to check the registry, which is available online. Even when contacting persons not on the registry, an agent must always honor requests not to be contacted again, may not block Caller ID, and may not call outside permissible calling hours.

EXPIRED LISTINGS. Real estate agents often keep an eye on listings that are about to expire. Expired listings can be opportunities in disguise. There are many reasons why a listing might not have sold: it was not marketed properly, minor repairs should have been made that were not, or the price was not reduced when it should have been. If so, a fresh approach may generate both the listing and a quick sale. (If the listing did not sell because the owners were not motivated, there is probably little that another agent can do to move the property.)

After a listing has expired, the new agent can approach the homeowners and see if they are interested in relisting their property. Note that these sellers may be wary of signing another listing agreement because they have just had one negative experience with a real estate agent.

Agents must never try to convince sellers to terminate an existing listing so that the seller can switch to another agent. Agents should also exercise extreme caution when discussing a previous agent's actions. Criticizing another agent's selling efforts is unprofessional. Instead, agents should focus on what they can do for their clients.

FOR SALE BY OWNERS. Another way to obtain listings is to call sellers who are trying to sell their homes on their own. Calling "for sale by owners" (FSBOs) can be very effective, as these homeowners have already decided to sell their homes. All the agent needs to do is convince the owner that the agent can do a better job selling the home, in a shorter period of time, and for a higher sales price with a greater net return.

Agents keep track of FSBOs by noting "For Sale" signs and reviewing listings on "by owner" online listing platforms. Some agents will contact the seller of any FSBO, while others have a more systematic method, such as only pursuing those in a certain price range or with a certain minimum number of days already on the market.

Agents approach FSBOs in a variety of different ways. One approach includes sending several letters to the homeowner that include helpful advice on selling a home. Another approach is to deliver free "service packages" to FSBOs. These packages may include helpful hints and articles on selling a home, and perhaps a preliminary CMA. Some agents may simply phone for an appointment or knock on the door. The key to any approach is to convince the homeowner that selling real estate is a complicated business that an agent can do better and faster.

Even agents who usually shy away from FSBOs may contact one if they have a particular buyer in mind. Under those circumstances, an agent can contact the FSBO and ask for a one-party listing. A **one-party listing** is a listing agreement that is valid only in regard to one particular buyer. FSBOs may be initially skeptical of agents who request one-party listings. They may not believe the agent actually has a particular buyer in mind. However, they will often agree to a one-party listing if they are convinced that there is a legitimate prospect.

REFERRALS. Perhaps the most effective way to get listings is through referrals. Referrals may come from other real estate or finance professionals, such as attorneys, accountants, mortgage brokers, or escrow officers; these people are often willing to recommend prospects to a real estate agent, with the hope that the agent will return the favor by referring clients who might need their services. Referrals may also come from satisfied clients or customers in the form of repeat business or word-of-mouth.

Seeking referrals is really no different from the sort of **networking** any job-seeker uses. The first step is for an agent to contact friends, family, professionals whose services he uses, and other people in the community, and inform them of the services the agent provides.

It may be particularly helpful for an agent to cultivate the friendship of influential persons in his neighborhood or community. These **centers of influence** can be a fruitful source of referrals, since they tend to have many acquaintances, some of whom might need an agent's services. When thinking of centers of influence, people often think of professionals such as attorneys, doctors, or public officials, but they can just as easily be store owners, bartenders, bank tellers, or anyone who interacts with a wide variety of people.

A key source for meeting centers of influence and other useful contacts is local community service groups. Many of the most successful agents build their referral networks through membership in groups such as the PTA, the Chamber of Commerce, religious organizations, political organizations, or fraternal groups. An agent should focus on deeper involvement in only one or two organizations, rather than superficial involvement in a wide number of groups. An agent's main focus, at first, should be on the group's mission rather than aggressively seeking referrals; the referrals will come naturally as one becomes more deeply involved in the community.

An agent can also use online referral services (generally for a fee). With one service, for example, sellers enter their property information and then receive listing proposals from competing agents. Zillow is a major player in this area, providing real estate agents with online leads for both sellers and buyers.

Regardless of what referral methods an agent uses, she should maintain a file of potential clients, preferably using a contact management database. These programs can generate either mass or personalized mailings and also remind the agent when it is time to write, text, or call in order to maintain steady contact.

SOCIAL MEDIA. Perhaps the most important lead-generation activity is building a social media presence on sites such as Facebook, Instagram, and LinkedIn. Social media gives agents a chance to showcase their expertise. Neighborhood networks such as Nextdoor are another type of social media that can be useful, since these networks are inherently focused on neighborhood concerns. Agents can build and leverage an online presence very efficiently with social media, but must be thoughtful in doing so.

LISTING PRESENTATIONS

Once you've identified a prospective seller, a **listing presentation** is almost always necessary to convince the owner to list the property with you. Many sellers "shop around" for a real estate agent by asking two or three agents to make listing presentations. (Such competition is built in if a seller uses an online referral platform to get competing proposals.) This allows sellers to judge the strengths and weaknesses of different agents before making a final choice, so it's essential to come across as professional and well prepared during your presentations.

Even if an owner needs no convincing and is ready to list, most agents use a listing presentation as an opportunity to discuss pricing. It's important to ensure that the owner is willing to put the property on the market at a competitive price.

BEFORE THE PRESENTATION. As soon as an agent has an appointment to make a listing presentation, he should begin preparing for it. He should complete a variety of tasks prior to the listing appointment, including:

- researching the property,
- visiting the property,
- completing a competitive market analysis, and
- preparing a marketing plan.

RESEARCH THE PROPERTY. The agent should gather basic information about the property, including the legal description, a plat map, tax information, and ownership information. This information often can be obtained from the MLS or a local title company. Property information sites (such as Zillow) can be a good starting point, but any information gleaned there should be verified by checking the original source.

VISIT THE PROPERTY. The agent should ask the owner if he can stop by to inspect the property prior to the listing appointment. During this visit, the agent counts and measures rooms, notes any special features (such as a gourmet kitchen or a dazzling view), and gets a general impression of the soundness of the construction. The agent also drives through the neighborhood to get a general feel for the area. Are neighboring homes well-kept? Are there nearby parks? How close are the schools?

COMPLETE A COMPETITIVE MARKET ANALYSIS. Once the agent has become familiar with the home and the neighborhood, it's time to complete a competitive market analysis. As you will recall from Chapter 4, a CMA is a comparison of the prices of homes that are similar in location, size, style, and amenities to the subject property. The purpose of a CMA is to help the seller set a realistic listing price; it is only by comparing the prices of similar homes that a seller can establish a reasonable price for her own home.

MARKETING PLAN. The agent should be prepared to discuss all the different ways she plans to promote the seller's property to prospective buyers. Most marketing plans will include a combination of traditional marketing practices (such as MLS listings and "For Sale" signs), as well as newer marketing practices (such as internet-based advertising and virtual tours of the home).

LISTING APPOINTMENT. The agent should arrive at the seller's home armed with the CMA, a complete marketing plan, a listing agreement ready for signature, an agency law pamphlet, a net proceeds to seller form (discussed later in this chapter), and information about the agent and the agent's firm. These items will help the agent explain the listing process to the seller and help the seller set a listing price. But the listing presentation is more than just an exchange of information; it is also the best opportunity the agent has to gain the seller's confidence and build rapport with the seller.

PRESENT THE CMA. A major benefit of a real estate agent's services is her ability to help establish a realistic listing price. The seller is probably more interested in hearing the agent's opinion of the value of the seller's home than any other piece of information.

All the information that was gathered and analyzed for the CMA should be presented to the seller, along with an explanation of how that information helps determine market value. A CMA enables the agent to present the information in an orderly, easily understood manner. Plus, a CMA makes it clear that the agent's estimate of value is based on facts, not merely personal opinion.

When the agent discusses value, it is best to focus on objective criteria: size, number of rooms, age, location, and terms of sale. This way, the seller (and the agent) won't get sidetracked with subjective issues, such as the fact that it took three years to complete the fancy deck.

Agents often present three figures to the seller. The first figure is the general price range. The second figure is a suggested listing price, which is typically higher than the estimated selling price, to leave room for negotiation. The third figure is what the agent believes the property will actually sell for—the estimated selling price. The estimated selling price should be close to the property's market value.

During the discussion of listing prices, the agent should emphasize that it is the seller, not the agent, who will ultimately decide the listing price. The agent can offer opinions and advice, but it is the seller who must set the price.

Many owners expect to receive more for their property than it is worth because of market misinformation, inflated expectations of value, or the owner's

FIG. 5.1   LISTING PRESENTATIONS

WHAT TO BRING TO YOUR LISTING PRESENTATION
- COMPETITIVE MARKET ANALYSIS
- MARKETING PLAN
- LISTING AGREEMENT
- AGENCY LAW PAMPHLET
- SELLER'S NET SHEET(S)
- INFORMATION ABOUT THE AGENT AND THE FIRM

personal attachment to the property. The information presented in the CMA can correct any misconceptions the seller has regarding current market conditions in his neighborhood, and force a more realistic approach to pricing.

PRESENT MARKETING PLAN. The agent should present a marketing plan to the seller. It's important for the agent to demonstrate what marketing tools she plans to use. For instance, if the agent will include a virtual tour in the listing, she should show the seller a tour that she recently made or, better yet, a quick demonstration using sample footage of the seller's home. The agent should explain each step in the marketing process, so the seller will know what to expect. For instance, the agent might explain to the seller that open houses rarely generate a buyer for the home, but they do provide valuable feedback as to pricing and presentation.

PROVIDE BACKGROUND INFORMATION. Sellers want to know something about the agent making the presentation and the firm the agent works for. The agent should discuss the success rate of his firm, its membership in the local MLS, and how the MLS operates. Information about the agent's career is also important, including number of years of experience, current sales statistics, any awards or achievements that have been earned, and any special certifications.

LISTING AGREEMENT. The agent should review the listing agreement with the seller. This includes going over the agreement's basic terms and answering any questions the seller has. It's a good idea to leave a copy of the form with the seller for a closer reading. (Of course, if the seller signs the agreement, the license law requires leaving a copy. Listing agreements are discussed in Chapter 2.)

AGENCY LAW PAMPHLET. If the seller decides to sign a listing agreement, the agent must provide the seller with a copy of the pamphlet that explains the provisions of Washington's Real Estate Brokerage Relationships Act (see Chapter 1). The agent should also talk to the seller about agency, explaining that the listing agreement will create a seller agency relationship between the seller and the agent's firm.

NET PROCEEDS TO SELLER. Along with the listing price, sellers are very interested in their net proceeds. They want to know how much cash they'll walk away with after the sale has closed and all the expenses have been paid. Agents use a "net proceeds to seller" form (often called a **seller's net sheet**) to arrive at the seller's bottom line. (Of course, at this point the expenses can only be estimated.) Most CMA software programs can prepare net sheets for you. Many agents leave the seller with three net sheets, showing estimated net proceeds for possible low, middle, and high selling prices. The steps for determining the net proceeds are discussed in Chapter 11, and a seller's net sheet is shown in Figure 11.5.

SERVICING THE LISTING

Once you get the listing, the work of servicing the listing begins. This includes helping prepare the property for showing, marketing the property, and maintaining ongoing communication with the seller. In some cases, servicing the listing also includes modifying the original listing agreement.

PREPARING THE PROPERTY. It is a rare house that is in prime condition and ready to go on the market. Most homes need at least some work, and many need a lot of work. At a minimum, homes must be cleaned thoroughly before they are shown to prospective buyers.

Both interiors and exteriors should be clean, freshly painted (if possible), and tidied up. Curb appeal—how a property looks from the street—is important. First impressions are often lasting impressions. Home interiors should be decorated in neutral colors. Closets should be cleaned and organized—bulging closets indicate a lack of storage space. All fixtures should work properly. Leaky faucets, squeaking doors, creaking floors, broken fences, or torn window screens should all be repaired.

Renovations can also make a home more marketable. For example, sellers can often expect to recoup more than 100% of what they spend on minor kitchen renovations.

The following are some tasks that should be completed before a home is shown. Some of these items need to be done on a regular basis to keep the property in top condition during the listing period:

- mow and water lawns;
- weed flower beds;
- plant extra flowers or shrubs (after removing all dead or damaged plantings);
- prune the trees and shrubs;
- rake up all old leaves and other debris;
- cover bare ground with bark chips or gravel;
- clean the roof and replace any missing shingles;
- mend broken fences or railings;
- clean up porches and decks;
- repaint when necessary (especially trim);
- remove children's toys and bikes from walkways and driveways;
- straighten up the garage and shed;
- fix broken door and window screens;
- replace or fix the mailbox;
- remove any old vehicles;
- clean and remove clutter from rooms;
- reorganize the closets, basement, attic, and other storage spaces;
- repaint any brightly colored walls in a neutral shade;
- replace any old or outdated carpeting and wallpaper;
- repair any cracks in the walls;
- fix leaky faucets;
- put new hardware on drawers and cabinets; and
- oil squeaky doors.

SECURITY. The seller should remove any small items of value, such as jewelry or coins, and keep them in a safety deposit box for the duration of the listing period. It may also be a good idea to rearrange or otherwise secure any delicate pieces of furniture or artwork.

KEYS AND KEYBOXES. The seller must provide the agent with a copy of keys to the property, which are generally stored in a lockbox attached to the front door.

MARKETING THE PROPERTY. Real estate agents market listed properties in many ways. One of the most important (and first) marketing activities occurs when the agent submits the listing to the MLS. Typically, this is done right after the listing agreement is signed. All the other MLS members become aware that the property is for sale and can begin looking for prospective buyers.

The internet is an important tool in real estate advertising. Brokerages and real estate organizations maintain **websites** with photos, video clips, and detailed information on listed properties. Many individual agents also maintain their own websites. Prospective buyers can search these websites to get a sense of what's available. If they find something that interests them, they can get in touch with an agent using the contact information on the website. Popular websites and phone apps like Zillow also provide accessible, searchable display advertising for listings.

"For Sale" signs are also an extremely effective form of marketing. Many prospective buyers drive around areas they are interested in, looking for "For Sale" signs. If they see a property they are interested in, they follow up with a phone call to their agent.

Flyers containing information about the property should be prepared and left in an obvious spot in the house (such as a kitchen counter, or a table in the entryway). That way, whenever any agent shows the home to a prospect, all the pertinent information about the house is close at hand. Flyers may also be placed in an information box attached to the "For Sale" sign in front of the home.

The flyer should include the price and other terms of sale, the number of bedrooms and bathrooms, and other pertinent information. It may also include a photograph or sketch of the property, an address for the agent's website featuring more details on the listing (such as photos and/or a virtual tour), and perhaps a QR code that can be scanned with a phone to link to the property's or agent's website.

Regardless of the marketing tools you use, you should always be sure that the money you spend on marketing activities is cost-effective. The key factor in any marketing strategy is to measure the dollars spent against the outcome achieved. Many agents find it helpful to keep a log of their marketing efforts. For example, an agent who spends $100 sending an email flyer about a new listing to 5,000 licensees will want to keep track of how many of those flyers result in showings, calls, offers, and/or sales. In her local market, she may find that the same $100 is better spent on a Facebook advertisement. Keeping track will help you determine which marketing strategies work best for a particular type of property in your area.

Real estate agents must be aware of federal and state laws that apply to real estate advertising. Some laws concern the truthfulness of ads, and others require certain information to be disclosed in ads. The laws apply both to traditional print ads and to internet advertising.

LICENSE LAW RESTRICTIONS. According to the real estate license law, all advertising must be truthful and not misleading. Most advertising must also include the brokerage firm's name as licensed; an ad that does not state the firm's name is a "blind ad" and a violation of the license law. (If a real estate agent is advertising his personally owned property, the firm's name need not be included but the ad must disclose that the owner is a real estate licensee.)

The Department of Licensing publishes a PDF booklet of real estate advertising guidelines that includes rules on the business use of the internet and social media.

TRUTH IN LENDING ACT. The federal Truth in Lending Act also contains provisions that apply to advertising. Generally, anyone placing a consumer credit advertisement must comply with the provisions of the act. This includes real estate agents who include financing information when advertising homes for sale.

Prior to passage of the act, an advertiser might have disclosed only the most attractive credit terms, thus distorting the true costs of the financing. For example, the advertisement could have described low monthly payments ("$450 a month") without indicating the large downpayment necessary to qualify for that payment level. The act requires the advertiser to include such pertinent details.

If an advertisement covered by the Truth in Lending Act contains any one of several terms listed in the act, that ad must also include certain disclosures. These terms are referred to as "triggering terms," because they trigger the disclosure requirement. In other words, if the advertiser uses a triggering term in the ad, the Truth in Lending Act disclosures must be made; if no triggering terms appear in the ad, then no disclosures are required. Triggering terms for real estate advertisements include:

- the amount of the downpayment ("Only 5% down");
- the amount of any payment ("Pay less than $1,700 per month");
- the number of payments ("260 monthly payments");
- the period of repayment ("30-year financing available"); and
- the amount of any finance charge ("1% finance charge").

> **EXAMPLE:** Agent Simms places a classified ad that reads "Fantastic buy! Three-bedroom, two-bath house in the Wildwood neighborhood. Buyer can assume seller's VA loan. Payments are only $1,525 a month!"
>
> This ad contains a triggering term, the amount of the monthly payment, so certain other loan terms must also be included in the ad.

If any triggering terms are used in the advertisement, all of the following disclosures must be made:

- the amount of the downpayment;
- the terms of repayment; and
- the annual percentage rate, using that term spelled out in full.

The **annual percentage rate** (APR) is the relationship of the finance charge to the amount of the loan, as an annualized percentage. The APR takes into account both the interest rate and the various fees charged by a lender to make a loan, such as the loan fee.

Some examples of phrases that would not trigger the required disclosures are:

- "No downpayment,"
- "8% Annual Percentage Rate loan available here,"
- "Easy monthly payments,"
- "Adjustable-rate financing available,"
- "VA and FHA financing available," and
- "Terms to fit your budget."

EXAMPLE: Returning to the previous example, Agent Simms decides that he does not want to clutter up the ad with a lot of disclosures, so he rewrites the ad to read: "Fantastic buy! Three-bedroom, two-bath house in the Wildwood neighborhood. Buyer can assume seller's VA loan and take advantage of low monthly payments." This ad complies with the requirements of the Truth in Lending Act; no additional disclosures are required.

Advertising is also subject to fair housing laws. See Chapter 3 for a full discussion of that topic.

HOLDING OPEN HOUSES. Most open houses do not directly result in the sale of the home, and some listing agents consider them a waste of time (at least in a hot market). However, most sellers expect their agent to hold an open house. From an agent's perspective, the main advantage of open houses is finding prospective buyers who might also be interested in other listed homes, or prospective sellers who are ready to list their own homes. That said, if the seller's house is above average and will clearly be in demand, an open house can generate extra buzz and cut down on the need for individual appointments.

The basic steps involved in holding an open house include arranging a day and time with the sellers when they can be out of the home, advertising the open house, preparing informational packets about the property, making sure the home is ready for showing, setting up open house directional signs, putting out a guest log, staying at the property during the scheduled open house hours, and following up with thank-you notes to those visitors who signed the guest log.

SETTING THE DAY AND TIME. Sellers should never remain in the house during an open house, so it is important for the agent to choose a day and time when it is convenient for the sellers to be away from their home. If a seller questions the need to be absent during an open house, the agent must tactfully explain that most buyers do not feel comfortable looking at a home when the owner is present.

ADVERTISING. After the date is set, the open house can be advertised on real estate apps, websites, and social media. Flyers are often sent to neighbors. Neighbors may know of someone in the market for a home, or may be interested in listing their own home (potential sellers like to know which agents are active in their neighborhood).

Flyer packets can be given to interested prospects who tour the home. These packages generally include a flyer about the home, the agent's business card, flyers on other listings in the area, and information about the agent.

PREPARING THE HOME. For an open house to accomplish anything, the listed property must be in top condition. The home should be sparkling clean, the rooms brightly lit and fresh-smelling. All clutter should be put away. The grounds should be mowed, trimmed, and tidied. Some sellers need an extra nudge to get their homes in shape for an open house. But for that all-important first impression, order and cleanliness are a must.

DIRECTIONAL SIGNS. "Open House" signs with arrows that point prospects in the right direction should be placed at strategic locations. Potential buyers may decide to drop in based on one of these signs.

GUEST LOGS. Guest logs are used to keep track of who views the property. A guest log can be a source of new leads as well as a security measure. Of course, not every prospect will want to sign the log; it is usually a mistake to try to push everyone to sign in.

PRESENCE DURING OPEN HOUSE HOURS. An agent should never leave an open house early, even if business is slow. Sellers are not very happy to come home to an empty house when they are expecting a positive report from an enthusiastic agent. Prospects that arrive at the property after the agent has left are sure to be disappointed and wary of dealing with that agent in the future. If an emergency arises and the agent must leave early, he should call another agent for backup. If business is slow, an agent can work on other aspects of the business during open house hours, such as calling FSBOs.

Of course, when the open house is over, it is imperative to lock up the home properly if the sellers have not yet returned.

FOLLOW-UP. Agents generally follow up on the leads who signed the guest log, in the form of a thank-you card or a personal note. It is especially important to keep any promises that were made. For instance, if an agent promised to go to a prospect's home and perform a CMA, it is vital that he contact the prospect to follow up on that promise.

SHOWING THE PROPERTY. Open houses occur only occasionally—usually when the property is first listed. And, as mentioned earlier, open houses rarely generate sales. The way most properties are sold is by showing them to individual prospects. Showing homes will be discussed in more detail later in the chapter.

LISTING MODIFICATIONS AND EXTENSIONS. Sometimes a property is listed at a price that both the real estate agent and seller believe reasonable, yet weeks pass without significant interest. This may be due to a slow real estate market, or may reflect a changing market. For example, if comparable homes have subsequently been put on the market at lower prices, this may decrease the interest in your listing. Of course, it's also possible that the listing simply was overpriced in the first place.

If pricing seems to be the problem, the agent should meet with the seller to discuss the situation and reevaluate the listing price. Many sellers resist the idea of lowering the price, so the agent should be prepared with data on new listings or comparable sales. Documentation of the agent's marketing efforts (such as flyers and screenshots or printouts of online advertising) may also be helpful.

Make modifications to a listing agreement, such as a change in listing price, using an appropriate form. (We discuss listing agreement modifications in Chapter 2. A sample modification form is shown in Figure 2.4.)

If the listing expiration date approaches and no sale is scheduled to close, the agent will want to obtain a listing extension. As with a listing modification, this involves meeting with the seller to discuss the efforts the agent has made and reasons why the property has not yet sold. The modification form shown in Figure 2.4 can be used to extend the listing agreement term.

COMMUNICATING WITH THE SELLER. An important aspect of servicing the listing is communication with the seller. Telling the seller what to expect and providing regular progress reports reassures the seller that the agent is working hard, and reduces the chance of misunderstandings.

The agent should provide the seller with regular updates summarizing the number of inquiries and/or showings on the property, and any advertising used. The reports may also include copies of advertisements for the property, and any comments from other agents or prospective buyers.

SELLING PRACTICES

Just as a listing agent must work to obtain and market listings, a selling agent must find prospective buyers. Once a prospective buyer is found, the buyer's agent must choose appropriate properties to show her, and work to maximize the appeal of those homes.

FINDING A BUYER

Buyers can be categorized in roughly five ways:

- first-time buyers,
- trade-up buyers,
- empty-nesters,
- retirees, and
- investors.

First-time buyers are the novices—typically they know little about buying a home, have limited funds, and are looking for smaller homes. They have lots of questions about buying a home and often rely on a parent or older friend for advice. Sometimes a parent will be helping to finance the home by giving the son or daughter some money toward a downpayment, or by co-signing the loan.

Trade-up buyers are selling one house in order to purchase a newer and/or larger house, so they may want to make the purchase contingent on the sale of their existing home. They are more experienced at buying a home, have a better idea of what they want, and rely less (if at all) on the advice of parents or friends.

Empty-nesters are parents whose children have left home. These buyers no longer need all the space in a large family home. They typically look for smaller homes that require less upkeep; at the same time, they often have considerable equity and may consider fairly expensive properties, such as a luxury condo.

Retirees are also looking for smaller, easily maintained homes. Monthly payments may be a concern, because many retirees have a fixed income. They may be interested in an inexpensive condominium or other attached housing; many are looking for homes with few or no stairs.

Investors are buyers who don't intend to live in the home. Instead, they're planning to rent it or to resell it at a profit. Some investors look for houses in poor condition that can be bought cheaply, renovated, and quickly resold at a higher price ("flipping"). Investors who plan to be landlords may also be interested in renovating fixer-uppers to turn them into rental homes; or they may simply be looking for homes in good condition that will appeal to potential renters in the area at competitive rents.

All types of buyers are found through some of the techniques previously discussed, such as advertising and open houses. Many buyers call real estate agents after seeing a "For Sale" sign posted on an attractive property, which is why most agents post their personal "name rider" on signs. Others find properties by browsing websites. And still others simply call or visit a real estate office because they want an agent to show them some properties. These "call-ins" or "walk-ins" are helped by the agent who is "working the floor" at the time.

Floor duty is the practice of assigning one agent to handle all the telephone calls and office visits for a specific period of time. If those calling or visiting do not ask to speak with a particular agent, the agent on floor duty can help them and, hopefully, retain them as clients. Some agents on floor duty use a prospect form (such as the one shown in Figure 5.2) that lets them quickly record pertinent information about the contact.

Social media can be a great way to find potential buyers (and sellers). Of course, to be successful you have to pick a form of social media that appeals to you, whether it's blogging, tweeting, or anything else. The internet is a rich source of information on how to use social media to build a clientele.

Regional or national companies often transfer workers from office to office. Transferees need agents to help them with both sides of the move: selling their present home and helping them to buy a home in a new community. Many real estate offices specialize in relocation or have relocation programs. These programs can be a lucrative source of business.

DETERMINING NEEDS. Buyers usually know what kind of home they want. Often, the difficult part is helping them prioritize their needs.

FIG. 5.2   WORKSHEET TO TRACK LEADS

Seller Prospect	
Name:	
Address:	
Phone: (H)	(W)
Reason for Selling:	
Must Sell By:	
Property Data	
Location:	
Age:	Family Room:
Lot size:	Square Footage:
Style:	Garage:
Bedroom:	Fireplace:
Bathroom:	Heating:
Dining Room:	Condition:
Asking Price:	Estimated Value:
Existing Financing:	
Minimum Net to Seller:	
Buyer Prospect	
Name:	
Address:	
Phone: (H)	(W)
Must Take Possession By:	
Property Desired	
Location:	Family Room:
Style:	Square Footage:
Bedroom:	Garage:
Bathroom:	Fireplace:
Dining Room:	Other:
Price Range: Maximum Downpayment:	Maximum Mortgage Payment:
Comments:	

EXAMPLE: Stan and Nancy Cook meet with Agent Sandin to discuss their housing needs. The Cooks have two children and a lot of out-of-town guests. They tell Agent Sandin that they need a four-bedroom, two-bathroom house. They need a large kitchen, a family room, at least one fireplace, a three-car garage, a large yard, and room for a kennel for their three dogs. "And a laundry room," says Stan. "And a tool shed," Nancy adds.

Agent Sandin knows there's no way he can find a house with all of these attributes in the Cooks' price range. After asking a lot of questions and listening carefully to the Cooks' answers, Agent Sandin says, "It sounds like four bedrooms, two bathrooms, and a large kitchen are the three most important criteria. The fourth item is room for your dogs, and the fifth is a large family room. Is that right?" After some thought, the Cooks agree. Now Agent Sandin can begin looking for a house that fits their needs.

Sometimes creative problem-solving can help meet a housing need.

EXAMPLE: Agent Sandin has found what he thinks is the perfect home for the Cooks, but it has only three bedrooms instead of four. However, the den could easily double as a guest room, especially since there is a third bathroom right off the den. The Cooks are willing to compromise on the guest bedroom and are pleased with a third bathroom.

An agent should never try to manipulate a buyer into considering a property just because that agent listed the home. If buyers feel they are being pressured to view homes that don't meet their needs, they will quickly find another agent who is more willing to accommodate them. If buyers sense a conflict of interest, they might even pursue disciplinary measures.

SHOWING PROPERTIES

The ability to show property effectively is vital to a successful real estate career. An agent should always take the time to research and plan his efforts, in order to make showings as efficient and useful as possible. Thorough preparation includes keeping current with the local market and general real estate trends.

SELECTING LISTINGS. When choosing properties to show a prospective buyer, only pick homes the buyer can afford. An agent can lose a sale by showing a buyer homes that are priced too high. Buyers should be preapproved to determine their affordable price range (we discuss preapproval in Chapter 9). However, sometimes buyers choose to spend less on housing than they can afford. An agent must respect the buyer's wishes—it is up to the buyer to decide how much to spend on a home.

Don't show too many houses on one trip. After five or six houses, most buyers begin to tire and may forget or confuse impressions and details. It does no good to show a home to a buyer who is not going to remember it.

PREVIEWING THE PROPERTIES. Before taking buyers on a showing, the agent should always preview the listed home and research the area. It's best to visit the property in person, rather than just relying on the internet. It's also a good idea to become familiar with school district boundaries and know the location of neighborhood shopping and recreational facilities.

INSIDE THE HOMES. It's important to read the buyer's signals. The buyer will let the agent know, either verbally or by body language, how she feels about the house. It's important for the agent to listen to what the buyer says and pick up any non-verbal cues. Is this the kind of house the buyer loves? Hates? The buyer's reaction to one house will guide the agent's choices in future showings.

Most buyers need to picture themselves in a house before they will make an offer on it. In order to do this, they need some time to themselves. Agents shouldn't talk nonstop during a showing. A little silence can be an effective sales tool.

MAKING AN OFFER

Once a buyer has found a house that she would like to buy, the selling agent's next step is to prepare an offer. To purchase real estate, an offer must be made in writing. Once the offer has been accepted by the seller, the offer forms a binding purchase and sale agreement. (We discuss offers and the purchase and sale agreement in greater detail in the next two chapters.)

OFFERS AND COUNTEROFFERS. Agents must submit any offer to the seller, even if that offer seems unreasonable. It is the seller who decides whether to accept an offer, not the real estate agent.

After a buyer's agent prepares an offer, it should be passed on to the listing agent, who then presents it to the seller. Typically, once an offer is presented to the seller, a period of negotiation begins. This is perhaps one of the most valuable services an agent can provide: shepherding the parties through the process of making offers and counteroffers, and helping the buyer and seller reach an agreement that satisfies them both.

NEGOTIATION. When presenting the offer, agents often present the most positive aspects first, and then the more negative aspects. This prevents the seller from immediately rejecting the offer before the seller has had a chance to listen to and carefully consider all the terms. Even if the seller is unwilling to accept a negative term (such as a low sales price or a quick closing date), the seller is more likely to counter with another offer than to reject the buyer outright.

During the negotiation process, agents should remember to maintain their professionalism and avoid hostility between the parties. It's also a good idea to talk to the other party's agent on the phone rather than relying completely on texts and emails. Most agents reveal more in casual conversation than they do in writing. And it's helpful to try to find out if any nonfinancial or "invisible" factors are motivating the other party—for example, perhaps the seller is moving to another part of the country soon and wants to sell the home quickly.

MULTIPLE OFFERS. In an active real estate market, a seller is likely to receive multiple offers, and in some cases more than one will be submitted at nearly the same time. In this situation, the listing agent should present all offers to the seller as soon as they come in. The seller can reject all the offers, accept one offer, make a counteroffer to one offer, or accept one offer and make a contingent backup counteroffer to another offer.

The seller's decision when faced with multiple offers is likely to hinge on the amount offered as a sales price, but there are ways to help a buyer's offer stand out from the crowd. Because a home sale is an emotional as well as financial decision, sometimes owners will give weight to a personal appeal from the buyers. Some selling agents, in a tight market, have prospective buyers write a brief statement about themselves and why the seller's house appeals to them. Sellers often feel some reluctance to sell, and may feel better about selling to someone they "know," who has articulated their enthusiasm for the property.

> **EXAMPLE:** A prospective buyer might write a statement such as this: "We are a young couple looking to purchase our first house, as we are planning to start a family and will soon need more room. My husband is an accountant with an investment firm, and I am a veterinarian. You might say we're both animal lovers; we have several dogs, as well as some smaller pets, and love that your house has a large yard for the dogs to play, as well as ample kennel space in the utility room. We were also won over by the lush landscaping and the terrific school district."

It's best to focus such a letter on what the buyers like about the property and not on details concerning their values, especially those implicating characteristics like religion, race, or national origin. While it's understandable to want to build goodwill between the parties, too much focus on cultural or social identity can backfire. For instance, a disgruntled buyer whose offer is rejected may allege discrimination. Whether or not the seller is guilty of discrimination, a letter from the successful bidder may provide accidental support for such a claim if it discusses these characteristics.

Also bear in mind that most buyers are interested in other properties as well, and—especially in a tight market—it can be helpful to tell a seller about other properties that the buyer is interested in. Not only does this remind the sellers that their house is competing against other properties, it also helps reassure the sellers that their house will be appreciated.

> **EXAMPLE:** A listing agent might inform the sellers: "The buyers were undecided between your home and a nearby property on Willow Way. While that property had a fourth bedroom and was about the same price, they opted for your property because they thought your home was in better condition, requiring less touching-up before they move in, and because they loved the big yard and the well-maintained landscaping."

AGENCY DISCLOSURE. Remember that Washington state law requires an agent to inform any party to a transaction which party that agent represents. This disclosure must be made to the buyer before the buyer signs the offer to purchase, and to the seller before the seller signs the offer in order to accept it. The disclosure must be made in writing, either as part of the purchase and sale agreement or in a separate document.

Even though the written disclosure isn't required until each party is about to sign the purchase and sale agreement, it's generally a good idea for an agent to explain his agency status to the parties sooner than that. For example, an agent who's representing the buyer (and only the buyer) should make sure the seller understands that early on in the negotiation process. That's especially important if it's a "for sale by owner" transaction, where the seller isn't represented by an agent of her own.

SAFETY ISSUES

Throughout the listing and selling process, real estate agents must take care to protect their own safety and the safety of clients and customers. For example, agents should never show buyers homes that are in the middle of construction. Instead, agents should arrange to have the contractor show the buyer the home. Construction sites are dangerous places. This is particularly true if the buyer is accompanied by young children.

Real estate agents should also take precautions to secure a seller's possessions during open houses or when showing the property. Sellers should be warned to remove valuable items from the home prior to showing. Agents should never leave prospects unattended in a home and should encourage all visitors to sign a log. Agents should be especially wary when a couple attends an open house and one partner keeps the agent occupied while the other partner disappears into another part of the house—this behavior is a signal that trouble may be brewing. And, naturally, agents must be sure to lock the property when they leave.

Keys and keyboxes pose special hazards. Agents must make every effort to keep house keys in a safe place, and to make sure that keyboxes are as secure as possible. For example, when a licensee terminates affiliation with a firm, the designated broker must be sure to notify the MLS immediately so that the agent's keybox code can be deactivated.

Real estate agents must also be conscious of their own safety. If at all possible, agents should work in pairs when showing properties or holding open houses. If that is not possible, agents should ask their customers to meet them at their offices. This avoids the dangers of meeting a stranger at an empty house. And when meeting with customers for the first time, it is wise to ask for photo ID.

Legitimate customers are generally happy to comply with brokerage safety rules. Customers who call up and insist on meeting the agent at the property, explaining they are pressed for time, should put the agent on guard.

When agents are showing properties, they should leave word with their office as to where they are going and when they will return. They can also arrange to check in with someone on a regular basis. Your firm may have additional safety suggestions.

In areas where crime is a problem and agents are worried about their personal safety, most local police departments provide training and give advice on ways to foster personal safety.

REAL ESTATE ASSISTANTS

Depending on the amount of business a real estate agent handles, she may decide to hire a real estate assistant. Many administrative and other tasks can be delegated to an assistant, freeing up more time for the agent to spend working face-to-face with clients. An assistant may work on a part-time or full-time basis, and is typically paid on a salary or salary-plus-commission basis.

Under the license law, many of the day-to-day activities performed by a real estate agent require a real estate license. Unlicensed assistants may not:

- show properties, answer questions, or interpret information about the property, price, or condition (except to repeat information from a pre-printed form);
- interpret information about listings, titles, financing, contracts, closing, or other information relating to a transaction;
- fill in legal forms or negotiate price or terms;
- hold or disburse trust funds; or
- perform any act with the intent to circumvent, or which results in the circumvention of, real estate licensing laws.

For this reason, when hiring a real estate assistant, an agent may want to consider hiring another real estate licensee.

For a variety of reasons, some licensees choose to work as real estate assistants instead of working as agents. For example, a new licensee might want more experience before taking on full-scale agent responsibilities; working as an assistant gives the licensee a chance to become more familiar with the business and to benefit from the knowledge and guidance of a mentor. Or a licensee might choose to work as an assistant because he can't afford to work full-time on a commission basis until he is more established and has a dependable stream of income. And some licensees simply find that they aren't comfortable performing the marketing and sales duties associated with being an agent.

If the agent decides to hire an assistant who is not a real estate licensee, both the agent and assistant must take care to ensure that none of the assistant's activities require a license.

TYPICAL DUTIES OF A REAL ESTATE ASSISTANT

A real estate agent may delegate various tasks to a real estate assistant, depending on how much experience the assistant has, and whether she is a real estate licensee. Business practices vary from firm to firm, but we'll discuss some common duties for a real estate assistant.

OFFICE ADMINISTRATION. Whether licensed or not, most real estate assistants help with basic office administration tasks. Real estate transactions generate a significant amount of paperwork; for example, the license law requires real estate firms to keep transaction records for a minimum of three years after closing. A transaction folder might include a listing agreement, a purchase and sale agreement, modifications or addenda to those agreements, and a settlement statement. By the time the transaction is completed, the folder might also hold photographs, disclosure forms, offers to purchase, an appraisal, escrow papers, and closing documents. An assistant will likely be responsible for organizing and filing these documents accordingly. If any documents must be duplicated and distributed to different parties, this task might also fall to an assistant.

In addition to handling paperwork, an assistant may answer and direct phone calls, and greet current or prospective clients visiting the office. When handling inquiries, an assistant can provide general information about listings, but should refer more complicated questions to the agent.

UPDATING INFORMATION. When a real estate agent takes a listing, the information should be given to the MLS as soon as possible. In addition, listing status changes must be updated with the MLS. If the listing information is not kept current, another agent may end up wasting time considering or showing a home that is no longer available. Failing to report a pending or closed sale is not only unprofessional, but may also subject the listing agent to a penalty. Most multiple listing services may impose fines for failing to report listing status changes promptly. An assistant can be invaluable in helping an agent to submit listing information to the MLS. However, depending on the requirements of the particular MLS, this task may require a real estate license.

If the agent maintains a website with listing information, it must also be updated regularly. Advertising homes that are no longer available (or failing to advertise homes that have come on the market) is unprofessional, as well as a violation of the DOL's guidelines on maintaining websites. If a prospective buyer is interested in a listing advertised on the agent's website, she will not be impressed to learn that it actually sold two months ago.

CLIENT COMMUNICATION. Keeping in contact with clients is essential to a successful real estate business, but can be extremely time-consuming. A busy agent might be able to handle exchanges with current clients, such as answering questions or providing updates. But the agent may not have time to stay in touch with former and prospective clients, even though this type of contact is an important component of marketing. An agent could delegate this work to an assistant. For example, the assistant could prepare and send newsletters, seasonal cards, or other promotional materials.

APPOINTMENTS AND OPEN HOUSES. Even the most organized agent may need help managing a busy schedule. An unlicensed assistant can coordinate the agent's appointments and remind the agent of upcoming meetings and showings.

However, an unlicensed assistant may not actually show properties, answer questions, or interpret information regarding property, price, or condition.

A licensed assistant can take on more responsibility. For instance, a licensed assistant could show homes and then actually write up an offer in the real estate agent's absence.

CHAPTER SUMMARY

1. Listing properties is a vital part of a real estate agent's business. Listings can be found by farming, by making cold calls, by approaching expired listings and FSBOs, and through online and personal referrals as well as social media.

2. Before making a listing presentation, the agent should research the property, visit the property, and prepare a competitive market analysis and marketing plan. At the listing presentation, the agent will present the competitive market analysis and marketing plan, tell the seller about the services the agent will provide, review the listing agreement, and discuss the net proceeds to the seller.

3. Once the listing is obtained, the agent must service the listing. This means advising the seller on preparing the property, advertising the property, holding an open house, and showing the home. If the listing does not sell, the listing agent and seller may agree to a listing modification or extension.

4. Agents need to find buyers for properties as well as listing properties. Buyers can be found by advertising, by holding open houses, and by working floor duty. When a prospective buyer is found, the agent needs to prioritize what the buyer wants in a home.

5. The agent must comply with license law rules regarding presenting offers and counteroffers. When making offers in a competitive market, it is important for a selling agent to paint a picture of the buyers and sell the buyers to the sellers; it is also important for buyers to be preapproved for financing.

6. An agent must be aware of a number of safety issues. Agents need to protect the physical safety of their clients and customers, protect the possessions of sellers, and protect themselves from danger.

7. An agent may need to hire a real estate assistant in order to make better use of her time. An assistant can help with maintaining files, updating listing information, communicating with clients, and setting up open houses. An agent must be careful that an unlicensed assistant does not perform any tasks that require a real estate license.

CHAPTER QUIZ

1. Agent Kalliwaki spends one hour every day randomly calling 20 homeowners to ask if they are interested in selling their homes. This practice is known as:

   a. farming
   b. cold calling
   c. FSBO-ing
   d. showing

2. An agent sees that another firm's listing will expire soon, and she'd like to list that property herself. The agent should:

   a. contact the current listing agent and ask for an assignment of the listing before it expires
   b. wait until after the current listing expires before contacting the sellers about listing their home with her firm instead
   c. contact the sellers as soon as possible and persuade them to terminate the current listing agreement
   d. send the sellers a letter pointing out the current agent's mistakes and short-comings

3. An agent should bring all of the following to a listing appointment, except for a:

   a. listing agreement
   b. marketing plan
   c. seller's net sheet
   d. loan estimate form

4. An agent is using the franchise name National Properties in his advertisements. The agent:

   a. is violating the real estate license law
   b. must also include his firm's licensed name in the advertisement
   c. must note that the agent is a licensed member of the franchise
   d. None of the above

5. The following ad is placed in a local newspaper: "Fixer-upper going cheap. Two bedrooms, one bathroom. Good foundation and plumbing, but needs a lot of TLC. Seller offers financing with small downpayment." This ad:

   a. violates the Truth in Lending Act
   b. must include the APR of the seller financing
   c. complies with the Truth in Lending Act
   d. must include the interest rate of the seller financing

6. Open houses:

    a. often generate potential buyers for other listings

    b. should be conducted with the sellers present

    c. are held just before the listing is submitted to the MLS

    d. are a good way to determine what repairs need to be completed before the house will sell

7. Agent Brown receives two offers on the same house in the same hour. One offer is full price; the other is $25,000 below the listing price.

    a. Brown must submit both offers to the seller immediately

    b. Brown need submit only the most advantageous offer to the seller

    c. Brown has the authority to accept the best offer on behalf of the seller

    d. Brown must submit the best offer immediately, but can wait until the following day to submit the less advantageous offer

8. Now that the Knolls' last child has moved out, they are looking for a smaller house with easier upkeep. They can afford a significant downpayment using the equity from their current house. The Knolls would be considered:

    a. first-time buyers

    b. trade-up buyers

    c. empty-nesters

    d. retirees

9. Which of the following is not a precaution that agents should take?

    a. Warn sellers to remove valuable items from the home prior to showing

    b. Request that customers meet them at the property rather than at their office

    c. Work in pairs when showing properties or holding open houses, when possible

    d. Leave word with the office where they are going and when they will return

10. Which of the following activities should an unlicensed real estate assistant not perform?

    a. Maintain information in transaction folders

    b. Prepare flyers for mass mailings

    c. Coordinate appointments

    d. Advise buyers about obtaining financing

ANSWER KEY

1. b. Cold calling is an unsolicited inquiry, usually by phone, made to a home-owner in order to obtain a listing.

2. b. As a general rule, agents shouldn't contact sellers directly while they are being represented by another firm. So this agent should wait until after the current listing expires to ask the sellers to list their home with her firm.

3. d. All of these are items that agents should bring to their listing appointments, except for a loan estimate. (A loan estimate is a disclosure form lenders are required to give residential loan applicants.)

4. b. An agent advertising under the name of a franchise must also include his firm's name in the advertisement.

5. c. The ad complies with the Truth in Lending Act, because it includes no triggering terms that would require additional information to be disclosed.

6. a. Most people who walk into an open house don't buy that particular home, but they are often interested in having the agent show them other homes.

7. a. Both offers must be submitted to the seller immediately. It is up to the seller to decide which offer to accept, not the agent.

8. c. The Knolls would be considered empty-nesters, since their children have moved out and they are looking for a smaller, easier-to-maintain property.

9. b. To be safe, agents should request that clients meet them at the brokerage office first, rather than at an empty house.

10. d. An unlicensed real estate assistant should not answer questions about financing; this should be done only by licensees.

NEGOTIATING THE OFFER AND ACCEPTANCE

MAKING AN OFFER TO PURCHASE

- Preparing an offer
- How offers are presented
- Multiple offers
- Backup offers
- Revoking an offer

COUNTEROFFERS AND NEGOTIATIONS

ACCEPTING AN OFFER

- Communicating acceptance
- Manner of acceptance
- Acceptance cannot change terms

CONTRACT AMENDMENTS

CONTRACT RESCISSION

EARNEST MONEY DEPOSITS

- Size of the deposit
- Form of the deposit
- Handling a deposit
- Refund or forfeiture

FAIR HOUSING CONSIDERATIONS

INTRODUCTION

When a buyer finds a house he wants and decides to make an offer on it, what happens next? How and when are offers presented to a seller? What is your role as negotiator? What if you're representing the seller instead of the buyer?

In this chapter, we will discuss preparing and presenting an offer to purchase, negotiating terms, and the point at which an offer becomes a binding contract. We will also explain the procedures for handling the earnest money that customarily accompanies an offer.

MAKING AN OFFER TO PURCHASE

You're helping your buyers—a married couple—look for a house that meets their needs: at least 1,800 square feet, three bedrooms, two baths, a large kitchen, and a double garage, in the $420,000 to $450,000 price range. After you've shown them several houses that fulfill these requirements, the buyers find one they are really interested in. You can tell, because they linger there a little longer, ask specific questions ("How old is the roof?" "How far is it to the elementary school?"), and mentally "move in" to the house, visualizing where their own furniture would go. They may make plans to come back and see the house again, perhaps bringing a third party—such as a parent or a more experienced friend— to examine the property with them.

After the buyers have had a chance to look at the property on their own and discuss it between themselves, you review the property's features and benefits and how well it meets their housing needs. You discuss a few concerns raised by the buyers, and ultimately they decide they are ready to make an offer to purchase the house. They ask you to write up their offer for them and present it to the seller.

PREPARING AN OFFER

Under the statute of frauds, an offer to purchase real property must be in writing and signed by the offeror (the buyer). The statute of frauds is the law that requires certain types of contracts to be in writing.

An offer to purchase residential property is usually written up on a standard purchase and sale agreement form (see Chapter 7). It must set forth all of the essential terms of the buyer's offer, including the purchase price, the amount of earnest money the buyer is willing to provide as an indication of good faith, how he will pay the purchase price, and the proposed closing date. It's important to include all of the terms on which the buyer is willing to purchase the property, because once the document is signed by both the buyer and the seller, it becomes a binding contract—their **purchase and sale agreement**.

What if a buyer wants to make an offer that is unrealistically low or contains too many conditions? As an agent, your job is to represent the client's best interests—naturally, this includes getting the best price possible, but it also includes helping write an offer that will be considered seriously by the seller. This is especially important in a situation where a seller is receiving multiple offers. (We'll discuss multiple offers in greater detail later in this chapter.)

Typically, price is the most important element of an offer, but other factors can make an offer more or less attractive to the seller. The seller wants to get the best price for his home, but is also interested in a smooth, problem-free transaction. Anything the buyer can do to demonstrate greater commitment to the purchase will be viewed favorably by the seller. For example, offering an unusually large earnest money deposit shows the seller that the buyer's interest in the property is sincere.

Similarly, an offer with few or no contingencies assures the seller of a greater chance of the sale closing smoothly. A "clean offer" with no conditions—such as no inspection contingency or financing contingency—is most attractive to sellers (although forgoing contingencies, especially an inspection contingency, can be risky for the buyer). Preapproval by a lender also makes an offer more attractive, since the buyer's ability to obtain financing is guaranteed (as long as the property meets the lender's standards).

An all-cash offer is highly attractive to sellers, since there's no financing contingency and no lender approval requirements that could stall or terminate the transaction. Some all-cash offers involve delayed financing. With delayed financing, the buyer liquidates investments—such as retirement funds or a stock portfolio—to provide funds for an all-cash offer. After closing, the buyer obtains financing secured by the new property, then uses the proceeds from the loan to replenish the liquidated investments.

It may be necessary to persuade your buyer to restructure her offer to make it more attractive. If the buyer wants to make a lowball offer, explain that the seller isn't likely to take the offer seriously and may in fact be offended. However, when discussing how to strengthen an offer, never encourage the buyer to eliminate an important contract condition or to make a higher offer than he can afford.

Who Can Prepare an Offer. Whose job is it to prepare the offer to purchase? A buyer could write her own offer; it is always legal (although generally not advisable) for the parties to a transaction to draw up their own contract. Or an attorney at law could draft the buyer's offer for her. What about you, the real estate agent? Can you prepare the buyer's offer?

When someone draws up a contract on behalf of others, he is considered to be practicing law. Only licensed attorneys may practice law, so as a general rule, contracts must be drafted by an attorney. However, there is an exception to this rule: real estate agents may fill in the blanks in routine purchase and sale agreements using standard forms that were originally written and approved by attorneys with expertise in real estate law. But this exception is limited; a real estate agent may only fill out a purchase and sale agreement form in connection with a transaction that he is handling. And a real estate agent cannot charge a separate fee (in addition to the brokerage commission) for completing the form.

Note that when you fill out a contract form, you will be held to the same standard of care that is required of a lawyer. If, through negligence, you make a mistake, you may be liable for any harm suffered by the buyer or the seller because of that mistake.

Also, remember that you are only allowed to fill in the blanks on a standard form. Writing special clauses to insert into the pre-printed form or advising the parties on the legal effect of certain provisions may constitute the unauthorized practice of law, which is a criminal offense.

Reviewing the Offer. After filling out the purchase and sale agreement form, check it over to see if it's complete and accurate. Then go over the form with the buyers, to make sure they understand and are satisfied with all of the terms. If they have questions about the legal consequences of particular provisions, refer them to a real estate lawyer.

When you review the financial aspects of the offer, you can use software to prepare a "Buyer's Estimated Net Cost" form to calculate the buyers' closing costs and show them approximately how much cash they'll need to close the transaction if the seller accepts their offer. (See Figure 11.4 in Chapter 11.)

After going through the offer with the buyers, have them sign it, and then immediately give them a copy of the signed document. At this point, the buyers will usually give you an earnest money deposit (discussed later in this chapter), which you will turn over to your designated broker.

LEGAL REQUIREMENTS. In addition to being in writing and signed, a buyer's offer must meet a few other legal requirements to serve as the basis for a binding contract. To be valid, the offer must be definite and certain in its terms, not vague or incomplete. If you fill out the purchase and sale agreement form properly, including the price, the closing date, and all of the other important terms, the buyer's offer will meet this requirement.

A valid offer must also clearly express a willingness to enter into a contract. Again, a standard purchase and sale agreement fulfills this requirement.

WHEN TO SEEK ADVICE. In filling out a purchase and sale agreement form, there are three key areas where problems most often occur:

- **Property description.** The property must be clearly described for the offer (and the subsequent sales contract) to be enforceable. A full legal description is not necessarily required, but one should be used whenever possible.

- **Method of payment.** The offer must state how the buyer intends to pay the purchase price. Will the buyer obtain institutional financing, pay cash, or take advantage of seller financing?

- **Contingencies or special arrangements.** If the offer is contingent (on loan approval or on inspection results, for example), the contingency provision must clearly state the circumstances under which the contingency is fulfilled. And any special arrangements that the buyer wants to make, such as taking possession before the closing date, need to be spelled out in the offer. Contingencies are discussed in greater detail in Chapter 8.

While you should pay extra attention to these areas, all of the terms of the offer are important. If, for any reason, you feel there may be a problem with the terms of the buyer's offer, ask your designated broker or branch manager for advice right away. Remember, you are preparing the offer as an agent of your firm, so your designated broker wants it to be problem-free.

Occasionally your designated broker or branch manager will decide that a real estate attorney's advice is needed. (Larger brokerages usually have a legal staff of their own.) Legal consultation is clearly required in any of these situations:

- Because of special terms in the offer, you can't use a pre-printed purchase and sale agreement or addendum. (Remember, you may not draft an agreement or even a simple clause.)
- You need legal documents, such as an easement or a road maintenance agreement, to be prepared.

HOW OFFERS ARE PRESENTED

It's usually the listing agent who presents an offer to the seller. (After all, it is the listing agent who represents the seller.) But the buyer's agent can also play an important role. We'll look at the presentation of a buyer's offer to a seller first from the buyer's agent's point of view and then from the listing agent's.

BUYER'S AGENT'S ROLE. If you are the buyer's agent and the listing agent is going to present the offer to the seller, you should thoroughly explain the offer to the listing agent. It's unusual, but it may even be possible to go along when the listing agent meets with the seller, so that you can answer questions about the buyer or the offer. Note that if you go along when the offer is presented to the seller, you must disclose your agency status to the seller.

Naturally, you'll give the seller the opportunity to discuss the offer privately with the listing agent. Whatever the seller decides to do about the offer, it is your job to convey that decision to the buyer.

If the buyer is especially likable, or in a situation that could evoke sympathy, it may be a good idea to ask the buyer to prepare a personal letter to give to the seller. Though financial considerations will be the primary basis for the seller's decision, he may view the offer more favorably if he thinks about the buyer as a real person rather than in the abstract. On the other hand, sellers receive a lot of these letters and some agents dispute their value.

LISTING AGENT'S ROLE. If you are the listing agent and receive a written offer to purchase, you should arrange to meet with the seller to discuss the offer right away. Any and all offers to purchase that you receive must be presented to the seller as soon as possible.

When you meet with the seller, you should go over all of the terms of the offer and make sure the seller understands them. When there is more than one seller, it's a good idea to give each of them a copy of the offer. For instance, if the sellers are a married couple, provide a copy of the offer to each spouse as you discuss it. Then go through the offer line by line, answering the sellers' questions. It is especially important to discuss the following provisions:

- the proposed closing date and date of possession;
- the list of included items (any personal property that would be transferred to the buyers along with the real property);

- any contingencies (such as whether the buyers need to sell their own house first); and
- any obligations the sellers would have to fulfill before closing, such as completing repairs or cleanup.

If the sellers have legal questions, recommend that they consult an attorney. Do not try to answer legal questions yourself.

The sellers may ask questions about the buyers—who they are, whether they can afford the home, and how motivated they are to buy. If you have any personal information about the buyers, be sure to avoid describing them in terms that might lead to a violation of the fair housing laws. Certain characteristics—race, national origin, religion, and so on—should not be mentioned.

When you review the financial aspects of the sale, it's helpful to use a "Seller's Estimated Net Proceeds" worksheet, which will make it easier to calculate the selling costs and the amount of cash the sellers can expect to receive at closing. (See Figure 11.5 in Chapter 11.)

MULTIPLE OFFERS

Sometimes a seller has more than one offer to consider at the same time. Two or more offers may come in simultaneously, or an additional offer may come in while the seller is considering an earlier one. The listing agent must present every offer received to the seller, even if the seller has already decided to accept another offer.

> **EXAMPLE:** You are the listing agent. You presented an offer to the sellers two days ago and they've been considering it very seriously. This morning they told you that they're almost sure they will accept it. They just want a little more time to think it over.
>
> A few minutes ago, a buyer's agent sent you another offer on the sellers' house. This offer is not nearly as attractive as the first one. Even so, you are required to present the new offer to the sellers right away. You can't wait around to see whether they accept or reject the first offer.

In competitive real estate markets, multiple offers are not uncommon. From a seller's point of view, multiple offer situations are desirable. Competing buyers may eliminate contingencies and increase offer amounts to make their offers more attractive, driving up the final sales price. For these same reasons, buyers usually try to avoid multiple offer situations.

BUYER'S AGENT'S ROLE. If you represent a buyer in a multiple offer situation, your goal is to work with the buyer to make the offer as attractive as possible, without compromising too much. Depending on your client's financial situation, this may mean increasing the amount of the earnest money deposit, or perhaps offering an unusually short closing period. As discussed in the previous chapter, a written statement or letter from the buyers may be helpful. Lender preapproval is almost a requirement; the seller is far less likely to consider an offer from an unapproved buyer if a similar offer has been submitted by an approved buyer. You may be able to find out from the seller's agent if the seller wants any special terms or concessions. For example, if the seller wants to sell quickly but remain in the home for an extra six months, you could add a sale-leaseback clause to your client's offer.

Help your buyer assess the offer to make sure any concessions made are worth it. It's easy for an anxious buyer to get caught up in a bidding war, and he may want to offer more than he can afford, or agree to unreasonable seller demands.

LISTING AGENT'S ROLE. On the other hand, if you represent the seller in a multiple offer situation, your goal is to ensure that the seller accepts an offer that maximizes her profit but minimizes the chance that the sale will fall through.

One possible pitfall of a bidding war can occur if the price is driven up beyond what the home is truly worth. The seller may accept the highest offer but see the deal fall through when the buyer's lender appraises the house for less than the offered amount. Or the sale may fail for a different reason, and when the seller begins the negotiating process again, she may have inflated expectations of her home's value.

It is the listing agent's job to explain to the seller that simply accepting the highest offer isn't necessarily the wisest move. It may make more sense, for example, to choose a lower, all-cash offer over a higher offer requiring lender approval.

When faced with multiple offers, a seller has a number of options. The seller may decide to:

- reject all of the offers,
- accept one of the offers and reject the others,
- make a counteroffer on one offer and reject the others, or
- accept one offer and make a contingent counteroffer on another.

The last of these alternatives, the contingent counteroffer, brings us to the subject of backup offers.

BACKUP OFFERS

Some buyers are so interested in a particular house that they are willing to make a backup offer—an offer that's contingent on the failure of a previous sales contract.

> **EXAMPLE:** You showed Clark's house to Lenihan a week ago, and this morning Lenihan called to say he wants to make an offer on it. You contact the listing agent and learn that the seller has already signed a purchase and sale agreement. Your client, Lenihan, is extremely disappointed. You explain that he can make a backup offer that is contingent on the failure of the first contract. He agrees to this, and you submit Lenihan's backup offer to the listing agent.

A listing agent is not only required to present additional offers received while the seller is already considering an offer, he must also present offers that come in after the seller has signed a contract, up until that sale actually closes. However, when an offer is submitted after the seller has signed a contract, it should be made contingent on the first sale's failure to close. Attaching a backup addendum such as the one shown in Figure 6.1 to the second buyer's offer is the best way to accomplish this.

CONTINGENT COUNTEROFFER. Suppose you're representing a seller who has already signed a purchase and sale agreement, and another buyer makes an offer. The seller is interested in accepting this as a backup offer, but it isn't contingent on the failure of the first contract. You should advise the seller to make a contingent counteroffer. The counteroffer will repeat the buyer's offer but add a contingency clause regarding the first contract.

> **EXAMPLE:** Your sellers have accepted an offer from the Browns. The Browns' offer is for the full listing price, but it's by no means certain that the Browns will qualify for the financing they need to complete the purchase. So when you present an offer from Finney, the sellers are very interested. Finney's offer is for $4,000 less than the Browns' offer, but Finney is already preapproved for the necessary loan.

FIG. 6.1   BACKUP OFFER ADDENDUM

Form 38A
Back-Up Addendum
Rev. 2/17
Page 1 of 1

BACK-UP ADDENDUM TO PURCHASE AND SALE AGREEMENT

The following is part of the Purchase and Sale Agreement dated _____ 1

between _____ ("Buyer") 2
　　　　　Buyer　　　　　　　　　　　　　　Buyer

and _____ ("Seller") 3
　　　Seller　　　　　　　　　　　　　　Seller

concerning _____ (the "Property"). 4
　　　　　　Address　　　　　　　　City　　　　　　State　Zip

1. **Property Already Sold.** Seller has previously sold the Property pursuant to a purchase and sale agreement　5
    dated _____ ("First Sale"). Seller reserves the right to change or amend the terms of the First Sale.　6

2. **Back-Up Agreement Subject to First Sale.** This "Back-Up Agreement" is subject to the First Sale. Seller is not　7
    obligated to sell to Buyer, unless the First Sale fails to close.　8

3. **Notice - If First Sale Fails to Close.** Seller shall give notice to Buyer within 3 days of learning that the First Sale　9
    will not close ("First Sale Failure Notice").　10

4. **Closing.** If the First Sale fails to close, the Closing Date of this Back-Up Agreement shall be _____ days　11
    (60 days if not filled in) from the date of delivery of the First Sale Failure Notice. The Closing Date in this　12
    Addendum supersedes the Closing Date in the Agreement.　13

5. **Expiration of Back-Up Agreement.** If Seller has not given the First Sale Failure Notice within _____ days　14
    (60 days if not filled in) after mutual acceptance of this Back-Up Agreement, this Back-Up Agreement shall　15
    terminate.　16

6. **Termination by Buyer.** Buyer may terminate this Back-Up Agreement any time prior to receiving the First Sale　17
    Failure Notice.　18

7. **Time.** For the purposes of computing time (except for paragraph 5 above), all timelines in this Back-Up　19
    Agreement, including the deposit of Earnest Money, shall begin on the date of delivery of the First Sale Failure　20
    Notice. If NWMLS Short Sale Addendum (Form 22SS) is a part of this Back-Up Agreement, all timelines shall　21
    begin on the date of delivery of the First Sale Failure Notice or Notice of Lender Consent, whichever occurs later.　22

8. **Other.**　23

　24
　25
　26
　27
　28
　29
　30
　31
　32
　33

_____　　_____
Buyer　　　　　　　　　　　Date　　　Seller　　　　　　　　　　Date

_____　　_____

The sellers want to accept Finney's offer as a backup offer. However, Finney's offer does not include a clause that makes it contingent on the failure of the first agreement. So you advise the sellers to make a counteroffer. They offer Finney the same terms set forth in his original offer, but they include a backup addendum making the sale to Finney contingent on the failure of the sale to the Browns. Finney accepts the sellers' counteroffer. Now if the Browns fail to qualify for financing, the sellers will have a binding contract with Finney.

BACKUP OFFERS AND BREACH OF CONTRACT. If a seller were to accept a second offer without a backup contingency clause, she would end up obligated under two different purchase and sale agreements. Because one contract couldn't be fulfilled without breaching the other, the seller would be liable for breach of contract to the potential buyer who didn't get the property.

> **EXAMPLE:** Returning to the previous example, suppose your sellers accepted Finney's offer without adding the contingency provision. They would then be obligated to sell the property both to Finney and to the Browns. Obviously, the sellers can only transfer the property to one of the buyers. So if the sale to the Browns closed, Finney could sue the sellers for breach of his contract.

Never try to convince a seller to break an existing agreement in order to accept another offer, even if the second offer is much better. If you were to do that, you could be found guilty of a tort (a civil wrong) called "tortious interference with a contractual relationship." You could be held liable for damages caused by the breach of contract.

> **EXAMPLE:** Now suppose that Finney's offer is substantially better than the Browns' offer. Finney is offering $15,000 more than the listing price, will pay all of the closing costs, and is preapproved for the necessary financing. The sellers would be better off with this offer, and so would you (your commission would be larger because of the higher purchase price). But you should not suggest that the sellers breach their contract with the Browns in order to accept Finney's offer. If you did, the Browns could sue you for damages, and you could also lose your real estate license.

If your clients express an interest in breaching a contract in favor of another offer, you should strongly recommend that they talk to a real estate attorney before taking any action.

NOTICE TO BACKUP BUYER. When a seller has accepted a backup offer and the first sale fails to close, the seller must notify the backup buyer that their purchase and sale agreement is now a binding contract. The seller can use a form such as the one shown in Figure 6.2 to notify the backup buyer that the first sale has failed.

REVOKING AN OFFER

A buyer can revoke an offer to purchase at any time before the seller properly communicates his acceptance of the offer. When the offer is accepted, a binding contract is created, and the buyer can't back out without breaching it.

Even if an offer gives the seller a specific length of time to consider it, the buyer can revoke the offer sooner than that, as long as she acts before the seller sends his acceptance.

EXAMPLE: Grant offers to buy Rush's house for $365,000. The offer states that it will terminate in 48 hours. If the 48 hours pass without an acceptance, Grant's offer terminates automatically. But if Grant changes her mind about buying the house before that (for example, 30 hours after making the offer) and Rush has not yet accepted it, Grant is free to revoke the offer. Rush cannot force her to keep the offer open for the full 48 hours.

If a time limit is not stated in the offer, it will terminate after a reasonable amount of time.

EXAMPLE: Now suppose that Grant's offer to Rush doesn't have a termination date. Rush doesn't respond to the offer for weeks. Finally, six weeks after receiving the offer, Rush notifies Grant that he's accepting it. It's too late, however. It's not reasonable to expect that an offer to purchase a house will be kept open for six weeks. If Grant has changed her mind about buying, she's no longer bound by her offer.

COUNTEROFFERS AND NEGOTIATIONS

Unless a buyer has made an offer that matches all of the seller's terms, there is likely to be some negotiation. In fact, negotiation is the norm rather than the exception. Under normal market conditions, sellers don't generally expect

FIG. 6.2   NOTICE TO BACKUP BUYER

Form 38B
Notice to Back-Up First Sale Fail
Rev. 8/11
Page 1 of 1

**FIRST SALE FAILURE NOTICE
TO BACK-UP BUYER**

©Copyright 2011
Northwest Multiple Listing Service
ALL RIGHTS RESERVED

The following is part of the Purchase and Sale Agreement dated _____ 1

between _____ ("Buyer") 2

and _____ ("Seller") 3

concerning _____ ("the Property"). 4

Pursuant to Paragraph 3 of the "Back-Up" Addendum (Form 38A), Seller gives notice to Buyer that the First Sale 5
failed to close ("First Sale Failure Notice"). This "Back-Up Agreement" is now a firm agreement for sale of the 6
Property. 7

_____ _____   _____ _____ 8
Seller   Date   Seller   Date

full-price offers, and buyers aren't surprised when the seller rejects their first offer and counters with another offer. The most common objections to initial offers concern:

- the price,
- the amount of earnest money,
- the closing date and date of possession,
- which furnishings or fixtures are included in the sale, and
- financing terms.

If the seller decides to counter the buyer's offer with another offer, you may be able to make the seller's changes on the original purchase and sale agreement form.

> **EXAMPLE:** Gordon has offered Lamont $275,000 for her house, with a closing date of June 16. He is making an earnest money deposit of $1,500. Lamont is pleased with nearly all of the terms of Gordon's offer, but she wants a larger deposit—$6,500. Lamont's agent simply crosses out the $1,500 earnest money figure on the form submitted by Gordon and writes in $6,500. Lamont initials the change, and her agent presents the counteroffer (the revised purchase and sale agreement form) to Gordon.

For simple changes such as the one in the example, this might work just fine. But it's usually better to use a separate counteroffer form, such as the one shown in Figure 6.3, especially when the changes are numerous or complicated. Otherwise the purchase and sale agreement may become confusing and, as a result, unenforceable.

On the counteroffer form in Figure 6.3, you identify the original offer by filling in the date it was signed by the buyer, the property description, and the names of the buyer and seller.

The counteroffer states that all of the terms of the original offer are acceptable to the seller, except for the changes noted. The form has lots of room to fill in the new terms the seller is proposing. There's space for setting a deadline, to indicate how long the buyer has to consider the counteroffer before it will terminate. The counteroffer is then signed by the seller and presented to the buyer for approval or rejection.

When your seller decides to make a counteroffer, be sure to explain that the counteroffer will terminate the original offer and all of the buyer's obligations under that offer.

FIG. 6.3   COUNTEROFFER FORM

Form 36
Counteroffer Addendum
Rev. 8/11
Page 1 of 1

**COUNTEROFFER ADDENDUM
TO REAL ESTATE PURCHASE AND SALE AGREEMENT**

All terms and conditions of the offer (Real Estate Purchase and Sale Agreement) dated _____ ,   1

concerning _____ (the "Property"),   2

by,_____ , as _____   3

and the undersigned _____ , as _____   4

are accepted, except for the following changes.   5

☐   **The Purchase Price** shall be $ _____   6

_____   7

☐   **Other.**   8

9
10
11
12
13
14
15
16
17
18
19
20
21
22
23
24
25
26
27

This counteroffer shall expire at 9:00 p.m. on _____ (if not filled in, two days after it is delivered),   28
unless it is sooner withdrawn. Acceptance shall not be effective until a signed copy is received by the counterofferor,   29
their broker or at the licensed office of their broker. If this counteroffer is not so accepted, it shall lapse and the   30
Earnest Money shall be refunded to Buyer.   31

All other terms and conditions of the above offer are incorporated herein by reference as though fully set forth.   32

_____ _____   _____ _____
Signature   Date   Signature   Date

The above counteroffer is accepted.

_____ _____   _____ _____
Signature   Date   Signature   Date

EXAMPLE: Returning to the previous example, suppose that Gordon rejects Lamont's counteroffer. He doesn't want to make a $6,500 earnest money deposit. In that case, Gordon has no further obligation to Lamont. That's because Lamont's counteroffer had the same effect as a rejection of Gordon's original offer would have had: it terminated the offer. So when Gordon refuses to pay a larger deposit, Lamont can't simply change her mind and decide to accept Gordon's original offer. His offer has already been terminated by rejection. If Gordon still wants to buy the property, he can renew his offer; however, if he no longer wants to buy it (or buy it on the terms he originally offered), he is not obligated to do so.

If you are presenting a counteroffer to a buyer, review every term the seller has altered. You may want to prepare another "Buyer's Estimated Costs" worksheet if the counteroffer changes the buyer's costs. If the buyer decides to accept the counteroffer, have him sign the counteroffer form. Then notify the seller that the counteroffer has been accepted.

In some cases, the parties will trade counteroffers back and forth a number of times. The negotiation process can be frustrating or even nerve-wracking. As always, maintain your professionalism and do what you can to keep the parties from becoming hostile. Refrain from making negative comments about either party. It's your responsibility to serve the best interests of your client, and a transaction that satisfies both parties is in your client's best interests, whether you're representing the buyer or the seller.

Don't forget to give the parties copies of any documents they sign when they sign them. Each party who makes a counteroffer should get a copy of it immediately after signing it, and both parties should get a copy of the final purchase and sale agreement as soon as it is signed.

Like any offer, a counteroffer can be revoked at any time before the other party accepts it. A form such as the one shown in Figure 6.4 can be used to withdraw a counteroffer.

ACCEPTING AN OFFER

When an offer (or a counteroffer) is accepted, a contract is formed and the parties are legally bound by it. There are three rules to keep in mind concerning the acceptance of an offer.

FIG. 6.4   WITHDRAWAL OF OFFER OR COUNTEROFFER

Form 36A
Offer/Counteroffer Withdrawal
Rev. 7/10
Page 1 of 1

©Copyright 2010
Northwest Multiple Listing Service
ALL RIGHTS RESERVED

WITHDRAWAL OF OFFER OR COUNTEROFFER

The following is part of the Purchase and Sale Agreement dated _____ 1

between _____ ("Buyer") 2

and _____ ("Seller") 3

concerning _____ (the "Property"). 4

TO: ❑   SELLER **AND** LISTING BROKER   5

           ❑   BUYER **AND** SELLING BROKER   6

THE ATTACHED ❑ OFFER OR ❑ COUNTEROFFER IS WITHDRAWN AND THE EARNEST MONEY SHOULD   7
BE RETURNED TO BUYER.   8

                                                                                       9

DATED: _____

                                              _____ 10

                                              _____ 11

RECEIPT OF THE ABOVE IS ACKNOWLEDGED AT _____   ON _____ 12

                                              _____ 13

                                              _____ 14

The acceptance:

1. must be communicated to the person who made the offer,
2. must be made in the specified manner, and
3. cannot change any of the terms of the offer.

COMMUNICATING ACCEPTANCE

To be effective and create a valid contract, the offeree's acceptance must be communicated to the offeror. (The offeree is the person to whom the offer was made, and the offeror is the person who made it.) A seller may have decided to accept a buyer's offer, but until the seller delivers the acceptance to the buyer, the buyer can still revoke it.

> **EXAMPLE:** White is selling his home. Hathaway makes an offer to buy it, and White's agent presents the offer to White.
>
> In the meantime, Hathaway finds another house she likes better. She immediately notifies White that she's revoking her offer.
>
> White protests, claiming that he had already signed Hathaway's offer before she revoked it. But since White hadn't given the signed contract to Hathaway yet, the acceptance was not communicated. As a result, Hathaway still had the right to revoke the offer.

TIME OF ACCEPTANCE. When the seller's acceptance is delivered to the buyer in person, acceptance is deemed to take place at the time of delivery. Traditionally, if a seller used the mail to notify the buyer of an acceptance, the "mailbox rule" applied: the acceptance created a binding contract when the seller dropped it in the mailbox. While postal mail is rarely used anymore to enter into a real estate agreement, the mailbox rule has been extended to other similar methods of communication, such as faxed messages.

In any case, most purchase agreement forms have a provision that trumps the mailbox rule. For example, the Northwest Multiple Listing Service purchase agreement form states that delivery, regardless of the method used (mail, email, fax, etc.) is effective only upon personal receipt.

COMMUNICATION TO AGENT. Acceptance is also considered to be communicated when the seller delivers it to the buyer's agent, even before the buyer's agent relays the acceptance to the buyer.

MANNER OF ACCEPTANCE

Because a contract to purchase real estate must be in writing, an offer to purchase real estate must be accepted in writing. A spoken acceptance does not create an enforceable contract.

EXAMPLE: Adams submits a written offer to purchase Baker's property. Baker finds the offer very attractive, so she immediately calls Adams and accepts the offer over the phone. Two hours later, Baker receives an even better offer. Baker can still withdraw her acceptance of the offer because the acceptance wasn't in writing.

Sometimes an offer calls for a particular manner of acceptance. If so, the acceptance must be made in the specified manner to be binding.

EXAMPLE: Wallace offers to buy Sanchez's property. But Wallace is leaving town shortly, so he includes the following provision in the offer: "This offer shall become a binding contract when written acceptance is hand-delivered to my attorney at 437 First Avenue, Suite 312." Sanchez can only accept the offer by having the acceptance hand-delivered to Wallace's attorney at the specified address.

If the offer does not call for a particular manner of acceptance, it may be accepted by any reasonable medium of communication. A medium is considered reasonable when it is the same one that was used by the buyer, it is one that is customarily used in similar transactions, or it has been used by the parties in previous transactions. For instance, if the buyer sent the offer to the seller by email, it's reasonable for the seller to send the acceptance to the buyer by email. (Note that if you email offers and acceptances, it's a good idea to get signed originals from both parties.)

ACCEPTANCE CANNOT CHANGE TERMS

To create a contract, the seller must accept the buyer's terms exactly as offered. The seller can't modify the terms of the offer or add any new terms. An acceptance with modifications is actually a counteroffer, not an acceptance.

CONTRACT AMENDMENTS

When an offer to purchase (or a counteroffer) is accepted in the proper manner, a contract is created. The terms of the contract can't be changed without the consent of both parties.

If the buyer and seller agree to modify their contract, you should use a separate form instead of writing the changes on the original purchase and sale agreement form. For example, amendments to the Northwest Multiple Listing Service purchase and sale agreement form are made with the optional clauses addendum shown in Chapter 7 (Figure 7.4).

The form used for an amendment should identify the original contract, provide space to write in the changes, and require the signatures of both parties. The signed amendment form should be attached to the original agreement. Each party should be given a copy of the amendment as soon as he signs it.

When you're filling out a form to amend a contract, remember that writing a special provision for the parties constitutes the unauthorized practice of law. When a transaction requires a special provision, ask your designated broker or branch manager. She is likely to have one or more standard clauses drafted by lawyers that are appropriate for your transaction.

CONTRACT RESCISSION

Sometimes both the buyer and the seller change their minds about going through with the transaction. If so, the parties can terminate their contract by mutual agreement. To do this, the buyer and the seller should sign a rescission agreement, which officially terminates the purchase and sale agreement. An example of a rescission form is shown in Figure 6.5.

A rescission agreement should describe how the earnest money deposit will be handled. When a purchase and sale agreement is rescinded by mutual agreement, the buyer and the seller may agree to let the listing and selling firms split the deposit in lieu of receiving the commission. Technically, the seller is still liable for the brokerage commission, but the firms are usually willing to share the earnest money instead.

For the firms' protection, a rescission agreement form may have an extender clause similar to the ones that appear in listing agreements. Under this type of provision, if the seller enters into a new purchase and sale agreement with this

FIG. 6.5   RESCISSION AGREEMENT FORM

Form 51
Rescission Agreement
Rev. 5/14
Page 1 of 1

RESCISSION AGREEMENT

The Purchase and Sale Agreement (the "Agreement") dated _____   1

between _____ ("Buyer")   2
       Buyer   Buyer

and _____ ("Seller"),   3
       Seller   Seller

concerning _____ (the "Property")   4
       Address   City   State Zip

is rescinded as follows: 5

1. **RELEASE**. The Agreement and all other agreements or undertakings between Buyer and Seller with respect to   6
the Property are rescinded. Each party releases the other and all real estate firms and brokers involved with   7
this sale from any and all liability in connection with the sale, except as agreed below. Nothing herein shall be   8
construed to terminate any existing agency relationships or related agreements unless otherwise agreed in   9
writing.   10

2. **EARNEST MONEY**. The party holding the earnest money is authorized and directed to disburse the earnest   11
money as follows: 12

    $_____ to Buyer.   13

    $_____ to Seller.   14

    $_____ to Listing Firm.   15

    $_____ to Selling Firm.   16

    $_____ to _____.   17

3. **COMMISSION**. If Seller shall, within six months from the date hereof, sell the Property to Buyer or someone   18
acting on Buyer's behalf, Seller shall pay Listing Firm the Total Commission as set forth in the Exclusive Listing   19
Agreement between Seller and Listing Firm, less any portion of the above earnest money retained by Listing   20
Firm. Listing Firm will pay Selling Firm's commission as set forth in the Exclusive Listing Agreement, less any   21
portion of the above earnest money retained by Selling Firm. Provided if a commission is paid to another   22
member(s) of a multiple listing service in conjunction with such a sale, the amount of commission payable to   23
Listing Firm and Selling Firm shall be reduced by the amount paid to such other member(s). "Sell" includes a   24
contract to sell; an exchange or contract to exchange; an option to purchase; and/or a lease with option to   25
purchase regardless of when it closes.   26

_____   _____   _____   _____   27
Buyer's Signature   Date   Seller's Signature   Date

_____   _____   _____   _____   28
Buyer's Signature   Date   Seller's Signature   Date

_____   _____   _____   29
Selling Firm   Listing Firm

_____   _____   _____   _____   30
Selling Broker's Signature   Date   Listing Broker's Signature   Date

same buyer within a specified period (such as six months) after rescinding their original agreement, the seller must pay the firms their full commission.

Rescission agreements are also used when a purchase and sale agreement terminates because a contingency has not been fulfilled. This is discussed in Chapter 8.

EARNEST MONEY DEPOSITS

An important part of helping a buyer make an offer to purchase a home is handling the earnest money deposit. It's traditional for the buyer to give the seller earnest money (sometimes called a good faith deposit) as evidence of the buyer's good faith intention to buy the property on the terms he has offered.

There's no law that requires a buyer to give the seller an earnest money deposit, but virtually every seller will expect one. A seller does not want to take her home off the market for weeks, possibly months, unless the buyer is actually going to follow through on his promise to buy the property. Since the buyer will usually forfeit the deposit if he backs out, the deposit gives the seller some assurance that the buyer really is ready, willing, and able to buy the property.

THE SIZE OF THE DEPOSIT

There is no "standard" deposit amount or percentage. In fact, the size of the earnest money deposit usually depends on the buyer's circumstances. A buyer who is planning on making a large cash downpayment generally won't have any trouble making a substantial deposit; the deposit will simply be applied toward the downpayment when the sale closes. On the other hand, if the buyer is planning to finance the purchase with a no-downpayment VA loan, he may not have enough cash for a big deposit.

As a general rule, the deposit should be large enough to give the buyer an economic incentive to complete the transaction. It should also be large enough to compensate the seller for the time and expense involved in taking the house off the market if the buyer fails to complete the transaction.

EXAMPLE: Bernhardt offers to buy Warren's property for $250,000. He makes a $800 deposit. Two weeks later, Bernhardt finds another property he likes more than Warren's for only $240,000. He decides to walk away from his contract with Warren, forfeit the $800 deposit, and purchase the other property.

Under the terms of the purchase and sale agreement, Warren can keep the deposit as payment for his time and trouble. But in this case, the deposit was too small to serve its purpose. The $800 deposit was not enough money to convince Bernhardt to honor his contract, nor was it enough to compensate Warren for the inconvenience of taking his property off the market for two weeks.

THE FORM OF THE DEPOSIT

A real estate agent who accepts an earnest money deposit from a buyer is required by law to tell the seller the amount of the deposit and what form it is in. Is it cash, a money order, a personal check, a cashier's check, a postdated check, or a promissory note? If you fail to disclose this information to the seller, you may be subject to disciplinary action. You may also face disciplinary action if you don't tell the seller that the earnest money check bounced or that the note was not paid. In addition, the seller could sue you for damages if you fail to make the proper disclosures and then the buyer does not come through with the deposit.

EXAMPLE: You're the listing agent for Peterson's house. When Thompson makes an offer, he tells you that he'll give you a $5,000 earnest money deposit. However, he explains that he can't write the earnest money check until he has transferred funds into his checking account. He assures you that he'll bring you a check tomorrow. He asks you to present the offer to Peterson right away.

When you present the offer, you tell Peterson that Thompson is making a $5,000 deposit, but neglect to mention that he hasn't given you the check yet. You could be subject to disciplinary action for failing to disclose this information.

Peterson accepts Thompson's offer without asking to see the check. She assumes that you already have it and will give it to your brokerage firm, in the usual way.

The next day, Thompson puts you off for one more day. The day after that, he refuses to give you the check and tells you he's decided to back out of his contract with Peterson. Now not only are you subject to disciplinary action, but Peterson could sue you and your firm for the money she should have received as compensation for Thompson's breach of contract.

Now let's consider the advantages and disadvantages of the different forms an earnest money deposit can take.

PERSONAL CHECKS. Most buyers make their earnest money deposit with a personal check. The check is usually made payable to the escrow agent or, lesson commonly, to the brokerage that will deposit the check if the buyer's offer is accepted. (Some firms require a cashier's check or a money order instead of a personal check.)

Sometimes a buyer wants to use a postdated check, which can't be deposited until the date on the check. However, some firms won't accept postdated checks. If you do accept a postdated check, you must tell the seller. It's wise to make this disclosure in writing.

As an alternative to using a postdated check, the buyer may choose to make a small initial earnest money deposit and include a provision in the offer that she will make an additional deposit within a certain period of time.

> **EXAMPLE:** Hassam wants to make an offer on a home. She has a certificate of deposit that will mature in ten days, and she's planning on using those funds for the downpayment. Right now, however, she only has enough cash available to make a $500 earnest money deposit. She doesn't want to cash in her certificate of deposit before it matures, because she would have to pay a penalty for early withdrawal. Instead, she gives you a $500 check with her offer and agrees in writing to make an additional earnest money deposit in the amount of $2,500 in ten days.

CASH. In rare cases, a buyer wants to make the earnest money deposit in cash. But accepting an earnest money deposit in cash carries risks for both the agent and the firm.

> **EXAMPLE:** A buyer wants to make an offer for a property on Friday night. He gives you a cash earnest money deposit of $2,200. You can't turn the cash over to your firm until Monday. What do you do with the cash over the weekend? You can't deposit it in your own account (that would be commingling trust funds with personal funds), but you will be responsible if the cash is lost or stolen.

Most brokerages won't accept cash deposits. If you do take a cash deposit, you must turn it over to the firm in its original cash form. You may not deposit it into your account and then write a check against the deposit. Nor may you purchase a money order or a cashier's check with the cash.

PROMISSORY NOTES. Although it's risky to accept a promissory note as an earnest money deposit, sometimes a seller is willing to do so. When you tell the seller that the deposit is in the form of a note, be sure he understands the risk. Should the buyer refuse to pay the note when it comes due, a lawsuit would be the only way to collect the money owed.

A form that can be used for an earnest money note is shown in Figure 6.6. This form provides that failure to pay the note as agreed is a breach of the purchase and sale agreement as well as a default on the note. It also provides that if it is necessary to sue the buyer to collect on the note, the buyer will have to pay reasonable attorney's fees and court costs.

PERSONAL PROPERTY. In unusual cases, a buyer may want to use an item of personal property as an earnest money deposit. For instance, you might encounter a buyer who wants to use stock certificates, bonds, or a boat as part or all of the deposit. It is up to the seller to decide whether to accept such an item as a deposit. The parties and your firm will have to arrange an appropriate method of safekeeping for the item in question.

HANDLING A DEPOSIT

When a buyer gives you an earnest money deposit, you're required to turn it over to your firm as soon as possible. How the firm handles the deposit is governed partly by the trust fund procedures set forth in the real estate license law, and partly by the terms of the purchase and sale agreement (the buyer's offer). Since most earnest money deposits take the form of a personal check, we'll focus on the procedures for handling a check.

HOLDING OR DEPOSITING THE CHECK. The purchase and sale agreement form shown in Figure 7.1 allows the buyer to specify whether the earnest money will be held by a closing agent or the selling firm. The buyer must deliver the check to the closing agent or selling broker within two days after the offer is accepted. If it's the selling broker who receives the check, she has three days either to pass it on to the closing agent or deposit it as directed by the purchase and sale agreement. Alternatively, the purchase and sale agreement may provide for the selling firm to hold an earnest money check until acceptance occurs; if acceptance doesn't occur, the check is returned to the buyer. Either method makes it easy for the buyer to get his money back if no deal is reached.

FIG. 6.6 EARNEST MONEY PROMISSORY NOTE FORM

Form 31
Earnest Money Promissory Note
Rev. 7/10
Pages 1 of 1

EARNEST MONEY PROMISSORY NOTE

$ _____ _____ , Washington 1

FOR VALUE RECEIVED, _____ ("Buyer") 2

agree(s) to pay to the order of _____ (Selling Firm or Closing Agent) 3

the sum of _____ Dollars 4

($ _____), as follows: 5

☐ within 3 days following mutual acceptance of the Purchase and Sale Agreement. 6

☐ * _____ . 7

This Note is evidence of the obligation to pay Earnest Money under a real estate Purchase and 8

Sale Agreement between the Buyer and _____ ("Seller") 9

dated _____. Buyer's failure to pay the Earnest Money 10

strictly as above shall constitute default on said Purchase and Sale Agreement as well as on this Note. 11

If this Note shall be placed in the hands of an attorney for collection, or if suit shall be brought to collect 12

any of the balance due on this Note, the Buyer promises to pay reasonable attorneys' fees, and all 13

court and collection costs. 14

Date: _____ 15

BUYER _____ 16

BUYER _____ 17

* "On closing" or similar language is not recommended. Use a definite date. 18

If the purchase and sale agreement does not require holding the check undeposited or turning it over to a closing agent, the law requires the check to be deposited into the firm's trust account by the end of the first banking day after receipt.

TRUST ACCOUNTS AND INTEREST. If the earnest money check is for $10,000 or less, the firm must keep it in a pooled trust account identified as a housing trust fund account, with interest paid to the state treasurer. If the check is for more than $10,000, it is usually placed in a separate trust account, with the interest paid to the buyer (the agreement could call for the interest to go to the seller, however). Before the buyer's check can be deposited into a separate account, the buyer must complete IRS form W-9.

FIRM'S RESPONSIBILITIES. Generally, the firm that receives the earnest money is the one responsible for handling the funds properly. Thus, the selling firm (the firm working with the buyer) is usually the one who is required to deposit the funds, deliver them to the closing agent, or hold them until the seller accepts the offer. Usually, the deposit is first given to the buyer's agent, who is supposed to turn the deposit over to her designated broker as soon as possible. Every firm must have procedures in place for handling deposits. For example, a designated broker should give his sales agents instructions on what to do if they receive an earnest money deposit when the office is closed.

BOUNCED OR STOPPED CHECKS. After the firm deposits an earnest money check into the appropriate trust account, problems can still arise. The check may fail to clear, or the buyer may stop payment for some reason.

> **EXAMPLE:** On Tuesday, Green made an offer on Bowen's property. Green gave you a $2,000 personal check for the earnest money, and you immediately turned it over to your designated broker.
>
> Wednesday morning, your designated broker deposited the check into her trust account. Wednesday evening, Bowen rejected Green's offer, so Green asked for a refund of his deposit. Thursday morning, your designated broker wrote Green a $2,000 check from her trust account.
>
> On Friday morning, the bank calls your designated broker to inform her that Green's check failed to clear his bank due to insufficient funds. Now Green has your firm's $2,000, your firm's trust account is overdrawn, and your designated broker may face disciplinary action for the shortfall.

To prevent this type of problem, the purchase and sale agreement can include a provision that requires the buyer to wait until his check clears before requesting a refund of the earnest money deposit. Of course, if the agreement provides that the firm will hold the deposit until the seller accepts the offer, this problem is avoided altogether.

Refund or Forfeiture of Earnest Money

If the buyer and seller have signed a purchase and sale agreement, but the sale fails to close, the earnest money will either be returned to the buyer or forfeited to the seller. The circumstances under which it will be refunded or forfeited should be stated clearly in the purchase and sale agreement. This is the best way to prevent a dispute between the buyer and the seller over who is entitled to the deposit.

Typically, the buyer is entitled to a refund of the deposit if:

- the seller rejects the offer;
- the buyer withdraws the offer before it is accepted;
- the buyer rescinds based on information in the seller disclosure statement or discovers a material inaccuracy concerning the property; or
- the seller accepts the offer, but a contingency provision is not fulfilled, so the contract is terminated.

Example: Lindor and Jones have a purchase and sale agreement that's contingent on Lindor obtaining a conventional loan to finance the purchase. Lindor applies to three lenders, but they all reject his loan application. The contingency hasn't been fulfilled, so the contract is terminated, and Lindor is entitled to a refund of the deposit.

On the other hand, the deposit will generally be forfeited to the seller if the seller accepts the offer, but then the buyer simply changes her mind and backs out of the sale. Most purchase and sale agreements provide that the deposit will be treated as liquidated damages if the buyer breaches the contract.

Washington has a statutory limit on liquidated damages in real estate transactions. When a buyer's earnest money deposit is treated as liquidated damages, the amount that the buyer forfeits cannot exceed 5% of the purchase price of the property.

FIG. 6.7   EARNEST MONEY RULES

BUYER'S EARNEST MONEY DEPOSIT

- MUST BE DEPOSITED INTO TRUST ACCOUNT BY END OF FIRST BANKING DAY AFTER RECEIPT, UNLESS OTHERWISE AGREED

- $10,000 OR LESS: MUST BE KEPT IN POOLED ACCOUNT, WITH INTEREST PAID TO STATE TREASURER

- MORE THAN $10,000: MAY BE KEPT IN SEPARATE ACCOUNT, WITH INTEREST PAID TO BUYER

If the brokerage firm is holding the earnest money, the firm should ask the parties to agree to the disbursement in writing. If they disagree as to which of them is entitled to the deposit, the firm must give written notice to both parties of the intent to distribute the funds within 30 days.

Some purchase and sale agreements provide that any expenses already incurred that were to be paid at closing will be deducted from the earnest money before it's forfeited to the seller. Also, listing agreements typically provide that the seller will pay half of the remainder of the deposit to the listing firm and selling firm in place of their commission.

Remember, it is the brokerage firm—not you—who is responsible for disbursing earnest money deposits. If a buyer or seller has questions about how the deposit will be handled, always refer her to your designated broker or branch manager. Never try to answer these questions yourself.

FAIR HOUSING CONSIDERATIONS

As we explained in Chapter 3, in Washington it's illegal to discriminate in real estate transactions based on race, color, creed, religion, national origin, sex, sexual orientation or gender identity, familial status, marital status, disability, use of a trained guide dog or service animal, honorably discharged veteran status, or military status. Chapter 3 covered discriminatory listing and marketing practices; this section discusses discrimination in the context of working with buyers and negotiating contracts.

The potential for illegal discrimination against a buyer begins with your first contact. Even before you show the buyer a house, prepare an offer, or negotiate a sale, you might engage in discriminatory conduct.

So keep in mind that you don't have to intend to discriminate in order to violate state or federal law. Simply acting in a discriminatory manner or with a discriminatory effect can be enough.

> **EXAMPLE:** An agent has some Vietnamese buyers who don't speak much English. She feels no prejudice against her clients but decides to show them properties around a part of town known as "Little Saigon" almost exclusively, genuinely believing that the family will be happier in an area where Vietnamese is commonly spoken. Regardless of her intent, the agent's actions constitute steering (see Chapter 3) and violate fair housing law.

A buyer's agent must avoid the same general kinds of discriminatory actions as a listing agent. In particular, a buyer's agent is prohibited from:

- refusing to receive or failing to transmit a bona fide offer;
- refusing to negotiate for the sale of property, or otherwise making it unavailable;
- changing the terms of the sale for different potential buyers;
- discriminating in providing services or facilities in connection with a real estate transaction;
- representing that a property is not available for inspection or sale when it is in fact available;
- failing to advise a prospect about a property listing;
- using any application form or making any record or inquiry which indicates, directly or indirectly, an intent to discriminate; and
- discriminating in negotiating or executing any service or item (such as title insurance or mortgage insurance) in connection with a real estate transaction.

The agent in the following example violated these prohibitions.

> **EXAMPLE:** Sarah has shown Hernandez, a Latino buyer, several houses. Hernandez asks to be shown a particular house that he noticed online. He thinks it might be just the place he's looking for. From office rumors, Sarah knows that the seller will probably refuse to accept an offer from any Latino buyer. She's anxious to avoid a confrontation, so she tells Hernandez that the seller

has already accepted an offer and the house is no longer available. Sarah has discriminated against Hernandez by representing that the property is not available when in fact it is.

Be sure to give all buyers the same quality of service. Obviously, it's discriminatory to ignore minority prospects when they enter your office, for instance, or to refuse to drive them to see the listed houses that interest them (if that's a service you ordinarily provide).

Your firm will have detailed sales procedures to help you ensure compliance with fair housing laws. Here are a few examples of guidelines to follow when talking to buyers, showing homes, and presenting and negotiating offers:

- Never imply that a person of a particular race, color, religion, national origin, etc., will have a harder time getting financing.
- Always offer to show your prospects all the listed properties in your market area that meet their objective criteria. Don't make assumptions about a buyer's housing needs or neighborhood preferences based on stereotypes.
- Be sure to treat all prospects equally when setting up showings, making appointments to present offers, or conducting negotiations.
- Report any suspected discriminatory act or statement on the part of a seller to your designated broker or another supervisor immediately. Ask the supervisor (or a lawyer, if necessary) what you should do about a rejection that seemed to be based on discriminatory reasons.

CHAPTER SUMMARY

1. As a real estate agent, you may fill out a standard purchase and sale agreement form, but only for a transaction you are handling, and you cannot charge a separate fee for the service. You may not draft special clauses or give advice about the legal effect of provisions in the form. If you have any questions or concerns when filling out a form, you should talk to your designated broker or a real estate attorney.

2. All offers to purchase, regardless of their merit, must be presented to the seller. You must even present offers received after the seller has already accepted another offer. (These backup offers should be made contingent on the failure of the first sales contract.) Offers are usually presented by the listing agent. You must disclose your agency status before presenting an offer to purchase.

3. When a seller "accepts" an offer with a few modifications, the seller is actually rejecting the offer and making a counteroffer. When a party wants to make a counteroffer, it is best to use a counteroffer form. When you present a counteroffer, be sure to explain each term that has been changed and discuss the financial ramifications of the changes.

4. If an offer does not have a time limit, it will terminate after a reasonable period of time. An offer can be revoked at any time up until it is accepted. An offer to purchase real property must be in writing. The acceptance also must be in writing.

5. When an acceptance is delivered, a binding contract is created. The contract cannot be modified without the written consent of both parties. The parties may mutually agree to terminate the contract, although the seller may still owe the firm the sales commission. If the contract is terminated, the parties should sign a rescission agreement.

6. You must disclose the amount and the form of the buyer's earnest money deposit to the seller and also disclose any problems with the deposit. Most deposits are personal checks, but they may also be in the form of cash, a money order, a cashier's check, a promissory note, or personal property.

7. Often the purchase and sale agreement provides that the deposit is to be held by the closing agent. Earnest money to be held by the firm must be deposited in the firm's trust account within one banking day of receipt, unless the purchase and sale agreement provides otherwise. Many agreements state that the buyer doesn't have to deliver the earnest money until after acceptance. If the sale closes, the earnest money will be credited against the buyer's downpayment. If the sale fails to close, the earnest money will either be returned to the buyer or forfeited to the seller, depending on the circumstances.

8. In showing homes, preparing offers, and negotiating sales, be sure you do not discriminate against the buyers you're representing. Discrimination does not have to be intentional to violate fair housing laws.

CHAPTER QUIZ

1. Which of the following statements about an offer to purchase real property is true?

    a. The offer needs to be in writing, but the acceptance does not

    b. Both the offer and the acceptance must be in writing

    c. Neither the offer nor the acceptance needs to be in writing, but the deed to transfer title must be in writing

    d. The offer does not have to be in writing, but the acceptance must include all of the terms of the offer

2. Which of the following statements about preparing an offer to purchase is true?

    a. The buyer cannot write her own offer without engaging in the unauthorized practice of law

    b. A real estate agent may write special clauses for the parties as long as they are inserted into a pre-printed form written and approved by attorneys

    c. A real estate agent may not prepare an offer if he represents one of the parties

    d. A real estate agent is held to the same standard of care as a lawyer when preparing an offer

3. A contingent counteroffer would be appropriate when:

    a. the seller has already signed a purchase and sale agreement, and then receives an attractive offer from another buyer

    b. the seller wants to accept the buyer's offer, but modify some of the terms

    c. the buyer wants to accept the seller's counteroffer, but isn't sure if he'll qualify for financing

    d. the seller has received multiple offers and wants to withdraw her previous counteroffer to one buyer and accept another buyer's offer

4. The seller's acceptance would be effective (so that the buyer could no longer withdraw his offer) in all of the following situations, except if the seller:

    a. accepts the buyer's offer over the phone

    b. uses a fax machine to transmit her acceptance

    c. sends her acceptance in the mail, but with delivery confirmation

    d. sends her acceptance via telegram

5. Once it has been signed by both the buyer and the seller, a purchase and sale agreement can be modified only if:

    a. a contingency clause is not fulfilled

    b. the buyer accepts the seller's counteroffer in writing

    c. both parties agree to the modifications in writing

    d. the seller failed to disclose certain information he was legally required to disclose

6. Which of the following is least likely to be found in a rescission agreement?

   a. An extender clause

   b. A notice to backup buyer

   c. An agreement to allow the listing and selling firms to share the earnest money deposit in lieu of a commission

   d. The signatures of both parties

7. After accepting an earnest money deposit from a buyer, you are required to tell the seller:

   a. what form the deposit is in

   b. whether the buyer actually has paid you the deposit funds

   c. the amount of the deposit

   d. All of the above

8. If you accept cash as an earnest money deposit, you:

   a. must turn the deposit over to the firm in its original cash form

   b. should use the cash to purchase a certified check, to prevent the funds from being lost or stolen

   c. should have the buyer's receipt notarized

   d. may face disciplinary action for violating the real estate license law

9. Some purchase and sale agreement forms have a provision allowing the firm to hold the earnest money check without depositing it for a specified period. One advantage of this is that:

   a. it gives the seller more time to consider the offer

   b. the firm can simply return the check to the buyer if the offer is rejected

   c. it ensures that the buyer has sufficient funds in her account

   d. the check can be postdated by a week or more

10. If the buyer forfeits the earnest money deposit as liquidated damages for breach of the purchase and sale agreement:

    a. the full amount of the deposit will be split between the selling firm and the listing firm in lieu of a commission

    b. any amount in excess of 5% of the purchase price must be refunded to the buyer

    c. any amount in excess of $10,000 must be refunded to the buyer

    d. the seller will be entitled to keep the entire amount, less any expenses incurred by the listing firm

Answer Key

1. b. The statute of frauds requires both an offer to purchase real property and the acceptance of the offer to be in writing.

2. d. When filling out a contract form, a real estate agent is held to the same standard of care that is required of a lawyer.

3. a. A contingent counteroffer allows a seller to accept a second offer, contingent on the failure of the first contract.

4. a. In order to form a contract to purchase real estate, the acceptance must be made in writing. Telephone communication is not a valid form of acceptance.

5. c. Once a contract has been formed, the terms of the contract can't be changed without the written consent of both parties. The parties may agree to amend the contract for any reason.

6. b. A contract rescission agreement should be signed by both parties and describe how the earnest money deposit will be handled. It may include an extender clause for the licensees' protection. If the seller has accepted a backup offer, the notice to the backup buyer will be handled separately.

7. d. A real estate agent who accepts an earnest money deposit is required to disclose the amount and form of the deposit to the seller. The agent must also inform the seller if the earnest money check bounces, the funds have not actually been paid, or a promissory note is not been paid.

8. a. If you accept an earnest money deposit in cash, you must turn the cash over to your firm so that it can be placed in the trust account in cash. Although accepting an earnest money deposit in cash increases the chance of loss or improper handling, it is not in itself grounds for disciplinary action.

9. b. Purchase and sale agreements may provide that the firm will hold the earnest money check without depositing it until the seller accepts the offer. This makes it easier to return the earnest money to the buyer if the offer is rejected.

10. b. If the buyer breaches the purchase and sale agreement, no more than 5% of the purchase price can be retained as liquidated damages. After expenses incurred by the firm have been deducted, the seller usually keeps half of the remainder and gives the listing firm the other half. The listing firm will usually split this portion with the selling firm.

PURCHASE AND SALE AGREEMENTS

REQUIREMENTS FOR A VALID AGREEMENT

PROVISIONS IN A RESIDENTIAL AGREEMENT

- Identifying the parties
- Property description
- Purchase price and method of payment
- Earnest money
- Included items
- Conveyance and title
- Information verification period
- Closing provisions
- Transfer of possession
- Default
- Time is of the essence
- Addenda
- Agency disclosure
- Lead-based paint disclosures
- Offer and acceptance
- Signatures

VACANT LAND PURCHASE AND SALE AGREEMENTS

INTRODUCTION

We've discussed a variety of techniques that will help you find potential buyers, show properties, and negotiate offers. Your designated broker or branch manager will undoubtedly give you training in these matters. However, learning the functions of a purchase and sale agreement and understanding its provisions are just as important to your career. If you make a mistake in filling out a purchase and sale agreement form, you could face the loss of your commission, a lawsuit by the buyer or the seller, and disciplinary action. This chapter describes the requirements for a valid purchase and sale agreement, the provisions typically found in a residential purchase and sale agreement form, and some of the addenda commonly used in residential transactions. At the end of the chapter, we'll look at a purchase and sale agreement for vacant land.

REQUIREMENTS FOR A VALID PURCHASE AND SALE AGREEMENT

When the seller signs the buyer's written offer, agreeing to the buyer's terms, a contract is formed. The contract holds the buyer and seller to their agreement until the sale closes. But the contract won't be enforceable unless it includes all of the terms that are legally required for a valid purchase and sale agreement.

To be enforceable, a purchase and sale agreement must meet the basic legal requirements for any contract. The parties must be competent, and there must be mutual consent (offer and acceptance), a lawful objective, and consideration (the seller's promise to sell and the buyer's promise to buy).

In addition, a purchase and sale agreement must:

1. be in writing;
2. identify the parties and describe the property;
3. state the price and method of payment;
4. provide for the payment of utilities and the proration of taxes, insurance, and liens;
5. state the type of deed and the condition of title;
6. list the liens or other encumbrances the buyer will assume or take title subject to;
7. describe any conditions or contingencies (such as a financing contingency); and
8. state the time for delivery of title and possession.

While these are the minimum requirements for validity, most purchase and sale agreement forms are quite detailed. It is important for the agreement between the parties to be stated fully and accurately; anything that isn't made clear at the outset can give rise to a dispute later on, and might prevent the transaction from closing.

TYPICAL PROVISIONS IN A RESIDENTIAL PURCHASE AND SALE AGREEMENT

There is no one purchase and sale agreement form that all real estate agents must use. A variety of forms are available from multiple listing services, other professional organizations, and legal form publishers. As an example, Figure 7.1 shows the residential purchase and sale agreement form that the Northwest Multiple Listing Service (NWMLS) uses. Of course, you need to become familiar with the terms of the purchase and sale agreement form that is used in your office. Our discussion will be an overview of the provisions found in most purchase and sale agreement forms.

To fill out a purchase and sale agreement form, you need to be able to answer these questions:

1. What information needs to be filled in?
2. Which provisions are pertinent to this transaction?
3. Which provisions should be crossed out?
4. What other provisions need to be attached to the form as addenda?

Remember that contract forms should always be filled in completely. If an entry doesn't apply to the transaction, write in "N/A," rather than leaving the space blank.

Also, a form must be used only for its intended purpose. For instance, the form in Figure 7.1 is intended for residential sales only. It shouldn't be used for any other type of transaction.

IDENTIFYING THE PARTIES

We generally refer to the parties to a purchase and sale agreement as the buyer and the seller. But in many transactions there's more than one buyer and/or more than one seller.

You must make sure that everyone who has an ownership interest in the property signs the contract. If any owner fails to sign it, the buyer may only be able

FIG. 7.1   RESIDENTIAL PURCHASE AND SALE AGREEMENT FORM

Form 21
Residential Purchase & Sale Agreement
Rev. 2/17
Page 1 of 5

©Copyright 2017
Northwest Multiple Listing Service
ALL RIGHTS RESERVED

RESIDENTIAL REAL ESTATE PURCHASE AND SALE AGREEMENT
SPECIFIC TERMS

1. **Date:** _____   **MLS No.:** _____   **Offer Expiration Date:** _____

2. **Buyer:** _____
   Buyer   Buyer   Status

3. **Seller:** _____
   Seller   Seller

4. **Property:** Legal Description attached as Exhibit A. Tax Parcel No(s).: _____, _____, _____,
   _____
   Address   City   County   State   Zip

5. **Included Items**: ❑ stove/range; ❑ refrigerator; ❑ washer; ❑ dryer; ❑ dishwasher; ❑ hot tub; ❑ fireplace insert; ❑ wood stove; ❑ satellite dish; ❑ security system; ❑ attached television(s); ❑ attached speaker(s); ❑ microwave; ❑ generator; ❑ other _____

6. **Purchase Price: $** _____ Dollars

7. **Earnest Money: $** _____   ❑ Check; ❑ Note; ❑ Other _____ (held by ❑ Selling Firm; ❑ Closing Agent)

8. **Default:** (check only one) ❑ Forfeiture of Earnest Money; ❑ Seller's Election of Remedies

9. **Title Insurance Company:** _____

10. **Closing Agent:** _____
    Company   Individual (optional)

11. **Closing Date:** _____; **Possession Date:** ❑ on Closing; ❑ Other _____

12. **Services of Closing Agent for Payment of Utilities:** ❑ Requested (attach NWMLS Form 22K); ❑ Waived

13. **Charges/Assessments Levied Before but Due After Closing:** ❑ assumed by Buyer; ❑ prepaid in full by Seller at Closing

14. **Seller Citizenship (FIRPTA):** Seller ❑ is; ❑ is not a foreign person for purposes of U.S. income taxation

15. **Agency Disclosure:**   Selling Broker represents: ❑ Buyer; ❑ Seller; ❑ both parties; ❑ neither party
    Listing Broker represents: ❑ Seller; ❑ both parties

16. **Addenda:** _____
    _____
    _____
    _____

Buyer's Signature Date	Seller's Signature Date
Buyer's Signature Date	Seller's Signature Date
Buyer's Address	Seller's Address
City, State, Zip	City, State, Zip
Phone No. Fax No.	Phone No. Fax No.
Buyer's E-mail Address	Seller's E-mail Address
Selling Firm MLS Office No.	Listing Firm MLS Office No.
Selling Broker (Print) MLS LAG No.	Listing Broker (Print) MLS LAG No.
Firm Phone No. Broker Phone No. Firm Fax No.	Firm Phone No. Broker Phone No. Firm Fax No.
Selling Firm Document E-mail Address	Listing Firm Document E-mail Address
Selling Broker's E-mail Address	Listing Broker's E-mail Address
Selling Broker DOL License No. Selling Firm DOL License No.	Listing Broker DOL License No. Listing Firm DOL License No.

Form 21
Residential Purchase & Sale Agreement
Rev. 2/17
Page 2 of 5

RESIDENTIAL REAL ESTATE PURCHASE AND SALE AGREEMENT
GENERAL TERMS
Continued

a. **Purchase Price**. Buyer shall pay to Seller the Purchase Price, including the Earnest Money, in cash at Closing, unless 1
otherwise specified in this Agreement. Buyer represents that Buyer has sufficient funds to close this sale in accordance 2
with this Agreement and is not relying on any contingent source of funds, including funds from loans, the sale of other 3
property, gifts, retirement, or future earnings, except to the extent otherwise specified in this Agreement. 4

b. **Earnest Money**. Buyer shall deliver the Earnest Money within 2 days after mutual acceptance to Selling Broker or to 5
Closing Agent. If Buyer delivers the Earnest Money to Selling Broker, Selling Broker will deposit any check to be held by 6
Selling Firm, or deliver any Earnest Money to be held by Closing Agent, within 3 days of receipt or mutual acceptance, 7
whichever occurs later. If the Earnest Money is held by Selling Firm and is over $10,000.00 it shall be deposited into an 8
interest bearing trust account in Selling Firm's name provided that Buyer completes an IRS Form W-9. Interest, if any, 9
after deduction of bank charges and fees, will be paid to Buyer. Buyer shall reimburse Selling Firm for bank charges 10
and fees in excess of the interest earned, if any. If the Earnest Money held by Selling Firm is over $10,000.00 Buyer 11
has the option to require Selling Firm to deposit the Earnest Money into the Housing Trust Fund Account, with the 12
interest paid to the State Treasurer, if both Seller and Buyer so agree in writing. If the Buyer does not complete an IRS 13
Form W-9 before Selling Firm must deposit the Earnest Money or the Earnest Money is $10,000.00 or less, the Earnest 14
Money shall be deposited into the Housing Trust Fund Account. Selling Firm may transfer the Earnest Money to Closing 15
Agent at Closing. If all or part of the Earnest Money is to be refunded to Buyer and any such costs remain unpaid, the 16
Selling Firm or Closing Agent may deduct and pay them therefrom. The parties instruct Closing Agent to provide written 17
verification of receipt of the Earnest Money and notice of dishonor of any check to the parties and Brokers at the 18
addresses and/or fax numbers provided herein. 19

Upon termination of this Agreement, a party or the Closing Agent may deliver a form authorizing the release of Earnest 20
Money to the other party or the parties. The party(s) shall execute such form and deliver the same to the Closing Agent. 21
If either party fails to execute the release form, a party may make a written demand to the Closing Agent for the Earnest 22
Money. Pursuant to RCW 64.04, Closing Agent shall deliver notice of the demand to the other party within 15 days. If 23
the other party does not object to the demand within 20 days of Closing Agent's notice, Closing Agent shall disburse the 24
Earnest Money to the party making the demand within 10 days of the expiration of the 20 day period. If Closing Agent 25
timely receives an objection or an inconsistent demand from the other party, Closing Agent shall commence an 26
interpleader action within 60 days of such objection or inconsistent demand, unless the parties provide subsequent 27
consistent instructions to Closing Agent to disburse the earnest money or refrain from commencing an interpleader 28
action for a specified period of time. Pursuant to RCW 4.28.080, the parties consent to service of the summons and 29
complaint for an interpleader action by first class mail, postage prepaid at the party's usual mailing address or the 30
address identified in this Agreement. If the Closing Agent complies with the preceding process, each party shall be 31
deemed to have released Closing Agent from any and all claims or liability related to the disbursal of the Earnest 32
Money. If either party fails to authorize the release of the Earnest Money to the other party when required to do so 33
under this Agreement, that party shall be in breach of this Agreement. For the purposes of this section, the term Closing 34
Agent includes a Selling Firm holding the Earnest Money. The parties authorize the party commencing an interpleader 35
action to deduct up to $500.00 for the costs thereof. 36

c. **Included Items**. Any of the following items, including items identified in Specific Term No. 5 if the corresponding box is 37
checked, located in or on the Property are included in the sale: built-in appliances; wall-to-wall carpeting; curtains, 38
drapes and all other window treatments; window and door screens; awnings; storm doors and windows; installed 39
television antennas; ventilating, air conditioning and heating fixtures; trash compactor; fireplace doors, gas logs and gas 40
log lighters; irrigation fixtures; electric garage door openers; water heaters; installed electrical fixtures; lighting fixtures; 41
shrubs, plants and trees planted in the ground; and other fixtures; and all associated operating remote controls. Unless 42
otherwise agreed, if any of the above items are leased or encumbered, Seller shall acquire clear title before Closing. 43

d. **Condition of Title**. Unless otherwise specified in this Agreement, title to the Property shall be marketable at Closing. 44
The following shall not cause the title to be unmarketable: rights, reservations, covenants, conditions and restrictions, 45
presently of record and general to the area; easements and encroachments, not materially affecting the value of or 46
unduly interfering with Buyer's reasonable use of the Property; and reserved oil and/or mining rights. Monetary 47
encumbrances or liens not assumed by Buyer, shall be paid or discharged by Seller on or before Closing. Title shall be 48
conveyed by a Statutory Warranty Deed. If this Agreement is for conveyance of a buyer's interest in a Real Estate 49
Contract, the Statutory Warranty Deed shall include a buyer's assignment of the contract sufficient to convey after 50
acquired title. 51

e. **Title Insurance**. Seller authorizes Buyer's lender or Closing Agent, at Seller's expense, to apply for the then-current 52
ALTA form of Homeowner's Policy of Title Insurance for One-to-Four Family Residence, from the Title Insurance 53
Company. If Seller previously received a preliminary commitment from a Title Insurance Company that Buyer declines 54
to use, Buyer shall pay any cancellation fees owing to the original Title Insurance Company. Otherwise, the party 55
applying for title insurance shall pay any title cancellation fee, in the event such a fee is assessed. If the Title Insurance 56
Company selected by the parties will not issue a Homeowner's Policy for the Property, the parties agree that the Title 57
Insurance Company shall instead issue the then-current ALTA standard form Owner's Policy, together with 58
homeowner's additional protection and inflation protection endorsements, if available. The Title Insurance Company 59

Buyer's Initials	Date	Buyer's Initials	Date	Seller's Initials	Date	Seller's Initials	Date

Form 21
Residential Purchase & Sale Agreement
Rev. 2/17
Page 3 of 5

RESIDENTIAL REAL ESTATE PURCHASE AND SALE AGREEMENT
GENERAL TERMS
Continued

shall send a copy of the preliminary commitment to Seller, Listing Broker, Buyer and Selling Broker. The preliminary 60
commitment, and the title policy to be issued, shall contain no exceptions other than the General Exclusions and 61
Exceptions in the Policy and Special Exceptions consistent with the Condition of Title herein provided. If title cannot be 62
made so insurable prior to the Closing Date, then as Buyer's sole and exclusive remedy, the Earnest Money shall, 63
unless Buyer elects to waive such defects or encumbrances, be refunded to the Buyer, less any unpaid costs described 64
in this Agreement, and this Agreement shall thereupon be terminated. Buyer shall have no right to specific performance 65
or damages as a consequence of Seller's inability to provide insurable title. 66

f. **Closing and Possession**. This sale shall be closed by the Closing Agent on the Closing Date. If the Closing Date falls 67
on a Saturday, Sunday, legal holiday as defined in RCW 1.16.050, or day when the county recording office is closed, 68
the Closing Agent shall close the transaction on the next day that is not a Saturday, Sunday, legal holiday, or day when 69
the county recording office is closed. "Closing" means the date on which all documents are recorded and the sale 70
proceeds are available to Seller. Seller shall deliver keys and garage door remotes to Buyer on the Closing Date or on 71
the Possession Date, whichever occurs first. Buyer shall be entitled to possession at 9:00 p.m. on the Possession Date. 72
Seller shall maintain the Property in its present condition, normal wear and tear excepted, until the Buyer is entitled to 73
possession. Seller shall either repair or replace any system or appliance (including, but not limited to plumbing, heat, 74
electrical, and all Included Items) that becomes inoperative or malfunctions prior to Closing with a system or appliance 75
of at least equal quality. Buyer reserves the right to walk through the Property within 5 days of Closing to verify that 76
Seller has maintained the Property and systems/appliances as required by this paragraph. Seller shall not enter into or 77
modify existing leases or rental agreements, service contracts, or other agreements affecting the Property which have 78
terms extending beyond Closing without first obtaining Buyer's consent, which shall not be unreasonably withheld. If 79
possession transfers at a time other than Closing, the parties shall execute NWMLS Form 65A (Rental 80
Agreement/Occupancy Prior to Closing) or NWMLS Form 65B (Rental Agreement/Seller Occupancy After Closing) (or 81
alternative rental agreements) and are advised of the need to contact their respective insurance companies to assure 82
appropriate hazard and liability insurance policies are in place, as applicable. 83

RCW 19.27.530 requires the seller of any owner-occupied single-family residence to equip the residence with a carbon 84
monoxide alarm(s) in accordance with the state building code before a buyer or any other person may legally occupy 85
the residence following the sale. The parties acknowledge that the Brokers are not responsible for ensuring that Seller 86
complies with RCW 19.27.530. Buyer and Seller shall hold the Brokers and their Firms harmless from any claim 87
resulting from Seller's failure to install a carbon monoxide alarm(s) in the Property. 88

g. **Section 1031 Like-Kind Exchange**. If either Buyer or Seller intends for this transaction to be a part of a Section 1031 89
like-kind exchange, then the other party shall cooperate in the completion of the like-kind exchange so long as the 90
cooperating party incurs no additional liability in doing so, and so long as any expenses (including attorneys' fees and 91
costs) incurred by the cooperating party that are related only to the exchange are paid or reimbursed to the cooperating 92
party at or prior to Closing. Notwithstanding the Assignment paragraph of this Agreement, any party completing a 93
Section 1031 like-kind exchange may assign this Agreement to its qualified intermediary or any entity set up for the 94
purposes of completing a reverse exchange. 95

h. **Closing Costs and Prorations and Charges and Assessments**. Seller and Buyer shall each pay one-half of the 96
escrow fee unless otherwise required by applicable FHA or VA regulations. Taxes for the current year, rent, interest, 97
and lienable homeowner's association dues shall be prorated as of Closing. Buyer shall pay Buyer's loan costs, 98
including credit report, appraisal charge and lender's title insurance, unless provided otherwise in this Agreement. If any 99
payments are delinquent on encumbrances which will remain after Closing, Closing Agent is instructed to pay such 100
delinquencies at Closing from money due, or to be paid by, Seller. Buyer shall pay for remaining fuel in the fuel tank if, 101
prior to Closing, Seller obtains a written statement from the supplier as to the quantity and current price and provides 102
such statement to the Closing Agent. Seller shall pay all utility charges, including unbilled charges. Unless waived in 103
Specific Term No. 12, Seller and Buyer request the services of Closing Agent in disbursing funds necessary to satisfy 104
unpaid utility charges in accordance with RCW 60.80 and Seller shall provide the names and addresses of all utilities 105
providing service to the Property and having lien rights (attach NWMLS Form 22K Identification of Utilities or 106
equivalent). 107

Buyer is advised to verify the existence and amount of any local improvement district, capacity or impact charges or 108
other assessments that may be charged against the Property before or after Closing. Seller will pay such charges that 109
are or become due on or before Closing. Charges levied before Closing, but becoming due after Closing shall be paid 110
as agreed in Specific Term No. 13. 111

i. **Sale Information**. Listing Broker and Selling Broker are authorized to report this Agreement (including price and all 112
terms) to the Multiple Listing Service that published it and to its members, financing institutions, appraisers, and anyone 113
else related to this sale. Buyer and Seller expressly authorize all Closing Agents, appraisers, title insurance companies, 114
and others related to this Sale, to furnish the Listing Broker and/or Selling Broker, on request, any and all information 115
and copies of documents concerning this sale. 116

_____ _____ _____ _____ _____ _____ _____ _____
Buyer's Initials   Date   Buyer's Initials   Date   Seller's Initials   Date   Seller's Initials   Date

Form 21
Residential Purchase & Sale Agreement
Rev. 2/17
Page 4 of 5

RESIDENTIAL REAL ESTATE PURCHASE AND SALE AGREEMENT
GENERAL TERMS
Continued

j. Seller Citizenship and FIRPTA. Seller warrants that the identification of Seller's citizenship status for purposes of U.S. 117
income taxation in Specific Term No. 14 is correct. Seller shall execute a certification (NWMLS Form 22E or equivalent) 118
under the Foreign Investment in Real Property Tax Act ("FIRPTA") at Closing and provide the certification to the Closing 119
Agent. If Seller is a foreign person for purposes of U.S. income taxation, and this transaction is not otherwise exempt 120
from FIRPTA, Closing Agent is instructed to withhold and pay the required amount to the Internal Revenue Service. 121

k. Notices and Delivery of Documents. Any notice related to this Agreement (including revocations of offers or 122
counteroffers) must be in writing. Notices to Seller must be signed by at least one Buyer and shall be deemed delivered 123
only when the notice is received by Seller, by Listing Broker, or at the licensed office of Listing Broker. Notices to Buyer 124
must be signed by at least one Seller and shall be deemed delivered only when the notice is received by Buyer, by 125
Selling Broker, or at the licensed office of Selling Broker. Documents related to this Agreement, such as NWMLS Form 126
17, Information on Lead-Based Paint and Lead-Based Paint Hazards, Public Offering Statement or Resale Certificate, 127
and all other documents shall be delivered pursuant to this paragraph. Buyer and Seller must keep Selling Broker and 128
Listing Broker advised of their whereabouts in order to receive prompt notification of receipt of a notice. 129

Facsimile transmission of any notice or document shall constitute delivery. E-mail transmission of any notice or 130
document (or a direct link to such notice or document) shall constitute delivery when: (i) the e-mail is sent to both Selling 131
Broker and Selling Firm or both Listing Broker and Listing Firm at the e-mail addresses specified on page one of this 132
Agreement; or (ii) Selling Broker or Listing Broker provide written acknowledgment of receipt of the e-mail (an automatic 133
e-mail reply does not constitute written acknowledgment). At the request of either party, or the Closing Agent, the 134
parties will confirm facsimile or e-mail transmitted signatures by signing an original document. 135

l. Computation of Time. Unless otherwise specified in this Agreement, any period of time measured in days and stated 136
in this Agreement shall start on the day following the event commencing the period and shall expire at 9:00 p.m. of the 137
last calendar day of the specified period of time. Except for the Possession Date, if the last day is a Saturday, Sunday 138
or legal holiday as defined in RCW 1.16.050, the specified period of time shall expire on the next day that is not a 139
Saturday, Sunday or legal holiday. Any specified period of 5 days or less, except for any time period relating to the 140
Possession Date, shall not include Saturdays, Sundays or legal holidays. If the parties agree that an event will occur on 141
a specific calendar date, the event shall occur on that date, except for the Closing Date, which, if it falls on a Saturday, 142
Sunday, legal holiday as defined in RCW 1.16.050, or day when the county recording office is closed, shall occur on the 143
next day that is not a Saturday, Sunday, legal holiday, or day when the county recording office is closed. If the parties 144
agree upon and attach a legal description after this Agreement is signed by the offeree and delivered to the offeror, then 145
for the purposes of computing time, mutual acceptance shall be deemed to be on the date of delivery of an accepted 146
offer or counteroffer to the offeror, rather than on the date the legal description is attached. Time is of the essence of 147
this Agreement. 148

m. Integration and Electronic Signatures. This Agreement constitutes the entire understanding between the parties and 149
supersedes all prior or contemporaneous understandings and representations. No modification of this Agreement shall 150
be effective unless agreed in writing and signed by Buyer and Seller. The parties acknowledge that a signature in 151
electronic form has the same legal effect and validity as a handwritten signature. 152

n. Assignment. Buyer may not assign this Agreement, or Buyer's rights hereunder, without Seller's prior written consent, 153
unless the parties indicate that assignment is permitted by the addition of "and/or assigns" on the line identifying the 154
Buyer on the first page of this Agreement. 155

o. Default. In the event Buyer fails, without legal excuse, to complete the purchase of the Property, then the following 156
provision, as identified in Specific Term No. 8, shall apply: 157

  i. Forfeiture of Earnest Money. That portion of the Earnest Money that does not exceed five percent (5%) of the 158
  Purchase Price shall be forfeited to the Seller as the sole and exclusive remedy available to Seller for such failure. 159

  ii. Seller's Election of Remedies. Seller may, at Seller's option, (a) keep the Earnest Money as liquidated damages 160
  as the sole and exclusive remedy available to Seller for such failure, (b) bring suit against Buyer for Seller's actual 161
  damages, (c) bring suit to specifically enforce this Agreement and recover any incidental damages, or (d) pursue 162
  any other rights or remedies available at law or equity. 163

p. Professional Advice and Attorneys' Fees. Buyer and Seller are advised to seek the counsel of an attorney and a 164
certified public accountant to review the terms of this Agreement. Buyer and Seller shall pay their own fees incurred for 165
such review. However, if Buyer or Seller institutes suit against the other concerning this Agreement the prevailing party 166
is entitled to reasonable attorneys' fees and expenses. 167

q. Offer. Buyer shall purchase the Property under the terms and conditions of this Agreement. Seller shall have until 9:00 168
p.m. on the Offer Expiration Date to accept this offer, unless sooner withdrawn. Acceptance shall not be effective until a 169
signed copy is received by Buyer, by Selling Broker or at the licensed office of Selling Broker. If this offer is not so 170
accepted, it shall lapse and any Earnest Money shall be refunded to Buyer. 171

_____   _____   _____   _____
Buyer's Initials   Date   Buyer's Initials   Date   Seller's Initials   Date   Seller's Initials   Date

Form 21
Residential Purchase & Sale Agreement
Rev. 2/17
Page 5 of 5

©Copyright 2017
Northwest Multiple Listing Service
ALL RIGHTS RESERVED

RESIDENTIAL REAL ESTATE PURCHASE AND SALE AGREEMENT
GENERAL TERMS
Continued

r. **Counteroffer**. Any change in the terms presented in an offer or counteroffer, other than the insertion of or change to 172
Seller's name and Seller's warranty of citizenship status, shall be considered a counteroffer. If a party makes a 173
counteroffer, then the other party shall have until 9:00 p.m. on the counteroffer expiration date to accept that 174
counteroffer, unless sooner withdrawn. Acceptance shall not be effective until a signed copy is received by the other 175
party, the other party's broker, or at the licensed office of the other party's broker. If the counteroffer is not so accepted, 176
it shall lapse and any Earnest Money shall be refunded to Buyer. 177

s. **Offer and Counteroffer Expiration Date**. If no expiration date is specified for an offer/counteroffer, the 178
offer/counteroffer shall expire 2 days after the offer/counteroffer is delivered by the party making the offer/counteroffer, 179
unless sooner withdrawn. 180

t. **Agency Disclosure**. Selling Firm, Selling Firm's Designated Broker, Selling Broker's Branch Manager (if any) and 181
Selling Broker's Managing Broker (if any) represent the same party that Selling Broker represents. Listing Firm, Listing 182
Firm's Designated Broker, Listing Broker's Branch Manager (if any), and Listing Broker's Managing Broker (if any) 183
represent the same party that the Listing Broker represents. If Selling Broker and Listing Broker are different persons 184
affiliated with the same Firm, then both Buyer and Seller confirm their consent to Designated Broker, Branch Manager 185
(if any), and Managing Broker (if any) representing both parties as dual agents. If Selling Broker and Listing Broker are 186
the same person representing both parties then both Buyer and Seller confirm their consent to that person and his/her 187
Designated Broker, Branch Manager (if any), and Managing Broker (if any) representing both parties as dual agents. All 188
parties acknowledge receipt of the pamphlet entitled "The Law of Real Estate Agency." 189

u. **Commission**. Seller and Buyer shall pay a commission in accordance with any listing or commission agreement to 190
which they are a party. The Listing Firm's commission shall be apportioned between Listing Firm and Selling Firm as 191
specified in the listing. Seller and Buyer hereby consent to Listing Firm or Selling Firm receiving compensation from 192
more than one party. Seller and Buyer hereby assign to Listing Firm and Selling Firm, as applicable, a portion of their 193
funds in escrow equal to such commission(s) and irrevocably instruct the Closing Agent to disburse the commission(s) 194
directly to the Firm(s). In any action by Listing or Selling Firm to enforce this paragraph, the prevailing party is entitled to 195
court costs and reasonable attorneys' fees. Seller and Buyer agree that the Firms are intended third party beneficiaries 196
under this Agreement. 197

v. **Cancellation Rights/Lead-Based Paint**. If a residential dwelling was built on the Property prior to 1978, and Buyer 198
receives a Disclosure of Information on Lead-Based Paint and Lead-Based Paint Hazards (NWMLS Form 22J) after 199
mutual acceptance, Buyer may rescind this Agreement at any time up to 3 days thereafter. 200

w. **Information Verification Period**. Buyer shall have 10 days after mutual acceptance to verify all information provided 201
from Seller or Listing Firm related to the Property. This contingency shall be deemed satisfied unless Buyer gives notice 202
identifying the materially inaccurate information within 10 days of mutual acceptance. If Buyer gives timely notice under 203
this section, then this Agreement shall terminate and the Earnest Money shall be refunded to Buyer. 204

x. **Property Condition Disclaimer**. Buyer and Seller agree, that except as provided in this Agreement, all representations 205
and information regarding the Property and the transaction are solely from the Seller or Buyer, and not from any Broker. 206
The parties acknowledge that the Brokers are not responsible for assuring that the parties perform their obligations 207
under this Agreement and that none of the Brokers has agreed to independently investigate or confirm any matter 208
related to this transaction except as stated in this Agreement, or in a separate writing signed by such Broker. In 209
addition, Brokers do not guarantee the value, quality or condition of the Property and some properties may contain 210
building materials, including siding, roofing, ceiling, insulation, electrical, and plumbing, that have been the subject of 211
lawsuits and/or governmental inquiry because of possible defects or health hazards. Some properties may have other 212
defects arising after construction, such as drainage, leakage, pest, rot and mold problems. Brokers do not have the 213
expertise to identify or assess defective products, materials, or conditions. Buyer is urged to use due diligence to 214
inspect the Property to Buyer's satisfaction and to retain inspectors qualified to identify the presence of defective 215
materials and evaluate the condition of the Property as there may be defects that may only be revealed by careful 216
inspection. Buyer is advised to investigate whether there is a sufficient water supply to meet Buyer's needs. Buyer is 217
advised to investigate the cost of insurance for the Property, including, but not limited to homeowner's, flood, 218
earthquake, landslide, and other available coverage. Buyer and Seller acknowledge that home protection plans may be 219
available which may provide additional protection and benefit to Buyer and Seller. Brokers may assist the parties with 220
locating and selecting third party service providers, such as inspectors or contractors, but Brokers cannot guarantee or 221
be responsible for the services provided by those third parties. The parties shall exercise their own judgment and due 222
diligence regarding third-party service providers. 223

_____ _____ _____ _____ _____ _____ _____ _____
Buyer's Initials   Date   Buyer's Initials   Date   Seller's Initials   Date   Seller's Initials   Date

to enforce the sale of a partial interest in the property, or the contract may not be enforceable at all.

> **EXAMPLE:** A property is owned by three cousins who inherited it from their grandfather. One of the cousins has lived in South America for several years, and the other two cousins manage the property. When they ask you to handle the sale of the property, you must be sure that the third cousin will be available to sign the sales contract, either in person or through a representative (such as an attorney in fact). Otherwise, a buyer would only be able to purchase a partial interest in the property. (Note that the absent cousin must also sign the listing agreement.)

You should also consider whether everyone who is signing the contract has contractual capacity. If one of the parties is a minor (younger than 18) or mentally incompetent, the contract should be signed by that party's legal guardian. Otherwise, the purchase and sale agreement will be either voidable or void.

MARITAL PROPERTY. Find out whether or not each buyer or seller who is going to sign the purchase and sale agreement is married. If so, have that party's spouse sign the agreement too. In Washington, when community real property is bought or sold, both spouses must join in the contract.

> **EXAMPLE:** Henry and Deborah's house is community property. They've been talking about selling it for some time. While Deborah's out of town, Henry decides to surprise her. He signs a purchase and sale agreement with the Bentleys, agreeing to sell their house for $525,000. When Deborah comes home and hears the news, she's aghast. She believes their house is worth much more than $525,000, and she isn't ready to move so soon. Deborah can call off the sale, because the house is community property and she didn't sign the contract.

Although a married person can sell his or her separate property without the spouse's consent, it's often difficult to know when real property owned by a married person is community property or separate property. It's not your job to determine the status of the property, so it's always best to get both spouses to sign all documents related to the transaction. If they have questions about the separate or community status of their property, they should consult an attorney.

In addition, if an agent knows there is a pending divorce action that may have an impact on a transaction, she should consult her managing broker or an attorney to make sure that all signed agreements are enforceable, and that the transaction will close. It is in the interests of all parties to make sure that there are no outstanding disputes that would prevent the sale from closing.

When filling in the names of a married couple, state each name separately: for example, "Edward K. Hardy and Joanna T. Hardy, a married couple."

OTHER FORMS OF CO-OWNERSHIP. When property is owned as a tenancy in common or in joint tenancy, all of the owners must sign the purchase and sale agreement in order to convey full ownership to the buyer. However, an individual tenant in common or joint tenant can convey her own interest without the consent of the other owner(s).

BUSINESS ENTITIES AS PARTIES. When one of the parties to the contract is a partnership, the names of all of the general partners (and their spouses) and the name of the partnership itself should appear in the contract. For partnerships, corporations, and limited liability companies, the entity's address and the state in which it is organized or incorporated should also be shown.

Legal authority to enter into the transaction must be established. Before closing, the escrow agent will require documentation proving that the person signing the contract on behalf of the entity is authorized to convey or purchase the property. For example, the documentation could be in the form of a power of attorney or a resolution of the board of directors. If there's any doubt about who needs to sign the documents, it's best to get the advice of a lawyer.

ESTATES AND TRUSTS. When property that is part of an estate is sold, the personal representative or executor of the estate must sign the purchase and sale agreement and other documents. To sell property that is part of a trust, the trustee must sign the documents.

BANKRUPTCY AND FORECLOSURE. If a buyer is purchasing property from a seller who is involved in personal bankruptcy proceedings, she should be prepared for a more complicated selling process. The property can be sold only with the approval of the bankruptcy court, it may be sold subject to existing liens and encumbrances, and it is often sold without title insurance or any warranties.

A property that is on the verge of mortgage foreclosure can be sold, but the transaction may be subject to the approval of the foreclosing lender, especially if it's a short sale (the proceeds won't be enough to pay off the loan balance). Even if the lender's approval is not required, the transaction may meet the criteria of a distressed home conveyance, and the provisions of Washington's Distressed Property Law may apply (see Chapter 3). Agents dealing with these types of transactions should always consult their designated broker and/or an attorney for advice on the appropriate way to proceed.

ATTORNEYS IN FACT. If a party to a contract is unavailable or unable to sign the contract documents, a personal representative may be authorized to sign on his behalf. Authorization to sign for someone else is granted by a written document called a **power of attorney**. The authorized person is referred to as an **attorney in fact**. The power of attorney is valid only while the person who granted it is still alive and mentally competent.

When an attorney in fact signs for another person, she usually signs that person's name and then writes her own name beneath it:

Michelle H. Plunkett
by Sarah R. Johnson, her Attorney in Fact

In a sale you're involved in, if an attorney in fact is going to sign any of the documents, ask to see a copy of the power of attorney and verify its validity by checking with the person who granted the power.

PROPERTY DESCRIPTION

To be enforceable, a purchase and sale agreement must have an unambiguous description of the property. A complete legal description should always be used. The street address is not enough. Tax parcel numbers are subject to change, and the description in the tax statement might be incomplete.

There usually isn't enough room for the property's legal description on the form, so an addendum containing the description should be attached. (The form already provides for this.) The legal description may be obtained from the MLS database, a title company, or the county recorder's website.

PURCHASE PRICE AND METHOD OF PAYMENT

The full purchase price, including any mortgages or other liens that the buyer is going to assume, should be stated in the agreement. For example, if the buyer is going to assume the seller's mortgage, which has a remaining principal balance of $347,000, and also give the seller $85,000 in cash at closing, then you should fill in $432,000 as the purchase price on the purchase and sale agreement form.

Many residential purchase and sale agreements are contingent on financing; in other words, the agreement will not be binding unless the buyer is able to obtain a loan. This requires a contingency provision, which is typically set forth in an addendum to the agreement. The financing contingency may specify the downpayment the buyer is willing to make and other terms of the loan he will apply for. The contingency may also state the buyer's duty to make a good faith effort to obtain financing. Financing contingencies are discussed in Chapter 8, and an example is shown in Figure 8.1.

Some transactions are financed completely or partially by the seller. The seller may accept a cash downpayment with a real estate contract or a deed of trust for all or part of the remainder of the purchase price. In that case, the interest rate, payment amount, and other terms for the seller financing must be included in the purchase and sale agreement, and a copy of the financing document forms (the real estate contract, or the promissory note and deed of trust) that the parties will be executing must be attached to the agreement. When a transaction involves seller financing, the parties should use an addendum such as the payment terms addendum shown in Figure 7.2. (For more information about seller financing, see Chapter 10.)

Finally, a significant number of residential real estate transactions are all-cash, with the buyer paying the entire purchase price out of her own funds. Because no financing is used, there's no need for the buyer to include a financing contingency in the offer; this makes all-cash offers especially appealing to sellers. In fact, while it's estimated that in recent years up to one-third of all home sales nationwide are all-cash, that figure is even higher in competitive markets.

EARNEST MONEY

The purchase and sale agreement form states how the deposit will be handled. As we explained in Chapter 6, the agreement should also state whether the deposit is in the form of cash, a money order, a check, or a promissory note.

In most cases, the purchase agreement provides that the buyer will give her agent a personal check for the deposit after the seller accepts the offer. The agreement directs the agent either to deposit the money in the firm's account or, more commonly, to deliver it to the escrow agent.

INCLUDED ITEMS

An "included items" paragraph states that certain items are included in the sale unless otherwise noted in the agreement. The list usually includes carpeting,

FIG. 7.2 PAYMENT TERMS ADDENDUM

**PAYMENT TERMS ADDENDUM
TO PURCHASE AND SALE AGREEMENT**

The following is part of the Purchase and Sale Agreement dated _____ 1

between _____ ("Buyer") 2

and _____("Seller") 3

concerning _____ (the "Property"). 4

1. **GENERAL TERMS** 5

    A. **Limited Use.** Buyer represents that the Property ❑ will; ❑ will not (will, if not filled in) be used for a 6
    residential dwelling. If the Property will be used for a residential dwelling, this Addendum may only be used if: 7

       i. Seller is a natural person (and not a loan originator), estate or trust; 8

      ii. Seller has not financed the sale of another property within the past 12 months; 9

     iii. Seller did not construct or act as a contractor for the construction of a residence on the Property in the 10
        ordinary course of Seller's business; 11

     iv. The repayment schedule does not result in a negative amortization; 12

      v. The financing has a fixed rate of interest or an adjustable rate of interest that is adjustable after five or 13
        more years, subject to reasonable annual and lifetime limitations on interest rate increases; and 14

     vi. Seller obtains a waiver from the Washington State Department of Financial Institutions ("DFI") under RCW 15
        31.04.025(3). 16

    B. **Limited Practice Board Forms.** The current version of any Limited Practice Board ("LPB") form referenced 17
    below shall be attached to this Agreement as a blank form. 18

    C. **Attorney Review.** Buyer and Seller are advised to seek the counsel of an attorney to review the terms of this 19
    Agreement and this Agreement is conditioned upon review and approval by counsel for Buyer and Seller. 20
    Unless a party gives written notice of disapproval of this Agreement within _____ days (5 days if not 21
    filled in) of mutual acceptance, this contingency shall be deemed satisfied (waived). 22

    D. **Attorney Review of Non-Standard Provisions.** If Buyer and Seller agree to financing terms that differ from 23
    the terms in this Addendum or an attached LPB form, including, but not limited to making interlineations or 24
    otherwise modifying or supplementing any pre-printed terms in this Addendum or attachments thereto, the 25
    parties shall have this Agreement reviewed by legal counsel. If Buyer and Seller do not give notice of 26
    approval of this Agreement by their counsel within _____ days (10 days if not filled in) of mutual 27
    acceptance, this Agreement shall terminate and the Earnest Money shall be refunded to Buyer. 28

    E. **Prior Indebtedness and Security.** Seller understands that Seller's security interest in the Property may be 29
    inferior to a third party's interest in the Property, such as a prior lender. 30

2. **DOWN PAYMENT AND INTEREST RATE** 31

    Buyer shall pay a down payment, including Earnest Money, at Closing of $ _____, which shall be 32
    applied to the Purchase Price. The balance of the Purchase Price (the "Indebtedness") shall accrue interest at 33
    _____ % per annum. Interest will begin to accrue on ❑ Closing; ❑ _____ (Closing if not checked). 34

_____   _____   _____   _____
Buyer's Initials   Date   Buyer's Initials   Date   Seller's Initials   Date   Seller's Initials   Date

**PAYMENT TERMS ADDENDUM
TO PURCHASE AND SALE AGREEMENT**
Continued

3. **PAYMENTS TO SELLER AND METHOD OF PAYMENT** 35

   A. **Payments to Seller**. Buyer shall pay (check applicable box): 36

      i. ❑ No installment payments are required. 37

      ii. ❑ Principal and interest installments of $_____. 38

      iii. ❑ Interest only payments on the outstanding principal balance. 39

   The installment payments, if any, shall begin on the _____ day of _____, and 40
shall continue on the _____ day of each succeeding (check applicable box): ❑ calendar month; ❑ third 41
calendar month; ❑ sixth calendar month; ❑ twelfth calendar month; ❑ Other: _____. 42

   B. ❑ **Promissory Note and Deed of Trust** 43

      i. **Security**. The Indebtedness shall be evidenced by a Promissory Note and a ❑ first; ❑ second; 44
❑ third (first, if not filled in) Deed of Trust, as set forth below. 45

      ii. **Promissory Note**. Buyer agrees to sign at Closing LPB Form 28A (Promissory Note). 46

      iii. **Deed of Trust**. Buyer agrees to sign at Closing the following selected form (check applicable box): 47

         a. ❑ LPB Form 22 (Deed of Trust) securing the Property; or 48

         b. ❑ LPB Form 22A (Deed of Trust with Due on Date) securing the Property. The parties 49
shall initial the Due on Sale clause, which provides: "The property described in this security 50
instrument may not be sold or transferred without the Beneficiary's consent. Upon breach of this 51
provision, Beneficiary may declare all sums due under the note and Deed of Trust immediately due 52
and payable, unless prohibited by applicable law." 53

      iv. **Due Date.** The balance of principal and accrued interest shall be due and payable in full on _____ 54
day of _____. 55

      v. **Default and Default Interest**. During any period of Buyer's default, the principal shall bear interest at the 56
rate of _____ % per annum (18% if not filled in) or the maximum rate allowed by law, whichever 57
is less. A late charge of $_____ or _____ % of any installment payment (5% of the 58
payment if neither is filled in) shall be added to any payment more than _____days late (15 days if 59
not filled in). If Buyer has not cured any default within _____ (30 days if not filled in) after written 60
notice, Seller may declare all outstanding sums immediately due and payable. 61

      vi. **Prepayment.** Buyer may prepay all or part of the balance owed under this Agreement at any time without 62
penalty. 63

      vii. ❑ **No Further Encumbrances.** Buyer shall not further encumber the Property until Seller has released 64
Seller's security interest in the Property. If selected, the Deed of Trust shall include the following 65
provision: 66

      As an express condition of Beneficiary making the loan secured by this Deed of Trust, Grantor shall not 67
further encumber, pledge, mortgage, hypothecate, place any lien, charge or claim upon, or otherwise give 68
as security the property or any interest therein nor cause or allow by operation of law the encumbrance of 69
the Trust Estate or any interest therein without the written consent of Beneficiary even though such 70
encumbrance may be junior to the encumbrance created by this Deed of Trust. Encumbrance of the 71
property contrary to the provisions of this provision shall constitute a default and Beneficiary may, at 72
Beneficiary's option, declare the entire balance of principal and interest immediately due and payable, 73
whether the same be created by Grantor or an unaffiliated third party asserting a judgment lien, 74
mechanic's or materialmen's lien or any other type of encumbrance or title defect. 75

_____ _____ _____ _____ _____ _____ _____ _____
Buyer's Initials   Date   Buyer's Initials   Date   Seller's Initials   Date   Seller's Initials   Date

Form 22C
Payment Terms Addendum
Rev. 2/14
Page 3 of 4

**PAYMENT TERMS ADDENDUM
TO PURCHASE AND SALE AGREEMENT**
Continued

C. ❑ **Real Estate Contract** 76

Note: If the Property is primarily for agricultural purposes, then a non-judicial foreclosure/forfeiture remedy 77
is available only by using a real estate contract. 78

i. **Real Estate Contract.** The parties agree to sign LPB Form 44 (Real Estate Contract). The parties agree 79
to initial and make applicable the following Optional Provisions in LPB Form 44 if the corresponding box is 80
checked: 81

a. ❑ Substitution and Security on Personal Property 82

b. ❑ Alterations 83

c. ❑ Due on Sale 84

d. ❑ Pre-Payment Penalties on Prior Encumbrances 85

e. ❑ Periodic Payments on Taxes and Insurance (The payments during the current year shall be 86
$ _____ per _____) 87

ii. ❑ **Cash Out.** The entire balance of principal and interest shall be due and payable in full not later than 88
_____ . 89

4. **ASSUMED UNDERLYING OBLIGATIONS AND METHOD OF PAYMENT** 90

A. ❑ **Assumed Obligations.** Buyer shall assume the following obligations $ _____ . 91

B. **Consent of Holder of Underlying Obligation.** If there is an existing Deed of Trust, Real Estate Contract or 92
other encumbrance which is to remain unpaid after Closing and its terms require the holder's consent to this 93
sale, Buyer agrees to promptly apply for such consent upon mutual acceptance of this Agreement. This 94
Agreement is subject to the written consent of the holder of the underlying obligation within _____ days 95
(15 days if not filled in) of mutual acceptance. If the holder's written consent to this Agreement is not obtained 96
by such date, this Agreement shall terminate, and the Earnest Money shall be refunded to Buyer. 97

C. ❑ **Seller Wrap of Existing Loan.** 98

Payments. From the payments by Buyer to Seller, Seller will pay the monthly payments of 99
$ _____ due on an existing loan by _____ (the lender) 100
having an approximate present principal balance of $ _____ with interest at 101
_____ % per annum computed on the unpaid principal and secured by the Property. Such balance 102
remains the obligation of the Seller and Seller agrees to pay such obligation in accordance with its terms and 103
conditions. Buyer shall have the right to remedy any default on the underlying obligation, provided Buyer is 104
not in default to Seller, and all sums so paid shall be credited to Buyer's payments to Seller. 105

D. ❑ **Cash Down to Existing Loan.** 106

i. **Type of Loan.** Buyer agrees to assume, at Closing, an existing ❑ Deed of Trust; ❑ Mortgage; 107
❑ Real Estate Contract securing the Property and to pay the balance of the Purchase Price in cash, 108
including Earnest Money, at Closing. The assumed loan ❑ is; ❑ is not an Adjustable Rate Mortgage 109
("ARM"). The monthly payments could increase or decrease if the assumed loan is an ARM. 110

_____ _____ _____ _____
Buyer's Initials Date Buyer's Initials Date Seller's Initials Date Seller's Initials Date

Form 22C
Payment Terms Addendum
Rev. 2/14
Page 4 of 4

**PAYMENT TERMS ADDENDUM
TO PURCHASE AND SALE AGREEMENT**
Continued

ii. **Loan Amount and Payments**. The assumed loan has a principal balance of approximately 111

$_____ and is payable in monthly installments of approximately 112

$_____ including interest at _____ % per annum computed on the declining 113
principal balance, and including ❏ real estate taxes; ❏ hazard insurance. Seller shall pay any 114
delinquencies at Closing. 115

iii. ❏ **Seller Warranty – Loan is Assumable**. Seller warrants that the assumed loan is assumable provided 116
that Buyer complies with and agrees to abide by any requirements or conditions imposed by the holder of 117
the assumed loan. 118

iv. ❏ **Buyer Review Period**. This Agreement is conditioned upon Buyer's review of the assumed loan. 119
Unless Buyer gives written notice to Seller of Buyer's disapproval of the assumed loan within _____ 120
days (5 days if not filled in) of mutual acceptance, this contingency shall be deemed satisfied (waived). 121

v. ❏ **Seller Review Period**. Seller understands that when a loan is "assumed," Seller may remain liable to 122
pay the holder of the assumed loan if the Buyer fails to do so. This Agreement is conditioned upon 123
Seller's review of the terms of the assumed loan. Unless Seller gives written notice to Buyer of Seller's 124
disapproval of the terms of the assumed loan within _____ days (5 days if not filled in) of mutual 125
acceptance, this contingency shall be deemed satisfied (waived). 126

5. **OTHER TERMS** (Check all that apply). 127

A. ❏ **Payments to Collection Account.** 128

i. **Collection Account.** Buyer's payments to or on behalf of Seller shall be made to a contract collection 129
account at _____ (the "Collection Account"), 130
❏ to be established and paid for by Buyer and Seller equally; or ❏ to be established and paid for as 131
follows: _____ (established and paid for equally if not filled in). 132
Closing Agent ❏ may; ❏ may not (may if not checked) collect Collection Account set-up fees and annual 133
escrow fees at Closing. 134

ii. ❏ **Escrow.** The Collection Account shall also serve as escrow for a request for reconveyance or 135
fulfillment deed (as applicable), which shall be fully executed by Seller at Closing and held by the 136
Collection Account pending payment of funds as provided for herein and shall be released to Buyer when 137
full payment of funds due and owing have been received by the Collection Account. 138

iii. ❏ **Taxes and Insurance.** In addition to payments for the principal and interest, additional amounts 139
determined by the Collection Account holder shall be paid by Buyer and applied to ❏ real property taxes; 140
❏ insurance, which amounts may change due to adjustments in taxes and insurance premiums. Closing 141
Agent ❏ may; ❏ may not (may if not checked) collect the initial deposit for taxes and insurance at 142
Closing. 143

B. ❏ **Seller's Review of Buyer's Finances Contingency.** This Agreement is conditioned upon Seller's review 144
and approval, in Seller's sole discretion, of (i) ❏ Buyer's credit report and score; (ii) ❏ Buyer's income tax 145
returns for the prior _____ years (3 years if not filled in); (iii) ❏ verification of Buyer's employment 146
from Buyer's employer; and (iv) ❏ other _____. 147
Buyer will provide Seller with all applicable information including a credit report and score (if applicable) 148
within _____ days (5 days if not filled in) of mutual acceptance. Unless Seller gives written notice to 149
Buyer of Seller's disapproval of the applicable conditions within _____ days (2 days if not filled in) 150
of the date the information is due, this contingency shall be deemed satisfied (waived). 151

C. ❏ **Title Insurance.** Buyer shall pay the cost of a lender's standard title insurance policy insuring Seller's 152
security interest and shall pay for an extended lender's title insurance policy if the cost of such extended 153
policy does not exceed the cost of a standard policy by more than ten percent (10%). 154

_____   _____   _____   _____   _____   _____   _____   _____
Buyer's Initials   Date   Buyer's Initials   Date   Seller's Initials   Date   Seller's Initials   Date

built-in appliances, window coverings, air conditioning equipment, shrubs, and so forth. Even without this provision in the agreement, many of the items listed would be considered fixtures or attachments and included in the sale, but the provision helps prevent disputes over this issue.

If the seller wants to remove an item listed in the provision or exclude an item that would normally be considered real property, you can attach an addendum specifying that the item is excluded from the sale. Similarly, if an item that is not listed in the provision will be included in the sale, you can attach an addendum stating that the item is included. Many forms provide a list of boxes that can be checked to include items that are not usually considered fixtures, but which are often included in the sale, such as a washer, dryer, or refrigerator.

CONVEYANCE AND TITLE

A purchase and sale agreement form includes provisions pertaining to the conveyance of the property and the condition of title. The type of deed that the seller will execute in favor of the buyer (ordinarily a statutory warranty deed) is specified. There is usually a clause in which the seller agrees to provide marketable title, free of undisclosed encumbrances, with a homeowner's policy of title insurance (if the transaction involves a one- to four-unit residential property). The seller also agrees to pay off any liens at closing (if not before), unless the buyer is assuming or taking title subject to an existing lien. Any unusual encumbrances that will remain after closing must be disclosed in the purchase and sale agreement.

Many agreements go into some detail about what will be considered marketable title. For example, an agreement might say that CC&Rs that apply to the entire neighborhood or subdivision will not make the title unmarketable, nor will easements that do not significantly interfere with the buyer's use of the property (an easement for underground wiring, for instance). There will be no problem if encumbrances of that type show up as exceptions on the preliminary title report. However, if the title report reveals other undisclosed encumbrances (such as an access easement that would interfere with the buyer's use of the property) and the seller cannot remove them before closing, then the title will be considered unmarketable and the buyer can refuse to go through with the purchase.

If the seller is a party to a legal action—such as a bankruptcy, a divorce, or a foreclosure action—the seller may not be able to convey clear title. This is a material fact and must be disclosed to the buyer. If the buyer has questions about the legal ramifications of the seller's court proceedings, the buyer should consult an attorney.

INFORMATION VERIFICATION PERIOD

The purchase and sale agreement may also contain a provision giving the buyer a certain amount of time to verify information about the property. During that period, the buyer should verify the facts provided by the seller and listing agent in the property listing, the seller disclosure statement, and any advertising. If the buyer finds any material inaccuracies, she has the right to terminate the agreement within the verification period. Alternatively, she may choose to waive that right and go ahead with the purchase.

CLOSING DATE

The closing date is the date when the proceeds of the sale are disbursed to the seller, the deed is delivered to the buyer, and all of the appropriate documents are recorded. The purchase and sale agreement usually sets a specific date for closing the transaction.

In setting a closing date, it's important to consider how long it will take to meet any conditions that the purchase and sale agreement may be contingent on (see Chapter 8) and any obligations it imposes. For example, even if the buyer has been preapproved for financing, the property still has to be appraised and the transaction evaluated before the lender will give final approval and make the loan funds available for closing. (The lender can probably give you some idea of how long this will take.) And after an inspection is performed, repairs may be necessary, followed by reinspection. The chosen closing date must allow enough time for the parties to fulfill these conditions and obligations.

If the closing date is approaching and repairs have not been completed, final loan approval has not been obtained, or some other contingency has not yet been satisfied, the parties may want to change the closing date by executing a written extension agreement. The purchase and sale agreement will terminate on the date set for closing, so try to get an extension agreement signed as soon as possible. Failure to extend the closing date may result in an unenforceable agreement. A dedicated form may be used for an extension agreement, or you can simply use a general amendment form that states that the parties agree to defer the closing to some later date.

EXAMPLE: Gopal is buying Harrison's home using financing from a local lender. The closing date is June 4. On June 2, Gopal's lender informs Gopal that because of unforeseen circumstances, his loan costs have increased significantly. Thus, the annual percentage rate on his loan will be higher than the rate the lender quoted at the time of application. Under the Truth in Lending Act and Regulation Z, the lender is required to give Gopal a new disclosure statement (see Chapter 9). The lender does so on June 3. Since this new statement must be provided to the borrower at least three days before closing, Gopal and Harrison must change their closing date to June 6. They can use a Regulation Z addendum to amend the purchase and sale agreement and delay the closing.

On the other hand, if all of the conditions and obligations in the purchase and sale agreement have been fulfilled well before the date set for closing, the buyer and seller may agree to move the closing date up. This amendment should also be in writing and signed by both parties.

CLOSING AGENT

The buyer should designate an escrow agent or other closing agent in the purchase and sale agreement. If the buyer is using financing, the lender's escrow department often serves as the closing agent.

Closing agents may perform a wide variety of tasks, such as ordering title insurance, arranging for liens to be paid off and released, and preparing documents on behalf of both the buyer and the seller. They also hold funds and documents in escrow for the parties, distributing them only when specified conditions have been fulfilled. (Escrow instructions and the closing process are discussed in Chapter 11.)

Most firms have policies concerning recommending particular escrow agents or other settlement service providers to the parties. Make sure any recommendations you make conform with these policies.

CLOSING COSTS

The purchase and sale agreement should state which party is responsible for paying the escrow agent's fee (it is typically split between the parties) and various other closing costs, such as the charges connected with the buyer's loan. In addition, the agreement should set forth how certain property expenses (for example, taxes and homeowners association dues) and any income (rent from tenants) will be shared between the parties. These items are ordinarily prorated as of the closing date, unless otherwise agreed.

TRANSFER OF POSSESSION

Most purchase and sale agreement forms have a space for filling in the date of possession, when the seller will relinquish possession of the property to the buyer. The seller usually agrees that the property will be maintained in its present condition until the buyer takes possession.

Possession is normally transferred to the buyer at closing. Sometimes the buyer wants to take possession a few days or even a few weeks earlier, or the seller wants a few extra days to vacate the property.

> **EXAMPLE:** Jenkins is buying Hahn's home. The sale will close on October 17. However, the sale of Jenkins's current home will close on September 10. Jenkins wants to move into Hahn's home on September 10 to avoid the nuisance of moving twice. Hahn agrees to move out by September 10.

If possession is transferred before (or after) the closing date, the parties should execute a separate rental agreement. An example of a rental agreement that can be used for occupancy before closing is shown in Figure 7.3. This agreement sets forth the dates of occupancy, the rental rate, and other terms that will govern possession during the rental period.

Transfer of possession to the buyer before closing may cause trouble for the seller if the sale fails to close. If the buyer/tenant refuses to vacate the property in accordance with the terms of the rental agreement, the seller might have to take legal action to evict him. Note that in the rental agreement in Figure 7.3, the Northwest Multiple Listing Service warns of risks associated with transferring possession to the buyer before closing and advises sellers to consult a lawyer before entering into such an arrangement.

While early transfer of possession may put the seller at risk, delayed transfer of possession may pose other problems for the parties. If a buyer allows a seller to remain in the home for more than 20 days after closing, he could risk turning the transaction into a distressed property conveyance (see discussion of the Distressed Property Law in Chapter 3). Of course, for this law to apply, the subject property would have to be a distressed property—one that is in danger of foreclosure. But if the property is a distressed home and the transfer of possession will be delayed, both the seller's agent and the buyer's agent should advise their clients to consult an attorney.

FIG. 7.3   RENTAL AGREEMENT FORM

Form 65A
Rental – Early Occupancy
Rev. 7/15
Page 1 of 2

RENTAL AGREEMENT
Buyer Occupancy Prior to Closing

©Copyright 2015
Northwest Multiple Listing Service
ALL RIGHTS RESERVED

Notice: There are many risks associated with giving a buyer the right to occupy a property prior to closing. Seller should consult with an attorney before entering into an agreement that provides a buyer with occupancy prior to closing.

Date: _____   1

Tenant(s) _____   2
              Buyer/Tenant   Buyer/Tenant

agree(s) to rent from Landlord _____   3
                                    Seller/Landlord   Seller/Landlord

the property commonly known as _____   4
                                      Address   City

_____ , (the "Property") on the following terms and conditions: 5
State   Zip   County

1. **RENT.** The rent shall be $_____ per _____. Landlord acknowledges receipt of rent in the amount   6
    of $ _____ for the period of _____. Future rents shall be payable as follows: 7

    Rent shall be payable to _____   8

    at _____ .   9

    Tenant is entitled to possession on _____ .   10

2. **TERM AND TERMINATION.** This Agreement shall terminate on _____. If Tenant   11
    purchases the Property from Landlord, then this Agreement shall terminate on closing of the sale. At the time of   12
    closing, advance rent paid to Landlord shall be pro-rated on a daily basis, and Tenant shall be credited with any   13
    unused portion thereof. If this Agreement is terminated prior to the termination date set forth in this paragraph,   14
    then any advance rent shall be pro-rated on a daily basis, and the unused portion refunded to Tenant immediately   15
    upon Tenant's vacating the Property.   16

3. **INSURANCE.** Landlord agrees to keep the Property insured against fire and other normal casualties. All proceeds   17
    of any such policy shall be payable to Landlord alone. Landlord shall have no responsibility for insuring anything   18
    in or on the Property which belongs to Tenant. Tenant is advised that renter's insurance is available to Tenant for   19
    coverage related to liability for bodily injury, property damage, and for the theft, loss, or damage to Tenant's   20
    personal property.   21

4. **UTILITIES.** Tenant agrees to pay for all utilities, including garbage collection charges, during the term of this   22
    Agreement.   23

5. **IMPROVEMENTS.** Tenant shall not be entitled to make any improvements or alterations in the Property, including   24
    painting, during the term of this Agreement without the written permission of Landlord. In the event this   25
    Agreement terminates for any reason other than Tenant's purchase of the Property, Tenant will return the   26
    Property to Landlord in as good a condition as it presently is, ordinary wear and tear excepted.   27

6. **LANDLORD - TENANT ACT.** This Agreement is subject to the provisions of the Residential Landlord - Tenant   28
    Act, RCW 59.18 and the Unlawful Detainer Statute, RCW 59.12. If Tenant and Landlord have entered into a   29
    purchase and sale agreement for the purchase of the Property, then a default under that purchase and sale   30
    agreement shall constitute a default under this Agreement, and Landlord shall be entitled to all remedies provided   31
    for in the Residential Landlord-Tenant Act, RCW 59.18, including but not limited to the exercise of all eviction   32
    proceedings authorized by RCW 59.12.   33

7. **SUBLETTING OR ASSIGNMENT.** Tenant may not sublet the Property and may not assign Tenant's rights under   34
    this Agreement.   35

8. **CITY OF SEATTLE RENTAL AGREEMENT REGULATION ORDINANCE.** If the Property is located within the   36
    City of Seattle then a copy of a summary of city and state landlord/tenant laws is attached. Tenant hereby   37
    acknowledges receipt of a copy of the summary.   38

_____   _____   _____   _____   _____   _____   _____   _____
Landlord's Initials   Date   Landlord's Initials   Date   Tenant's Initials   Date   Tenant's Initials   Date

Form 65A
Rental – Early Occupancy
Rev. 7/15
Page 2 of 2

RENTAL AGREEMENT
Buyer Occupancy Prior to Closing
(Continued)

9. **RELEASE OF REAL ESTATE FIRMS.** Landlord and Tenant release all real estate firms and brokers involved 39
with this Agreement between Landlord and Tenant and agree to indemnify all real estate firms and brokers from 40
any and all claims arising under this Agreement. 41

10. **ATTORNEYS' FEES.** In the event either party employs an attorney to enforce any terms of this Agreement and is 42
successful, the other party agrees to pay reasonable attorneys' fees. In the event of trial, the amount of fees shall 43
be as fixed by the court. 44

11. **SMOKE DETECTOR.** Tenant acknowledges and Lessor certifies that the Property is equipped with a smoke 45
detector(s) as required by RCW 43.44.110 and that the detector(s) has/have been tested and is/are operable. It is 46
Tenant's responsibility to maintain the smoke detector(s) as specified by the manufacturer, including replacement 47
of batteries, if required. In addition, if the Property is a multi-family building (more than one unit), Lessor makes 48
the following disclosures: 49

    (a) The smoke detection device is ❑ hard-wired ❑ battery operated. 50
    (b) The Building ❑ does ❑ does not have a fire sprinkler system. 51
    (c) The Building ❑ does ❑ does not have a fire alarm system. 52
    (d) ❑   The building has a smoking policy, as follows: 53

        _____ 54
        _____ 55

      ❑   The building does not have a smoking policy 56

    (e) ❑   The building has an emergency notification plan for occupants, a copy of which is attached to this 57
        Agreement. 58
      ❑   The building does not have an emergency notification plan for occupants. 59

    (f) ❑   The building has an emergency relocation plan for occupants, a copy of which is attached to this 60
        Agreement. 61
      ❑   The building does not have an emergency relocation plan for occupants. 62

    (g) ❑   The building has an emergency evacuation plan for occupants, a copy of which is attached to this 63
        Agreement. 64
      ❑   The building does not have an emergency evacuation plan for occupants. 65

    Tenant hereby acknowledges receipt of a copy of the building's emergency evacuation routes. 66

12. **CARBON MONOXIDE ALARMS.** Landlord shall equip the Property with carbon monoxide alarm(s) in accordance 67
with the state building code as required by RCW 19.27.530. The parties acknowledge that the real estate firms 68
and brokers are not responsible for ensuring that Landlord complies with RCW 19.27.530. 69

13. **LEAD-BASED PAINT.** If the Property includes housing that was built before 1978, then the Addendum entitled 70
"Disclosure of Information on Lead-Based Paint and Lead-Based Paint Hazards" (NWMLS Form 22J or 71
equivalent), must be attached to this Agreement unless this lease/rental transaction is exempt from all applicable 72
federal regulations. 73

14. **MOLD DISCLOSURE.** Tenant acknowledges receipt of the pamphlet entitled "A Brief Guide to Mold, Moisture, 74
and Your Home." 75

_____	_____	_____	_____
Landlord	Date	Tenant	Date

_____	_____	_____	_____
Landlord	Date	Tenant	Date

DEFAULT

A purchase and sale agreement usually states the remedies available to the buyer or the seller if the other party defaults, and explains how the earnest money deposit will be treated in case of default.

The default provision in the NWMLS form shown in Figure 7.1 gives the parties two options: the seller's sole remedy may be to keep the earnest money deposit as liquidated damages, or the seller may be allowed to choose what remedy to pursue. The possible remedies include keeping the deposit, suing the buyer for damages, or suing for specific performance.

LIQUIDATED DAMAGES LIMIT. Under Washington law, no more than 5% of the property's sales price can be treated as liquidated damages in a purchase and sale agreement. So if the buyer's earnest money deposit was more than 5% of the price, the seller will be required to return the excess to the buyer if the buyer forfeits the earnest money.

DISPOSITION OF EARNEST MONEY. A purchase and sale agreement may provide that if the buyer is entitled to have the earnest money deposit returned, the closing agent may first deduct expenses that have already been incurred on the buyer's behalf.

If the buyer forfeits the earnest money to the seller, the listing firm is usually entitled to half of the money the seller receives (but not more than the firm would have been paid as a commission if the sale had closed). This is usually provided for in the listing agreement rather than the purchase and sale agreement (see Chapter 2). In practical terms, this usually means that the seller gets half of the deposit, the listing firm gets 25% of the deposit, and the selling firm gets 25% of the deposit.

> **EXAMPLE:** Bowen agreed to sell her house to Wilder for $175,000. The earnest money deposit was $10,000. Now Wilder has defaulted on the purchase and sale agreement by backing out of the transaction with no legal excuse.
>
> Under the terms of the agreement Bowen is entitled to keep Wilder's earnest money deposit as liquidated damages. However, the law allows a seller to keep no more than 5% of the sales price. In this case, that's $8,750 ($175,000 × 5% = $8,750), so Bowen must return $1,250 to Wilder ($10,000 − $8,750 = $1,250).
>
> When she listed her property, Bowen agreed to give 50% of any forfeited earnest money deposit to the listing firm, Cunningham Realty. As a result,

Bowen and Cunningham Realty each get $4,375. Under the terms of a commission split agreement, Cunningham Realty is required to split its share with the selling firm. Thus, each of the firms ends up with $2,187.50.

ATTORNEY'S FEES. A purchase and sale agreement typically includes an attorney's fees provision. Under this provision, if one party has to sue the other party to enforce the contract, the prevailing party's attorney's fees and related expenses must be paid by the losing party.

TIME IS OF THE ESSENCE

A purchase and sale agreement usually states that "time is of the essence of this agreement." This phrase doesn't simply mean that the parties hope the sale progresses as quickly as possible; it means they are legally required to meet all deadlines set in the agreement. Performance on or before the specified dates (not just within a reasonable time thereafter) is considered one of the essential terms of the agreement. Failure to meet any of the deadlines is a breach of contract.

ADDENDA

A provision headed "Addenda" indicates whether there are attachments to the purchase and sale agreement that contain additional contract provisions. The attachments might include one of the addendum forms we've already discussed, such as the payment terms addendum, or any of a number of others. The optional clauses addendum, shown in Figure 7.4, is used in many transactions. To incorporate the addenda into the agreement, the names of the forms should be listed in the space provided, the forms should be attached to the main document, and the parties must sign or initial and date each page of the attachments.

AGENCY DISCLOSURE

As we discussed in Chapter 1, Washington law requires real estate licensees to give the parties a written agency disclosure statement. A listing agent must inform both the buyer and the seller which party (or parties) she is representing in the transaction. If there is a selling agent as well as a listing agent, the selling agent must also disclose this information. The disclosures must be made to the buyer before the buyer signs the offer to purchase, and to the seller before the seller signs the buyer's offer. The disclosures must be in writing, and they must appear either in the purchase and sale agreement or in a separate agency disclosure form.

FIG. 7.4 OPTIONAL CLAUSES ADDENDUM

Form 22D
Optional Clauses Addendum
Rev. 2/17
Page 1 of 2

©Copyright 2017
Northwest Multiple Listing Service
ALL RIGHTS RESERVED

**OPTIONAL CLAUSES ADDENDUM TO
PURCHASE & SALE AGREEMENT**

The following is part of the Purchase and Sale Agreement dated _____ 1

between _____ ("Buyer") 2
　　　　　　Buyer　　　　　　　　　　　　　　　　　Buyer

and _____("Seller") 3
　　　　　Seller　　　　　　　　　　　　　　　　　Seller

concerning _____ (the "Property"). 4
　　　　　　　Address　　　　　　　　　　　City　　　　　　　State　Zip

CHECK IF INCLUDED: 5

1. ☐ **Square Footage/Lot Size/Encroachments.** The Listing Broker and Selling Broker make no representations 6
concerning: (a) the lot size or the accuracy of any information provided by the Seller; (b) the square footage of 7
any improvements on the Property; (c) whether there are any encroachments (fences, rockeries, buildings) on 8
the Property, or by the Property on adjacent properties. Buyer is advised to verify lot size, square footage and 9
encroachments to Buyer's own satisfaction. 10

2. **Title Insurance.** The Title Insurance clause in the Agreement provides Seller is to provide the then-current ALTA 11
form of Homeowner's Policy of Title Insurance. The parties have the option to provide less coverage by selecting 12
a Standard Owner's Policy or more coverage by selecting an Extended Coverage Policy: 13

　　☐ **Standard Owner's Coverage.** Seller authorizes Buyer's lender or Closing Agent, at Seller's expense, to 14
　　apply for the then-current ALTA form of Owner's Policy of Title Insurance, together with homeowner's 15
　　additional protection and inflation protection endorsements, if available at no additional cost, rather than 16
　　the Homeowner's Policy of Title Insurance. 17

　　☐ **Extended Coverage.** Seller authorizes Buyer's lender or Closing Agent, at Seller's expense to apply for 18
　　an ALTA or comparable Extended Coverage Policy of Title Insurance, rather than the Homeowner's 19
　　Policy of Title Insurance. Buyer shall pay the increased costs associated with the Extended Coverage 20
　　Policy, including the excess premium over that charged for Homeowner's Policy of Title Insurance and 21
　　the cost of any survey required by the title insurer. 22

3. ☐ **Seller Cleaning.** Seller shall clean the interiors of any structures and remove all trash, debris and rubbish 23
from the Property prior to Buyer taking possession. 24

4. ☐ **Personal Property.** Unless otherwise agreed, Seller shall remove all personal property from the Property 25
prior to the Possession Date. Any personal property remaining on the Property thereafter shall become the 26
property of Buyer, and may be retained or disposed of as Buyer determines. 27

5. ☐ **Utilities.** To the best of Seller's knowledge, Seller represents that the Property is connected to a: 28
☐ public water main; ☐ public sewer main; ☐ septic tank; ☐ well (specify type) _____ ; 29
☐ irrigation water (specify provider) _____ ; ☐ natural gas; ☐ telephone; 30
☐ cable; ☐ electricity; ☐ other _____ . 31

6. ☐ **Insulation - New Construction**. If this is new construction, Federal Trade Commission Regulations require 32
the following to be filled in. If insulation has not yet been selected, FTC regulations require Seller to furnish 33
Buyer the information below in writing as soon as available: 34

WALL INSULATION: TYPE: _____ THICKNESS: _____ R-VALUE: _____ 35

CEILING INSULATION: TYPE: _____ THICKNESS: _____ R-VALUE: _____ 36

OTHER INSULATION DATA: _____ 37

7. ☐ **Leased Property Review Period and Assumption.** Buyer acknowledges that Seller leases the following 38
items of personal property that are included with the sale: ☐ propane tank; ☐ security system; ☐ satellite 39
dish and operating equipment; ☐ other _____ . 40

_____　_____　_____　_____　_____　_____　_____　_____
Buyer's Initials　　　Date　Buyer's Initials　　　Date　Seller's Initials　　　Date　Seller's Initials　　　Date

Form 22D
Optional Clauses Addendum
Rev. 2/17
Page 2 of 2

OPTIONAL CLAUSES ADDENDUM TO
PURCHASE & SALE AGREEMENT
Continued

Seller shall provide Buyer a copy of the lease for the selected items within _____ days (5 days if not filled   41
in) of mutual acceptance. If Buyer, in Buyer's sole discretion, does not give notice of disapproval within   42
_____ days (5 days if not filled in) of receipt of the lease(s) or the date that the lease(s) are due, whichever   43
is earlier, then this lease review period shall conclusively be deemed satisfied (waived) and at Closing, Buyer   44
shall assume the lease(s) for the selected item(s) and hold Seller harmless from and against any further   45
obligation, liability, or claim arising from the lease(s), if the lease(s) can be assumed. If Buyer gives timely   46
notice of disapproval, then this Agreement shall terminate and the Earnest Money shall be refunded to Buyer.   47

8. ☐ **Homeowners' Association Review Period.** If the Property is subject to a homeowners' association or any   48
other association, then Seller shall, at Seller's expense, provide Buyer a copy of the following documents (if   49
available from the Association) within _____ days (10 days if not filled in) of mutual acceptance: 50

    a. Association rules and regulations, including, but not limited to architectural guidelines;   51
    b. Association bylaws and covenants, conditions, and restrictions (CC&Rs);   52
    c. Association meeting minutes from the prior two (2) years;   53
    d. Association Board of Directors meeting minutes from the prior six (6) months; and   54
    e. Association financial statements from the prior two (2) years and current operating budget.   55

If Buyer, in Buyer's sole discretion, does not give notice of disapproval within _____ days (5 days if not   56
filled in) of receipt of the above documents or the date that the above documents are due, whichever is   57
earlier, then this homeowners' association review period shall conclusively be deemed satisfied (waived). If   58
Buyer gives timely notice of disapproval, then this Agreement shall terminate and the Earnest Money shall be   59
refunded to Buyer.   60

9. ☐ **Homeowners' Association Transfer Fee.** If there is a transfer fee imposed by the homeowners' association   61
or any other association (e.g. a "move-in" or "move-out" fee), the fee shall be paid by the party as provided for   62
in the association documents. If the association documents do not provide which party pays the fee, the fee   63
shall be paid by ☐ Buyer; ☐ Seller (Seller if not filled in).   64

10. ☐ **Excluded Item(s).** The following item(s), that would otherwise be included in the sale of the Property, is   65
excluded from the sale ("Excluded Item(s)"). Seller shall repair any damage to the Property caused by the   66
removal of the Excluded Item(s). Excluded Item(s):   67

    68
    69

11. ☐ **Home Warranty.** Buyer and Seller acknowledge that home warranty plans are available which may provide   70
additional protection and benefits to Buyer and Seller. Buyer shall order a one-year home warranty as follows: 71

    a. Home warranty provider: _____   72
    b. Seller shall pay up to $_____ ($0.00 if not filled in) of the cost for the home warranty, together   73
       with any included options, and Buyer shall pay any balance.   74
    c. Options to be included: _____   75
    _____ (none, if not filled in).   76
    d. Other:_____.   77

12. ☐ **Other.**   78

    79
    80
    81
    82
    83
    84
    85

_____ _____   _____ _____   _____ _____   _____ _____
Buyer's Initials   Date   Buyer's Initials   Date   Seller's Initials   Date   Seller's Initials   Date

LEAD-BASED PAINT DISCLOSURES

Residential purchase and sale agreements have a disclosure provision or addendum concerning lead-based paint. In transactions that involve housing built before 1978, federal law requires the seller to disclose information about lead-based paint on the property to potential buyers. Many of the homes built before 1978 contain some lead-based paint. The paint is usually not dangerous if properly maintained, but if it deteriorates and is ingested, it may cause brain damage and organ damage in young children.

The seller of a dwelling built before 1978 must do all of the following:

- disclose the location of any lead-based paint in the home that he is aware of;
- provide a copy of any report concerning lead-based paint in the home, if the home has been inspected;
- give buyers a copy of a pamphlet on lead-based paint prepared by the U.S. Environmental Protection Agency; and
- allow buyers at least a ten-day period in which to have the home tested for lead-based paint.

Specific warnings must be included in the purchase and sale agreement, along with signed statements from the parties acknowledging that the requirements of this law have been fulfilled. The signed acknowledgments must be kept for at least three years as proof of compliance. An addendum like the one in Figure 7.5 may be used to satisfy these legal requirements.

AGENT'S RESPONSIBILITIES. A real estate agent is required to ensure that the seller knows her obligations under the lead-based paint disclosure law and fulfills those obligations. It is also the agent's responsibility to make sure that the purchase agreement contains the required warnings, disclosures, and signatures.

PENALTIES. Sellers and real estate agents who fail to fulfill their obligations under the lead-based paint disclosure law may be ordered to pay the buyer treble damages (three times the amount of any actual damages suffered by the buyer). Civil and criminal penalties may also be imposed.

OFFER AND ACCEPTANCE

A purchase and sale agreement form includes space in which to set a deadline for acceptance of the offer. The manner in which the seller is required to

FIG. 7.5   LEAD-BASED PAINT DISCLOSURE FORM

Disclosure of Information on Lead-Based Paint and/or Lead-Based Paint Hazards

Lead Warning Statement

Every purchaser of any interest in residential real property on which a residential dwelling was built prior to 1978 is notified that such property may present exposure to lead from lead-based paint that may place young children at risk of developing lead poisoning. Lead poisoning in young children may produce permanent neurological damage, including learning disabilities, reduced intelligence quotient, behavioral problems, and impaired memory. Lead poisoning also poses a particular risk to pregnant women. The seller of any interest in residential real property is required to provide the buyer with any information on lead-based paint hazards from risk assessments or inspections in the seller's possession and notify the buyer of any known lead-based paint hazards. A risk assessment or inspection for possible lead-based paint hazards is recommended prior to purchase.

Seller's Disclosure

(a) Presence of lead-based paint and/or lead-based paint hazards (check (i) or (ii) below):

    (i) _____ Known lead-based paint and/or lead-based paint hazards are present in the housing (explain).

    _____

    (ii) _____ Seller has no knowledge of lead-based paint and/or lead-based paint hazards in the housing.

(b) Records and reports available to the seller (check (i) or (ii) below):

    (i) _____ Seller has provided the purchaser with all available records and reports pertaining to lead-based paint and/or lead-based paint hazards in the housing (list documents below).

    _____

    (ii) _____ Seller has no reports or records pertaining to lead-based paint and/or lead-based paint hazards in the housing.

Purchaser's Acknowledgment (initial)

(c) _____ Purchaser has received copies of all information listed above.

(d) _____ Purchaser has received the pamphlet *Protect Your Family from Lead in Your Home.*

(e) Purchaser has (check (i) or (ii) below):

    (i) _____ received a 10-day opportunity (or mutually agreed upon period) to conduct a risk assessment or inspection for the presence of lead-based paint and/or lead-based paint hazards; or

    (ii) _____ waived the opportunity to conduct a risk assessment or inspection for the presence of lead-based paint and/or lead-based paint hazards.

Agent's Acknowledgment (initial)

(f) _____ Agent has informed the seller of the seller's obligations under 42 U.S.C. 4852(d) and is aware of his/her responsibility to ensure compliance.

Certification of Accuracy

The following parties have reviewed the information above and certify, to the best of their knowledge, that the information they have provided is true and accurate.

Seller	Date	Seller	Date
Purchaser	Date	Purchaser	Date
Agent	Date	Agent	Date

communicate acceptance may also be specified. In the NWMLS form, for example, the seller's acceptance is not effective until a copy of the agreement signed by the seller is received by the buyer, by the selling agent, or at the selling agent's office.

A purchase and sale agreement may also set a deadline for the buyer's acceptance of a counteroffer. Remember that a counteroffer isn't an acceptance, so the buyer isn't contractually bound unless he accepts the seller's counteroffer.

SIGNATURES

Of course, space is provided for each party's signature. The buyer's signature makes the form an offer to purchase, and the seller's signature turns it into a binding contract. On many forms, the listing and selling agents are also supposed to sign and fill in the names of their brokerages.

With some purchase and sale agreement forms, when the seller signs the form to accept the buyer's offer, the seller is also agreeing to pay the real estate commission. This gives the firm a safety net, in case the listing agreement was invalid for some reason. The clause in the purchase and sale agreement satisfies the statute of frauds and allows the firm to sue the seller for the commission, if necessary.

VACANT LAND PURCHASE AND SALE AGREEMENTS

The purchase and sale agreement shown in Figure 7.1 should be used only for improved residential property—land and a house. If your buyer is making an offer on vacant land, use a vacant land purchase and sale agreement instead, such as the NWMLS form shown in Figure 7.6.

Many of the provisions in a vacant land purchase and sale agreement are similar or identical to those in a residential agreement. Most of the special provisions in a vacant land agreement relate to the planned or potential development of the property.

SUBDIVISION PROVISIONS

Development of vacant land often involves the subdivision of a large parcel into smaller parcels. For example, a 25-acre tract of land might be subdivided into 100 residential lots, each intended for a single-family house.

Before land can be subdivided legally, various procedural requirements must be met. One of these requirements is submission of a plat to the planning

FIG. 7.6   VACANT LAND PURCHASE AND SALE AGREEMENT

Form 25
Vacant Land Purchase & Sale
Rev. 2/17
Page 1 of 5

VACANT LAND PURCHASE AND SALE AGREEMENT
SPECIFIC TERMS

©Copyright 2017
Northwest Multiple Listing Service
ALL RIGHTS RESERVED

1. **Date:** _____   MLS No.: _____   Offer Expiration Date: _____

2. **Buyer:** _____
   Buyer   Buyer   Status

3. **Seller:** _____
   Seller   Seller

4. **Property:** Legal Description attached as Exhibit A.   Tax Parcel No(s).: _____, _____, _____,
   _____
   Address   City   County   State   Zip

5. **Purchase Price:** $ _____Dollars

6. **Earnest Money:** $ _____ ❑ Check; ❑ Note; ❑ Other _____ (held by ❑ Selling Firm; ❑ Closing Agent)

7. **Default:** (check only one) ❑ Forfeiture of Earnest Money; ❑ Seller's Election of Remedies

8. **Title Insurance Company:** _____

9. **Closing Agent:** _____
   Company   Individual (optional)

10. **Closing Date:** _____; **Possession Date:** ❑ on Closing; ❑ Other _____

11. **Services of Closing Agent for Payment of Utilities:** ❑ Requested (attach NWMLS Form 22K); ❑ Waived

12. **Charges/Assessments Levied Before but Due After Closing:** ❑ assumed by Buyer; ❑ prepaid in full by Seller at Closing

13. **Seller Citizenship (FIRPTA):** Seller ❑ is; ❑ is not a foreign person for purposes of U.S. income taxation

14. **Subdivision:** The Property: ❑ must be subdivided before_____; ❑ is not required to be subdivided

15. **Feasibility Contingency Expiration Date:** ❑____days after mutual acceptance; ❑ Other _____

16. **Agency Disclosure:** Selling Broker represents: ❑ Buyer; ❑ Seller; ❑ both parties; ❑ neither party
    Listing Broker represents: ❑ Seller; ❑ both parties

17. **Addenda:** _____

Buyer's Signature   Date   Seller's Signature   Date

Buyer's Signature   Date   Seller's Signature   Date

Buyer's Address   Seller's Address

City, State, Zip   City, State, Zip

Phone No.   Fax No.   Phone No.   Fax No.

Buyer's E-mail Address   Seller's E-mail Address

Selling Firm   MLS Office No.   Listing Firm   MLS Office No.

Selling Broker (Print)   MLS LAG No.   Listing Broker (Print)   MLS LAG No.

Firm Phone No.   Broker Phone No.   Firm Fax No.   Firm Phone No.   Broker Phone No.   Firm Fax No.

Selling Firm Document E-mail Address   Listing Firm Document E-mail Address

Selling Broker's E-mail Address   Listing Broker's E-mail Address

Selling Broker DOL License No.   Selling Firm DOL License No.   Listing Broker DOL License No.   Listing Firm DOL License No.

Form 25
Vacant Land Purchase & Sale
Rev. 2/17
Page 2 of 5

©Copyright 2017
Northwest Multiple Listing Service
ALL RIGHTS RESERVED

VACANT LAND PURCHASE AND SALE AGREEMENT
GENERAL TERMS
Continued

a. **Purchase Price.** Buyer shall pay to Seller the Purchase Price, including the Earnest Money, in cash at Closing, unless 1
otherwise specified in this Agreement. Buyer represents that Buyer has sufficient funds to close this sale in accordance 2
with this Agreement and is not relying on any contingent source of funds, including funds from loans, the sale of other 3
property, gifts, retirement, or future earnings, except to the extent otherwise specified in this Agreement. 4

b. **Earnest Money.** Buyer shall deliver the Earnest Money within 2 days after mutual acceptance to Selling Broker or to 5
Closing Agent. If Buyer delivers the Earnest Money to Selling Broker, Selling Broker will deposit any check to be held by 6
Selling Firm, or deliver any Earnest Money to be held by Closing Agent, within 3 days of receipt or mutual acceptance, 7
whichever occurs later. If the Earnest Money is held by Selling Firm and is over $10,000.00 it shall be deposited into an 8
interest bearing trust account in Selling Firm's name provided that Buyer completes an IRS Form W-9. Interest, if any, 9
after deduction of bank charges and fees, will be paid to Buyer. Buyer shall reimburse Selling Firm for bank charges 10
and fees in excess of the interest earned, if any. If the Earnest Money held by Selling Firm is over $10,000.00 Buyer 11
has the option to require Selling Firm to deposit the Earnest Money into the Housing Trust Fund Account, with the 12
interest paid to the State Treasurer, If both Seller and Buyer so agree in writing. If the Buyer does not complete an IRS 13
Form W-9 before Selling Firm must deposit the Earnest Money or the Earnest Money is $10,000.00 or less, the Earnest 14
Money shall be deposited into the Housing Trust Fund Account. Selling Firm may transfer the Earnest Money to Closing 15
Agent at Closing. If all or part of the Earnest Money is to be refunded to Buyer and any such costs remain unpaid, the 16
Selling Firm or Closing Agent may deduct and pay them therefrom. The parties instruct Closing Agent to provide written 17
verification of receipt of the Earnest Money and notice of dishonor of any check to the parties and Brokers at the 18
addresses and/or fax numbers provided herein. 19

Upon termination of this Agreement, a party or the Closing Agent may deliver a form authorizing the release of Earnest 20
Money to the other party or the parties. The party(s) shall execute such form and deliver the same to the Closing Agent. 21
If either party fails to execute the release form, a party may make a written demand to the Closing Agent for the Earnest 22
Money. Pursuant to RCW 64.04, Closing Agent shall deliver notice of the demand to the other party within 15 days. If 23
the other party does not object to the demand within 20 days of Closing Agent's notice, Closing Agent shall disburse the 24
Earnest Money to the party making the demand within 10 days of the expiration of the 20 day period. If Closing Agent 25
timely receives an objection or an inconsistent demand from the other party, Closing Agent shall commence an 26
interpleader action within 60 days of such objection or inconsistent demand, unless the parties provide subsequent 27
consistent instructions to Closing Agent to disburse the earnest money or refrain from commencing an interpleader 28
action for a specified period of time. Pursuant to RCW 4.28.080, the parties consent to service of the summons and 29
complaint for an interpleader action by first class mail, postage prepaid at the party's usual mailing address or the 30
address identified in this Agreement. If the Closing Agent complies with the preceding process, each party shall be 31
deemed to have released Closing Agent from any and all claims or liability related to the disbursal of the Earnest 32
Money. If either party fails to authorize the release of the Earnest Money to the other party when required to do so 33
under this Agreement, that party shall be in breach of this Agreement. For the purposes of this section, the term Closing 34
Agent includes a Selling Firm holding the Earnest Money. The parties authorize the party commencing an interpleader 35
action to deduct up to $500.00 for the costs thereof. 36

c. **Condition of Title.** Unless otherwise specified in this Agreement, title to the Property shall be marketable at Closing. 37
The following shall not cause the title to be unmarketable: rights, reservations, covenants, conditions and restrictions, 38
presently of record and general to the area; easements and encroachments, not materially affecting the value of or 39
unduly interfering with Buyer's reasonable use of the Property; and reserved oil and/or mining rights. Monetary 40
encumbrances or liens not assumed by Buyer, shall be paid or discharged by Seller on or before Closing. Title shall be 41
conveyed by a Statutory Warranty Deed. If this Agreement is for conveyance of a buyer's interest in a Real Estate 42
Contract, the Statutory Warranty Deed shall include a buyer's assignment of the contract sufficient to convey after 43
acquired title. If the Property has been short platted, the Short Plat number is in the Legal Description. 44

d. **Title Insurance.** Seller authorizes Buyer's lender or Closing Agent, at Seller's expense, to apply for the then-current 45
ALTA form of standard form owner's policy of title insurance from the Title Insurance Company. If Seller previously 46
received a preliminary commitment from a Title Insurance Company that Buyer declines to use, Buyer shall pay any 47
cancellation fees owing to the original Title Insurance Company. Otherwise, the party applying for title insurance shall 48
pay any title cancellation fee, in the event such a fee is assessed. The Title Insurance Company shall send a copy of 49
the preliminary commitment to Seller, Listing Broker, Buyer and Selling Broker. The preliminary commitment, and the 50
title policy to be issued, shall contain no exceptions other than the General Exclusions and Exceptions in said standard 51
form and Special Exceptions consistent with the Condition of Title herein provided. If title cannot be made so insurable 52
prior to the Closing Date, then as Buyer's sole and exclusive remedy, the Earnest Money shall, unless Buyer elects to 53
waive such defects or encumbrances, be refunded to the Buyer, less any unpaid costs described in this Agreement, and 54
this Agreement shall thereupon be terminated. Buyer shall have no right to specific performance or damages as a 55
consequence of Seller's inability to provide insurable title. 56

e. **Closing and Possession.** This sale shall be closed by the Closing Agent on the Closing Date. "Closing" means the 57
date on which all documents are recorded and the sale proceeds are available to Seller. If the Closing Date falls on a 58
Saturday, Sunday, legal holiday as defined in RCW 1.16.050, or day when the county recording office is closed, the 59
Closing Agent shall close the transaction on the next day that is not a Saturday, Sunday, legal holiday, or day when the 60

Buyer's Initials	Date	Buyer's Initials	Date	Seller's Initials	Date	Seller's Initials	Date

Form 25
Vacant Land Purchase & Sale
Rev. 2/17
Page 3 of 5

©Copyright 2017
Northwest Multiple Listing Service
ALL RIGHTS RESERVED

VACANT LAND PURCHASE AND SALE AGREEMENT
GENERAL TERMS
Continued

county recording office is closed. Buyer shall be entitled to possession at 9:00 p.m. on the Possession Date. Seller shall 61
maintain the Property in its present condition, normal wear and tear excepted, until the Buyer is entitled to possession. 62
Buyer reserves the right to walk through the Property within 5 days of Closing to verify that Seller has maintained the 63
Property as required by this paragraph. Seller shall not enter into or modify existing leases or rental agreements, 64
service contracts, or other agreements affecting the Property which have terms extending beyond Closing without first 65
obtaining Buyer's consent, which shall not be unreasonably withheld. 66

f. **Section 1031 Like-Kind Exchange.** If either Buyer or Seller intends for this transaction to be a part of a Section 1031 67
like-kind exchange, then the other party shall cooperate in the completion of the like-kind exchange so long as the 68
cooperating party incurs no additional liability in doing so, and so long as any expenses (including attorneys' fees and 69
costs) incurred by the cooperating party that are related only to the exchange are paid or reimbursed to the cooperating 70
party at or prior to Closing. Notwithstanding the Assignment paragraph of this Agreement, any party completing a 71
Section 1031 like-kind exchange may assign this Agreement to its qualified intermediary or any entity set up for the 72
purposes of completing a reverse exchange. 73

g. **Closing Costs and Prorations and Charges and Assessments**. Seller and Buyer shall each pay one-half of the 74
escrow fee unless otherwise required by applicable FHA or VA regulations. Taxes for the current year, rent, interest, 75
and lienable homeowner's association dues shall be prorated as of Closing. Buyer shall pay Buyer's loan costs, 76
including credit report, appraisal charge and lender's title insurance, unless provided otherwise in this Agreement. If any 77
payments are delinquent on encumbrances which will remain after Closing, Closing Agent is instructed to pay such 78
delinquencies at Closing from money due, or to be paid by, Seller. Buyer shall pay for remaining fuel in the fuel tank if, 79
prior to Closing, Seller obtains a written statement from the supplier as to the quantity and current price and provides 80
such statement to the Closing Agent. Seller shall pay all utility charges, including unbilled charges. Unless waived in 81
Specific Term No. 11, Seller and Buyer request the services of Closing Agent in disbursing funds necessary to satisfy 82
unpaid utility charges in accordance with RCW 60.80 and Seller shall provide the names and addresses of all utilities 83
providing service to the Property and having lien rights (attach NWMLS Form 22K Identification of Utilities or 84
equivalent). 85

Buyer is advised to verify the existence and amount of any local improvement district, capacity or impact charges or 86
other assessments that may be charged against the Property before or after Closing. Seller will pay such charges that 87
are or become due on or before Closing. Charges levied before Closing, but becoming due after Closing shall be paid 88
as agreed in Specific Term No.12. 89

h. **Sale Information**. Listing Broker and Selling Broker are authorized to report this Agreement (including price and all 90
terms) to the Multiple Listing Service that published it and to its members, financing institutions, appraisers, and anyone 91
else related to this sale. Buyer and Seller expressly authorize all Closing Agents, appraisers, title insurance companies, 92
and others related to this Sale, to furnish the Listing Broker and/or Selling Broker, on request, any and all information 93
and copies of documents concerning this sale. 94

i. **Seller Citizenship and FIRPTA.** Seller warrants that the identification of Seller's citizenship status for purposes of U.S. 95
income taxation in Specific Term No. 13 is correct. Seller shall execute a certification (NWMLS Form 22E or equivalent) 96
under the Foreign Investment In Real Property Tax Act ("FIRPTA") at Closing and provide the certification to the Closing 97
Agent. If Seller is a foreign person for purposes of U.S. income taxation, and this transaction is not otherwise exempt 98
from FIRPTA, Closing Agent is instructed to withhold and pay the required amount to the Internal Revenue Service. 99

j. **Notices and Delivery of Documents.** Any notice related to this Agreement (including revocations of offers or 100
counteroffers) must be in writing. Notices to Seller must be signed by at least one Buyer and shall be deemed delivered 101
only when the notice is received by Seller, by Listing Broker, or at the licensed office of Listing Broker. Notices to Buyer 102
must be signed by at least one Seller and shall be deemed delivered only when the notice is received by Buyer, by 103
Selling Broker, or at the licensed office of Selling Broker. Documents related to this Agreement, such as NWMLS Form 104
17C, Information on Lead-Based Paint and Lead-Based Paint Hazards, Public Offering Statement or Resale Certificate, 105
and all other documents shall be delivered pursuant to this paragraph. Buyer and Seller must keep Selling Broker and 106
Listing Broker advised of their whereabouts in order to receive prompt notification of receipt of a notice. 107

Facsimile transmission of any notice or document shall constitute delivery. E-mail transmission of any notice or 108
document (or a direct link to such notice or document) shall constitute delivery when: (i) the e-mail is sent to both Selling 109
Broker and Selling Firm or both Listing Broker and Listing Firm at the e-mail addresses specified on page one of this 110
Agreement; or (ii) Selling Broker or Listing Broker provide written acknowledgment of receipt of the e-mail (an automatic 111
e-mail reply does not constitute written acknowledgment). At the request of either party, or the Closing Agent, the 112
parties will confirm facsimile or e-mail transmitted signatures by signing an original document. 113

k. **Computation of Time**. Unless otherwise specified in this Agreement, any period of time measured in days and stated 114
in this Agreement shall start on the day following the event commencing the period and shall expire at 9:00 p.m. of the 115
last calendar day of the specified period of time. Except for the Possession Date, if the last day is a Saturday, Sunday 116
or legal holiday as defined in RCW 1.16.050, the specified period of time shall expire on the next day that is not a 117
Saturday, Sunday or legal holiday. Any specified period of 5 days or less, except for any time period relating to the 118

_____ _____ _____ _____
Buyer's Initials   Date   Buyer's Initials   Date   Seller's Initials   Date   Seller's Initials   Date

Form 25
Vacant Land Purchase & Sale
Rev. 2/17
Page 4 of 5

**VACANT LAND PURCHASE AND SALE AGREEMENT
GENERAL TERMS**
Continued

Possesion Date, shall not include Saturdays, Sundays or legal holidays. If the parties agree that an event will occur on a 119
specific calendar date, the event shall occur on that date, except for the Closing Date, which, if it falls on a Saturday, 120
Sunday, legal holiday as defined in RCW 1.16.050, or day when the county recording office is closed, shall occur on the 121
next day that is not a Saturday, Sunday, legal holiday, or day when the county recording office is closed. If the parties 122
agree upon and attach a legal description after this Agreement is signed by the offeree and delivered to the offeror, then 123
for the purposes of computing time, mutual acceptance shall be deemed to be on the date of delivery of an accepted 124
offer or counteroffer to the offeror, rather than on the date the legal description is attached. Time is of the essence of 125
this Agreement. 126

l.   **Integration and Electronic Signatures.** This Agreement constitutes the entire understanding between the parties and 127
supersedes all prior or contemporaneous understandings and representations. No modification of this Agreement shall 128
be effective unless agreed in writing and signed by Buyer and Seller. The parties acknowledge that a signature in 129
electronic form has the same legal effect and validity as a handwritten signature. 130

m. **Assignment.** Buyer may not assign this Agreement, or Buyer's rights hereunder, without Seller's prior written consent, 131
unless the parties indicate that assignment is permitted by the addition of "and/or assigns" on the line identifying the 132
Buyer on the first page of this Agreement. 133

n.   **Default.** In the event Buyer fails, without legal excuse, to complete the purchase of the Property, then the following 134
provision, as identified in Specific Term No. 7, shall apply: 135

   i.   **Forfeiture of Earnest Money**. That portion of the Earnest Money that does not exceed five percent (5%) of the 136
   Purchase Price shall be forfeited to the Seller as the sole and exclusive remedy available to Seller for such failure. 137

   ii. **Seller's Election of Remedies**. Seller may, at Seller's option, (a) keep the Earnest Money as liquidated damages 138
   as the sole and exclusive remedy available to Seller for such failure, (b) bring suit against Buyer for Seller's actual 139
   damages, (c) bring suit to specifically enforce this Agreement and recover any incidental damages, or (d) pursue 140
   any other rights or remedies available at law or equity. 141

o.   **Professional Advice and Attorneys' Fees**. Buyer and Seller are advised to seek the counsel of an attorney and a 142
certified public accountant to review the terms of this Agreement. Buyer and Seller shall pay their own fees incurred for 143
such review. However, if Buyer or Seller institutes suit against the other concerning this Agreement the prevailing party 144
is entitled to reasonable attorneys' fees and expenses. 145

p.   **Offer.** Buyer shall purchase the Property under the terms and conditions of this Agreement. Seller shall have until 9:00 146
p.m. on the Offer Expiration Date to accept this offer, unless sooner withdrawn. Acceptance shall not be effective until a 147
signed copy is received by Buyer, by Selling Broker or at the licensed office of Selling Broker. If this offer is not so 148
accepted, it shall lapse and any Earnest Money shall be refunded to Buyer. 149

q.   **Counteroffer**. Any change in the terms presented in an offer or counteroffer, other than the insertion of or change to 150
Seller's name and Seller's warranty of citizenship status, shall be considered a counteroffer. If a party makes a 151
counteroffer, then the other party shall have until 9:00 p.m. on the counteroffer expiration date to accept that 152
counteroffer, unless sooner withdrawn. Acceptance shall not be effective until a signed copy is received by the other 153
party, the other party's broker, or at the licensed office of the other party's broker. If the counteroffer is not so accepted, 154
it shall lapse and any Earnest Money shall be refunded to Buyer. 155

r.   **Offer and Counteroffer Expiration Date**. If no expiration date is specified for an offer/counteroffer, the 156
offer/counteroffer shall expire 2 days after the offer/counteroffer is delivered by the party making the offer/counteroffer, 157
unless sooner withdrawn. 158

s.   **Agency Disclosure**. Selling Firm, Selling Firm's Designated Broker, Selling Broker's Branch Manager (if any) and 159
Selling Broker's Managing Broker (if any) represent the same party that Selling Broker represents. Listing Firm, Listing 160
Firm's Designated Broker, Listing Broker's Branch Manager (if any), and Listing Broker's Managing Broker (if any) 161
represent the same party that the Listing Broker represents. If Selling Broker and Listing Broker are different persons 162
affiliated with the same Firm, then both Buyer and Seller confirm their consent to Designated Broker, Branch Manager 163
(if any), and Managing Broker (if any) representing both parties as dual agents. If Selling Broker and Listing Broker are 164
the same person representing both parties then both Buyer and Seller confirm their consent to that person and his/her 165
Designated Broker, Branch Manager (if any), and Managing Broker (if any) representing both parties as dual agents. All 166
parties acknowledge receipt of the pamphlet entitled "The Law of Real Estate Agency." 167

t.   **Commission**. Seller and Buyer shall pay a commission in accordance with any listing or commission agreement to 168
which they are a party. The Listing Firm's commission shall be apportioned between Listing Firm and Selling Firm as 169
specified in the listing. Seller and Buyer hereby consent to Listing Firm or Selling Firm receiving compensation from 170
more than one party. Seller and Buyer hereby assign to Listing Firm and Selling Firm, as applicable, a portion of their 171
funds in escrow equal to such commission(s) and irrevocably instruct the Closing Agent to disburse the commission(s) 172
directly to the Firm(s). In any action by Listing or Selling Firm to enforce this paragraph, the prevailing party is entitled to 173

_____   _____   _____   _____   _____   _____   _____   _____
Buyer's Initials   Date   Buyer's Initials   Date   Seller's Initials   Date   Seller's Initials   Date

VACANT LAND PURCHASE AND SALE AGREEMENT
GENERAL TERMS
Continued

court costs and reasonable attorneys' fees. Seller and Buyer agree that the Firms are intended third party beneficiaries under this Agreement. 174–175

u. Feasibility Contingency. It is the Buyer's responsibility to verify before the Feasibility Contingency Expiration Date identified in Specific Term No.15 whether or not the Property can be platted, developed and/or built on (now or in the future) and what it will cost to do this. Buyer should not rely on any oral statements concerning this made by the Seller, Listing Broker or Selling Broker. Buyer should inquire at the city or county, and water, sewer or other special districts in which the Property is located. Buyer's inquiry should include, but not be limited to: building or development moratoriums applicable to or being considered for the Property; any special building requirements, including setbacks, height limits or restrictions on where buildings may be constructed on the Property; whether the Property is affected by a flood zone, wetlands, shorelands or other environmentally sensitive area; road, school, fire and any other growth mitigation or impact fees that must be paid; the procedure and length of time necessary to obtain plat approval and/or a building permit; sufficient water, sewer and utility and any service connection charges; and all other charges that must be paid. Buyer and Buyer's agents, representatives, consultants, architects and engineers shall have the right, from time to time during and after the feasibility contingency, to enter onto the Property and to conduct any tests or studies that Buyer may need to ascertain the condition and suitability of the Property for Buyer's intended purpose. Buyer shall restore the Property and all improvements on the Property to the same condition they were in prior to the inspection. Buyer shall be responsible for all damages resulting from any inspection of the Property performed on Buyer's behalf. If the Buyer does not give notice to the contrary on or before the Feasibility Contingency Expiration Date identified in Specific Term No. 15, it shall be conclusively deemed that Buyer is satisfied as to development and/or construction feasibility and cost. If Buyer gives notice this Agreement shall terminate and the Earnest Money shall be refunded to Buyer, less any unpaid costs. 176–194

Seller shall cooperate with Buyer in obtaining permits or other approvals Buyer may reasonably require for Buyer's intended use of the Property; provided that Seller shall not be required to incur any liability or expenses in doing so. 195–196

v. Subdivision. If the Property must be subdivided, Seller represents that there has been preliminary plat approval for the Property and this Agreement is conditioned on the recording of the final plat containing the Property on or before the date specified in Specific Term No. 14. If the final plat is not recorded by such date, this Agreement shall terminate and the Earnest Money shall be refunded to Buyer. 197–200

w. Information Verification Period. Buyer shall have 10 days after mutual acceptance to verify all information provided from Seller or Listing Firm related to the Property. This contingency shall be deemed satisfied unless Buyer gives notice identifying the materially inaccurate information within 10 days of mutual acceptance. If Buyer gives timely notice under this section, then this Agreement shall terminate and the Earnest Money shall be refunded to Buyer. 201–204

x. Property Condition Disclaimer. Buyer and Seller agree that except as provided in this Agreement, all representations and information regarding the Property and the transaction are solely from the Seller or Buyer, and not from any Broker. The parties acknowledge that the Brokers are not responsible for assuring that the parties perform their obligations under this Agreement and that none of the Brokers has agreed to independently investigate or confirm any matter related to this transaction except as stated in this Agreement, or in a separate writing signed by such Broker. In addition, Brokers do not guarantee the value, quality or condition of the Property and some properties may contain building materials, including siding, roofing, ceiling, insulation, electrical, and plumbing, that have been the subject of lawsuits and/or governmental inquiry because of possible defects or health hazards. Some properties may have other defects arising after construction, such as drainage, leakage, pest, rot and mold problems. Brokers do not have the expertise to identify or assess defective products, materials, or conditions. Buyer is urged to use due diligence to inspect the Property to Buyer's satisfaction and to retain inspectors qualified to identify the presence of defective materials and evaluate the condition of the Property as there may be defects that may only be revealed by careful inspection. Buyer is advised to investigate whether there is a sufficient water supply to meet Buyer's needs. Buyer is advised to investigate the cost of insurance for the Property, including, but not limited to homeowner's, flood, earthquake, landslide, and other available coverage. Brokers may assist the parties with locating and selecting third party service providers, such as inspectors or contractors, but Brokers cannot guarantee or be responsible for the services provided by those third parties. The parties shall exercise their own judgment and due diligence regarding third-party service providers. 205–222

_____ _____ _____ _____ _____ _____ _____ _____
Buyer's Initials   Date   Buyer's Initials   Date   Seller's Initials   Date   Seller's Initials   Date

commission for approval. A plat is a map that shows the location and boundaries of the proposed lots, streets, and public areas within the subdivision; it may also provide information about easements, utilities, and other site features.

A vacant land purchase and sale agreement commonly has provisions that address subdivision issues. For instance, paragraph v on page 5 in the NWMLS form provides that if the property must be subdivided, the agreement is contingent on the recording of the final plat by a specified date.

DEVELOPMENT AND CONSTRUCTION FEASIBILITY

The cost of developing the property is crucial in nearly every decision to buy vacant land, so a provision concerning development and construction costs is typically included in the purchase and sale agreement. The agreement in Figure 7.6 states that it's the buyer's responsibility to determine whether the property can be platted, developed, and built upon, and what it will cost to do so. The buyer is supposed to fill in the number of days it will take to decide if development is feasible. To gather the necessary information, the buyer should consult the county and/or city and various utility districts. The feasibility provision goes on to list some of the specific information the buyer should find out about, including applicable building moratoriums, special building requirements, environmental concerns, growth mitigation restrictions or fees, plat approval requirements, and utility connection charges.

Unless the buyer gives the seller notice within the stated number of days, the buyer is deemed to be satisfied with the feasibility and cost of development and construction. If the buyer notifies the seller that he is not satisfied, the agreement will terminate and the earnest money will be refunded (less any unpaid costs).

CHAPTER SUMMARY

1. A properly signed purchase and sale agreement is a binding contract that holds the parties to the terms of their agreement until all conditions have been fulfilled and the transaction closes.

2. The parties to a purchase and sale agreement are the buyer(s) and the seller(s). All parties must have contractual capacity. Everyone with an interest in the property must sign the agreement. The spouse of any married seller or buyer should also sign.

3. Every purchase and sale agreement must have an adequate description of the property, specify the total purchase price and the method of payment, set a closing date and date of possession, and state by what type of deed and in what condition title will be conveyed.

4. In most cases, the purchase agreement provides that the buyer will give her agent a personal check for the deposit after the seller accepts the offer. The agreement directs the agent to either deposit the money in the firm's account or, more commonly, deliver it to the escrow agent.

5. Purchase and sale agreements almost always contain a "time is of the essence" clause, which makes the closing date a material term of the contract. Closing must take place on or before the date stated in the agreement, unless the parties agree in writing to an extension.

6. In Washington, a purchase and sale agreement should include an agency disclosure paragraph, stating that the real estate agents involved in the transaction have made the required disclosures concerning which party or parties they were representing.

7. A vacant land purchase and sale agreement should be used when a buyer makes an offer to purchase unimproved property. Provisions regarding subdivision and development feasibility are important in a transaction involving vacant land.

CHAPTER QUIZ

1. If the seller is a minor, the purchase and sale agreement should be signed by:
   a. the seller's husband or wife
   b. both the seller and the seller's spouse
   c. the seller's legal guardian
   d. both the seller and the seller's attorney in fact

2. The purchase price stated in the purchase and sale agreement should include:
   a. mortgages or other liens being assumed by the buyer
   b. seller financing
   c. any loan amount contingent on buyer obtaining financing
   d. All of the above

3. A buyer usually gives the earnest money deposit either to the escrow agent or to the:
   a. selling agent
   b. seller
   c. listing agent
   d. escrow agent

4. The "included items" paragraph is used to:
   a. disclose the encumbrances on the property
   b. list the documents that are being attached to the agreement
   c. determine how closing costs will be allocated
   d. specify what fixtures or other property will be part of the sale

5. In choosing a closing date, you should take into account all of the following except:
   a. when the next installment of the property taxes will be due
   b. how long the seller needs to make any necessary repairs
   c. whether the buyer needs to sell her current home
   d. the time needed to clear away any liens

6. Which document should be prepared if the buyer plans to take possession before the closing date?

   a. Rental agreement

   b. Sale of buyer's home contingency

   c. Bump notice

   d. Backup offer

7. Under federal law, the seller of a home built before 1978 must:

   a. remove all lead-based paint from the property

   b. have the home inspected for lead-based paint

   c. provide a copy of any report about lead-based paint in the home

   d. repaint any areas where lead-based paint was used

8. Which of the following might interfere with the seller's ability to convey clear title to the property?

   a. The existence of fixtures on the property

   b. An easement for underground wiring

   c. The seller is going through a divorce

   d. CC&Rs that apply to the entire neighborhood

9. In a real estate transaction in Washington, liquidated damages cannot exceed what percentage of the property's purchase price?

   a. 1%

   b. 3%

   c. 5%

   d. 10%

10. All of the following provisions are unique to a vacant land agreement except:

    a. development and construction feasibility

    b. default provisions

    c. property's subdivision status

    d. drainage test

ANSWER KEY

1. c. If one of the parties to a contract is a minor (under 18 years of age), the contract should be signed by that party's legal guardian.

2. d. The purchase price stated in the agreement should be the full price being paid for the property, including the downpayment, any mortgages or liens the buyer is assuming, and any part of the price that the buyer is financing.

3. a. In most cases, the buyer will give the earnest money deposit to the selling agent (and the deposit will be held in trust or delivered to an escrow agent by the selling agent).

4. d. The "included items" paragraph lists items that are included in the sale unless otherwise noted. (Many of the items listed would be considered fixtures or attachments to the real property and included in the sale even without this provision.)

5. a. In setting a closing date, it's important to consider how long it will take the parties to fulfill their obligations and satisfy any contingencies in the purchase and sale agreement.

6. a. If the parties plan to transfer possession of the property either before or after the closing date, they should sign a rental agreement that includes rental terms and rate.

7. c. The seller of a home built before 1978 must provide a copy of any report concerning lead-based paint in the home and disclose the location of any lead-based paint that he is aware of.

8. c. If the seller is a party to a legal action, such as a divorce or bankruptcy, the seller may not be able to convey clear title to the property.

9. c. Washington law limits liquidated damages to no more than 5% of the purchase price.

10. b. All of the provisions are unique to vacant land transactions with the exception of the default provisions, which are the same in both the residential purchase and sale agreement and the vacant land agreement form.

CONTINGENT TRANSACTIONS

HOW CONTINGENCIES WORK

- Termination or waiver
- Good faith effort required
- Basic elements of a contingency clause

TYPES OF CONTINGENCIES

- Financing contingencies
  - Financing terms
  - Financing timelines
  - Loan information
  - Loan cost provisions
  - Earnest money
  - Lender-required inspections
  - Appraisal provisions
  - Truth in Lending Act
  - Seller financing
- Inspection contingencies
  - Approval or disapproval of inspection report
  - Opportunity to repair vs. buyer's satisfaction
  - Neighborhood review
  - Code violations
  - "As is" sales
- Sale of buyer's home contingencies
  - Elements
  - Bump clauses

RESCISSION

INTRODUCTION

In many cases, a buyer wants to make an offer on a house, but does not want to become bound by a contract with the seller unless a particular event occurs first. For instance, the buyer may need to get a purchase loan approved, or she may want to have the house inspected by an expert. However, the buyer doesn't want to wait until that event occurs before making an offer on the house—by that time, the seller might have sold the property to someone else. In this situation, the buyer needs to make her offer conditional (or contingent) on the occurrence of the event in question.

To help a buyer prepare a contingent offer, you need to know how contingency clauses work, the essential elements of a contingency, the common types of contingencies, and the various pre-printed forms you can use to establish a contingency.

HOW CONTINGENCIES WORK

Many purchase and sale agreements are enforceable only if a certain event occurs. The event is called a **contingency**, or a **condition** of the sale. If the specified event occurs, then both the buyer and the seller are bound to carry out the terms of their contract. If the specified event does not occur, the agreement may be terminated and, in most cases, the buyer is entitled to a refund of the earnest money deposit.

TERMINATION OR WAIVER

A contingency provision is typically included in a contract for the benefit of one of the parties rather than both of them. If the contingency is not fulfilled—if the specified event does not happen—the party that benefits has two choices. He may:

1. terminate the contract without penalty, or
2. waive the condition and proceed with the contract.

Only the benefiting party has the right to choose between terminating the contract or waiving the condition. If he is willing to waive the condition, the other party cannot refuse to go through with the sale just because the condition has not been met.

EXAMPLE: Suppose a purchase and sale agreement is contingent on the buyer obtaining a fixed-rate conventional loan with a $20,000 downpayment within 30 days of the seller's acceptance of the offer. This contingency benefits the buyer. It protects the buyer from being forced to complete the purchase if he can't get the financing he needs.

If the buyer gets the loan within the 30-day period, he is obligated to buy the seller's property. If the buyer got the loan but refused to purchase the property anyway, the seller would be able to keep the buyer's earnest money deposit as liquidated damages or (depending on the terms of their agreement) sue the buyer.

On the other hand, if he doesn't get the loan, the buyer can take one of two courses of action. He can give the seller notice that the condition has not been met, terminate the agreement, and get his deposit back. Alternatively, he can waive the financing contingency and go ahead with the transaction. This would mean that he would have to come up with the purchase price from some other source by the closing date, or else forfeit his deposit.

If the buyer decides to go ahead with the purchase, the seller cannot refuse to complete the transaction because the financing condition was not met. Since the condition was included in the purchase and sale agreement for the benefit of the buyer, only the buyer can choose whether to waive the condition or terminate the sale.

In the unusual case when a contingency clause benefits both parties to a contract, the condition can be waived only with the consent of both parties.

FOR THE BUYER'S BENEFIT. Contingency provisions in a purchase and sale agreement are usually for the benefit of the buyer. They protect the buyer from becoming obligated to go through with the purchase if problems arise, or if it turns out that the property is unsuitable in some way—for instance, because it can't be subdivided, or it's infested with termites, or the well water is contaminated. Common contingency provisions in real estate transactions concern the buyer's financing (as in the example above); the sale of property the buyer currently owns; a satisfactory pest, soil, septic, well, or structural inspection; obtaining approval for a rezone, variance, or subdivision from the local planning commission; or the issuance of some sort of license needed to operate an establishment (such as a liquor license).

GOOD FAITH EFFORT REQUIRED

Whenever a contract contains a contingency clause, the benefiting party has an implied legal obligation to make a reasonable, good faith effort to fulfill the contingency.

EXAMPLE: Hanson's agreement to purchase Moore's house is contingent on Hanson getting a 30-year, 90%, fixed-rate loan at 5% interest. Three days after signing the agreement, Hanson decides she doesn't want to buy Moore's property after all, so she doesn't even bother to apply for a loan. Hanson then tells Moore that she's terminating the contract because the contingency hasn't been fulfilled, and she demands the return of her earnest money.

However, Hanson had a legal obligation to make a reasonable effort to get a loan. Because she didn't fulfill that obligation, she breached the purchase and sale agreement and is not entitled to a refund of her deposit.

If the responsible party does not make a good faith effort to satisfy the contingency, then it is dropped from the contract. That party is bound by the contract even though the condition has not been met. Under these circumstances, as in the example above, the seller could keep the deposit if the buyer failed to go through with the purchase.

Although the obligation to make a good faith effort to fulfill a condition is always implied in the contract, the contingency clause should spell out that obligation. For example, the Northwest Multiple Listing Service financing contingency addendum, which we'll discuss later in this chapter, includes the following clause:

If Buyer has not waived the Financing Contingency, and is unable to obtain financing by Closing after a good faith effort then, on Buyer's notice, this Agreement shall terminate. The Earnest Money shall be refunded to Buyer...

BASIC ELEMENTS OF A CONTINGENCY CLAUSE

Any type of contingency provision, whether it's a financing contingency, an inspection contingency, or some other type, should contain all of the following elements:

1. An exact statement of the condition and what is required to fulfill it.
2. The procedure for notifying the other party of the condition's satisfaction or waiver.

3. The deadline by which the condition must be met or waived.

4. The rights of the parties if the condition is not met or waived by the specified date.

While it's important to know the elements a contingency clause should have, you shouldn't try to draft one yourself. As with the purchase and sale agreement itself, you should use a pre-printed, attorney-approved contingency form that can be attached as an addendum to the agreement. If you were to write your own provision instead of using a pre-printed form, that would probably be considered the unauthorized practice of law.

TYPES OF CONTINGENCIES

In purchase and sale agreements for residential transactions, there are three common types of contingency clauses: financing contingencies, inspection contingencies, and contingencies that concern the sale of the buyer's home.

FINANCING CONTINGENCIES

Most residential purchase and sale agreements are contingent on whether the buyer can obtain the financing needed in order to be able to pay the seller the agreed price. Standard contract forms may either include a financing contingency clause in the purchase and sale agreement itself, or require an addendum that sets forth the terms of the financing contingency.

The primary purpose of a financing contingency is to allow the buyer to be released from the agreement and get her deposit back if she can't get the necessary financing.

A financing contingency usually states the type of financing the buyer will apply for, sets deadlines for the loan application and fulfillment or waiver of the contingency, specifies the notice periods, and describes how lender-required inspections and repairs will be handled.

FINANCING TERMS. The financing terms set forth in the contingency clause may be general or specific. In this regard, the parties have conflicting interests. The buyer may want the contract to be contingent on a specific and very favorable financing arrangement, one that is as affordable as possible. On the other hand, the seller—who wants to hold the buyer to the agreement, or to keep the deposit if the buyer backs out—would prefer a financing contingency that simply calls for an institutional loan that's typical for the current marketplace. The seller probably won't agree to a financing contingency that specifies a below-market interest rate or unusually low loan fees, because it's much less likely that the buyer will be able to obtain that type of financing.

Figure 8.1 shows the financing addendum designed for use with the Northwest Multiple Listing Service purchase and sale agreement that appears in Chapter 7 (Figure 7.1). The financing terms set forth in this addendum are fairly general. In the first paragraph, you're supposed to indicate the type of financing the buyer will seek, and state the amount of the buyer's downpayment. The buyer is required to apply for a loan to pay the balance of the purchase price.

A more specific financing contingency could include any or all of these additional terms for the buyer's loan: the interest rate, and whether the rate is fixed or variable; the loan term, and whether the loan will be fully or partially amortized; and the maximum monthly payment amount. Again, a very specific financing contingency is ordinarily to the buyer's advantage and the seller's disadvantage.

Many financing contingencies state which party will pay the costs and fees associated with the loan application; this is usually the buyer's responsibility.

FINANCING TIMELINES. A financing contingency usually states that the buyer must apply for the loan within a certain number of days. In addition, the contingency provision may establish a time period after which the seller may give notice of his right to terminate their agreement. Once the buyer receives this notice, she might have, for instance, three days (as on the NWMLS form) to decide whether to waive the contingency; if she chooses not to waive it, the seller may terminate the agreement.

LOAN INFORMATION. Once a certain amount of time has passed after mutual acceptance of the agreement (10 days is the default if the blank is not filled in), the seller can give notice requesting that the buyer provide information about the status of his loan application. The request can be made once per transaction. The buyer then has three days to reply with information that includes the date of the application, the name of the lender, a list of the information that the buyer has given the lender, and a warranty that the buyer has provided the lender with all required information. If the buyer fails to provide the seller with the information by the deadline, the seller can terminate the agreement.

LOAN COST PROVISIONS. The financing contingency usually allows the parties to negotiate whether the seller will pay any of the buyer's loan or closing costs.

FIG. 8.1 FINANCING CONTINGENCY ADDENDUM

Form 22A
Financing Addendum
Rev. 2/17
Page 1 of 3

©Copyright 2017
Northwest Multiple Listing Service
ALL RIGHTS RESERVED

FINANCING ADDENDUM TO
PURCHASE & SALE AGREEMENT

The following is part of the Purchase and Sale Agreement dated _____ 1

between _____ ("Buyer") 2
        Buyer   Buyer

and _____ ("Seller") 3
      Seller   Seller

concerning _____ (the "Property"). 4
         Address   City   State   Zip

1. LOAN APPLICATION/WAIVER OF CONTINGENCY. 5

    a. Loan Application. This Agreement is contingent on Buyer obtaining the following type of loan or loans to 6
    purchase the Property (the "Loan(s)"): ❑ Conventional First; ❑ Conventional Second; ❑ Bridge; ❑ VA; ❑ FHA; 7
    ❑ USDA; ❑ Home Equity Line of Credit; ❑ Other _____ 8
    (the "Financing Contingency"). Buyer shall pay ❑ $ _____; or ❑ _____ % of the Purchase 9
    Price down, in addition to the Loans. Buyer shall make application for the Loans to pay the balance of the 10
    Purchase Price and pay the application fee, if required, for the subject Property within _____ days (5 11
    days if not filled in) after mutual acceptance of this Agreement. For the purposes of this Addendum, 12
    "application" means the submission of Buyer's financial information for the purposes of obtaining an extension 13
    of credit including Buyer's name, income, social security number (if required), the Property address, purchase 14
    price, and the loan amount. 15

    b. Waiver of Financing Contingency. If Buyer (i) fails to make application for financing for the Property within 16
    the agreed time; (ii) changes the type of loan at any time without Seller's prior written consent; or (iii) changes 17
    the lender without Seller's prior written consent after the agreed upon time to apply for financing expires, then 18
    the Financing Contingency shall be deemed waived. Buyer's waiver of the Financing Contingency under this 19
    Paragraph 1(b) also constitutes waiver of Paragraph 7 (Appraisal Less Than Sales Price). For purposes of 20
    this Addendum, "lender" means either the party to whom the application was submitted or the party funding 21
    the loan. 22

2. LOAN INFORMATION. 23

    a. Seller's Request for Loan Information. At any time _____ days (10 days if not filled in) after mutual 24
    acceptance, Seller may give, once, a notice requesting information related to the status of Buyer's loan 25
    application ("Request for Loan Information"). NWMLS Form 22AL may be used for this notice. 26

    b. Buyer's Loan Information Notice. Within _____ days (3 days if not filled in) of receiving Seller's Request 27
    for Loan Information, Buyer shall give notice of the status of Buyer's loan application ("Loan Information 28
    Notice"). Buyer's notice shall be on NWMLS Form 22AP and shall include the date of application, the name 29
    of lender, a list of the information that Buyer has provided to lender, and a warranty that Buyer has provided 30
    all information requested by lender. 31

    c. Failure to Provide Loan Information Notice. If Buyer fails to timely give to Seller a completed Loan 32
    Information Notice, Seller may give the Right to Terminate Notice described in Paragraph 3 (Seller's Right to 33
    Terminate) at any time after the date that the Loan Information Notice is due. 34

3. SELLER'S RIGHT TO TERMINATE. 35

    a. Right to Terminate Notice. At any time _____ days (30 days if not filled in) after mutual acceptance, 36
    Seller may give notice that Seller may terminate the Agreement at any time 3 days after delivery of that notice 37
    (the "Right to Terminate Notice"). NWMLS Form 22AR may be used for this notice. 38

    b. Termination Notice. If Buyer has not previously waived the Financing Contingency, Seller may give notice of 39
    termination of this Agreement (the "Termination Notice") any time following 3 days after delivery of the Right 40
    to Terminate Notice. If Seller gives the Termination Notice before Buyer has waived the Financing 41
    Contingency, this Agreement is terminated and the Earnest Money shall be refunded to Buyer. NWMLS Form 42
    22AR shall be used for this notice. If not waived, the Financing Contingency shall survive the Closing Date. 43

    c. Appraisal Less Than Sales Price. Buyer's waiver of the Financing Contingency under this Paragraph 3 ❑ will; 44
    or ❑ will not (will, if not filled in) constitute waiver of Paragraph 7 (Appraisal Less Than Sales Price). 45

_____   _____   _____   _____
Buyer's Initials   Date   Buyer's Initials   Date   Seller's Initials   Date   Seller's Initials   Date

Form 22A
Financing Addendum
Rev. 2/17
Page 2 of 3

FINANCING ADDENDUM TO
PURCHASE & SALE AGREEMENT
Continued

4. **LOAN COST PROVISIONS.** Seller shall pay up to ❑ $ _____ ; or ❑ _____ % of the Purchase   46
   Price ($0.00 if not filled in), which shall be applied to Buyer's Loan(s) and settlement costs, including prepaids, loan   47
   discount, loan fee, interest buy down, financing, closing or other costs allowed by lender. That amount shall include   48
   the following costs that lender is prohibited from collecting from Buyer: (a) up to $300.00 for Buyer's Loan(s) and   49
   settlement costs for FHA/USDA/VA loans; and (b) Buyer's share of the escrow fee for a VA loan. Seller shall pay the   50
   costs for (a) and (b), even if the amount agreed upon in this Paragraph 4 is insufficient to pay for those costs.   51

5. **EARNEST MONEY.** If Buyer has not waived the Financing Contingency, and is unable to obtain financing by   52
   Closing after a good faith effort then, on Buyer's notice, this Agreement shall terminate. The Earnest Money shall   53
   be refunded to Buyer after lender confirms in writing (a) the date Buyer's loan application for the Property was   54
   made, including a copy of the loan estimate that was provided to Buyer; (b) that Buyer possessed sufficient funds   55
   to close; and (c) the reasons Buyer was unable to obtain financing by Closing. If Seller terminates this Agreement,   56
   the Earnest Money shall be refunded without need for such confirmation.   57

6. **INSPECTION.** Seller shall permit inspections required by lender, including but not limited to structural, pest,   58
   heating, plumbing, roof, electrical, septic, and well inspections. Seller is not obligated to pay for such inspections   59
   unless otherwise agreed.   60

7. **APPRAISAL LESS THAN SALE PRICE.**   61
   a. **Notice of Low Appraisal.** If lender's appraised value of the Property is less than the Purchase Price, Buyer   62
      may, within 3 days after receipt of a copy of lender's appraisal, give notice of low appraisal, which shall   63
      include a copy of lender's appraisal. NWMLS Form 22AN may be used for the notices in this Paragraph 7.   64
   b. **Seller's Response.** Seller shall, within 10 days after Buyer's notice of low appraisal, give notice of: 65
      (i) A reappraisal or reconsideration of value, at Seller's expense, by the same appraiser or another appraiser   66
      acceptable to lender, in an amount not less than the Purchase Price. Buyer shall promptly seek lender's   67
      approval of such reappraisal or reconsideration of value. The parties are advised that lender may elect   68
      not to accept a reappraisal or reconsideration of value;   69
      (ii) Seller's consent to reduce the Purchase Price to an amount not more than the amount specified in the   70
      appraisal or reappraisal by the same appraiser, or an appraisal by another appraiser acceptable to   71
      lender, whichever is higher. (This provision is not applicable if this Agreement is conditioned on FHA, VA,   72
      or USDA financing. FHA, VA, and USDA financing does not permit the Buyer to be obligated to buy if the   73
      Seller reduces the Purchase Price to the appraised value. Buyer, however, has the option to buy at the   74
      reduced price.);   75
      (iii) Seller's proposal to reduce the Purchase Price to an amount more than the amount specified in the   76
      appraisal and for Buyer to pay the necessary additional funds (the amount the reduced Purchase Price   77
      exceeds the appraised value) to close the sale; or   78
      (iv) Seller's rejection of Buyer's notice of low appraisal.   79

      If Seller timely delivers notice of (i) reappraisal, reconsideration of value; or (ii) consent to reduce the   80
      Purchase Price to an amount not more than the amount specified in the appraisal, and lender accepts Seller's   81
      response, then Buyer shall be bound by Seller's response.   82

   c. **Buyer's Reply.**   83
      (i) Buyer shall have 3 days from either Seller's notice of rejection of low appraisal or, if Seller fails to respond,   84
      the day Seller's response period ends, whichever is earlier, to (a) waive the Financing Contingency; or (b)   85
      terminate the Agreement, in which event the Earnest Money shall be refunded to Buyer.   86
      (ii) If Seller proposes to reduce the Purchase Price to an amount more than the appraised value, Buyer shall   87
      have 3 days to (a) accept and represent that Buyer has sufficient funds to close the sale in accordance with   88
      this provision; or (b) terminate the Agreement, in which event the Earnest Money shall be refunded to Buyer.   89

      Buyer's inaction during this reply period shall result in termination of the Agreement and return of the Earnest   90
      Money to Buyer. The Closing Date shall be extended as necessary to accommodate the foregoing times for   91
      notices.   92

_____   _____   _____   _____   _____   _____   _____   _____
Buyer's Initials   Date   Buyer's Initials   Date   Seller's Initials   Date   Seller's Initials   Date

Form 22A
Financing Addendum
Rev. 2/17
Page 3 of 3

**FINANCING ADDENDUM TO
PURCHASE & SALE AGREEMENT**
Continued

8. **FHA/VA/USDA - Appraisal Certificate.** If this Agreement is contingent on Buyer obtaining FHA, VA, or USDA   93
financing, notwithstanding any other provisions of this Agreement, Buyer is not obligated to complete the   94
purchase of the Property unless Buyer has been given in accordance with HUD/FHA, VA, or USDA requirements   95
a written statement by FHA, VA, USDA or a Direct Endorsement lender, setting forth the appraised value of the   96
Property (excluding closing costs). Buyer shall pay the costs of any appraisal. If the appraised value of the   97
Property is less than the Purchase Price, Paragraph 7 above shall apply.   98

    Purpose of Appraisal. The appraised valuation is arrived at only to determine the maximum mortgage FHA, VA,   99
or USDA will insure. FHA, VA, or USDA do not warrant the value or the condition of the Property. Buyer agrees to   100
satisfy himself/herself that the price and condition of the Property are acceptable.   101

9. **EXTENSION OF CLOSING.** If, through no fault of Buyer, lender is required by 12 CFR 1026 to give corrected   102
disclosures to Buyer due to (a) a change in the Annual Percentage Rate ("APR") of Buyer's Loan(s) by .125% or   103
more for a fixed rate loan or .250% or more for an adjustable rate loan; (b) a change in the loan product; or (c) the   104
addition of a prepayment penalty, then upon notice from Buyer, the Closing Date shall be extended for up to 4 days   105
to accommodate the requirements of Regulation Z of the Truth in Lending Act. This paragraph shall survive Buyer's   106
waiver of this Financing Contingency.   107

SAMPLE

_____   _____   _____   _____   _____   _____   _____   _____
Buyer's Initials   Date   Buyer's Initials   Date   Seller's Initials   Date   Seller's Initials   Date

In addition, the contingency often includes special provisions concerning FHA, VA, and USDA financing. The regulations that govern these financing programs prevent the buyer from paying certain loan and closing costs, so the seller agrees to pay these costs if the buyer is applying for an FHA, VA, or USDA loan. FHA, VA, and USDA transactions also require certain provisions concerning the property appraisal.

EARNEST MONEY. The financing contingency will also state the seller's obligation to return the earnest money to the buyer if the purchase agreement is terminated because the buyer's good faith loan application is denied. To receive a refund of the earnest money, the buyer must provide the seller with a written confirmation from the buyer's lender stating that the buyer's loan application was denied and the reasons for the denial.

LENDER-REQUIRED INSPECTIONS. Before approving a loan application, many lenders require that the property be inspected, so a financing contingency may describe how a lender-required inspection will be handled. The contingency will state that the seller agrees to allow this type of inspection. It will also say whether the seller will pay for the inspection (usually not).

If the inspection report says that repairs are needed, the lender may require the repairs to be completed as a condition of loan approval. If the seller opts not to pay for these repairs, the buyer can cancel the agreement without losing the good faith deposit.

APPRAISAL PROVISIONS. Because the buyer's loan amount depends in part on the appraised value of the property, the financing contingency usually addresses the parties' options in the event of a low appraisal. Typically, the contingency states that if the appraised value is lower than the price the buyer agreed to pay, the seller must either obtain a reappraisal that matches or exceeds the agreed price, or else reduce the price to the appraised amount. Otherwise, the buyer can terminate the purchase and sale agreement without forfeiting the earnest money. The contingency form may also give the buyer the option of waiving the financing contingency without waiving the provision that protects the buyer in the event of a low appraisal.

Note that if there is a low appraisal in an FHA, VA, or USDA transaction, the buyer can't be required to go through with the purchase even if the seller is willing to reduce the price to the appraised value (although the buyer may choose to buy the property at the reduced price).

See Chapter 4 for a more general discussion of the low appraisal problem.

TRUTH IN LENDING ACT. Under the federal Truth in Lending Act, if the annual percentage rate (APR) on the buyer's loan differs significantly from the APR that was initially disclosed to the buyer in the loan estimate, the lender must disclose this change to the buyer at least three days before closing. The financing contingency may contain a provision that will extend closing by up to four days, if necessary, to accommodate this requirement. This provision remains effective even if the buyer waives the financing contingency.

SELLER FINANCING. If the seller is going to provide the buyer's financing, the purchase and sale agreement normally won't have a financing contingency. A different type of addendum, such as the payment terms addendum in Chapter 7 (Figure 7.2), should be used to set forth the terms of the seller financing. The financing forms that are going to be used—the real estate contract, or the promissory note and deed of trust—must also be attached to the purchase and sale agreement. It will be a breach of contract if the seller fails to provide financing on the agreed terms.

INSPECTION CONTINGENCIES

Another very common type of contingency in residential purchase and sale agreements is an inspection contingency. (See Figure 8.2.) The contract can be made contingent on one or more expert inspections of the property: for example, a structural or mechanical inspection of the property's improvements, compliance with building or zoning codes, a geological inspection, a hazardous substances inspection, a video inspection of the sewer line, and/or a pest control inspection.

An inspection contingency should establish:

- which party is responsible for ordering and paying for the inspection,
- when and how the buyer will give the seller notice of disapproval of the inspection report,
- whether the seller has the option of making repairs, and
- a time limit for reinspection by the buyer if the seller makes repairs.

FIG. 8.2   INSPECTION CONTINGENCY ADDENDUM

Form 35
Inspection Addendum
Rev. 5/14
Page 1 of 2

©Copyright 2014
Northwest Multiple Listing Service
ALL RIGHTS RESERVED

INSPECTION ADDENDUM TO PURCHASE AND SALE AGREEMENT

The following is part of the Purchase and Sale Agreement dated _____ 1

between _____ ("Buyer") 2
             Buyer   Buyer

and _____ ("Seller") 3
         Seller   Seller

concerning _____ (the "Property"). 4
           Address   City   State   Zip

1. ❑ **a. INSPECTION CONTINGENCY.** This Agreement is conditioned on Buyer's subjective satisfaction with 5
inspections of the Property and the improvements on the Property. Buyer's inspections may include, at 6
Buyer's option and without limitation, the structural, mechanical and general condition of the improvements 7
to the Property, compliance with building and zoning codes, an inspection of the Property for hazardous 8
materials, a pest inspection, and a soils/stability inspection. The inspection must be performed by Buyer or a 9
person licensed (or exempt from licensing) under Chapter 18.280 RCW. 10

Sewer Inspection. Buyer's inspection of the Property ❑ may; ❑ may not (may, if not checked) include an 11
inspection of the sewer system, which may include a sewer line video inspection and assessment and may 12
require the inspector to remove toilets or other fixtures to access the sewer line. 13

Buyer's Obligations. All inspections are to be (a) ordered by Buyer, (b) performed by inspectors of Buyer's 14
choice, and (c) completed at Buyer's expense. Buyer shall not alter the Property or any improvements on the 15
Property without first obtaining Seller's permission. Buyer is solely responsible for interviewing and selecting 16
all inspectors. Buyer shall restore the Property and all improvements on the Property to the same condition 17
they were in prior to the inspection. Buyer shall be responsible for all damages resulting from any inspection 18
of the Property performed on Buyer's behalf. 19

BUYER'S NOTICE. This inspection contingency SHALL CONCLUSIVELY BE DEEMED WAIVED unless 20
within _____ days (10 days if not filled in) after mutual acceptance of this Agreement (the "Initial 21
Inspection Period"), Buyer gives notice (1) approving the inspection and waiving this contingency; (2) 22
disapproving the inspection and terminating the Agreement; (3) that Buyer will conduct additional 23
inspections; or (4) proposing repairs to the property or modifications to the Agreement. If Buyer disapproves 24
the inspection and terminates the Agreement, the Earnest Money shall be refunded to Buyer. If Buyer 25
proposes repairs to the property or modifications to the Agreement, including adjustments to the purchase 26
price or credits for repairs to be performed after closing, the parties shall negotiate as set forth in paragraph 27
1.c, below. The parties may use NWMLS Form 35R to give notices required by this Addendum. 28

ATTENTION BUYER: If Buyer fails to give timely notice, then this inspection contingency shall be deemed 29
waived and Seller shall not be obligated to make any repairs or modifications. 30

b. Additional Inspections. If an inspector so recommends, Buyer may obtain further evaluation of any 31
item by a specialist at Buyer's option and expense if, on or before the end of the Initial Inspection Period, 32
Buyer provides Seller a copy of the inspector's recommendation and notice that Buyer will seek additional 33
inspections. If Buyer gives timely notice of additional inspections, Buyer shall have _____ (5 days if 34
not filled in) after giving the notice to obtain the additional inspection(s) by a specialist. 35

c. Buyer's Requests for Repairs or Modifications. If Buyer requests repairs or modifications under 36
paragraph 1.a or 1.b. above, the parties shall negotiate as set forth in this paragraph. All requests, 37
responses, and replies made in accordance with the following procedures are irrevocable for the time period 38
provided. 39

    (i) Seller's Response to Request for Repairs or Modifications. Seller shall have _____ days 40
(3 days if not filled in) after receipt of Buyer's request for repairs or modifications to give notice that 41
Seller (a) agrees to the repairs or modifications proposed by Buyer; (b) agrees to some of the repairs or 42
modifications proposed by Buyer; (c) rejects all repairs or modifications proposed by Buyer; or (d) offers 43
different or additional repairs or modifications. If Seller agrees to the terms of Buyer's request for repairs 44
or modifications, this contingency shall be satisfied and Buyer's Reply shall not be necessary. If Seller 45
does not agree to all of Buyer's repairs or modifications, Buyer shall have an opportunity to reply, as 46
follows: 47

_____ _____ _____ _____ _____ _____ _____ _____
Buyer's Initials   Date   Buyer's Initials   Date   Seller's Initials   Date   Seller's Initials   Date

Reprinted courtesy of Northwest Multiple Listing Service. All rights reserved.

Form 35
Inspection Addendum
Rev. 5/14
Page 2 of 2

INSPECTION ADDENDUM TO PURCHASE AND SALE AGREEMENT
Continued

(ii) Buyer's Reply. If Seller does not agree to all of the repairs or modifications proposed by Buyer, 48
Buyer shall have _____ days (3 days if not filled in) from either the day Buyer receives Seller's 49
response or, if Seller fails to respond, the day Seller's response period ends, whichever is earlier, to (a) 50
accept the Seller's response at which time this contingency shall be satisfied; (b) agree with the Seller on 51
other remedies; or (c) disapprove the inspection and terminate the Agreement, in which event, the 52
Earnest Money shall be refunded to Buyer. 53

ATTENTION BUYER: These time periods for negotiating repairs or modifications shall not repeat. The 54
parties must either reach a written agreement or Buyer must terminate this Agreement by the Buyer's Reply 55
deadline set forth in paragraph 1.c.ii. Buyer's inaction during Buyer's reply period shall result in waiver of this 56
inspection condition, in which case Seller shall not be obligated to make any repairs or modifications 57
whatsoever AND THIS CONTINGENCY SHALL BE DEEMED WAIVED. 58

d. Repairs. If Seller agrees to make the repairs proposed by Buyer, then repairs shall be accomplished at 59
Seller's expense in a commercially reasonable manner prior to the Closing Date. In the case of hazardous 60
materials, "repair" means removal or treatment (including but not limited to removal or, at Seller's option, 61
decommissioning of any oil storage tanks) of the hazardous material at Seller's expense as recommended by 62
and under the direction of a licensed hazardous material engineer or other expert selected by Seller. Seller's 63
repairs are subject to reinspection and approval, prior to Closing, by the inspector who recommended the repair, 64
if Buyer elects to order and pay for such reinspection. If Buyer agrees to pay for any repairs prior to closing, the 65
parties are advised to seek the counsel of an attorney to review the terms of that agreement. 66

e. Oil Storage Tanks. Any inspection regarding oil storage tanks or contamination from such tanks shall be 67
limited solely to determining the presence or non-presence of oil storage tanks on the Property, unless otherwise 68
agreed in writing by Buyer and Seller. 69

2. **ON-SITE SEWAGE DISPOSAL SYSTEMS ADVISORY:** Buyer is advised that on-site sewage disposal systems, 70
including "septic systems," are subject to strict governmental regulation and occasional malfunction and even 71
failure. Buyer is advised to consider conducting an inspection of any on-site sewage system in addition to the 72
inspection of the Property provided by this Form 35 by including an appropriate on-site sewage disposal 73
inspection contingency such as NWMLS Form 22S (Septic Addendum). 74

3. ❑ **NEIGHBORHOOD REVIEW CONTINGENCY:** Buyer's inspection includes Buyer's subjective satisfaction 75
that the conditions of the neighborhood in which the Property is located are consistent with the Buyer's 76
intended use of the Property (the "Neighborhood Review"). The Neighborhood Review may include Buyer's 77
investigation of the schools, proximity to bus lines, availability of shopping, traffic patterns, noise, parking and 78
investigation of other neighborhood, environmental and safety conditions the Buyer may determine to be 79
relevant in deciding to purchase the Property. If Buyer does not give notice of disapproval of the 80
Neighborhood Review within _____ (3 days if not filled in) of mutual acceptance of the Agreement, 81
then this Neighborhood Review condition shall conclusively be deemed satisfied (waived). If Buyer gives a 82
timely notice of disapproval, then this Agreement shall terminate and the Earnest Money shall be refunded to 83
Buyer. 84

4. ❑ **PREINSPECTION CONDUCTED.** Buyer, prior to mutual acceptance of this Agreement, conducted a 85
building, hazardous substances, building and zoning code, pest or soils/stability inspection of the Property, 86
and closing of this Agreement is not conditioned on the results of such inspections. Buyer elects to buy the 87
Property in its present condition and acknowledges that the decision to purchase the property was based on 88
Buyer's prior inspection and that Buyer has not relied on representations by Seller, Listing Broker or Selling 89
Broker. 90

5. ❑ **WAIVER OF INSPECTION.** Buyer has been advised to obtain a building, hazardous substances, building 91
and zoning code, pest or soils/stability inspection, and to condition the closing of this Agreement on the 92
results of such inspections, but Buyer elects to waive the right and buy the Property in its present condition. 93
Buyer acknowledges that the decision to waive Buyer's inspection options was based on Buyer's personal 94
inspection and Buyer has not relied on representations by Seller, Listing Broker or Selling Broker. 95

_____ _____ _____ _____ _____ _____ _____ _____
Buyer's Initials   Date   Buyer's Initials   Date   Seller's Initials   Date   Seller's Initials   Date

APPROVAL OR DISAPPROVAL. Most inspection contingencies provide that if the buyer fails to notify the seller that he disapproves the inspection report before the deadline, the buyer is deemed to have approved the report.

If the buyer disapproves the inspection report, the seller may be given the opportunity to repair the problems noted in the report. If so, the seller has a certain period—three days, for example—to notify the buyer whether she will make the requested repairs. If the seller chooses to make the repairs, the purchase and sale agreement becomes binding and the buyer must go ahead with the purchase.

The seller's repairs are generally subject to reinspection and approval by the same inspector who prepared the original report. The reinspection is usually paid for by the buyer.

If the seller decides not to make the requested repairs, the buyer then must choose whether to waive the condition and proceed with the transaction, or else terminate the purchase and sale agreement.

Sometimes a seller responds to the buyer by offering to make only some of the requested repairs, or by offering to modify their contract in some way (for example, by lowering the purchase price). It is then up to the buyer to accept or reject the seller's offer. The parties may go back and forth in this way several times before a compromise is reached or the buyer decides to give up and terminate the contract.

OPPORTUNITY TO REPAIR VS. BUYER'S SATISFACTION. After the buyer receives an inspection report, whether he's required to give the seller an opportunity to make repairs will depend on the terms of the inspection contingency that they included in their purchase and sale agreement.

If an inspection contingency form provides that the seller must be given an opportunity to make repairs if she chooses to do so, the form typically requires the buyer's requests for repairs to be based on problems revealed in the inspection report. The seller may be entitled to a copy of the relevant parts of the report that justify the buyer's requests. If the report shows that the inspector didn't find any problems, then the buyer is usually required to go ahead with the transaction.

Other inspection contingency forms have no such requirements. For example, the Northwest Multiple Listing Service inspection contingency addendum in Figure 8.2 allows the buyer to terminate the transaction without offering the seller a chance to make repairs. It makes the purchase and sale agreement contingent on the buyer's subjective satisfaction with the inspection report. After

FIG. 8.3   INSPECTION RESPONSE FORM

Form 35R
Inspection Response for Form 35
Rev. 7/08
Page 1 of 1

INSPECTION RESPONSE FOR FORM 35

©Copyright 2008
Northwest Multiple Listing Service
ALL RIGHTS RESERVED

The following is part of the Purchase and Sale Agreement dated _____   1

between _____ ("Buyer")   2
                        Buyer   Buyer

and _____ ("Seller")   3
                        Seller   Seller

concerning _____ (the "Property").   4
                        Address   City   State   Zip

I.   BUYER'S RESPONSE OR REQUEST FOR REPAIRS OR MODIFICATION   5
❑   Buyer's inspection of the Property is approved and the inspection contingency is satisfied.*   6
❑   Buyer's inspection of the Property is disapproved and the Agreement is terminated. The Earnest Money shall be   7
      refunded to Buyer.*   8
❑   Buyer gives notice of an additional inspection. The inspector's recommendation is attached. The time for Buyer's   9
      response to the initial and additional inspection is extended as provided in paragraph 1(b) of Form 35.*   10
❑   Buyer requests the following modifications and/or repairs. If Seller agrees to these modifications or repairs, the   11
      inspection contingency shall be deemed satisfied.**   12

_____   13
_____   14
_____   15
_____   16
_____   17
_____   18
_____   19

_____   _____   _____   _____
Buyer   Date   Buyer   Date

If Buyer requests modifications and/or repairs, this Form 35R and any other addenda or notice pertaining to the   20
modifications and/or repairs and amendment to the Agreement related to or resulting from the request for   21
modifications and/or repairs shall become a part of the Agreement.   22

II.   SELLER'S RESPONSE TO BUYER'S REQUEST FOR REPAIRS OR MODIFICATION.   23
      Seller acknowledges receipt of Buyer's request for modification or repair, and responds as follows: 24
❑   Seller agrees to all of the modifications or repairs in Buyer's request for modification or repair. The inspection contingency   25
      is satisfied, the parties agree to proceed to Closing as provided in the Agreement, and Buyer's reply, below, is not   26
      necessary.**   27
❑   Seller offers to correct only the following conditions:**   28

_____   29
_____   30

❑   Seller rejects all proposals by Buyer.*   31
❑   Seller rejects all proposals by Buyer, but proposes the following alternative modifications or repairs:**   32

_____   33
_____   34

_____   _____   _____   _____   35
Seller   Date   Seller   Date

III. BUYER'S REPLY TO SELLER'S RESPONSE.   36
❑   Buyer accepts Seller's response and agrees to proceed to Closing as provided in the Agreement.**   37
❑   Buyer rejects Seller's response. Buyer disapproves of the inspection and this Agreement is terminated. The   38
      Earnest Money shall be refunded to Buyer.*   39
❑   Buyer rejects Seller's response, but offers the attached alternative proposal for modification or repair. Buyer   40
      acknowledges that the inspection contingency will be waived unless Buyer and Seller reach written agreement or   41
      Buyer gives notice disapproving the inspection and terminating the Agreement before the deadline in paragraph   42
      1(c)(ii) of the inspection contingency (NWMLS Form 35).**   43

_____   _____   _____   _____   44
Buyer   Date   Buyer   Date

* This is a notice which requires only one Buyer's or one Seller's initials.   45
** This is not a notice and requires all Buyer's or Seller's initials.   46

reviewing the report, the buyer may choose to ask the seller to make repairs or to modify their contract, but the buyer is under no obligation to continue with the transaction if he has changed his mind about buying the property. He can withdraw even if the inspection report indicates that there are no problems with the property whatsoever. In fact, the seller isn't entitled to see a copy of the report if the buyer doesn't want to show it to her.

NOTIFICATION FORM. The NWMLS inspection addendum form has a corresponding notification form, which is shown in Figure 8.3. The buyer uses this form to give the seller notice of her approval or disapproval of the inspection report. The buyer also uses the notification form to request repairs if she chooses to do so, and the seller will use the same form to respond.

NEIGHBORHOOD REVIEW. In addition to inspecting characteristics of the property itself, the buyer may also want to inspect the neighborhood. The NWMLS inspection addendum contains a neighborhood review contingency, which gives the buyer an opportunity to perform a neighborhood review, looking at characteristics such as schools, public transportation, and traffic patterns. The buyer has three days to notify the seller that he disapproves of the neighborhood; otherwise the contingency is waived.

CODE VIOLATIONS. Sellers should be aware that if an inspection reveals violations of the building code or other laws, public authorities could order them to correct the violations, whether or not the sale to the buyer proceeds.

"AS IS" SALES. Of course, a buyer might want to purchase the seller's property "as is," without having any expert inspections done. If so, the inspection addendum form shown in Figure 8.2 has a waiver of inspection provision that can be checked. In this provision, the buyer acknowledges that his decision to waive his inspection options was based on his own inspection of the property, not on any representations made by the seller or the real estate licensees.

SALE OF BUYER'S HOME CONTINGENCIES

Unless you're helping them buy their first home, your buyers will usually have to sell their current home before buying a new one. For one thing, they probably need to sell their current home to generate the cash for the downpayment on the new home. Also, few buyers can afford the mortgage payments on two houses at the same time. For both of these reasons, it's very common to make the sale of the buyer's current home a condition of the contract for the purchase of the new home.

Depending on the terms of the purchase and sale agreement, this condition may actually be a "hidden contingency." In other words, the agreement may be contingent on the sale of the buyer's home even though that contingency is not expressly stated in the agreement.

EXAMPLE: Wilder has agreed to purchase Greenbaum's home. The sale is contingent on financing: unless Wilder obtains a purchase loan from an institutional lender, the contract will not be binding.

When Wilder applies for a loan, she doesn't have enough cash for the downpayment she'll be required to make. She plans to sell her current home to get the necessary cash. The lender processes the application and approves the loan on the condition that Wilder obtain the necessary cash before closing. If Wilder is unable to sell her home before the closing date set in her contract with Greenbaum, she won't have the cash for the downpayment and the lender will refuse to fund the loan. Thus, the sale of Greenbaum's home is actually contingent on the sale of Wilder's home, even though this contingency was not stated in their purchase and sale agreement.

Naturally, it's important to state the terms of any contingency clearly rather than leave it unstated or hidden behind another contingency. The seller needs to be aware of all the contingencies of the sale before he can make an informed decision about whether or not to accept the buyer's offer. This is particularly important when the buyer must sell her own property before completing the purchase. If this contingency is not made clear to the seller, the seller may believe that the buyer has a much better chance of getting a loan than she actually does. If the transaction doesn't close because the buyer is unable to sell her home (and thus get the loan), the seller could claim that by failing to disclose the hidden contingency, you misrepresented the buyer's financial ability to complete the purchase.

ELEMENTS. Some purchase and sale agreements have pre-printed clauses to fill out in order to make the offer contingent on the sale of the buyer's home. Or an addendum may be used, such as the one shown in Figure 8.4. In any case, the contingency provision should address the issues that exist with any contingency (how a party fulfills the contingency, relevant deadlines, method of notifying the parties, and what happens if a party fulfills or waives the contingency). In addition, with a sale of buyer's home contingency, the parties need to state what will happen if the seller gets another offer during the contingency period.

FIG. 8.4   SALE OF BUYER'S PROPERTY CONTINGENCY ADDENDUM

**BUYER'S SALE OF PROPERTY CONTINGENCY
ADDENDUM TO PURCHASE & SALE AGREEMENT**

The following is part of the Purchase and Sale Agreement dated _____   1

between _____ ("Buyer")   2
           Buyer   Buyer

and _____ ("Seller")   3
         Seller   Seller

concerning _____ (the "Property").   4
        Address   City   State   Zip

1. **CONTINGENT ON SALE OF BUYER'S PROPERTY.** This Agreement is contingent on Buyer selling Buyer's   5
    property at _____   6
    City of _____ , State of _____ (the "Buyer's Property")   7
    on or before _____ (if not filled in, 45 days after mutual acceptance of this Agreement) (the   8
    "Contingency Period"). Buyer shall list Buyer's Property for sale on a multiple listing service in the area serving the   9
    property with a licensed real estate firm within 5 days after mutual acceptance of this Agreement. If Buyer fails to   10
    do so, this contingency shall be deemed waived and Paragraph 6(d) shall apply. If Buyer has not sold Buyer's   11
    Property or given notice waiving this contingency by the end of the Contingency Period, then this Agreement shall   12
    terminate and the Earnest Money shall be refunded to Buyer. For the purposes of this Addendum, the terms "sell,"   13
    "selling" and "sold" shall mean that Buyer has entered into a valid and enforceable agreement for the purchase   14
    and sale of Buyer's Property.   15

2. **WHEN SELLER'S CONSENT IS REQUIRED ON SALE OF BUYER'S PROPERTY.** Buyer must obtain Seller's   16
    written consent before Buyer accepts any offer for the sale of Buyer's Property that: 17
    (a) is contingent on the sale or closing of that (second) buyer's property; and/or   18
    (b) has a closing date less than 30 or more than 60 days from the date of mutual acceptance of the offer on   19
        Buyer's Property.   20

    If Buyer accepts any such offer without Seller's prior written consent, Seller shall have three days to terminate this   21
    Agreement from Buyer's notice that the contingency is satisfied (which notice shall include a complete copy of the   22
    purchase and sale agreement for the sale of Buyer's Property) and, upon Seller's termination, Buyer shall be in   23
    default and Seller shall be entitled to remedies as provided for in the Agreement. If Seller does not timely   24
    terminate, the Agreement shall not be affected.   25

3. **LOAN APPLICATION.** If this Agreement is contingent on Buyer obtaining financing pursuant to Form 22A   26
    (Financing Addendum), Buyer shall make written application for the Loan(s) (defined in Form 22A) and pay the   27
    application fee, if required, for the subject Property ☐ within _____ days (5 days if not filled in) after mutual   28
    acceptance of this Agreement, or ☐ within _____ days (5 days if not filled in) after Buyer satisfies the   29
    contingency in this Addendum (from mutual acceptance if neither box checked). If Buyer is not required to apply   30
    for the Loan(s) until after satisfaction of this contingency, the timelines in Form 22A shall not begin until that time.   31
    This Paragraph 3 supersedes the requirement for Buyer's loan application in Form 22A.   32

4. **PROPERTY REMAINS ON MARKET.** Seller may keep the Property on the market in the "Contingent" status until   33
    Seller has received notice that Buyer has satisfied or waived this contingency. If prior to that time, Seller accepts   34
    another offer, Seller shall give notice to Buyer and shall give Buyer _____ days (5 days if not filled in) or   35
    by the expiration of the contingency in Paragraph 1, whichever is earlier (the "Bump Period") to waive or satisfy   36
    this contingency. If Buyer does not timely waive or satisfy this contingency, this Agreement shall terminate and   37
    the Earnest Money shall be refunded to the Buyer. Seller's notice shall be on the Bump Notice (Form 44) or   38
    similar form, and Buyer's reply shall be on Bump Reply (Form 46) or similar form.   39

5. **CONTINGENCY SATISFIED.** Buyer shall give notice to Seller within 2 days of entering into an agreement to sell   40
    Buyer's Property (i.e., the contingency is "satisfied"). Buyer's notice shall include a complete copy of the purchase   41
    and sale agreement for the sale of Buyer's Property. The sale of the Property shall close 3 days after the closing   42
    of the sale of Buyer's Property. Buyer's notice shall be on the Contingency Property Notice (Form 90K) or similar   43
    form. Buyer may not extend the closing date for the sale of Buyer's Property without Seller's written consent.   44

_____ _____ _____ _____ _____ _____ _____ _____
Buyer's Initials   Date   Buyer's Initials   Date   Seller's Initials   Date   Seller's Initials   Date

Form 22B
Buyer's Property Contingency Addendum
Rev. 2/17
Page 2 of 2

**BUYER'S SALE OF PROPERTY CONTINGENCY
ADDENDUM TO PURCHASE & SALE AGREEMENT**
Continued

6. BUYER'S PROPERTY – FAILURE TO CLOSE.   45

   (a) <u>Notice to Seller</u>. Buyer shall give notice to Seller within 2 days of learning that the sale of Buyer's Property   46
has failed. If Buyer does not give such timely notice, then Buyer shall be in default. Such notice must be given   47
regardless of whether Buyer chooses to proceed with this Agreement.   48

   (b) <u>Contingency Survives</u>. If the sale of Buyer's Property fails to close through no fault of Buyer before expiration   49
of the Contingency Period in Paragraph 1, then this contingency shall be reinstated until the Contingency   50
Period has expired.   51

   (c) <u>Agreement Terminates</u>. If the sale of Buyer's Property fails to close through no fault of Buyer after expiration   52
of the Contingency Period, then this Agreement shall terminate and the Earnest Money shall be refunded to   53
Buyer.   54

   (d) <u>Waiver by Buyer</u>. If the sale of Buyer's Property fails to close through no fault of Buyer after expiration of the   55
Contingency Period, Buyer shall have the option of waiving the contingency and proceeding with the   56
Agreement. By waiving this contingency, Buyer also waives all other conditions in this Agreement (including   57
financing or any other contingency). If Buyer waives this contingency (whether after failure of Buyer's Property   58
to close or otherwise), the sale of the Property shall close 30 days after Buyer's waiver.   59

   (e) <u>Waiver by Buyer – New Construction</u>. If at the time of Buyer's waiver, a Certificate of Occupancy (CO) or its   60
equivalent for the Property has not been issued by the applicable government authority, then Buyer shall   61
close within _____ days (5 days if not filled in) of notice from Seller that a Certificate of Occupancy,   62
or equivalent, has been issued or within 30 days of waiver, whichever is later.   63

7. CLOSING DATE. The Closing Date set forth in this Addendum shall supersede the Closing Date set forth in the   64
Agreement.   65

                                     66

8. OTHER.   67

68
69
70
71
72
73
74
75
76
77
78
79
80
81
82
83
84
85
86
87
88
89
90
91
92

Buyer's Initials	Date	Buyer's Initials	Date	Seller's Initials	Date	Seller's Initials	Date

ACCEPTANCE OR CLOSING. There are two ways to set up this type of contingency provision. The sale can be made contingent on the buyer's acceptance of an offer to buy his current home, or on the closing of the sale of his current home. The seller will usually prefer to base fulfillment of the contingency on the buyer's acceptance of an offer. That way, the seller doesn't have to wait until the buyer's sale closes to know whether she and the buyer have a binding contract. If the buyer doesn't get an acceptable offer for his house within a certain period—for example, 45 days—then his agreement with the seller can be terminated.

From the buyer's point of view, it's preferable to base fulfillment of the contingency on the actual closing of his sale and the receipt of enough cash from that sale to close the transaction with the seller.

EXAMPLE: Whitfield is offering to buy Mayer's home for $389,000, with a $78,000 downpayment. The purchase and sale agreement will be contingent on the sale of Whitfield's current home.

Whitfield wants the contingency clause to be written so that the condition will be fulfilled only if the sale of his home actually closes within 90 days and he nets enough cash to make his $78,000 downpayment. He's afraid of what would happen if the condition were fulfilled when he accepted an offer for his home, but that sale failed to close for some reason. He wouldn't be able to go through with his purchase of Mayer's home (because he wouldn't have the money for the downpayment). As a result, Whitfield would be in default on the purchase and sale agreement, and he would forfeit his earnest money deposit to Mayer.

On the other hand, Mayer wants the contingency clause to be written so that the condition will be fulfilled if Whitfield accepts an offer on his current home within 45 days of signing the purchase and sale agreement with Mayer. Mayer doesn't want to wait up to 90 days to see whether Whitfield's sale is actually going to close. He wants to know that they have an enforceable contract much sooner than that. Otherwise, he would rather wait for another offer.

Many contingency forms try to address both of these conflicting needs. For instance, the form shown in Figure 8.4 states that the contingency will be fulfilled when the buyer accepts an offer on his house. However, if the sale of the buyer's house fails to close through no fault of the buyer, the purchase and sale agreement terminates and the earnest money deposit will be refunded to the buyer.

Another way the buyer can handle the problem of purchase funds being tied up in her current home is by applying to a lender for a **swing loan**, also called a bridge loan or gap loan. This loan provides the buyer with the funds to close the purchase of the new home, secured by the equity in the buyer's old home. The lender has a lien against the old home until the swing loan is paid off. The buyer will pay it off out of the proceeds when the sale of the old home eventually closes.

DEADLINES. The conflicting interests of the buyer and the seller are also apparent when you fill in the time periods in this type of contingency clause or addendum. The buyer generally wants as much time as possible to fulfill the contingency, so that her house can be sold for the highest possible price. The seller, on the other hand, usually wants the present transaction to close as soon as possible so that he'll have the money from the sale more quickly. So the parties must agree on a compromise that will give the buyer a reasonable length of time to market her house without delaying the resolution of the present transaction (either a successful closing or the failure of the contingency) for too long.

It's extremely important to make sure that the dates in the contingency clause agree with the other dates in the purchase and sale agreement. For example, the contingency should not give the buyer 90 days to sell her home if the current sale is supposed to close within 45 days.

BUMP CLAUSES. When a purchase and sale agreement is contingent on the sale of the buyer's home, it's common to include a provision that gives the seller the right to keep the house on the market and to accept another offer. This provision, known as a "bump clause," may be used with any type of contingency, but is most commonly used with offers that are contingent on the sale of the buyer's home. That's because this contingency tends to involve greater uncertainty and a longer wait than other types of contingencies. While you can usually predict whether a buyer will be able to get a loan or whether a pest inspection will be satisfactory, it's harder to predict whether a buyer will be able to sell his home by a certain date on terms that will generate a certain amount of cash.

A bump clause helps reconcile the buyer's need for time to sell his current home with the seller's need for a timely resolution of her contingent contract with the buyer. It allows the seller to accept an uncertain offer without having to take her property off the market.

The sale of buyer's home contingency addendum in Figure 8.4 includes a bump clause. This bump clause states that the seller will continue to actively market her property until the buyer notifies the seller that the contingency has been satisfied or waived. If the seller receives a second offer during this period, the seller will notify the buyer of her intention to accept the second offer. The

FIG. 8.5   SECOND BUYER'S ADDENDUM

Form 39
Second Buyer's Addendum
Rev. 7/15
Page 1 of 1

©Copyright 2015
Northwest Multiple Listing Service
ALL RIGHTS RESERVED

SECOND BUYER'S ADDENDUM

The following Addendum is part of the Purchase and Sale Agreement dated _____ 1

(the "Second Sale Agreement") between _____ ("Seller") 2
Seller   Seller

and _____ ("Second Buyer") 3
2ⁿᵈ Buyer   2ⁿᵈ Buyer

concerning _____ (the "Property"). 4
Address   City   State Zip

1. **Property Subject to Prior Contingent Sale.** Second Buyer acknowledges that the Property is subject to a 5
prior purchase and sale agreement (the "Prior Sale") between Seller and _____ 6
("First Buyer"). The Prior Sale is contingent on First Buyer entering into an agreement for the sale of First 7
Buyer's property ("Buyer's Property") on or before _____. The Prior Sale provides if Seller accepts another 8
offer to sell the Property, then notice of Seller's acceptance of a second offer shall be given to First Buyer (the 9
"Bump Notice"). If, after receipt of the Bump Notice, First Buyer does not give timely notice that (i) First Buyer 10
has sold Buyer's Property; or (ii) that First Buyer waives the Buyer's Sale of Property Contingency, then the Prior 11
Sale will terminate, and this Second Sale Agreement shall proceed to Closing. Seller shall not amend the terms 12
of the Prior Sale after mutual acceptance and prior to termination of this Second Sale Agreement. 13

2. **Second Buyer's Waiver of Contingencies.** The Bump Notice will not be given to First Buyer until Seller has 14
received notice of Second Buyer's waiver or satisfaction of the contingencies selected below. 15
   ❑ a. Second Buyer's approval of a "Seller Disclosure Statement" (Form 17). 16
   ❑ b. Second Buyer's approval of an inspection of the Property and the improvements on the Property, including 17
       but not limited to structural, roof, pest, soils/stability, and septic inspections, e.g., Inspection Addendum 18
       (Form 35) and Septic Addendum (Form 22S). 19
   ❑ c. Second Buyer's approval of a review of the Property to determine if the Property can be used in a manner 20
       consistent with Second Buyer's intended use, e.g., Feasibility Contingency Addendum (Form 35F). 21
   ❑ d. Second Buyer's approval of a Condominium Resale Certificate (Form 27). 22
   ❑ e. Second Buyer's Financing Addendum (Form 22A). 23
   ❑ f. Second Buyer's approval of _____ . 24

3. **Bump Notice.** Within _____ days (1 day if not filled in) of Second Buyer's notice that all contingencies 25
selected in Paragraph 2 of this Addendum have been satisfied or waived, a Bump Notice shall be given to First 26
Buyer. Seller shall inform Second Buyer of the results of First Buyer's response to the Bump Notice. If Second 27
Buyer terminates this Second Sale Agreement, without legal cause, after the Bump Notice is given to First Buyer, 28
then Second Buyer shall be in default. 29

4. **First Buyer's Contingency Satisfied or Waived.** If First Buyer responds to the Bump Notice and satisfies or 30
waives First Buyer's Sale of Property Contingency, then Seller shall provide Second Buyer with notice of the 31
same within 1 day and this Second Sale Agreement shall terminate and the Earnest Money shall be refunded to 32
Second Buyer. Seller's notice may be given on the Contingency Property Notice (Form 90K) or similar form. 33

5. **First Buyer's Contingency Not Satisfied or Waived.** If First Buyer responds to the Bump Notice by terminating 34
the Prior Sale, then Seller shall provide Second Buyer with notice of the same within 1 day ("Seller's Notice – 35
First Buyer Terminated Prior Sale") and this Second Sale Agreement shall proceed to Closing. Seller's notice 36
may be given on the Contingency Property Notice (Form 90K) or similar form. 37

6. **Computation of Time.** For the purposes of computing time (except for the timelines in this Addendum and the 38
deposit of earnest money), all timelines shall begin on Seller's Notice – First Buyer Terminated Prior Sale. 39

7. **This Addendum Controls.** All other terms and conditions of the Second Sale Agreement remain in full force and 40
effect. In the event of conflict between the terms of this Addendum and any other term of this Second Sale 41
Agreement, this Addendum shall control. 42

Buyer's Initials Date	Buyer's Initials Date	Seller's Initials Date	Seller's Initials Date

FIG. 8.6 BUMP NOTICE (FROM SELLER TO FIRST BUYER)

BUMP NOTICE
(Notice that Seller has accepted another offer)

The following is part of the Purchase and Sale Agreement dated _____ 1

between _____ ("Buyer") 2
          Buyer   Buyer

and _____("Seller") 3
      Seller   Seller

concerning _____ (the "Property"). 4
          Address   City   State   Zip

Seller gives notice that Seller has accepted another offer to purchase the Property as permitted by the Buyer's Sale of 5
Property Contingency Addendum (Form 22B). 6

Unless Buyer gives notice before expiration of the Bump Period that Buyer has satisfied or waived the contingency, 7
the Agreement shall terminate and the Earnest Money shall be refunded to Buyer. Buyer should use the Bump 8
Response (Form 46) to respond to this notice. 9

_____   _____ 10
Seller   Date   Seller   Date

FIG. 8.7   BUMP REPLY (FROM FIRST BUYER TO SELLER)

BUMP RESPONSE

The following is part of the Purchase and Sale Agreement dated _____ 1

between _____ ("Buyer") 2
         Buyer   Buyer

and _____ ("Seller") 3
     Seller   Seller

concerning _____ (the "Property"). 4
            Address   City   State   Zip

Bump Response. In response to notice that Seller has accepted another offer to purchase the Property (the "Bump 5
Notice"), Buyer gives notice as follows: 6

❑ **Buyer's Property Sold – Contingency Satisfied.** Buyer has accepted an offer to sell Buyer's Property that 7
is not contingent on the sale or closing of another property and that will close no less than 30 days and no 8
more than 45 days from the date Buyer accepted the offer (or as otherwise consented to by Seller). 9

For this notice to be effective, Buyer shall attach a copy of the complete purchase and sale agreement for the 10
sale of Buyer's Property. If the sale of Buyer's Property fails to close, Buyer will give notice to Seller within two 11
days, as required by the Buyer's Sale of Property Contingency Addendum (Form 22B). 12

❑ **Buyer's Property Not Sold – Contingency Waived.** Buyer has not accepted an offer to sell Buyer's 13
Property; however, Buyer waives the contingency in Buyer's Sale of Property Contingency Addendum (Form 14
22B). Buyer understands that by waiving this contingency, Buyer waives all other contingencies in the 15
Agreement (including inspection, financing, etc.). 16

❑ **Buyer's Property Not Sold – Agreement Terminated.** Buyer has not accepted an offer to sell Buyer's 17
Property. The Agreement is terminated and the Earnest Money shall be refunded to Buyer. 18

_____   _____ 19
Buyer   Date   Buyer   Date

buyer is given a short period of time—the default period is five days in the form shown—to notify the seller that the contingency has been either satisfied or waived. Otherwise, the transaction will terminate and the deposit will be returned to the buyer.

SECOND BUYER'S ADDENDUM. Before the seller sends the first buyer a bump notice, the seller may require the second buyer to waive any contingencies the second sales agreement is subject to. This will protect the seller against bumping one contingent buyer in order to enter into a contract with another contingent buyer and ultimately losing both buyers. A form such as the one shown in Figure 8.5 can be used for this purpose. This second buyer's addendum states that the property is subject to a first sales agreement that is contingent on the buyer selling his current home. It goes on to say that before the seller sends the first buyer a bump notice, the second buyer must waive all the contingencies checked off on the form.

After the seller receives the second buyer's waiver, the seller will send the first buyer the bump notice and then notify the second buyer of the first buyer's response. If the first buyer fulfills or waives the contingency, the second sales agreement terminates and the seller will return the second buyer's earnest money. On the other hand, if the first buyer does not fulfill or waive the contingency, the first sale will terminate and the second sale will proceed.

BUMP NOTICE. An example of a bump notice—the seller's notice to the first buyer about the second offer—is shown in Figure 8.6. This notice states that the seller has accepted another offer as a backup, and gives the first buyer a certain amount of time to satisfy or waive the contingency. The notice also states that if the first buyer fails to remove the contingency, her purchase and sale agreement will terminate.

Upon receiving the seller's bump notice, the first buyer must decide fairly quickly whether to waive the contingency or terminate the agreement. (It's unlikely that the buyer will be able to satisfy the contingency in such a short time.) If the buyer decides to terminate the agreement, he is entitled to a refund of the earnest money. If the buyer decides to waive the contingency, he must proceed with the transaction whether or not his home sells.

BUMP REPLY. Once the first buyer makes his decision, he then gives the seller notice of what he intends to do. This is sometimes called a bump reply. A form such as the one shown in Figure 8.7 may be used for this purpose.

RESCISSION

When a purchase and sale agreement is terminated because a contingency was neither satisfied nor waived, the seller usually wants to put the property back on the market. In some cases, the seller has already entered into a backup agreement that is conditioned on the termination of the first agreement. But uncertainties about the rights and obligations of the buyer and seller under the first agreement may cause problems for a subsequent sale. Thus, a second sale should not proceed until the first agreement has been officially terminated and it is clearly established that the first buyer has no right to enforce that earlier agreement. This is done by having the first buyer and the seller sign a rescission agreement.

As explained in Chapter 6, a rescission agreement formally terminates a purchase and sale agreement. It should authorize the designated broker or other party who is keeping the earnest money in trust to disburse it to the appropriate party. If a dispute arises over the earnest money, the law requires the designated broker holding the deposit to give all parties notice of her intent to disburse the deposit, and then distribute the funds within 30 days of that notice. An example of a rescission agreement is shown in Chapter 6 (Figure 6.5). A safety clause in the form requires a commission to be paid if the buyer and seller enter into another purchase and sale agreement within six months after signing the rescission agreement.

CHAPTER SUMMARY

1. Most purchase and sale agreements are contingent on the occurrence of a specified event (or events). Unless the event occurs, the party benefiting from the contingency (usually the buyer) is not obligated to follow through with the transaction. The party benefiting from the contingency has an obligation to make a good faith effort to fulfill it.

2. A contingency provision should include a statement of what the condition is and what has to occur to fulfill it, the procedure for notifying the other party of satisfaction or waiver of the condition, the time limit for fulfilling or waiving the condition, and what happens if the condition is not fulfilled or waived.

3. The three most common types of contingencies in residential purchase and sale agreements are financing contingencies, inspection contingencies, and sale of the buyer's home contingencies.

4. A financing contingency gives the buyer the right to be released from the agreement without forfeiting her deposit if she can't get the financing she needs. Sometimes, a financing contingency will specify in detail the terms of the loan the buyer will apply for.

5. An inspection contingency conditions the sale on a satisfactory structural, pest, soil, geological, or hazardous substances inspection. The inspection contingency should state who is responsible for ordering and paying for the inspection, when and how the buyer will notify the seller of disapproval of the report, whether the seller has the option to perform any necessary repairs, and the time limit for reinspection if the seller makes repairs.

6. An offer may be conditioned on the sale of the buyer's current home. The contingency provision should state whether the condition will be fulfilled by the acceptance of an offer or when the sale of the buyer's home closes; the deadline for fulfillment or waiver of the contingency; the notification requirements; what happens if the contingency is not met or waived; and what happens if the seller gets another offer during the contingency period.

7. A bump clause allows the seller to continue actively marketing her property during the contingency period. If the seller intends to accept another offer, the seller notifies the first buyer and gives the first buyer a short time to either meet or waive the contingency, or the first contract will terminate.

8. If a contingent transaction fails, the buyer and the seller should sign a rescission agreement. A rescission agreement formally terminates the purchase and sale agreement, authorizes the disbursement of the earnest money deposit, and may provide for a commission to be paid if the buyer and seller enter into another sales agreement within a specified period. Once a rescission agreement has been signed by the first buyer and the seller, the seller can safely enter into a purchase and sale agreement with another buyer.

CHAPTER QUIZ

1. If a contingency clause benefits both parties to a contract, it:
    a. can only be waived with the consent of both parties
    b. cannot be waived by either party
    c. can be waived by either party
    d. can be waived by the buyer, but not by the seller

2. All of the following are typically found in contingency provisions except:
    a. a procedure for notifying the other party that the condition has been waived or satisfied
    b. a deadline for waiving or satisfying the condition
    c. statutorily required language advising the parties to seek legal advice
    d. the rights of the parties if a condition isn't waived or satisfied

3. Which of the following is usually not included in a financing contingency provision?
    a. The parties' options in case of a low appraisal
    b. The amount of the buyer's downpayment
    c. The terms of the seller financing arrangement
    d. A clause making the sale dependent on the buyer's ability to get homeowner's insurance

4. If an inspection reveals building code violations, which of the following is true?
    a. The buyer's lender may require the seller to correct the violations as a condition of loan approval
    b. The buyer may require the seller to correct the violations before proceeding with the contract
    c. Public authorities may order the seller to correct the violations whether or not the transaction closes
    d. All of the above

5. The purchase and sale agreement required the seller to order a pest inspection. The inspector found an infestation, and remedial action was required. Which party was responsible for paying to fix the problem?
    a. Only the buyer
    b. The brokerage
    c. The buyer and seller were required to split the cost
    d. Whichever party agreed to pay for the expense in the purchase and sale agreement

6. After an inspection, the buyer requests that the seller make certain repairs. Which of the following is not one of the ways in which the seller can respond?

    a. Waiving the inspection contingency
    b. Refusing to make the requested repairs
    c. Offering to modify the contract
    d. Offering to make only some of the requested repairs

7. A sale of buyer's home contingency usually states:

    a. a price at which the buyer will be required to accept an offer on his current home
    b. that the seller may continue to market her property until the contingency is waived or fulfilled
    c. that all contingencies must be waived on any offer on the buyer's current home
    d. a deadline for applying for a swing loan

8. With a sale of buyer's home contingency, the common approaches to resolving the conflicting needs of the buyer and seller do not include:

    a. having the buyer get the funds to close the purchase of the seller's home with a swing loan
    b. making the contract contingent on the buyer's acceptance of an offer, but allowing the buyer to terminate if the sale of the buyer's home fails to close
    c. a bump clause
    d. a rescission agreement

9. The purpose of a second buyer's addendum is to:

    a. inform a second buyer that the seller's property is already subject to a contingent purchase and sale agreement
    b. notify the contingent buyer of the seller's intention to accept another offer
    c. create a contingency for secondary financing
    d. notify the seller that the sale of buyer's home contingency has been satisfied

10. A rescission agreement commonly contains a safety or extender clause for the protection of the:

    a. first buyer
    b. second buyer
    c. real estate agent
    d. seller

ANSWER KEY

1. a. When a contingency clause benefits both parties to a contract, the condition can only be waived with the consent of both parties. If the condition isn't satisfied, either party can terminate the contract.

2. c. Generally, contingency provisions don't require language advising the parties to seek counsel, although obtaining legal advice is often a good idea.

3. c. If the seller is going to provide financing for the buyer, the terms should be set forth in another addendum, and the financing forms that will be used must be attached. (Seller financing is not ordinarily treated as a contingency.)

4. d. If an inspection reveals violations of the building code or other laws, public authorities could order the seller to correct the violations, regardless of whether the sale to the buyer proceeds.

5. d. If a purchase and sale agreement is contingent on the results of an inspection, the parties also should specify in the contract how repairs will be handled.

6. a. The inspection contingency is for the benefit of the buyer, so only the buyer has the ability to waive it.

7. b. A typical sale of buyer's home contingency usually includes a bump clause, which allows the seller to keep her property on the market and consider other offers.

8. d. A rescission agreement terminates a purchase and sale agreement, so it would only be used if the contingency is not fulfilled.

9. a. A seller uses a second buyer's addendum to inform the second buyer that the property is subject to a prior contingent purchase agreement. It requires the second buyer to waive certain contingencies before the seller will send the first buyer a bump notice.

10. c. A rescission agreement may include an extender clause (safety clause), which obligates the seller to pay the commission if the seller sells the property to the same buyer within a certain period of time.

INTRODUCTION

While financing the sale is the buyer's responsibility, and judging the creditworthiness of the buyer is the lender's responsibility, it's still important for you to understand the loan approval process in case your buyers have questions. This chapter explains loan preapproval, then describes the underwriting process lenders use to evaluate the creditworthiness of mortgage loan applicants. It also discusses how loan applicants can compare different loans.

PREAPPROVAL

Most buyers apply for a loan and get preapproved before they start house-hunting in earnest. In a **preapproval**, the lender carefully evaluates the buyer's financial situation, then decides on a maximum loan amount—how much the lender is willing to loan this buyer for a home purchase. Armed with this information, the buyer can shop for houses with a very clear idea of what price range he can afford. (Note that buyers can get a rough idea of their maximum loan amount without actually applying for preapproval by using one of the "prequalification" calculators found on many mortgage lender websites.)

Preapproval is especially important in an active market, when sellers rarely even consider offers from buyers who aren't preapproved. Even in a slower market, an offer may not get serious consideration unless the buyer has been preapproved. Buyer's agents typically urge their clients to get preapproved no matter what the market is like; few agents want to spend time showing clients properties they can't afford.

THE PREAPPROVAL PROCESS

To get preapproved, buyers must complete a loan application and provide the required supporting documentation, just as if they were applying for a loan after finding a house. Much of this can be accomplished online.

The lender evaluates an application for preapproval in the same way as an ordinary loan application, with this exception: there's no property appraisal or title report at this point, since the buyers have not yet chosen a home to buy. If the buyers are creditworthy, the lender uses their income and net worth information to set a maximum loan amount. The lender gives the buyers a **preapproval letter**, agreeing to loan them up to the specified amount when they find the home they want to buy, as long as the property and the property title meet the lender's standards. The preapproval letter will expire at the end of a specified period—for example, after 60 or 90 days. If the buyers haven't found the house they want by then, the lender may agree to an extension.

ADVANTAGES OF PREAPPROVAL

A preapproval letter can be an extremely useful tool in negotiating with a seller. It gives the seller confidence that if he accepts the buyers' offer, the financing contingency isn't likely to be a problem; absent something unforeseen, the buyer will be able to buy.

However, there is one thing for the buyer to consider: the lender's letter will ordinarily state the maximum amount that the buyer is preapproved for. This is fine if the buyer is looking for a home near the upper limit of her price range, but it can be a drawback if she is making an offer on a home that's well within the limit.

> **EXAMPLE:** The buyer has a preapproval letter that says she's financially qualified to purchase property worth up to $485,000. But the buyer is interested in a home that's listed for only $452,000, and she wants to make a starting offer of $440,000. The seller will be able to tell from the buyer's preapproval letter that the buyer could easily afford to pay the full listing price for his home. That's likely to make the seller less inclined to accept a lower offer than he might otherwise be.
>
> There is a way around this problem. To make an offer on this property, the buyer could ask her lender for a special version of the preapproval letter indicating that the buyer is preapproved to purchase a $455,000 home. This would assure the seller that the buyer is financially qualified to buy his home, without revealing the buyer's full purchasing power.

Preapproval also helps simplify the closing process. The lender has already evaluated the buyers, and while there will be a recheck before closing to make sure the buyer's finances haven't changed for the worse, much of the paperwork has been taken care of, making this step go smoothly.

THE UNDERWRITING PROCESS

Before you can discuss financing options with your buyers, you need to understand the criteria a lender uses to qualify a buyer for a loan. These criteria are referred to as **qualifying standards** or **loan underwriting standards**.

Loan underwriting is the process a lender goes through to evaluate the buyer and the property to determine whether the proposed loan would be a good risk. The lender has employees called loan underwriters (or credit underwriters) who carry out the underwriting process and decide whether to accept or reject the loan application.

Every loan carries some risk of default. To evaluate this risk, the underwriter asks two questions during the underwriting process:

1. Can the borrower be expected to make the monthly loan payments on time, based on her overall financial situation?
2. If the borrower defaults, will the security property generate enough money in a foreclosure sale to pay off the loan balance?

To help answer these two questions, the underwriter applies underwriting standards to both the prospective borrower (the buyer) and the property. The underwriter's evaluation of the property is based on an appraisal. The appraisal process is similar to that used by an agent in preparing a CMA for pricing a property (discussed in Chapter 4), but it is more rigorous. In this chapter, we will focus on the standards that are applied to the borrower.

Although lenders may establish their own qualifying standards, the standards set by Fannie Mae and Freddie Mac, the government-sponsored entities that participate in the secondary market, are very influential. Lenders want to be able to sell their loans on the secondary market, and conventional loans that don't meet the standards set by Fannie Mae and Freddie Mac (referred to as **nonconforming** loans) are more difficult to sell. Also, lenders who want to make loans through a particular loan program must comply with the program's qualifying standards. For example, a loan will be eligible for FHA insurance or a VA guaranty only if it meets FHA or VA standards.

While qualifying standards vary, the underwriting process is basically the same no matter what type of loan the buyer has applied for. This section focuses on the basic underwriting process. The specific qualifying standards for the major loan programs are discussed in the next chapter.

Lenders handle most aspects of the underwriting process by computer. This is known as **automated underwriting**. The software analyzes the loan application and credit report and makes a recommendation for or against approval. However, the analysis of a loan application can't be entirely automated. As a general rule, the ultimate decision whether or not to approve the loan is still made by people.

The information in the loan application and the credit report can be broken down into three basic categories:

1. income,
2. net worth, and
3. credit reputation.

INCOME ANALYSIS

Underwriting requires analyzing a loan applicant's income to see if the applicant earns or receives enough money to reliably make the monthly mortgage payment for the requested loan. To decide how large a mortgage payment a loan applicant can afford, the lender only considers the applicant's **stable monthly income**: income that has been earned for at least two years and which is expected to continue for at least another three years.

ACCEPTABLE TYPES OF INCOME. Let's look at the various types of income that may qualify as stable monthly income.

PERMANENT EMPLOYMENT INCOME. Usually, a loan applicant needs to have been continuously employed for at least two years for her employment income to be considered stable. However, under some extenuating circumstances, income may count as stable even without a two-year work history (for example, if the applicant has recently finished college, completed job training, or left the armed services). A loan applicant with an inadequate employment history should include a brief explanation of any extenuating circumstances in her loan application.

VARIABLE EMPLOYMENT INCOME. Bonuses, commissions, and part-time earnings may qualify as stable income if the loan applicant has earned this income for at least one—but preferably two—years. Lenders won't count overtime as stable income unless it's clearly a regular part of the applicant's earnings.

> **EXAMPLE:** Schwinn's salary is $4,500 a month. Over the last three months, she worked many hours of overtime. She averaged an additional $1,000 a month in overtime during those three months. A lender will not count that additional $1,000 a month as stable income, because Schwinn only earned it for three months.
>
> However, if Schwinn could show that she earned an average of $1,000 a month in overtime over the previous 14 months, the lender might count that income. Or if Schwinn could show that she earned an average of $3,000 a year in seasonal overtime from September to November every year for the

past three years, and that this pattern is likely to continue, the lender would probably count the overtime.

SELF-EMPLOYMENT INCOME. Generally, a self-employed loan applicant must have been in business for at least two years in order for his business income to be used to qualify for a loan. However, the lender may count the income of a self-employed loan applicant who has been in business for less time if there are offsetting positive factors, such as a history of employment in the same field or a convincing, comprehensive business plan.

SECONDARY INCOME SOURCES. There are other acceptable income sources besides employment income. For example, **pension** and **social security** payments are also considered part of a loan applicant's stable monthly income.

Alimony or **spousal maintenance** payments are only considered stable income if the payments are reliable. So the underwriter will look to see whether the payments are required by a court decree, how long the loan applicant has been receiving the payments, the financial status of the ex-spouse, and the applicant's ability to compel payment.

Child support payments are accepted as stable income under the same conditions: if they are required by a court decree and there is proof of regular payment. If payments are missed, or regularly late, the underwriter may decide to exclude the child support from the loan applicant's stable income. Also, child support payments typically stop when the child turns 18. Since stable income is income that will last for at least three years, the lender is unlikely to include child support for a child who is older than 15.

> **EXAMPLE:** Martinez gets court-ordered child support for her daughter, who is 16, and for her son, who is 13. Martinez has received the child support regularly for three years. The lender will probably consider only the child support for her son as part of her stable monthly income. The child support for the daughter will last only another two years, so it won't be counted.

Income from **public assistance** programs may also be acceptable income. The Equal Credit Opportunity Act prohibits lenders from discriminating against loan applicants on the basis that all or part of their income is from a public assistance program, such as welfare or food stamps. Public assistance payments are considered stable income only if they are expected to continue for a sufficiently long time (at least the first few years of the loan term). If the loan applicant's eligibility for the program will terminate shortly, the lender is unlikely to treat the income as part of the loan applicant's stable income.

EXAMPLE: A loan applicant receives monthly income from a public assistance program. Although the lender generally treats public assistance payments as stable monthly income, the loan applicant's eligibility for this particular program will run out in just about a year. The payments won't last long enough to be counted in calculating the applicant's stable monthly income.

Dividends or **interest** from investments are also part of stable monthly income, unless the loan applicant needs to cash in the investment to have enough funds for a downpayment or to pay for closing costs.

Net income from **rental property** can count as stable income. This may be property the loan applicant already owns or the property being purchased. When possible, the lender uses detailed information about the property's income and expenses to determine a monthly net income figure. In other cases, the lender might use a certain percentage (for example, 75%) of the gross rent as a rough estimate of the net income.

EXAMPLE: Your buyer is purchasing a duplex. She is planning to occupy one unit; the other is currently leased for $2,000 per month. To allow for maintenance expenses and possible vacancies or rent collection losses, the lender will count only 75% of the gross rent, or $1,500, as stable monthly income.

UNACCEPTABLE TYPES OF INCOME. Some types of income don't qualify as stable monthly income. As mentioned earlier, **unemployment benefits** last only for a limited period of time, so they are virtually never considered stable income.

Also, lenders are generally not interested in the **earnings of family members** other than the loan applicants themselves. For instance, if a married couple is applying for a loan, the lender will take into account the income of both spouses. However, income that the couple's teenage children earn will not be considered, because the children won't necessarily be sharing their parents' home for much longer.

Income from full- or part-time **temporary work** generally isn't considered stable monthly income because of its short-term nature. However, income from temporary work may be accepted if the loan applicant has supported herself through a particular type of temporary work for years. The income from temporary work is then considered self-employment income.

EXAMPLE: Ingraham works in the computer industry as a temporary employee. She goes from job to job, helping to set up databases. Each job is temporary. However, Ingraham has supported herself for four years with this kind of temporary work. At this point, a lender might regard these temporary jobs as a form of self-employment and consider Ingraham's earnings to be stable monthly income.

VERIFYING INCOME. Lenders verify the income information given to them by loan applicants. A lender may send an income verification form (containing a release signed by the applicant) directly to the applicant's employer. The employer fills out the form and sends it directly back to the lender.

Alternatively, the lender may ask the loan applicant for W-2 forms for the previous two years, and payroll stubs or vouchers for the previous 30-day period. The lender then confirms the employment and income information with a phone call to the employer.

In addition to verifying the applicant's regular wages or salary, the lender also needs to verify any other types of income included in the applicant's stable monthly income. For example, if the applicant is relying on commission income, the lender will require copies of the applicant's federal income tax returns for the previous two years.

A self-employed loan applicant is usually required to give the lender audited financial statements and federal income tax returns for the two years prior to the loan application.

For alimony or child support income, the lender will require a copy of the court decree and proof that the payments are received. A bank statement showing that the checks have been deposited into the applicant's account may be good enough, or the lender might require copies of the deposited checks.

To verify rental income, the loan applicant usually has to submit copies of recent income tax returns. The lender may also require additional documentation, such as copies of leases.

CALCULATING MONTHLY INCOME. The lender wants to know the amount of the loan applicant's income in monthly terms. If a buyer works full-time (40 hours per week) for an hourly wage, monthly income is calculated by multiplying the hourly wage by 173.33.

EXAMPLE: The buyer makes $17.50 an hour. To calculate her monthly earnings, multiply $17.50 by 173.33. $17.50 × 173.33 = $3,033.28. She earns $3,033 per month.

If a buyer gets paid twice a month, simply multiply the amount of the pay-check by two.

> **EXAMPLE:** The buyer gets paid $2,700 twice a month. $2,700 × 2 = $5,400. His monthly income is $5,400.

It's a little more complicated if the buyer gets paid every two weeks. First, you must multiply the payment by 26 to get the annual income figure, and then you must divide that figure by 12 to get the monthly income figure.

> **EXAMPLE:** The buyer gets paid $2,700 every two weeks. $2,700 × 26 = $70,200. His annual income is $70,200. Now divide $70,200 by 12. $70,200 ÷ 12 = $5,850. His monthly income is $5,850.

CO-BORROWERS AND COSIGNERS. When two people apply for a loan together, they may be referred to as **co-borrowers**, or as borrower and co-borrower. The underwriter takes into account the income and assets of both applicants, along with their debts and credit reputations. If the loan is approved, both borrowers become fully liable for repaying the lender.

Most co-borrowers are couples who occupy the property together. In some cases, though, one of the borrowers occupies the property and the co-borrower (usually a parent or other family member) is a non-occupant. The non-occupant co-borrower may or may not also be a co-owner of the property.

A co-borrower who won't have an ownership interest in the property is called a **cosigner**. A cosigner signs the promissory note but not the mortgage, since she doesn't have an ownership interest. A cosigner with a good income and credit score can help a marginal borrower obtain a loan. Conversely, a cosigner with poor numbers can do more harm than good to an application.

USING INCOME RATIOS. After determining the amount of stable monthly income, it's necessary to decide whether that income is enough to cover the expenses the homeowner is likely to face.

The lender usually uses two percentages, called **income ratios** or qualifying ratios, to measure the buyer's income. If a loan applicant's regular expenses exceed a certain percentage of his income, the risk of default is considered unacceptably high. The lender wants some assurance that the applicant can make the mortgage payment and still have enough income left over for other expenses, such as food, clothing, medical bills, car payments, and other necessities.

There are two income ratios:

1. a debt to income ratio, and
2. a housing expense to income ratio.

A debt to income ratio measures the monthly mortgage payment plus any other regular debt payments against the pre-tax monthly income. A housing expense to income ratio measures only the monthly mortgage payment against the monthly income. For the purposes of income ratios, the monthly mortgage payment includes principal, interest, property taxes, and hazard insurance, plus mortgage insurance and homeowners association dues, if any. This is often called the **PITI** payment, which stands for principal, interest, taxes, and insurance. (If homeowners association dues are included, it may be called the PITIA payment.)

Each ratio is expressed as a percentage. For instance, a loan applicant's housing expense to income ratio would be 29% if her proposed mortgage payment represented 29% of her monthly income.

Each loan program has its own income ratio requirements. For example, the maximum acceptable debt to income ratio might be 36% or 41%, depending on the program. We'll discuss the income ratio limits used for various loan programs in the next chapter. For now, just to show you how income ratios work, we'll use the general rule that the monthly mortgage payment should not exceed 28% of the loan applicant's income.

EXAMPLE: Robinson's annual salary is $62,000. During the last four months, she made an extra $300 per month in overtime. For the past three years, she has received an annual bonus of $2,600. And two years ago she inherited a rental house that rents for $2,100 a month.

First decide which portions of Robinson's employment income a lender is likely to count. Her salary is stable monthly income, but you should exclude the overtime, because it hasn't been a regular part of her earnings history. You can include her annual bonus, because she's received a bonus for at least two years in a row. So add $2,600 to her annual salary of $62,000.

$$\$62,000 + \$2,600 = \$64,600$$

To calculate Robinson's stable monthly income from employment, divide this annual figure by 12 to arrive at a monthly figure.

$$\$64,600 \div 12 = \$5,383$$

Now take 75% of her regular rental income (to allow for maintenance expenses and vacancy or rent collection losses) and add that to her monthly employment income.

$$\$2,100 \times .75 = \$1,575$$
$$\$1,575 + \$5,383 = \$6,958$$

Robinson's stable monthly income totals $6,958. To get a rough idea of the maximum loan payment she would qualify for, multiply her stable monthly income by 28%.

$$\$6,958 \times .28 = \$1,948$$

Robinson could probably qualify for a monthly housing payment of $1,948. About 15% of that ($292) would go to taxes and insurance; the rest ($1,656) is her maximum principal and interest payment.

NET WORTH

Along with income, a lender also analyzes the buyer's net worth. Net worth is the buyer's "bottom line"—the value of his financial holdings less his liabilities.

EXAMPLE: Brown owns a house, a car, and some furniture, and he has $2,900 in savings. The total value of these assets is $277,000. Brown owes $5,000 on the car and $243,000 on the house; he owns the furniture free and clear.

To calculate Brown's net worth, subtract the money he owes (his liabilities) from the value of his assets. $277,000 − $248,000 = $29,000. Brown's net worth is $29,000.

Net worth is important for a number of reasons. First, if a loan applicant has accumulated a significant amount of net worth, that's a sign that she is a good credit risk. A healthy net worth is especially important if the loan application is weak in another area. For instance, if a loan applicant's income is marginal, an above-average net worth can mean the difference between loan approval and rejection.

Significant net worth—particularly cash—also tells the lender that the loan applicant has sufficient funds to complete the purchase. The applicant needs enough cash to cover the downpayment, the closing costs, and any other expenses involved in buying the property.

Also, a certain amount of net worth over and above the amount needed to close is usually necessary—that's because many lenders require a loan applicant to have **reserves** left over after making the downpayment and paying the closing costs. Typically, the reserves must be enough to cover two or three months' worth of mortgage payments. Reserves give the lender confidence that the applicant could handle a temporary financial emergency without defaulting on the loan.

TYPES OF ASSETS. A buyer should list all of his assets on the loan application. An asset is anything of value, including real estate, cars, furniture, jewelry, stocks, bonds, or the cash value in a life insurance policy.

LIQUID ASSETS. Liquid assets are generally more important to an underwriter than non-liquid assets. Liquid assets include cash and any other assets that can be quickly converted to cash. For example, stocks (which can easily be sold) are preferred over real estate. And cash in the bank is best of all.

REAL ESTATE. When a buyer is selling one home in order to buy another (usually more expensive) home, she can use her **net equity** in the home she is selling as a liquid asset. Net equity is the market value of the property minus the sum of the liens against the property and the selling expenses. In other words, net equity is the money the buyer expects to receive from the sale of her current home.

To estimate the amount of equity the buyer can apply toward the new purchase, take the appraised value of the current home (or the sales price, if a sale is already pending), subtract any outstanding mortgages or other liens, and then subtract the estimated selling costs (which are commonly between 10% and 13% of the sales price).

EXAMPLE: The buyer's current home is worth $350,000. There's a mortgage with a $294,000 balance to be paid off when the home is sold. To calculate the buyer's gross equity, subtract the mortgage balance from the market value.

$$\$350,000 - \$294,000 = \$56,000$$

The gross equity is $56,000. From the gross equity, deduct the estimated selling expenses, which are $38,500.

$$\$56,000 - \$38,500 = \$17,500$$

Your buyer will have approximately $17,500 in net equity to apply to the purchase of a new home.

Sometimes equity in other property is the primary source of the cash that the buyer will use to purchase the new property. In this situation, the lender will probably require proof that the property has been sold and that the buyer has received the sale proceeds before it will make the new loan.

A buyer may also own real estate that she is not planning to sell. The property may be a rental house, a small apartment building, or vacant land. In any case, the property must be included in the loan application. Again, it is the equity in this other real estate that is important, not just the appraised value. If the buyer has little or no equity in the property, the lender may view it as a liability rather than an asset.

VERIFYING ASSETS. The lender has to verify the existence of the assets listed on the loan application. For example, the lender must verify that the loan applicant has the money in his bank account that he claims to have. The lender can send a "Request for Verification of Deposit" to the bank (along with a release signed by the loan applicant), to be returned directly to the lender. Alternatively, many lenders will accept original bank statements from the applicant for the previous three months. (Account statements are also used to verify assets such as stocks or mutual funds.)

Part of the bank account verification process involves checking to see whether the account was opened recently or has a higher balance than normal. Either one strongly suggests that the loan applicant borrowed the funds for the downpayment and closing costs, something that generally isn't allowed. However, if the funds are a gift, the lender may find this acceptable. (See the discussion of gift funds, below.)

LIABILITIES. As we explained earlier, to determine net worth, the lender subtracts liabilities from assets. So after listing all his assets on the loan application, a buyer must then list all his liabilities.

Liabilities include balances owing on credit cards, charge accounts, student loans, car loans, and other installment debts. Other types of debts, such as income taxes that are currently payable, are also liabilities.

GIFT FUNDS. Sometimes a buyer has enough income to qualify for a loan, but lacks the liquid assets necessary to close the loan. (In other words, she doesn't have enough cash for the downpayment and other expenses.) In some cases, the buyer's family is willing to make up the deficit. Most lenders allow that, as long as the money supplied by the family is a gift and not a loan.

A gift of money from a relative must be confirmed with a **gift letter**. The letter should clearly state that the money is a gift to the buyer and does not have to be repaid, and it must be signed by the donor. Lenders often have their own form for gift letters and may require the donor to use their form.

The lender will have to verify the gift funds, so the donor should give them to the buyer as soon as possible.

Many loan programs have limits on the amount of gift funds that can be used in a transaction. These limits are intended to ensure that the buyer invests at least a small amount of his own money in the property he's buying.

CREDIT REPUTATION

The third part of the qualifying process is analyzing the loan applicant's credit reputation. The lender does this by obtaining a credit report from a credit reporting agency. The applicant (the buyer) normally pays the fee for the credit report(s).

A personal credit report includes information about an individual's debts and repayment history for the preceding seven years. A credit report primarily covers credit cards and loans. Other bills, such as utility bills, usually aren't listed unless they were turned over to a collection agency.

DEROGATORY CREDIT INFORMATION. If a loan applicant's credit report shows a history of slow payment or other credit problems, the loan application could be declined. Derogatory credit information includes all of the following.

- **Slow payments.** If the loan applicant is chronically late in paying bills, this will show up on the credit report. Slow payments may be a sign that the applicant is unable to pay on time, perhaps because she is already financially overextended. Or they may be a sign that she does not take debt repayment seriously.

- **Debt consolidation and refinancing.** A pattern of continually increasing liabilities and periodic "bailouts" through refinancing and debt consolidation is a red flag to a lender. It suggests that the loan applicant has a tendency to spend beyond a prudent level.

- **Collections.** After several attempts to get a debtor to pay a bill, a frustrated creditor may turn the bill over to a collection agency. Collections show up on the debtor's credit report for seven years.

- **Repossessions.** If someone purchases personal property on credit and fails to make the payments, the creditor may be able to repossess the item. Repossessions stay on the debtor's credit report for seven years.

- **Foreclosure.** A real estate foreclosure stays on the debtor's credit report for seven years. (Some alternatives to foreclosure, such as a short sale, will also appear on a credit report.)

- **Bankruptcy.** Not surprisingly, lenders look at bankruptcy—a federal court procedure that can eliminate certain types of debts—with disfavor. A bankruptcy also stays on the debtor's credit report longer than other credit problems (for ten years instead of seven).

CREDIT SCORES. Underwriters use credit scores to help evaluate a loan applicant's credit history. A credit reporting agency calculates an individual's credit score using the information that appears in his credit report and a quantitative model developed by a national credit scoring company. Credit scoring models for use by mortgage lenders, which are based on statistical analysis of large numbers of mortgages, are designed to predict the likelihood of successful repayment of (or default on) a mortgage. In general, someone with a poor credit score is much more likely to default than someone with a good credit score.

There are a variety of credit scoring models in use. The most widely used credit scores are FICO® scores. FICO® scores range from under 300 to over 800. A relatively high FICO® score (for example, over 700) is a positive sign.

HOW CREDIT SCORES ARE USED. In some cases, underwriters use credit scores to decide what level of review to apply to a loan applicant's credit history. For example, if an applicant has a very good credit score, the underwriter might perform a basic review, simply confirming that the information in the credit report is complete and accurate without investigating further. The underwriter probably won't question the applicant about any derogatory information in the report, because it's already been taken into account in calculating the credit score. On the other hand, if the applicant has a mediocre or poor credit score, the underwriter will perform a more complete review, looking into the circumstances that led to credit problems.

A loan applicant's credit score may also be a factor in determining the interest rate that will apply if the loan is approved. If the credit score is mediocre, instead of rejecting the application, the lender might approve the loan but charge a higher interest rate or additional loan fees (called loan level price adjustments) to make up for the increased risk of default.

MAINTAINING A GOOD CREDIT SCORE. Any information that appears on a person's credit report may affect his credit score, but credit activity within the last two years has the greatest impact.

Unsurprisingly, chronically late payments and collection problems will hurt someone's credit rating, but less obvious factors can also do so. For example, with a revolving credit card, maintaining a balance near the credit limit ("maxing out" the card) will have a negative impact on the cardholder's credit score, even if she always makes the minimum monthly payment on time.

Applying for too much credit can also have a negative effect. Each time a person applies for credit (a store charge card, a car loan, a home equity loan, and so on), the creditor makes a "credit inquiry" that becomes part of the applicant's credit history. Occasional inquiries are fine, but more than a few inquiries within the past year can detract from the applicant's credit score. From a lender's point of view, too many credit inquiries may indicate that the applicant is becoming overextended.

An exception applies when a number of credit inquiries are made within a short period of time. This could happen, for example, if someone were applying for a car loan or mortgage loan from various lenders, intending to compare loan offers and accept the best one. To allow for that type of situation, all of the credit inquiries within a certain period (ranging from 14 to 45 days) are treated as a single inquiry when the loan applicant's credit score is calculated.

OBTAINING CREDIT INFORMATION. It's a good idea for prospective home buyers to obtain their credit reports and find out their credit scores well before they apply for a mortgage. (Obtaining a copy of your own credit report does not count as a credit inquiry.) A credit report may contain incorrect information, and the Fair Credit Reporting Act, a federal law, requires credit reporting agencies to investigate complaints and make corrections. This process can take a month or more.

There are three major credit reporting agencies: Equifax, Experian, and TransUnion. A buyer should obtain a credit report from each of the three agencies (reports can be obtained with a single online request). Credit scores should also be requested; they aren't always automatically part of the credit report.

EXPLAINING CREDIT PROBLEMS. A negative credit report or a poor credit score won't necessarily prevent a buyer from getting a loan at a reasonable interest rate. Credit problems can often be explained. If the lender is convinced that the past problems don't reflect the buyer's overall attitude toward credit and that the circumstances leading to the problems were temporary and are unlikely to recur, the loan application may well be approved. By obtaining her credit report before

FIG. 9.1   QUALIFYING A BUYER FOR A MORTGAGE LOAN

INCOME ANALYSIS

- STABLE MONTHLY INCOME
- INCOME VERIFICATION
- INCOME RATIOS MEASURE ADEQUACY OF STABLE MONTHLY INCOME

NET WORTH

- ASSETS MINUS LIABILITIES
- LIQUID VS. NON-LIQUID ASSETS
- RESERVES AFTER CLOSING
- ASSET VERIFICATION
- GIFT FUND LIMITS

CREDIT REPUTATION

- CREDIT REPORTS
- CREDIT SCORES
- MITIGATING CIRCUMSTANCES FOR PAST PROBLEMS

applying for a mortgage loan, the buyer can be prepared to discuss any problems with the lender.

Most people try to meet their credit obligations on time; when they don't, there's usually a reason. Loss of a job, divorce, hospitalization, prolonged illness, or a death in the family can create extraordinary financial pressures and adversely affect bill-paying habits. If a buyer has a poor credit score, it may be possible to show that the credit problems occurred during a specific period for an understandable reason, and that the buyer has handled credit well both before and since that period. The buyer should put this explanation in writing and be prepared to provide supporting documentation (such as hospital records) from a third party.

When a buyer explains a credit problem to a lender, it's a mistake to blame the problem on the creditor. Lenders hear too many excuses from loan applicants who refuse to accept responsibility for their own actions. The lender's reaction is predictable: skepticism and rejection of the loan application. The lender will reason that someone who won't take responsibility for previous credit problems won't take responsibility for future ones, either.

Even serious credit problems can be resolved with time. Buyers who've had credit problems in the past shouldn't assume that they can't qualify for a good loan. They should speak to a lender or a mortgage broker and get an expert opinion.

LOW-DOCUMENTATION LOANS

At times, some lenders have been willing to make low-documentation ("low-doc") loans to certain buyers. For example, if a buyer with a high credit score could make a large downpayment, a lender might waive some of the requirements for proof of income and assets in exchange for a higher interest rate. This is convenient for self-employed buyers and others with complicated financial situations.

However, the practice got out of hand during the subprime boom (see below). Some lenders made low-doc and even "no doc" loans to less creditworthy buyers, including some who claimed income and assets they didn't actually have. Many of these borrowers eventually defaulted. Low-doc loans are much less common now, and no-doc loans have virtually disappeared for the typical buyer.

SUBPRIME LENDING

Buyers who won't qualify for a loan under standard underwriting requirements may be able to obtain a subprime mortgage. Subprime lenders apply more flexible underwriting standards, taking on riskier borrowers and riskier loans. To offset the increased risk, subprime lenders charge significantly higher interest rates and fees. In addition, subprime loans are more likely to involve prepayment penalties, balloon payments, and negative amortization.

Many subprime borrowers are buyers with poor or limited credit histories. However, subprime financing has also been used by buyers who:

- can't (or would rather not have to) meet the income and asset documentation requirements of prime lenders;
- have more debt than prime lenders allow; or
- want make a smaller downpayment than prime lenders would allow.

Beginning in the late 1990s, the mortgage industry experienced a boom in subprime lending, enabling many subprime borrowers to buy homes. However, by 2008, a significant number of these borrowers were defaulting on their loans. The resulting wave of foreclosures hurt housing prices generally and the economy as a whole. It is now more difficult to get subprime financing.

CHOOSING A LOAN

Usually a borrower has a choice of different loans from a given lender, as well as from competing lenders. Comparing the loans and choosing between them can be a challenge. The buyer must compare the cost of the loans and also consider how the structure of each loan (the downpayment, repayment period, and other features) would affect his financial situation in both the short and long term.

TRUTH IN LENDING ACT

To tell which of two or more possible loans is the least expensive, it isn't enough to compare the quoted interest rates. Loan fees and other financing charges also need to be taken into account.

The federal **Truth in Lending Act** (TILA), requires lenders to disclose information about loan costs in consumer credit transactions. The disclosures help loan applicants compare credit costs and shop around for the best terms.

TILA is implemented by **Regulation Z**, and is enforced by the Consumer Financial Protection Bureau. The law does not set limits on interest rates or other finance charges, but it does regulate the disclosure of these charges.

The most important disclosure required under TILA is the loan's **annual percentage rate** (APR). The APR expresses the relationship between the finance charge and the amount financed as an annualized percentage. The finance charge that's used to calculate the APR is the sum of all fees charged for the loan. It includes interest, the loan origination fee, any discount points that will be paid by the borrower, and mortgage insurance premiums (see Chapter 10).

Because it takes into account these other charges as well as the interest, the APR for a real estate loan is virtually always higher than the quoted interest rate. For example, a loan that bears an annual interest rate of 4% might have a 4.25% APR, because of the origination fee and mortgage insurance.

By comparing only the interest rates quoted by different lenders, a buyer could easily be misled. For instance, a lender might quote a very low interest rate, but charge a large origination fee or several discount points. In that case, the total cost of the loan may actually exceed the total cost of a loan from a competitor with a higher interest rate. The APRs of the two loans will reveal this difference in cost.

To help prospective borrowers evaluate and compare loans, TILA and the Real Estate Settlement Procedures Act (discussed in Chapter 11) require lenders in most residential transactions to give the loan applicant a form called a **loan estimate**. The form discloses key information about the loan, including the APR, monthly payment amount, finance charges, and other closing costs, along with a list of services the borrower can shop around for, such as title insurance.

The lender has three business days after receiving the loan application to mail or deliver the loan estimate form. Most lenders give the estimate to the applicant at the time of application. If any of the estimated figures change over the course of the transaction, the lender has three days to give the borrower an updated estimate. Generally the lender must do this at least four days before the buyer becomes contractually obligated to the lender (which usually occurs at closing or just before).

While a buyer won't get the loan estimate form until after actually applying for a loan, it's possible to find out the estimated APR and other loan details with a phone call to the lender or by checking the lender's website.

LOCKING IN THE INTEREST RATE. If a buyer chooses a lender because of a low interest rate, she should consider asking the lender to **lock in** the rate for a certain period. If the rate is not locked in, the lender may change it at any time before closing. So even if the rate is 4.25% when the loan application is submitted, by the time the loan closes, the rate could be 4.5%. The buyer might end up with a much higher monthly loan payment than originally anticipated—even an unaffordable payment.

A buyer who wants to lock in the interest rate typically pays a lock-in fee or a slightly higher rate of interest. If the closing date gets postponed, the buyer may have to pay an extension fee to maintain the rate lock.

A rate lock can be expensive. If the buyer thinks market interest rates may drop in the next few weeks, it doesn't make sense to lock in the rate. The lender may charge the buyer the locked-in rate even if market rates have gone down in the period before closing. (To avoid this risk, the buyer may be able to add a **float down provision** to the rate lock agreement for an additional charge.)

OTHER CONSIDERATIONS IN CHOOSING A LOAN

The interest rate and the overall cost of a loan are important considerations for any buyer, but they are by no means the only ones. In comparing different financing options, buyers should think about a variety of other issues: How much money will they have left in savings after the loan closes? How much spending money will they have left over each month after paying their mortgage payment?

How long do they plan to stay in the home they're buying? With income ratios and other qualifying standards, a lender takes certain aspects of the buyers' situation into account before agreeing to make a loan. But only the buyers themselves can decide which financing alternative is most comfortable for them and fits in best with their own financial plans.

Some buyers are only planning to live in the house they're purchasing for a few years. These buyers generally want to minimize the short-term cost of the property, and they're less concerned with the long-term over-all cost. For example, a buyer who plans to sell the property in less than five years might be a candidate for an adjustable-rate mortgage with a five-year fixed-rate period at the outset. IIe can take advantage of the lower starting interest rate without worrying about how high market rates may rise in the future.

Buyers who hope to retire early or reduce their workload may be most concerned with building equity and paying off their mortgage as soon as possible. They might prefer a loan with a 15-year or 20-year term, rather than the standard 30-year term, even though it means they will qualify for a smaller loan amount and have to buy a less expensive home than they otherwise would.

Some first-time buyers with limited buying power want to purchase the largest home they can afford. They may be interested in financing arrangements that

---

FIG. 9.2 BUYER'S CONSIDERATIONS IN CHOOSING A LOAN

- INTEREST RATE AND LOAN FEES

- SHORT-TERM COST OF FINANCING VS. OVERALL LONG-TERM COST

- SAVINGS REMAINING AFTER HOME PURCHASE

- SPENDING MONEY REMAINING AFTER MONTHLY MORTGAGE PAYMENT

- HOW LONG DOES THE BUYER INTEND TO OWN THIS HOME?

- HOW RAPIDLY WILL EQUITY BUILD?

- HOW SOON WILL THE MORTGAGE BE PAID OFF?

- HOW MUCH HOUSE WILL THIS FINANCING ENABLE THE BUYER TO PURCHASE?

- WHAT ALTERNATIVE INVESTMENT OPPORTUNITIES ARE AVAILABLE?

can boost their price range: an adjustable interest rate, a high loan-to-value ratio, a 40-year loan term, discount points, or secondary financing.

On the other hand, some buyers don't want to borrow as much money for a house as lenders would allow. They may want to invest their money differently, or they may simply prefer to avoid the financial stress that the maximum monthly mortgage payment would represent for them.

In short, buyers must evaluate every potential loan in light of their own goals and preferences. The downpayment and other cash requirements, a fixed or adjustable interest rate, the monthly payment amount, and the loan term are all variables to consider in choosing a loan. We'll be discussing these and other loan features in the next chapter.

PREDATORY LENDING

We can't end our discussion of loan qualifying without mentioning predatory lending. The term predatory lending is used to describe an array of mortgage practices used to take advantage of unsophisticated borrowers. Predatory lenders tend to target elderly or minority borrowers, especially those with limited income or limited English skills.

Examples of predatory lending practices include:

- **Predatory steering.** Steering a buyer toward a more expensive loan when the buyer could qualify for a less expensive one.
- **Fee packing.** Charging interest rates, points, or processing fees that far exceed the norm and aren't justified by the cost of the services provided.
- **Loan flipping.** Encouraging repeated refinancing even though there is no benefit to the borrower. (The predatory lender benefits from the loan fees.)
- **Disregarding borrower's ability to pay.** Making a loan based on the property's value, without using appropriate qualifying standards to determine the borrower's ability to afford the loan payments.
- **Balloon payment abuses.** Making a partially amortized or interest-only loan with low monthly payments, without disclosing to the borrower that a large balloon payment will be required after a short period.
- **Fraud.** Misrepresenting or concealing unfavorable loan terms or excessive fees, falsifying documents, or using other fraudulent means to induce a prospective borrower to enter into a loan agreement.

Predatory lending is often associated with subprime mortgages, and it's considered to have contributed to the subprime mortgage crisis. Many states now have anti-predatory lending laws, including Washington. The state **Mortgage Broker Practices Act** (MBPA), which regulates mortgage brokers, contains provisions that are intended to help prevent certain fraudulent practices in lending.

Under the Mortgage Broker Practices Act, mortgage brokers have a fiduciary duty to borrowers. Among other things, they are prohibited from:

- defrauding or misleading borrowers, lenders, or third parties;
- engaging in unfair or deceptive practices;
- misrepresenting available rates, points, or financing terms; and
- failing to make required disclosures to loan applicants and other parties

Note that the MBPA also places restrictions on a real estate licensee acting as a mortgage broker in his own transaction or a transaction handled by another licensee working for the same brokerage. In this situation, the licensee must make a written disclosure to the borrower regarding his role(s) in the transaction and the borrower's right to choose a different mortgage broker. The licensee must also comply with rules regarding business practices, office location, and signage that help ensure separation between his real estate activities and mortgage broker activities.

An individual harmed by a violation of the MBPA may bring a civil action against the mortgage broker's bond for actual damages suffered. In addition, a violation of the MBPA is also a violation of the Consumer Protection Act (CPA). Individuals may bring actions under the CPA for up to three times the amount of actual damages.

CHAPTER SUMMARY

1. Home buyers usually get preapproved by a lender before beginning their house hunt. Preapproval requires submission of a loan application and all supporting documentation, just like applying for a loan after finding the property.

2. When a mortgage loan application is submitted to a lender, the lender's underwriters evaluate it to determine whether the applicant is a good credit risk and can afford the proposed loan. The underwriter analyzes the applicant's income, net worth, and credit reputation.

3. A lender looks at a loan applicant's stable monthly income to determine how big a mortgage payment the applicant can afford. Stable income is income that has been earned for at least two years and which is expected to continue for at least another three. Verified income from employment, pensions, social security, spousal maintenance, child support, public assistance, dividends, interest, and rental property may be counted as stable monthly income.

4. Income ratios are used to measure the adequacy of a loan applicant's income. In many cases, the underwriter will apply both a debt to income ratio and a housing expense to income ratio. A debt to income ratio states the applicant's monthly mortgage payment (PITI), plus any other monthly obligations, as a percentage of her stable monthly income. A housing expense to income ratio states the PITI payment alone as a percentage of stable monthly income.

5. Net worth is calculated by subtracting liabilities from assets. A loan applicant's net worth indicates to a lender whether the applicant knows how to manage money, has the cash required for closing, and has adequate reserves in case of a financial emergency. Liquid assets are generally more helpful to a loan application than non-liquid assets. If the loan applicant owns real estate, the lender will be concerned with the applicant's net equity. Lenders place limits on the amount of gift funds a buyer can use to close the transaction.

6. A credit report lists credit problems that have occurred within the past seven years (ten years for a bankruptcy). A loan applicant's credit score provides an overall measure of creditworthiness and may be used to determine the level of review applied to the application. It may also be a factor in setting the loan's interest rate.

7. Subprime lending involves making riskier loans, usually in exchange for higher interest rates and fees. Many subprime borrowers have poor or limited credit histories; others simply want to purchase nonstandard properties that prime lenders don't regard as acceptable collateral.

8. The Truth in Lending Act and the Real Estate Settlement Procedures Act require residential lenders to provide loan applicants with a loan estimate form within three days after receiving an application. The form must disclose the annual percentage rate (APR) of the proposed loan and provide estimates of finance charges and the monthly payment amount.

9. It is not always a good idea for buyers to borrow the maximum loan amount and buy the most expensive home they can. Buyers need to consider their entire financial situation, short-term and long-term, when choosing a home to buy and a loan to finance the purchase.

10. Predatory lenders take advantage of unsophisticated borrowers, often targeting elderly or minority borrowers. Predatory lending practices include predatory steering, fee packing, loan flipping, disregarding a borrower's ability to pay, balloon payment abuses, and fraud.

CHAPTER QUIZ

1. When a potential buyer approaches a lender prior to looking for a house, in order to obtain a promise of a loan up to a certain amount, this is known as:

   a. prequalification
   b. predetermination
   c. preapproval
   d. prepayment

2. A buyer will find it useful to have a preapproval letter because it:

   a. does not commit the lender to making a loan
   b. gives the seller confidence that the financing contingency won't be a problem
   c. tells the seller the maximum amount the buyer can afford
   d. allows the buyer to extend the closing process

3. If a loan applicant's primary source of income is self-employment, the lender will consider this stable monthly income if the loan applicant:

   a. does not have any other source of income
   b. also has secondary sources of income
   c. has been self-employed for at least one year
   d. has a history of employment in the same field and can document a reasonable chance for success

4. Which of the following would a lender consider an acceptable secondary income source?

   a. Rental income, with a percentage deducted for vacancies or uncollected rent
   b. Interest on investments that the loan applicant will cash in to pay for closing costs
   c. Child support payments for the loan applicant's 17-year-old daughter
   d. Regular monthly income from a public assistance program, if the loan applicant's eligibility will expire at the end of the year

5. In contrast to a debt to income ratio, a housing expense to income ratio:

   a. takes into account principal and interest on the mortgage, but not taxes and insurance
   b. is based on the monthly mortgage payment alone, not on all of the loan applicant's debt payments
   c. uses the applicant's current housing expense instead of the proposed mortgage payment
   d. takes into account the loan applicant's net worth as well as monthly income

6. Which of the following is true about how a lender evaluates net worth?

    a. When verifying bank accounts, the lender wants the present balance to be significantly higher than the average balance in the past

    b. The lender prefers non-liquid assets to liquid assets

    c. The lender is primarily concerned with the appraised value of the real estate that the loan applicant owns

    d. If the loan applicant's income is marginal, the lender may approve the loan anyway if the applicant has significant net worth

7. How would a lender calculate the net equity in real estate the loan applicant owns?

    a. Take the market value of the property and deduct the sum of the liens against the property, plus the selling expenses

    b. Subtract the balance of the existing mortgage from the assessed value of the property

    c. Take the market value of the property and subtract between 10% and 13% for the estimated selling costs

    d. Add the buyer's downpayment to the market value of the property, then subtract the sum of the liens against the property

8. Which of the following would be most likely to have a negative effect on an individual's credit rating?

    a. Obtaining a copy of his own credit report

    b. Unemployment

    c. Debt consolidation

    d. A high FICO® score

9. The APR for a real estate loan:

    a. must be disclosed before a loan application is submitted

    b. expresses the relationship of the finance charges to the total amount financed

    c. includes interest, points, lock-in fees, closing costs, and the downpayment

    d. is usually lower than the quoted interest rate

10. Fee packing, loan flipping, and balloon payment abuses are all examples of:

    a. preapproval techniques

    b. derogatory credit information

    c. rate lock-ins

    d. predatory lending practices

ANSWER KEY

1. c. A buyer who would like to be preapproved will go directly to a lender and submit a loan application.

2. b. Preapproval makes a buyer's offer more attractive because it gives the seller confidence that the buyer will qualify for financing. (The lender isn't obligated to make the loan unless the chosen property meets the lender's standards, however.)

3. d. A lender will count the income of a self-employed loan applicant who has been in business for a short time, but only if the loan applicant has a history of employment in the same field and can document a reasonable chance for success with financial statements and a good business plan.

4. a. Income from sources besides employment must still be stable. Rental income is acceptable if the loan applicant can prove that rental payments are made regularly, but the lender will usually only consider a certain percentage because vacancies and rent collection problems are unpredictable.

5. b. A housing expense to income ratio measures the adequacy of the loan applicant's income using only the monthly mortgage payment (principal, interest, taxes, and insurance). A debt to income ratio also takes payments on other debts into account.

6. d. Above-average net worth can mean the difference between approval and rejection if the loan applicant's income is marginal.

7. a. Net equity is the amount of money the loan applicant can expect to receive from the sale of the property. This is often the primary source of cash that will be used to buy the new property.

8. c. A pattern of increasing liabilities followed by debt consolidation suggests that the individual tends to live beyond his means.

9. b. The annual percentage rate (APR) helps loan applicants compare the overall cost of different loans. A loan's APR expresses the relationship between the finance charge (interest rate and loan fees) and the amount financed.

10. d. These are all examples of predatory lending practices.

CHAPTER 10

FINANCING PROGRAMS

BASIC LOAN FEATURES

- Repayment period
- Amortization
- Loan-to-value ratios
- Secondary financing
- Loan fees
- Fixed and adjustable interest rates

CONVENTIONAL LOANS

- Conventional loans and the secondary market
- Characteristics of conventional loans
- Underwriting conventional loans
- Making conventional loans more affordable

GOVERNMENT-SPONSORED LOAN PROGRAMS

- FHA-insured loans
- VA-guaranteed loans

SELLER FINANCING

- How seller financing works
- Types of seller financing
- Other ways sellers can help

INTRODUCTION

As discussed in the previous chapter, the size of loan that a particular buyer can get depends on the buyer's income, net worth, and credit reputation. But it also depends on the features of the loan and the way it's structured. How long is the repayment period? How much of a downpayment does the lender require? Is the interest rate fixed or adjustable? Changes in loan features that residential lenders offer reflect the changing conditions in the mortgage finance market. Lenders want to make loans that will enable buyers to purchase homes, but they have to structure the loans to control the risk of default and protect their investments. The mortgage loans that make business sense to a lender vary with the state of the market: Are interest rates high or low, and are they headed up or down? Is this a buyer's market or a seller's market?

As a real estate agent, you can help your buyers get the financing they need by keeping abreast of currently available options. Lenders will frequently send you information about their latest loan programs, and you should keep an eye out for new developments. First-time buyers are especially likely to benefit from special programs. This chapter will provide you with the background information needed to understand the various types of loans lenders offer.

In the first part of the chapter, we'll review the basic features of a mortgage loan; it is differences in these features that distinguish the various loan programs. In the second part of the chapter, we'll look at the main categories of mortgage loan programs: conventional loans and government-sponsored loans. We'll also discuss seller financing.

BASIC LOAN FEATURES

The basic features of a mortgage loan include the repayment period; amortization; the loan-to-value ratio; a secondary financing arrangement (in some cases); loan fees; and a fixed or adjustable interest rate.

REPAYMENT PERIOD

The repayment period of a loan is the number of years the borrower has to repay the loan. The repayment period may also be referred to as the loan term.

Thirty years is generally considered the standard repayment period for a residential mortgage, but many lenders also offer 15-year and 20-year loans. In some programs, a term as short as 10 years or as long as 40 years is allowed.

The length of the repayment period affects two important aspects of a mortgage loan:

1. the amount of the monthly payment, and
2. the total amount of interest paid over the life of the loan.

To see the impact that the repayment period has on the monthly payment and the total interest paid, let's compare a 30-year loan with a 15-year loan.

MONTHLY PAYMENT AMOUNT. The main reason 30 years became the standard term for a residential mortgage is that a longer repayment period reduces the amount of the monthly payment. Thus, a 30-year loan is more affordable than a 15-year loan.

> **EXAMPLE:** The monthly payment on a $100,000 30-year loan at 7% interest is $665.30. The monthly payment on the same loan amortized over a 15-year period is $898.83. (The numbers for this example and similar following examples cannot be determined using a standard calculator; they can only be derived using online amortization software or a specialized financial calculator.)

The higher monthly payment required for a 15-year loan means that the borrower will build equity in the home much faster. But the higher payment also makes it much more difficult to qualify for a 15-year loan than for the same size loan with a 30-year term. A buyer who wants a 15-year loan and has sufficient funds might decide to make a larger downpayment and borrow less money in order to make the monthly payment amount more affordable. Or the buyer might choose instead to buy a much less expensive home than what he could afford with a 30-year loan.

TOTAL INTEREST. The biggest advantage of a shorter repayment period is that it substantially decreases the amount of interest paid over the life of the loan. With a 15-year mortgage, a borrower will end up paying less than half as much interest over the life of the loan as a 30-year mortgage would require.

> **EXAMPLE:** Let's look at our $100,000 loan at 7% interest again. By the end of a 30-year loan term, the borrower will pay a total of $239,509. But by the end of a 15-year term, the borrower will pay only $161,789. After deducting the original $100,000 principal amount, you can see that the 30-year loan will require $139,509 in interest, while the 15-year loan will require only $61,789 in interest.

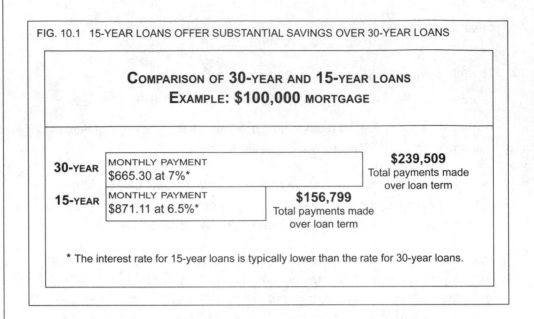

FIG. 10.1   15-YEAR LOANS OFFER SUBSTANTIAL SAVINGS OVER 30-YEAR LOANS

COMPARISON OF 30-YEAR AND 15-YEAR LOANS
EXAMPLE: $100,000 MORTGAGE

30-YEAR   MONTHLY PAYMENT
$665.30 at 7%*

$239,509
Total payments made
over loan term

15-YEAR   MONTHLY PAYMENT
$871.11 at 6.5%*

$156,799
Total payments made
over loan term

* The interest rate for 15-year loans is typically lower than the rate for 30-year loans.

So the 30-year mortgage has more affordable payments, but requires the borrower to pay a lot more interest over the life of the loan. On the other hand, the 15-year loan has much higher monthly payments, but allows the borrower to pay far less interest over the life of the loan.

INTEREST RATES FOR 15-YEAR LOANS. To simplify our comparison of a 15-year loan and a 30-year loan, we applied the same interest rate—7%—to both loans. However, a lender is likely to charge a significantly lower interest rate on a 15-year loan than it charges for a comparable 30-year loan. That's because a 15-year loan represents less of a risk for the lender.

The interest rate on a 15-year loan might be half a percentage point lower than the rate on a 30-year loan. If the interest rate on the 15-year loan in our example were only 6.5% instead of 7%, the monthly payment would be $871.11. The total interest paid over the life of the loan would be $56,799.

AMORTIZATION

Amortization refers to how the principal and interest are paid over a loan's repayment period. Most loans made by institutional lenders like banks and savings and loans are **fully amortized**. A fully amortized loan is completely paid off by the end of the repayment period by means of regular monthly payments. The amount of the monthly payment remains the same throughout the repayment period. Each monthly payment includes both a principal portion and an interest portion. As each payment is made, the principal amount of the debt is reduced. With each succeeding payment, a slightly smaller portion of the payment is applied to interest and a slightly larger portion is applied to the principal, until at last the final payment pays off the loan completely.

In the early years of a fully amortized loan, the principal portion of the payment is quite small, so it takes several years for the borrower's equity to increase significantly through debt reduction. But toward the end of the loan period, the borrower's equity increases more rapidly.

> **EXAMPLE:** A fully amortized, 30-year $100,000 loan at 6% interest calls for monthly payments of $599.55. Only $99.55 of the first payment is applied to the principal. But by the twentieth year of the loan term, $327.89 of the $599.55 payment is applied to the principal.

The alternatives to fully amortized loans include partially amortized loans and interest-only loans. Like a fully amortized loan, a **partially amortized** loan requires monthly payments of both principal and interest. However, the monthly payments are not enough to completely pay off the debt by the end of the repayment period.

FIG. 10.2 PAYMENTS FOR A FULLY AMORTIZED LOAN

EXAMPLE: **$100,000** LOAN @ **6%, 30**-YEAR TERM, MONTHLY PAYMENTS

PAYMENT NUMBER	BEGINNING BALANCE	TOTAL PAYMENT	INTEREST PORTION	PRINCIPAL PORTION	ENDING BALANCE
1	$100,000.00	$599.55	$500.00	$99.55	$99,900.45
2	$99,900.45	$599.55	$499.50	$100.05	$99,800.40
3	$99,800.40	$599.55	$499.00	$100.55	$99,699.85
4	$99,699.85	$599.55	$498.50	$101.05	$99,598.80
5	$99,598.80	$599.55	$497.99	$101.56	$99,497.24

At the end of the repayment period, some principal remains unpaid. It must then be paid off in one lump sum called a **balloon payment**.

> **EXAMPLE:** A partially amortized $400,000 loan might have a $171,000 balance at the end of the loan term. The borrower will have to make a balloon payment of $171,000 to pay off the loan.

In most cases, the borrower comes up with the funds for the balloon payment by refinancing. (Refinancing means using the funds from a new mortgage loan to pay off an existing mortgage.)

The term **interest-only loan** may be used in two different ways. In the first of these, an interest-only loan is one that calls for payments during the loan term that cover only the interest accruing on the loan, without paying off any of the principal. The entire principal amount—the amount originally borrowed—is due at the end of the term. For example, in this sense, someone who borrows $600,000 on an interest-only basis will make monthly interest payments to the lender during the loan term; at the end of the term, the borrower will be required to repay the lender the entire $600,000 principal amount as a lump sum.

In the alternative usage, an interest-only loan is one that allows the borrower to make interest-only payments for a specified period at the beginning of the loan term. At the end of this period, the borrower must begin making amortized payments that will pay off all of the principal, along with the additional interest that accrues, by the end of the term. Though popular for a few years, this type of loan led to many foreclosures and is no longer widely available.

LOAN-TO-VALUE RATIOS

A **loan-to-value ratio** (LTV) expresses the relationship between the loan amount and the value of the home being purchased. If a buyer is purchasing a $100,000 home with an $80,000 loan and a $20,000 downpayment, the loan-to-value ratio is 80%. If the loan amount were $90,000 and the downpayment were $10,000, the LTV would be 90%. The higher the LTV, the larger the loan amount and the smaller the downpayment.

A loan with a low LTV is generally less risky than one with a high LTV. The borrower's investment in her home is greater, so she'll try harder to avoid defaulting on the loan and losing the home. And if the borrower does default, the outstanding loan balance is less, so it's more likely that the lender will be able to recoup the entire amount in a foreclosure sale.

Lenders use LTVs to set maximum loan amounts. For example, under the terms of a particular loan program, the maximum loan amount might be 95% of the sales price or appraised value of the property, whichever is less. The borrower would be required to make a downpayment of at least 5%.

SECONDARY FINANCING

Sometimes a buyer may want to get two loans at the same time. One of the loans is a **primary loan** for most of the purchase price, and the other is generally used to pay part of the downpayment or closing costs required for the first loan. The second loan is referred to as **secondary financing**.

Secondary financing can come from a variety of sources. It may come from the same lender who is making the primary loan, it may come from a second institutional lender, it may come from the seller, or it may come from a private third party.

A lender making a primary loan will usually place restrictions on the type of secondary financing arrangement the borrower may enter into. The borrower generally must be able to qualify for the combined payment on the primary and secondary loans. And in most cases the borrower must make at least a minimum downpayment out of his own funds.

LOAN FEES

Of course, lenders don't loan money free of charge. For mortgage loans, lenders not only charge borrowers interest on the principal, they also charge points. The term "point" is short for "percentage point." A point is one percentage point (1%) of the loan amount. For example, on a $100,000 loan, one point would be $1,000; six points would be $6,000. Any lender charges that are a percentage of the loan amount may be referred to as points; the chief examples are loan origination fees and discount points.

ORIGINATION FEES. A loan origination fee covers administrative costs the lender incurs in processing a loan; it is sometimes called a service fee, an administrative charge, or simply a loan fee. An origination fee is charged in almost every residential loan transaction, with the exception of "no-fee" loans (which usually carry a slightly higher interest rate over the entire loan term instead). The buyer usually pays the origination fee.

DISCOUNT POINTS. Discount points are used to increase the lender's upfront yield, or profit, on the loan. By charging discount points, the lender not only

---

FIG. 10.3 BASIC FEATURES OF MORTGAGE LOANS

BASIC LOAN FEATURES

- REPAYMENT PERIOD
- AMORTIZATION
- LOAN-TO-VALUE RATIO
- SECONDARY FINANCING (IN SOME CASES)
- LOAN FEES
  - ORIGINATION FEE (NEARLY ALWAYS)
  - DISCOUNT POINTS (IN SOME CASES)
- INTEREST RATE: FIXED OR ADJUSTABLE

---

gets interest throughout the loan term, it collects an additional sum of money up front, when the loan is funded. As a result, the lender is willing to "discount" the loan—that is, make the loan at a lower interest rate than it would have without the discount points. In effect, the borrower pays the lender a lump sum at closing to avoid paying more interest later. A lower interest rate also translates into a lower monthly payment.

Discount points are not charged in all loan transactions, but they are quite common. The number of discount points charged usually depends on how the loan's interest rate compares to market interest rates. Typically, a lender that offers an especially low rate charges more points to make up for it.

FIXED AND ADJUSTABLE INTEREST RATES

A loan's interest rate can be either fixed or adjustable. With a fixed-rate loan, the interest rate charged on the loan remains constant throughout the entire loan term. If a borrower obtains a 30-year home loan with a 7% fixed interest rate, the interest rate remains 7% for the whole 30-year period, no matter what happens to market interest rates during that time. If market rates increase to 9%, or if they drop to 5%, the interest rate charged on the loan will still be 7%.

Until the early 1980s, virtually all mortgage loans had fixed interest rates. During the 1980s, however, market interest rates rose dramatically and fluctuated constantly. Suddenly, many borrowers could no longer afford a home loan. And many lenders, unable to predict future interest rates, became uncomfortable lending money for 30 years at a fixed rate. The **adjustable-rate mortgage** (ARM) was introduced as the solution to both of these problems.

An ARM allows the lender to periodically adjust the loan's interest rate to reflect changes in market interest rates. The lender's ability to change the loan's interest rate during the loan term passes on the risk of interest rate increases to the borrower. Because of this shift in risk, lenders are often willing to charge a lower rate on ARMs. For example, if a borrower could get a fixed-rate loan at 6%, he might be able to get an ARM at an initial rate between 5% and 5.5%.

Of course, while a lower initial interest rate may make an adjustable-rate loan attractive, the borrower is assuming the risk that he'll have to pay a significantly higher rate later on. If market rates go up, the borrower's interest rate and monthly payment amount will also go up. On the other hand, there's also the possibility of a lower rate later on: if market rates decrease, the borrower's interest rate and monthly payment will also decrease.

ARM FEATURES. The features of an adjustable-rate loan include the note rate, the index, the margin, the rate adjustment period, and the payment adjustment period. There may also be rate caps, a payment cap, a negative amortization cap, and a conversion option.

NOTE RATE. The note rate is the ARM's initial interest rate. It's commonly referred to as the note rate because it's the rate stated in the promissory note.

INDEX. An index is a widely published statistical report that is considered a reliable indicator of changes in the cost of money. Examples include the one-year Treasury securities index, the Eleventh District cost of funds index, and the LIBOR index.

MARGIN. An ARM's margin is the difference between the index rate and the interest rate the lender charges the borrower. The margin is how the lender earns a profit on the loan. A typical margin is between two and three percentage points.

> **EXAMPLE:** Suppose the current index rate is 2.5% and the lender's margin is 2%. 2.5% + 2% = 4.5%. The lender charges the borrower 4.5% on the loan. The 2% margin is the lender's income from the loan.

RATE ADJUSTMENT PERIOD. An ARM's rate adjustment period determines how often the lender has the right to adjust the loan's interest rate. The most common rate adjustment period is one year. But the rate adjustment period may be every six months, every three years, or some other time period. At the end of each period, the lender checks the index. If the index rate has increased, the lender can increase the borrower's interest rate. If the index rate has decreased, the lender must decrease the borrower's interest rate.

Some ARMs have a two-tiered rate adjustment structure. They provide for a longer initial period before the first rate adjustment, with more frequent rate adjustments after that. These are sometimes called **hybrid ARMs**, because they are a cross between adjustable-rate and fixed-rate mortgages.

> **EXAMPLE:** The borrowers are financing their home with a 30-year ARM that has an initial rate adjustment period of three years, with annual rate adjustments from then on. The interest rate charged on their loan won't change during the first three years of the repayment period, but it will change each year after that.

The loan in the example would be called a 3/1 ARM. There are also 5/1 ARMs, 7/1 ARMs, and 10/1 ARMs. In each case, the first number is the number of years in the initial rate adjustment period, and the second number means that subsequent rate adjustments will occur once a year. Some borrowers who choose these types of loans intend to sell or refinance their home before the end of the initial adjustment period. As a general rule, the longer the initial adjustment period, the higher the initial interest rate. However, the initial rate will still often be lower than the rate for a comparable fixed-rate loan. As a result, some borrowers choose hybrid ARMs because they intend to sell or refinance their home before the end of the initial adjustment period.

MORTGAGE PAYMENT ADJUSTMENT PERIOD. An ARM's mortgage payment adjustment period determines when the lender changes the amount of the borrower's monthly payment to reflect a change in the interest rate charged on the loan. For most ARMs, the payment adjustment period coincides with the interest rate adjustment period. In that case, when the lender increases the interest rate on the loan, the payment amount immediately goes up as well. And when the lender decreases the loan's interest rate, the payment amount immediately goes down.

RATE CAPS. ARM borrowers may run the risk of "payment shock." Payment shock occurs when interest rates rise so rapidly that an ARM borrower can no longer afford her monthly mortgage payment. This could happen to an ARM borrower if there is a sharp jump in market interest rates, or if market rates keep rising steadily over an extended period.

To help borrowers avoid payment shock, lenders generally include interest rate caps in their ARMs. A rate cap limits how much the interest rate on the loan can go up, regardless of what its index does; and limiting interest rate increases prevents the monthly payment from increasing too much.

FIG. 10.4 COMMON FEATURES OF ADJUSTABLE-RATE MORTGAGES

ARM FEATURES

- NOTE RATE: INITIAL INTEREST RATE
- INDEX: CHANGES IN ARM'S INTEREST RATE ARE TIED TO INDEX
- MARGIN: DIFFERENCE BETWEEN INDEX RATE AND ARM RATE
- RATE ADJUSTMENT PERIOD: HOW OFTEN ARM INTEREST RATE MAY CHANGE
- PAYMENT ADJUSTMENT PERIOD: HOW OFTEN PAYMENT AMOUNT MAY CHANGE
- RATE CAPS: LIMIT RATE INCREASES (PER ADJUSTMENT AND LIFE-OF-LOAN)
- PAYMENT CAP: DIRECTLY LIMITS INCREASES IN MONTHLY PAYMENT AMOUNT
- NEGATIVE AMORTIZATION CAP: LIMITS HOW MUCH INTEREST CAN BE ADDED TO PRINCIPAL BALANCE
- CONVERSION OPTION: ALLOWS BORROWER TO CONVERT TO FIXED RATE

Many ARMs have two kinds of rate caps. One limits the amount that the interest rate can increase in any one adjustment period. The other limits the amount that the interest rate can increase over the entire life of the loan. For example, rate caps might be 2% per year and 6% over the life of the loan.

PAYMENT CAP. A mortgage payment cap serves the same purpose as a rate cap: limiting how much the borrower's monthly mortgage payment can increase. A payment cap directly limits how much the lender can raise the monthly mortgage payment, regardless of what is happening to the mortgage interest rate. For example, a payment cap might limit payment increases to 7.5% annually. However, a payment cap unaccompanied by a rate cap may lead to negative amortization. We'll discuss that issue next.

NEGATIVE AMORTIZATION CAP. If an ARM has a payment cap but no rate cap, payment increases don't always keep up with increases in the loan's interest rate. The same thing can happen if the payment adjustment period differs from the rate adjustment period. As a result, the monthly payments don't cover the full amount of the interest that has accrued. So the lender adds the unpaid interest to the loan's principal balance. This is called **negative amortization**. A loan's principal balance ordinarily declines steadily over the loan term, but negative amortization makes the balance go up instead of down. The borrower can end up owing the lender more money than the original loan amount.

Most ARMs today are structured to prevent negative amortization in the first place. In loans that aren't, however, a negative amortization cap limits the amount of unpaid interest that can be added to the principal balance. A typical negative amortization cap might limit the total amount a borrower can owe to 110% of the original loan amount (although caps can go as high as 125%).

CONVERSION OPTION. An ARM may have a conversion option that allows the borrower to convert it to a fixed-rate loan. Most conversion options give the borrower a limited time in which to convert. For example, the borrower may be able to convert the ARM to a fixed-rate loan anytime between the first and fifth year of the loan term. Conversion is usually considerably less expensive than refinancing the loan.

ARM CHECKLIST. Adjustable-rate loans are complicated. To help your buyers understand ARMs and get all the information they need, you can give them the following list of questions to ask the lender:

- What will my initial interest rate be?
- How often will my interest rate change? Is the first rate adjustment period longer than later adjustment periods?
- How often will my payment change?
- Is there any limit to how much my interest rate can be increased?
- Is there any limit to how much my payment can be increased at any one time?
- Is negative amortization a possibility with my loan?
- Can my ARM be converted to a fixed-rate loan?

CONVENTIONAL LOANS

Now let's turn our attention to loan programs. Loans made by institutional lenders (such as banks, savings and loans, or mortgage companies) can be divided into two main categories: conventional loans and government-sponsored loans. A **conventional loan** is any institutional loan that is not insured or guaranteed by a government agency. For example, a loan that is made by a commercial bank and insured by a private mortgage insurance company is a conventional loan. A loan that is insured by the FHA (Federal Housing Administration) or guaranteed by the VA (Department of Veterans Affairs) is not a conventional loan. We'll discuss conventional loans first, and then look at the FHA and VA.

CONVENTIONAL LOANS AND THE SECONDARY MARKET

Lenders sometimes make conventional "portfolio" loans. A portfolio loan is one that the lender plans on keeping in its own portfolio of investments, as opposed to selling it on the secondary market. With some limitations, portfolio loans can be made according to the lender's own underwriting standards.

However, lenders generally want to have the option of selling their loans on the secondary market instead of keeping them in portfolio. Conventional loans are much easier to sell if the lender makes them in accordance with the underwriting standards and other rules set by the government-sponsored enterprises that operate in the secondary market, Fannie Mae and Freddie Mac. Loans that conform to the rules of Fannie Mae and/or Freddie Mac are called **conforming loans**; by contrast, loans that don't meet Fannie Mae or Freddie Mac's standards are **nonconforming loans**.

Because the standards of Fannie Mae and Freddie Mac have been very influential, our discussion of conventional loans is primarily based on their rules.

CHARACTERISTICS OF CONVENTIONAL LOANS

A conventional loan's characteristics are determined by rules concerning loan amounts, loan-to-value ratios, private mortgage insurance, risk-based loan fees, secondary financing, prepayment penalties, and assumption.

CONVENTIONAL LOAN AMOUNTS. In order for a loan to be eligible for purchase by Fannie Mae or Freddie Mac, the loan amount must not exceed the applicable **conforming loan limit**. Conforming loan limits for dwellings with one, two, three, or four units are set by the Federal Housing Finance Agency (the agency that oversees the secondary market entities) based on median housing prices nationwide. The limits may be adjusted annually to reflect changes in median prices.

For 2019, the conforming loan limit for single-family homes and other one-unit dwellings in most parts of the country is $484,350. In high-cost areas—areas where housing is more expensive—there are higher limits based on area median housing prices, up to a maximum of $726,525.

Although they're generally ineligible for sale to Fannie Mae and Freddie Mac, conventional loans that exceed the conforming loan limits are also available in many areas. For these larger loans, sometimes called **jumbo loans**, lenders generally charge higher interest rates and fees and apply stricter underwriting standards.

CONVENTIONAL LTVs. A mortgage loan for 80% of the property's sales price or appraised value is generally regarded as a very safe investment for the lender. The 20% downpayment gives the borrower a substantial incentive to avoid default, and if foreclosure becomes necessary, the lender is likely to recover the full amount owed.

Traditionally, 80% was the standard loan-to-value ratio for conventional loans. That started changing in the 1980s. More and more lenders became comfortable making conventional loans with higher LTVs. By the late 1990s, high-LTV loans had become more common than 80% loans. Lenders routinely made conventional loans with LTVs up to 95%, requiring only a 5% downpayment.

By the 2000s, some lenders were even making 100% conventional loans, allowing the borrowers to put no money down. In 2007 and 2008, when home values began dropping around the country, many high-LTV borrowers who had started out with little or no equity soon ended up with "negative equity." In other words, they owed their lenders more than their homes were worth. If borrowers in that situation could no longer afford to pay their mortgage, they often lost their homes to foreclosure, and their lenders often incurred serious losses. As we discussed in the previous chapter, a nationwide foreclosure crisis developed. Because of the crisis, conventional loans with LTVs over 95% are no longer common, although some lenders still offer them through special programs. (See the discussion of low-downpayment programs later in this chapter.)

Conventional loans with loan-to-value ratios up to 95% are still generally available, however. Applicants for conventional loans with LTVs over 90% typically must meet stricter qualifying standards than they'd have to for a lower-LTV loan, and they can expect to pay a higher interest rate and higher loan fees. Some lenders also require these loans to have a fixed interest rate, because the unpredictability of changes in the interest rate and monthly payment amount of an adjustable-rate mortgage makes default more likely with an ARM than with a fixed-rate loan.

PRIVATE MORTGAGE INSURANCE. With a conventional loan, if the downpayment is less than 20% of the property's value, the lender requires the borrower to purchase private mortgage insurance (PMI). The mortgage insurance protects the lender against the extra risk that a higher loan-to-value ratio represents. Fannie Mae and Freddie Mac both require PMI on all conventional loans they purchase that have loan-to-value ratios over 80%.

With PMI, the mortgage insurance company insures the lender against losses that might result if the borrower defaults on the loan. The mortgage insurance covers only the upper portion of the loan amount—for example, it might cover the upper 25%. In this way, the insurance company assumes only part of the risk of loss rather than the entire risk.

> **EXAMPLE:** Wilson is buying a $400,000 home. She's financing the purchase with a $360,000 loan, so the loan-to-value ratio is 90%. Because the LTV is over 80%, the lender requires Wilson to purchase PMI. In exchange for the PMI premiums, the mortgage insurance company insures the top 25% of the loan amount, or $90,000. The insurance company is assuming the risk that the lender may lose up to $90,000 on a foreclosure sale in the event that Wilson defaults.

If the borrower defaults on a loan covered by PMI, the lender has two options. The lender can foreclose on the property, and if the foreclosure sale results in a loss, file a claim with the insurance company to cover the loss, up to the policy amount. Or the lender can simply relinquish the property to the insurer and make a claim for actual losses up to the policy amount. Most lenders choose the first option.

PREMIUMS. The premiums for private mortgage insurance can be paid by the lender or another party, but they are usually paid by the borrower. (As in the example above, the lender requires the borrower to purchase the insurance as a condition of making the loan.) Mortgage insurers offer various payment plans, such as:

- a flat monthly premium amount added to the monthly mortgage payment;
- an initial premium paid at closing, plus annual renewal premiums; or
- a one-time premium paid at closing or financed along with the loan amount.

CANCELLATION OF PMI. If all goes well, the borrower will gradually pay off the principal. And unless the property depreciates in value, as the principal balance goes down, the loan-to-value ratio will decrease. Eventually the mortgage insurance should no longer be necessary.

A federal law called the Homeowners Protection Act requires lenders to cancel a conventional loan's PMI and refund any unearned premium to the borrower once certain conditions are met.

Here are the basic rules for standard loans covered by PMI (different rules apply to loans classified as high-risk and outside standard guidelines):

- The lender must automatically cancel the PMI when the loan's principal balance is scheduled to reach 78% of the home's original value, unless the borrower is delinquent on the payments.
- The borrower may send the lender a written request to cancel the PMI earlier, when the principal balance is scheduled to reach 80% of the original value. The request must be granted if the borrower's payment history is good, the value of the home has not decreased, and the borrower has not taken out any other loans on the home.

The Homeowners Protection Act requires lenders to send all borrowers with private mortgage insurance an annual notice concerning their PMI cancellation rights.

RISK-BASED LOAN FEES. Conventional borrowers are nearly always expected to pay an origination fee, and they may also agree to pay discount points. In addition, if their loan is going to be sold to Fannie Mae or Freddie Mac, the lender will probably charge one or more loan-level price adjustments (LLPAs). Loan-level price adjustments shift some of the risk (that is, the cost) of mortgage default to the borrower. As a general rule, the riskier the loan, the more the borrower is required to pay in LLPAs. The lender then passes this cost along to the borrower, though usually in the form of a slightly higher interest rate on the loan, rather than a one-time fee paid at closing.

Nearly all loans sold to the secondary market entities are subject to an LLPA. The amount of the LLPA varies depending on the borrower's credit score and the loan-to-value ratio; the riskier the loan, the larger the LLPA. For instance, a borrower with a credit score of 660 and a 90% loan-to-value ratio might be required to pay an LLPA of 2.25% of the loan amount at closing, while a borrower with a credit score of 730 and an 80% loan might be charged only 0.50%.

There are also LLPAs for certain types of transactions that involve more risk, such as investor loans, loans with secondary financing, and interest-only loans. One or more of these LLPAs may be charged in addition to the one that's based on the credit score and loan-to-value ratio.

FIG. 10.5 FEATURES OF CONVENTIONAL LOANS

CONVENTIONAL LOAN FEATURES

- LOAN-TO-VALUE RATIOS UP TO 95% GENERALLY AVAILABLE
- PRIVATE MORTGAGE INSURANCE REQUIRED IF LTV IS OVER 80%
- BORROWERS MAY BE REQUIRED TO PAY RISK-BASED LOAN FEES (LOAN-LEVEL PRICE ADJUSTMENTS)
- SECONDARY FINANCING ALLOWED IF CERTAIN RULES ARE MET
- PREPAYMENT PENALTIES NOT STANDARD
- ASSUMPTION: LENDER'S PERMISSION USUALLY REQUIRED

SECONDARY FINANCING AND CONVENTIONAL LOANS. Secondary financing can be used in conjunction with conventional loans, but most lenders require a series of rules to be met. These rules are designed to keep the borrower from overextending himself, thus reducing the risk that he will default on the primary loan. For example, a second loan generally isn't allowed to have a repayment period of less than five years. This prevents the second lender from requiring the borrower to make a balloon payment in the first five years of the loan term, when the risk of default on the primary loan is the greatest. If your buyer is interested in secondary financing, he should check with the lender to see what types of secondary financing arrangements are acceptable.

PREPAYMENT PENALTIES. Some mortgage loan agreements allow the lender to charge the borrower a prepayment penalty if the borrower pays off all of the principal, or a substantial portion of it, before it is due. A prepayment penalty is not considered a standard provision in a conventional loan. However, some lenders offer reduced loan fees or a lower interest rate in exchange for including a prepayment penalty provision in the loan agreement. While this can be a reasonable arrangement, the borrower should carefully consider the consequences before agreeing to a prepayment penalty.

Lenders usually charge a prepayment penalty only if the loan is prepaid during the first few years of the loan term. The borrower should find out how many years the prepayment penalty provision will be in effect. She also needs to ask under what circumstances the penalty will be charged. Will she have to pay the penalty if the loan is paid off early because she has sold the property, or only if she refinances? And how much will the penalty be? Imposing a heavy prepayment penalty with unreasonable terms is a predatory lending practice.

The federal Dodd-Frank Act of 2010 placed new limitations on prepayment penalties on loans secured by dwellings with up to four units. In adjustable-rate mortgages and "higher-priced" loans (those that exceed average rates and fees by a certain amount), prepayment penalties are prohibited. For other loans secured by a dwelling, a prepayment penalty can be charged only during the first three years of the loan term, and the amount of the penalty is limited.

ASSUMPTION. A conventional loan usually includes a due-on-sale clause (alienation clause), which means the loan can be assumed only with the lender's permission. The lender will evaluate the new buyers to make sure they are creditworthy. The buyers will be expected to pay an assumption fee.

The lender may also raise the interest rate on a conventional loan. (The rate isn't increased when an FHA or VA loan is assumed.) Raising the interest rate largely defeats the purpose of assuming a loan, so assumption of conventional loans is fairly rare.

UNDERWRITING CONVENTIONAL LOANS

Now let's look at the underwriting guidelines Fannie Mae and Freddie Mac require lenders to follow in qualifying a buyer for a conforming conventional loan.

Based on both credit score and loan-to-value ratio, Fannie Mae ranks a proposed loan as having a low, moderate, or high primary risk, and this ranking determines the level of review applied to the rest of the loan application. Other aspects of the application, such as the applicant's debt to income ratio and cash reserves, are weighed as factors that may increase or decrease the risk of default.

Freddie Mac's approach involves a separate evaluation of each of the main components of creditworthiness: credit reputation, income, net worth, and property value. Strength in one component may compensate for weakness in another.

In practice, Freddie Mac's and Fannie Mae's approaches are similar. In both approaches, each aspect of the application is considered as part of the overall picture, and positive factors may offset negative ones and vice versa.

CREDIT SCORES. Both Fannie Mae and Freddie Mac expect lenders to use applicants' credit scores as a key tool in evaluating creditworthiness. In addition, as

FIG. 10.6 UNDERWRITING CONVENTIONAL LOANS

CONVENTIONAL UNDERWRITING

- CREDIT SCORE AND LTV MAY BE TREATED AS PRIMARY RISK FACTORS TO DETERMINE LEVEL OF REVIEW, WITH OTHER ASPECTS OF APPLICATION AS CONTRIBUTORY RISK FACTORS
- UNDERWRITER EVALUATES OVERALL RISK
- INCOME RATIOS
  - BENCHMARK DEBT TO INCOME RATIO: 36%
  - BENCHMARK HOUSING EXPENSE TO INCOME RATIO: 28%
  - HIGHER RATIOS ALLOWED WITH COMPENSATING FACTORS
- RESERVES TO COVER AT LEAST TWO MONTHS OF MORTGAGE PAYMENTS ARE DESIRABLE BUT NOT NECESSARILY REQUIRED
- GIFT FUNDS ALLOWED, BUT LIMITED IF LOAN HAS A HIGH LTV

explained earlier, credit scores are used in determining the risk-based loan fees (loan-level price adjustments) that borrowers will be charged.

Fannie Mae won't buy loans made to borrowers with credit scores below 620. Depending on the type of loan and the LTV, Freddie Mac will consider borrowers with scores below 620, although many Freddie Mac loan programs require higher scores. Loans made to borrowers with lower credit scores have higher LLPAs.

INCOME RATIOS. As with any type of loan, the first step in the income analysis for a conventional loan is calculating the applicant's stable monthly income. (See Chapter 9.) The next step is measuring the adequacy of the stable monthly income using income ratios. Both Fannie Mae and Freddie Mac require lenders to use the first ratio we'll discuss: the debt to income ratio.

The debt to income ratio measures the relationship between the loan applicant's monthly income and his total monthly debt. The total monthly debt is made up of the proposed housing expense (which includes PITI: principal, interest, property taxes, hazard insurance, and any mortgage insurance or homeowners association dues), plus any other recurring liabilities. These other recurring liabilities fall into three categories:

- installment debts (which have a definite beginning and ending date and fixed monthly payments);
- revolving debts (such as credit card payments); and
- other obligations (such as child support or spousal maintenance).

Note that an installment debt usually counts as part of the applicant's monthly obligations only if there are more than ten payments remaining.

EXAMPLE: George has applied for a conventional loan. Among other debts, he has a student loan that requires payments of $108 per month. However, he only has to make ten more payments to pay off the loan. As a result, the $108 payment won't be included in George's total monthly debt.

That rule also applies to child support or spousal maintenance (alimony): if the required payments will end in ten months or less, they don't count as part of the loan applicant's monthly obligations.

There is an exception to the ten-payment rule, however. Even if there are no more than ten payments remaining on a debt, if the payment amount is large enough to potentially interfere with the borrower's ability to pay the mortgage, then the debt should be counted in calculating the debt to income ratio.

The standard or benchmark debt to income ratio for conventional loans is 36%. In other words, a loan applicant's income is generally considered adequate for a conventional loan if the total monthly debt does not exceed 36% of the applicant's stable monthly income (although this ratio can go much higher, as we'll explain next).

EXAMPLE: The Browns' stable monthly income is $4,800. Their monthly debts include a $40 minimum payment on a credit card, a $250 car loan payment, and a $150 personal loan payment.

To estimate how large a mortgage payment the Browns might qualify for if they apply for a conventional loan, first multiply $4,800 by 36%. $4,800 × .36 = $1,728. The benchmark 36% debt to income ratio would allow them to have up to $1,728 in monthly obligations, including their housing expense.

Now subtract the Browns' monthly payments on their debts from that figure: $1,728 − $40 charge card payment − $250 car loan payment − $150 personal loan payment = $1,288. So $1,288 is the maximum monthly housing expense the Browns could afford under the 36% debt to income ratio guideline.

Freddie Mac guidelines (although not Fannie Mae guidelines) also call for lenders to consider a second ratio: the loan applicant's housing expense to income ratio. The proposed housing expense generally should not exceed 28% of the applicant's stable monthly income.

EXAMPLE: Let's go back to the Browns' situation. Their stable monthly income is $4,800. To apply the housing expense to income ratio, simply multiply $4,800 by 28%, or .28. $4,800 × .28 = $1,344. So $1,344 is the maximum housing expense the Browns could afford under the 28% housing expense to income ratio guideline.

The maximum housing expense figure arrived at with the debt to income ratio is compared to the one arrived at with the housing expense to income ratio, and the smaller of the two figures is treated as the maximum allowable housing expense. In our example, the Browns' maximum housing expense would be $1,288 (the figure indicated by the debt to income ratio) rather than $1,344.

It's important to understand that both Fannie Mae and Freddie Mac consider their income ratios as benchmarks or guidelines rather than rigid limits. They may be willing to purchase a loan even though the borrower's debt to income ratio exceeds 36%, as long as there are compensating factors that justify making the loan in spite of the higher income ratio. For example, one or more of the following factors (especially either of the first two) might offset the extra risk:

- a large downpayment;
- substantial net worth;
- demonstrated ability to incur few debts and accumulate savings;
- ability to devote extra income to housing expenses;
- education, job training, or employment history that indicates strong potential for increased earnings; or
- significant energy-efficient features in the home being purchased.

On the other hand, when a proposed loan would involve other factors that represent increased rather than decreased risk, then a debt to income ratio in excess of 36% is generally unacceptable. For example, many lenders would be unwilling to accept a high debt to income ratio for a loan with a loan-to-value ratio over 90% or for an adjustable-rate loan.

In a case where compensating factors make a debt to income ratio over 36% acceptable, how much higher than the benchmark can the ratio be? If the loan application is manually underwritten, neither Fannie Mae nor Freddie Mac will accept a debt to income ratio over 45%, no matter how many compensating factors are present. If the application is submitted to an automated underwriting system, Fannie Mae may consider a ratio as high as 50%.

RESERVES. Conventional loan applicants generally should have the equivalent of at least two months of mortgage payments in reserve after making the downpayment and paying all closing costs. That's not necessarily treated as a strict requirement, but less than that in reserve will weaken an application, and more will strengthen it. Some lenders do require at least two months of reserves, and some require even more for riskier loans. For example, a lender might require three months of reserves for a 95% loan on a principal residence, or six months of reserves for an investor loan. The reserves must be cash or liquid assets that could easily be converted to cash if necessary (for example, the cash value of a life insurance policy, or the vested portion of a retirement account).

GIFT FUNDS. Lenders also apply a number of rules regarding the use of gift funds to close a transaction financed with a conventional loan. The donor usually must be someone who has a particular connection with the borrower—for example, a family member, fiancé, or employer. A nonprofit organization or a municipality may also be an acceptable donor. The donor is usually required to sign a **gift letter** to confirm that the funds are a gift and not a loan. And for a high-LTV loan, the borrower is often required to make a downpayment of at least 5% out of her own funds.

MAKING CONVENTIONAL LOANS MORE AFFORDABLE

Sometimes a buyer can't qualify for a standard fixed-rate loan and wouldn't be comfortable with an adjustable-rate loan. There are quite a few other options that can make a conventional loan more affordable. These include buydowns; low-downpayment programs; programs targeted at first-time buyers, public employees, low-income borrowers, or low-income neighborhoods; and loans with lower initial payments.

BUYDOWN PLANS. One of the easiest ways to make a loan less expensive is with a buydown. A buydown lowers the borrower's monthly payment and can make it easier to qualify for the loan. When the loan is made, the seller or a third party pays the lender a lump sum that is used to reduce the borrower's payments either early in the loan term or throughout the loan term.

A buydown has the same effect as discount points (mentioned earlier in the chapter). The lump sum payment at closing increases the lender's upfront yield on the loan, and in return the lender charges a lower interest rate, which lowers the amount of the borrower's monthly mortgage payment. But a buydown is typically proposed to the lender by the parties; unlike ordinary discount points, it's not a component of the lender's initial rate quote.

Note that when a seller agrees to pay for a buydown, he doesn't have to come up with cash to do so. The amount of the buydown is simply deducted from the seller's net proceeds at closing and transferred to the lender. As you might expect, buydowns are especially popular when market interest rates are high.

A buydown can be permanent or temporary. With a permanent buydown, the borrower pays the lower interest rate (and a lower monthly payment) for the entire loan term. With a temporary buydown, the interest rate and the monthly payment are reduced only during the first years of the loan term.

PERMANENT BUYDOWNS. If a borrower's interest rate is bought down permanently, the buydown reduces the note rate, which is the interest rate stated in the promissory note. The cost of a permanent buydown depends on how much the interest rate is reduced; the greater the rate reduction, the higher the cost.

> **EXAMPLE:** Bowen needs to borrow $150,000 to buy Sanderson's property. The lender quoted a 10% interest rate, and Bowen can't quite qualify for the loan at that rate. Sanderson offers to buy down Bowen's interest rate by 1% to help her qualify for the loan.
>
> Based on market conditions, the lender estimates it will take about six points to increase the yield on a 30-year loan by 1%. So the lender agrees to make the buydown for six points, or 6% of the loan amount. To determine how much the buydown will cost Sanderson, multiply the loan amount by 6%. $150,000 × .06 = $9,000. At closing, the lender will withhold approximately $9,000 from the loan funds, reducing Sanderson's proceeds from the sale.
>
> The 1% buydown will reduce Bowen's mortgage payment by more than $100 per month, enabling her to qualify for the loan. The lender will charge Bowen 9% interest instead of 10% throughout the 30-year loan term, which will save Bowen nearly $39,400 over the life of the loan. In that way, the buydown is of much greater value to Bowen than simply reducing the purchase price by $9,000 (although a lower purchase price might have meant a somewhat smaller downpayment).

As the example indicates, the cost of a buydown is affected by market conditions, including market interest rates and the average time loans are outstanding before they are paid off. The amount that the lender will actually charge should be confirmed before the parties sign an agreement.

TEMPORARY BUYDOWNS. A temporary buydown reduces the buyer's monthly payment in the early years of the loan. Temporary buydowns appeal to buyers who believe they can grow into a larger payment, but need time to get established. They also cost sellers less than permanent buydowns.

There are two types of temporary buydown plans: level payment and graduated payment. A **level payment plan** calls for an interest reduction that stays the same throughout the buydown period. For example, a seller might buy a buyer's interest rate down by 2% for two years. The buyer would pay the lower interest rate during the first two years, and then the lender would begin charging the note rate at the start of the third year.

With a **graduated payment plan**, the interest rate reduction changes at set points during the buydown period. For example, one graduated payment plan is the 3-2-1 buydown. It calls for a 3% reduction in the interest rate during the first year, 2% during the second year, and 1% during the third year. The lender begins charging the note rate in the fourth year. This gives the buyer the chance to get used to higher payments gradually.

With a temporary buydown, because the buyer will eventually have to afford a larger payment based on the full note rate, the lender generally uses the note rate rather than the buydown rate to qualify the buyer. (Special rules may apply to adjustable-rate loans.)

LIMITS ON BUYDOWNS AND OTHER CONTRIBUTIONS. Fannie Mae and Freddie Mac limit the financial contributions a buyer may accept from the seller or another interested party, such as the builder or a real estate agent involved in the transaction. The limits are based on a percentage of the property's sales price or appraised value, whichever is less. These limits apply to buydowns, to payment of closing costs ordinarily paid by the buyer, and to similar contributions.

LOW-DOWNPAYMENT PROGRAMS. For many potential home buyers, especially first-time buyers, coming up with enough cash is the biggest challenge in buying a home. They have a steady, reliable income, but they don't have the savings to cover the downpayment, closing costs, and reserves required for a standard conventional loan. Even the 5% downpayment required for a 95% loan may be beyond their means. Buyers in this situation may want to consider special programs that have reduced cash requirements and allow them to draw on alternative sources for the cash they need.

The details of these programs vary. But, for example, it's possible to obtain a loan with a 97% LTV, with a 3% downpayment coming from the borrower or from gifts or grants.

Some of these programs don't require the borrower to have any reserves after closing. Others require only one month's mortgage payment in reserve.

TARGETED PROGRAMS. Although some conventional low-downpayment programs are open to any prospective home buyer, many are targeted at low- and moderate-income buyers. As a general rule, a buyer can qualify for one of these targeted programs if his stable monthly income does not exceed the median income in the metropolitan area in question. (An increased income limit applies in a high-cost area such as Seattle.) To make it even easier for low- and moderate-income buyers to get a mortgage, these programs may allow a debt to income ratio of 38% or even 40% without compensating factors, and may have no maximum housing expense to income ratio.

To encourage neighborhood revitalization, the targeted programs often waive their income limits for buyers who are purchasing homes in low-income or run-down neighborhoods. Thus, a buyer whose income is well above the area median could still qualify for a targeted low-downpayment program if she's buying a home in a neighborhood that meets the program's standards.

Other conventional low-downpayment programs are offered to groups such as teachers, police officers, and firefighters. These programs encourage public employees to live in the communities where they work. Special programs for first-time buyers are generally meant to stimulate the housing market.

LOANS WITH LOWER INITIAL PAYMENTS. Some borrowers have adequate funds for a downpayment, but don't have enough income to qualify for a loan with high monthly payments. If these borrowers expect their income to increase steadily (for example, perhaps they're young adults just starting out on their careers), so that they'll be able to grow into larger payments later on, they might be able to afford a more expensive home by getting a loan with lower initial payments.

We've already discussed some types of loans that fall into this category. The most common type is the hybrid ARM, an adjustable-rate mortgage with a two-tiered rate adjustment schedule, such as a 5/1 ARM: the interest rate and payment amount start out lower than the rate and payment for a fixed-rate loan, and they don't change during the first five years; the lender makes annual adjustments after that.

FIG. 10.7   MAKING CONVENTIONAL LOANS MORE AFFORDABLE

CONVENTIONAL AFFORDABILITY PLANS AND PROGRAMS

- BUYDOWNS: PERMANENT OR TEMPORARY
- LOW-DOWNPAYMENT PROGRAMS
  - TYPICALLY ALLOW LTVS UP TO 97%
  - BORROWER MAY USE SOME FUNDS FROM ALTERNATIVE SOURCES
  - TARGETED PROGRAMS: PUBLIC EMPLOYEES, FIRST-TIME BUYERS, LOW- OR MODERATE-INCOME BUYERS, OR LOW-INCOME NEIGHBORHOODS
- LOW INITIAL PAYMENT PROGRAMS

Another option (also discussed earlier) is the type of interest-only loan where the borrower pays only interest on the loan balance during the early years of the loan term, and later must start making amortized payments that will pay off the balance by the end of the term. This switch will cause the monthly payments to rise considerably. Interest-only loans fell into disfavor as a result of the foreclosure crisis. Hybrid ARMs satisfy most of the demand today for loans with low initial payments.

GOVERNMENT-SPONSORED LOAN PROGRAMS

Now let's turn to government-sponsored mortgage loan programs. The two major programs established by the federal government are the FHA-insured loan program and the VA-guaranteed loan program. We'll look at each of these in turn. (Another federal program, administered by the U.S. Department of Agriculture's Rural Housing Service, offers additional financing possibilities for low-income buyers in many rural areas; these are often called USDA loans.)

FHA-INSURED LOANS

The federal government created the Federal Housing Administration (FHA) in 1934, during the Great Depression, to help people with low and moderate incomes buy homes. For much of the twentieth century, the FHA-insured loan program was the main source of low-downpayment mortgage loans for U.S. home buyers.

The FHA is an agency within the U.S. Department of Housing and Urban Development. The FHA does not make loans; it insures loans made by banks and other institutional lenders. In effect, the FHA is a giant mortgage insurance agency. Its insurance program, the Mutual Mortgage Insurance Plan, is funded with premiums paid by FHA borrowers. If a lender that makes an FHA-insured loan suffers a loss because the borrower defaults, the FHA will compensate the lender for its loss.

In exchange for insuring a loan, the FHA regulates most of the loan's terms and conditions. The FHA has various programs for specific types of mortgage loans, such as home rehabilitation loans and energy efficiency loans. But the central program for single-family home purchase loans is the 203(b) program. The rules we'll be discussing here apply to loans made through the 203(b) program.

CHARACTERISTICS OF FHA LOANS. Here are some of the key characteristics of FHA loans:

- Although FHA programs are intended to help home buyers with low or moderate incomes, there are no maximum income limits. (Instead, the maximum loan amount rules ensure that FHA loans can generally only be used to purchase relatively modest homes.)
- An FHA loan requires a comparatively small downpayment, and the loan fees and other charges may be lower than they would be for a typical conventional loan. Overall, an FHA borrower may need significantly less cash for closing.
- FHA loan amounts can't exceed specified maximums that are based on median housing prices. In some areas, the FHA maximum loan amounts are considerably lower than the maximums for conforming conventional loans.
- The qualifying standards for an FHA loan are not as strict as those for a standard conventional loan.
- The property purchased with an FHA loan may have up to four dwelling units. The borrowers must intend to occupy it as their primary residence. The FHA does not insure loans made to investors, as opposed to owner-occupants.
- If there are any other mortgage liens against the property, the FHA loan must have first lien position.
- The interest rate on an FHA loan may be fixed or adjustable.
- Most FHA loans have 30-year terms, although 15-year loans are also available. (However, if the interest rate is adjustable, the term must be 30 years.)
- In addition to an origination fee, an FHA borrower may be charged discount points, which can be paid by either the borrower or the property seller.

- Mortgage insurance is required on all FHA loans.
- FHA loans never call for a prepayment penalty; they can be paid off at any time with no penalty.

FHA LOAN AMOUNTS. The loan amount for a transaction financed with an FHA loan can't exceed the local limit that applies in the area where the property is located. Local limits are based on median housing prices and tied to the conforming loan limits for conventional loans. They may be adjusted annually.

For 2019, the FHA maximum loan amount for single-family homes and other one-unit dwellings is generally $314,827, but it can be as much as $726,525 in high-cost areas.

LOAN-TO-VALUE RATIOS. The loan amount for a particular transaction is determined not just by the FHA loan ceiling for the local area, but also by the FHA's rules concerning loan-to-value ratios.

The maximum loan-to-value ratio for an FHA loan depends on the borrower's credit score. If the borrower's credit score is 580 or above, the maximum LTV is 96.5%. If his score is 500 to 579, the maximum LTV is 90%. Someone with a score below 500 isn't eligible for an FHA loan.

MINIMUM CASH INVESTMENT. The difference between the maximum loan amount and the appraised value or sales price (whichever is less) is called the borrower's minimum cash investment. In effect, the minimum cash investment is the required downpayment for an FHA loan. In a transaction with maximum financing (a 96.5% LTV), the borrower must make a minimum cash investment of 3.5%. Closing costs, discount points, and prepaid expenses (interim interest on the loan and impounds for taxes and insurance) don't count toward the minimum cash investment.

FHA INSURANCE PREMIUMS. The mortgage insurance premiums for FHA loans are called the MIP. Usually, an FHA borrower pays both a one-time premium and annual premiums.

UPFRONT PREMIUM. The one-time premium is called the **upfront MIP**. Either the borrower or the seller can pay the upfront premium in cash at closing. The borrower also has the option of financing the upfront premium over the loan term. When the upfront premium is financed, it's simply added to the base loan amount (the amount determined by the maximum loan amount and minimum cash investment rules). The monthly payments are then set to pay off the total amount financed by the end of the loan term. When the upfront premium is financed in this way, the total loan amount (the base loan amount plus the upfront premium) can't exceed 100% of the property's appraised value. Currently, the upfront premium for FHA purchase loans is 1.75% of the loan amount.

ANNUAL PREMIUM. In addition to the upfront MIP, an annual premium is also required for most FHA loans. The annual premium ranges from about 0.5% to a little over 1% of the loan balance, depending on the principal balance, loan term, and the loan-to-value ratio. The annual premium is paid in monthly installments: one-twelfth of the annual premium is added to each monthly payment.

If the original LTV is over 90%, the annual MIP must be paid for the entire loan term. If the original LTV is 90% or less, the annual MIP gets canceled after 11 years. (The mortgage insurance remains in effect throughout the life of the loan, however.)

SELLER CONTRIBUTIONS. As you've seen, to make the home more affordable, sometimes a seller agrees to buy down the buyer's interest rate. Or the seller might help pay all or part of the buyer's closing costs. When the sale is financed with an FHA loan, contributions from the seller—or from another interested party, such as a real estate agent—may not exceed 6% of the sales price or the appraised value, whichever is less. Any amount over that limit must be subtracted from the sales price before applying the loan-to-value ratio and calculating the minimum cash investment.

SECONDARY FINANCING. Secondary financing is allowed in conjunction with FHA loans. In fact, the amount of the first and second mortgages added together can exceed the FHA's local loan ceiling, so in some cases secondary financing makes it possible to buy a more expensive house. As a general rule, however, the combined loan-to-value ratio can't exceed the FHA's maximum allowable LTV. That means secondary financing ordinarily can't be used for the minimum cash investment. (There are exceptions to this rule when the secondary financing is provided by a family member, nonprofit, or a governmental agency.)

A number of other restrictions apply to secondary financing supplementing an FHA loan. For example, the second loan can't require a balloon payment within a certain number of years after closing, and it can't have a prepayment penalty.

UNDERWRITING FHA LOANS. Qualifying a buyer for an FHA loan involves essentially the same steps as conventional qualifying: the lender analyzes the applicant's income, net worth, and credit reputation. However, it's important to note that the FHA's underwriting standards are not as strict as the standards used for conventional loans. The less stringent FHA standards make it easier for low- and moderate-income home buyers to qualify for a mortgage.

INCOME RATIOS. The FHA's term for stable monthly income is **effective income**. An FHA loan applicant's effective income is his monthly gross income from all sources that can be expected to continue for the first three years of the loan term.

Two ratios are applied to evaluate the adequacy of the applicant's effective income. These are the fixed payment to income ratio (which is the same concept as the "debt to income ratio" in the conventional loan context) and the housing expense to income ratio. As a general rule, an FHA loan applicant's fixed payment to income ratio may not exceed 43%. In addition, the applicant's housing expense to income ratio may not exceed 31%. The applicant must qualify under both ratios.

The fixed payment to income ratio takes into account the proposed monthly housing expense plus all recurring monthly charges. The housing expense includes principal and interest (based on the total amount financed), property taxes, hazard insurance, one-twelfth of the annual premium for the FHA mortgage insurance, and any dues owed to a homeowners association. Recurring monthly charges include the monthly payments on any debt with ten or more payments remaining. Alimony and child support payments, installment debt payments, and payments on revolving credit accounts are all counted.

EXAMPLE: Miriam is applying for an FHA loan. She has a reliable monthly salary of $2,750. She also receives $740 a month in Social Security payments for her young children, which began when their father died three years ago. Miriam's effective income totals $3,490 a month. She pays the following monthly recurring charges: a $235 car payment, a $50 minimum Master-Card payment, and a $125 personal loan payment.

To get a general idea of how large a house payment Miriam can qualify for with FHA financing, use the FHA's two income ratios. First multiply her effective income by 43% to see how much she can spend per month on her total monthly obligations. $3,490 × .43 = $1,501. Then subtract her recurring monthly charges from her maximum monthly obligations. $1,501 − $235 car payment – $50 MasterCard payment – $125 personal loan payment = $1,091. Miriam could qualify for a $1,091 monthly housing expense under the debt to income ratio.

Next, apply the housing expense to income ratio by multiplying Miriam's effective income by 31%. $3,490 × .31 = $1,082. So $1,082 is the maximum monthly housing expense Miriam could qualify for under this ratio. Since Miriam must qualify under both ratios, $1,082 is her maximum monthly housing expense for an FHA loan.

If an FHA loan applicant's income ratios exceed the 43% and 31% limits, the application will be subject to manual underwriting. The underwriter can still approve the loan if there are compensating factors that will reduce the risk of default. For example, if the applicant has a conservative attitude toward credit and will have at least three months of mortgage payments in reserve after closing, the underwriter might approve the loan even though the applicant has a 44% fixed payment to income ratio or a 33% housing expense to income ratio.

A temporary buydown can be used with an FHA loan, as long as the loan has a fixed interest rate. However, the FHA underwriter will use the note rate to qualify the borrower. So even if the interest rate on the loan were bought down from 4% to 3% for the first two years of the loan term, the buyer would still be required to qualify for the loan at 4%, the note rate.

FUNDS FOR CLOSING. At closing, an FHA borrower must have enough cash to cover the minimum cash investment, discount points, prepaid expenses, and other out-of-pocket expenses. Ordinarily, no reserves are required. The borrower may use gift funds to help close the transaction. The donor of the gift funds must be the borrower's employer or labor union, a close relative, a close friend with a clearly defined interest in the borrower, a charitable organization, or a government agency.

An FHA borrower also has other options for coming up with the necessary funds. As we discussed earlier, a close family member may provide secondary financing to cover the minimum cash investment and other funds needed for closing. This loan may be secured by a second mortgage on the property being purchased, secured by other collateral, or even unsecured (made without any collateral).

Also, the borrower may be permitted to borrow the cash needed for closing from someone other than a family member, as long as the loan is secured by collateral other than the property being purchased with the FHA mortgage. For example, if the applicant can borrow money against his car or vacation property, the loan funds may be used to close the sale. Note that this loan must be from an

FIG. 10.8 FEATURES OF FHA-INSURED LOANS

FHA LOAN FEATURES

- FOR RESIDENTIAL PROPERTIES WITH ONE TO FOUR UNITS
- BORROWER MUST OCCUPY PROPERTY AS PRIMARY RESIDENCE
- FHA MORTGAGE INSURANCE (MIP) ON ALL LOANS
- MAXIMUM LOAN AMOUNT BASED ON LOCAL MEDIAN HOUSING PRICES
- BORROWER'S MINIMUM CASH INVESTMENT: 3.5% OF PRICE OR VALUE, OR 10% IF CREDIT SCORE IS BELOW 580
- MINIMUM CREDIT SCORE 500
- SECONDARY FINANCING ALLOWED
- INCOME RATIO GUIDELINES:
  - 43% FIXED PAYMENT TO INCOME RATIO
  - 31% HOUSING EXPENSE TO INCOME RATIO
- ASSUMPTION: LENDER'S APPROVAL REQUIRED

independent third party, not from the seller or a real estate agent involved in the transaction. It must be clear that the loan is a bona fide business transaction and that the collateral is truly worth the loan proceeds.

ASSUMPTION. FHA loans contain due-on-sale clauses, and various limitations on assumption apply. With some exceptions, the buyer must intend to occupy the property as his primary residence. The lender will review the creditworthiness of the buyer before agreeing to the assumption.

VA-GUARANTEED LOANS

The VA home loan program allows veterans to finance the purchase of their homes with low-cost loans that offer a number of advantages over conventional and FHA loans. A VA loan, like an FHA loan, is made by an institutional lender, not a government agency. However, the loan is guaranteed by the Department of Veterans Affairs (VA), and that significantly reduces the lender's risk. If the borrower defaults, the VA will reimburse the lender for its losses, up to the guaranty amount.

A VA loan can be used to finance the purchase or construction of an owner-occupied single-family residence, or a multifamily residence with up to four units, as long as the veteran will occupy one of the units.

CHARACTERISTICS OF VA LOANS. One of the biggest advantages of VA financing is that, unlike most loans, a typical VA loan does not require a downpayment. Within certain limitations, a VA loan can equal the sales price or appraised value of the home, whichever is less. This allows many veterans who would otherwise be unable to buy homes to do so.

Equally important to many veterans, the underwriting standards for VA loans are more relaxed than the standards for conventional loans. So not only will a veteran need less cash to buy a home with a VA loan, it will also be easier to qualify for the loan.

There are no income limits on VA borrowers, nor are there official restrictions on the size of a VA loan. This means that VA loans aren't limited to low- or moderate-income buyers.

VA loans are fully amortized and typically have 30-year terms. The lender may not impose any prepayment penalties.

The VA doesn't set a maximum interest rate for VA loans; the interest rate is negotiable between the lender and borrower. The lender may charge the borrower a flat fee of no more than 1% of the loan amount to cover administrative costs (the equivalent of an origination fee). The lender may also charge reasonable discount points, which can be paid by the borrower, the seller, or a third party.

VA loans do not require mortgage insurance. The borrower doesn't have to pay for the private mortgage insurance required for many conventional loans, or the MIP required for all FHA-insured loans. However, a VA borrower usually has to pay a **funding fee**, which the lender will remit to the VA. (Veterans with service-connected disabilities are exempt.) The fee is generally about 2%, but decreases with a downpayment.

Another important feature of VA loans is the leniency extended to VA borrowers who are experiencing temporary financial difficulties, such as illness, injury, unemployment, or the death of a spouse. A VA loan officer can help a borrower whose loan becomes delinquent to negotiate a repayment plan.

ELIGIBILITY. To obtain a VA loan, a veteran must have a Certificate of Eligibility issued by the VA. To be eligible, the veteran must have served a certain minimum amount of time on active duty. The minimum amount varies depending on when the veteran served, and it ranges from 90 days to two years of active duty. Buyers who want to determine whether they're eligible for a VA loan may do so online or check with the local VA office.

VA GUARANTY. Like private mortgage insurance, the VA guaranty covers only a portion of the loan amount. The guaranty amount available for a particular transaction depends on the loan amount. For larger loans, it also depends on median home prices in the county where the property being purchased is located.

For example, for a VA loan used to purchase a one-unit property, if the loan amount is over $144,000 and up to $484,350, the guaranty amount is 25% of the loan amount. (So that's a $121,087.50 guaranty for a $484,350 loan.) For loan amounts over $484,350, the guaranty is 25% of the loan amount, up to the maximum specified for the county.

In Washington, the 2019 maximum guaranty ranges from $121,087.50 (for most counties) up to $181,631.25 (for the most expensive counties).

LOAN AMOUNT. The amount of a VA loan can't exceed the appraised value of the home or the sales price. The VA puts no other restrictions on the loan amount. However, most lenders do have rules about VA loan amounts. The most common rule is that for a no-downpayment VA loan, most lenders require the guaranty amount to equal at least 25% of the value or sales price of the property, whichever is less. For example, with a guaranty amount of $121,087.50 (the 2019 maximum in most places that don't have high housing prices), this restriction means that most lenders won't make a no-downpayment VA loan for more than $484,350 ($121,087.50 ÷ 25% = $484,350).

Lenders who follow that rule will still approve a larger loan if the borrower can make a downpayment. They typically want the total of the guaranty amount and the veteran's downpayment to equal 25% of the value or the sales price, whichever is less. This 25% rule means that the downpayment a veteran may have to make is still likely to be fairly modest.

> **EXAMPLE:** Sharon Vincent is eligible for a VA loan. She wants to buy a home for $497,350. The maximum guaranty amount in her county is $121,087.50, so her lender won't make a no-downpayment VA loan larger than $484,350. That means Sharon will have to make a downpayment in order to purchase the home.
>
> However, because of the lender's 25% rule, Sharon doesn't have to pay the difference between the $497,350 sales price and $484,350 to get the

loan. Her downpayment only has to equal 25% of the difference. The combination of the guaranty and the downpayment must equal 25% of the sales price. 25% of $497,350 is $124,337.50. $124,377.50 – $121,087.50 guaranty amount = $3,250. Sharon only has to make a $3,250 downpayment in order to purchase the home.

The other situation in which a VA borrower has to make a downpayment is when the property's sales price exceeds its appraised value. The borrower must make up the difference out of his own funds.

SECONDARY FINANCING. If he doesn't have enough cash, a VA borrower can obtain secondary financing to cover a downpayment required by the lender. The total financing (the VA loan plus the secondary financing) can't exceed the appraised value of the property, the borrower must be able to qualify for the payments on both loans, and the second loan cannot have more stringent conditions than the VA loan.

Secondary financing that meets these standards can be used for the borrower's closing costs, as well as for a downpayment required by the lender. But secondary financing cannot be used when the downpayment is required because the sales price exceeds the property's appraised value.

ASSUMPTION AND RELEASE OF LIABILITY. A VA loan can be assumed by anyone, either a veteran or a non-veteran, as long as the person is creditworthy. The VA must give prior approval to the parties. The interest rate on a VA loan is not changed on assumption.

The original borrower is released from further liability in connection with the loan if the following conditions are met:

1. the loan payments are current,
2. the new buyer is an acceptable credit risk, and
3. the new buyer contractually assumes the veteran's obligations on the loan.

RESTORATION OF ENTITLEMENT. The guaranty amount available to a particular veteran is sometimes called the veteran's "entitlement." After using his entitlement, a veteran can obtain another VA loan only if the entitlement is restored.

EXAMPLE: Joe McDowell used a VA loan to buy a home in 2002. This year Joe decided to sell the property. He paid off his VA loan out of the sale proceeds. When he repaid the loan, Joe's guaranty entitlement was restored. If Joe decides to buy another home, he can use his entitlement to get another VA loan.

It's possible for a veteran to have his entitlement restored even if the loan is assumed instead of paid off when the home is sold. For this to work, the new home buyer must also be a veteran who agrees to substitute her entitlement for the seller's entitlement. The loan payments must be current, and the buyer must also be an acceptable credit risk. If all of these conditions are met, the veteran can formally request a substitution of entitlement from the VA.

QUALIFYING FOR A VA LOAN. To qualify for a VA loan, a veteran must meet the underwriting standards set by the Department of Veterans Affairs. A VA loan ap-

FIG. 10.9 VA RESIDUAL INCOME REQUIREMENTS

Table of Residual Incomes by Region
For loan amounts of $79,999 and below

Family Size	Northeast	Midwest	South	West
1	$390	$382	$382	$425
2	$654	$641	$641	$713
3	$788	$772	$772	$859
4	$888	$868	$868	$967
5	$921	$902	$902	$1,004
Over 5: Add $75 for each additional member up to a family of 7.				

Table of Residual Incomes by Region
For loan amounts of $80,000 and above

Family Size	Northeast	Midwest	South	West
1	$450	$441	$441	$491
2	$755	$738	$738	$823
3	$909	$889	$889	$990
4	$1,025	$1,003	$1,003	$1,117
5	$1,062	$1,039	$1,039	$1,158
Over 5: Add $80 for each additional member up to a family of 7.				

plicant's income is analyzed with two different methods, an income ratio method and a residual income method. The veteran must qualify under both methods.

The income ratio method for analyzing a veteran's income is similar to the method used for conventional and FHA loans. Only one ratio—the debt to income ratio—is used. As a general rule, a veteran's debt to income ratio should not be more than 41%.

> **EXAMPLE:** Robert Garcia is eligible for a VA loan. He makes $2,800 a month, and his total monthly obligations add up to $375 a month. To estimate how large a house payment he can qualify for, multiply $2,800 by 41%. $2,800 × .41 = $1,148. Now subtract his monthly obligations of $375 from $1,148. $1,148 − $375 = $773. Robert could qualify for a $773 monthly housing expense under the debt to income ratio.

The second method used to qualify a VA loan applicant is the **residual income method,** also called cash flow analysis. This method uses the **monthly shelter expense,** which is the proposed housing expense (the PITI payment), plus estimated property maintenance and utility costs (with the estimate based on the square footage of the home being purchased). The monthly shelter expense, all other recurring obligations, and certain taxes (including federal income tax, any state or local income tax, Social Security tax, Medicare tax, and any other taxes deducted from the veteran's paychecks) are subtracted from the veteran's gross monthly income to determine his residual income.

The loan applicant's residual income should be at least one dollar more than the VA's minimum requirement. The minimum requirement varies, depending on where the veteran lives, his family size, and the size of the proposed loan (see Figure 10.9). For example, the residual income required for a family of four living in Washington when the loan amount is $80,000 or more is $1,117.

> **EXAMPLE:** Robert lives in Washington; he's divorced and has one child. He wants to buy a 1,500 square-foot home that costs $307,000. The VA requires him to have at least $823 in residual income to qualify for a loan.
>
> To calculate Robert's residual income, start with his monthly gross income, $2,800. Subtract his federal income tax, which is $350. There's no state or local income tax where he lives, but Social Security and Medicare taxes do have to be subtracted; they total $214. Next, subtract his recurring monthly obligations, which are $375. Calculate the monthly maintenance

FIG. 10.10 FEATURES OF VA-GUARANTEED LOANS

VA LOAN FEATURES

- FOR RESIDENTIAL PROPERTIES WITH ONE TO FOUR UNITS
- BORROWER MUST OCCUPY PROPERTY AS PRIMARY RESIDENCE
- 100% FINANCING ALLOWED — NO DOWNPAYMENT REQUIRED
- 1% ORIGINATION FEE AND DISCOUNT POINTS ALLOWED
- FUNDING FEE, BUT NO MORTGAGE INSURANCE
- NO MAXIMUM LOAN AMOUNT
- MAXIMUM GUARANTY IS TIED TO COUNTY MEDIAN HOME PRICE AND VARIES WITH LOAN AMOUNT
- LENDER MIGHT REQUIRE DOWNPAYMENT IF GUARANTY IS LESS THAN 25% OF LOAN AMOUNT
- SECONDARY FINANCING ALLOWED FOR DOWNPAYMENT
- LOAN CAN BE ASSUMED BY CREDITWORTHY VETERAN OR NON-VETERAN (WITH LENDER'S APPROVAL)
- RESTORATION OF ENTITLEMENT: LOAN MUST BE PAID OFF UNLESS ASSUMED BY ANOTHER VETERAN
- INCOME RATIO GUIDELINE: 41% DEBT TO INCOME RATIO
- RESIDUAL INCOME REQUIREMENTS

and utility costs ($0.14 × 1,500 square feet = $210) and subtract that figure. Then subtract Robert's proposed housing expense (PITI), which is, at most, $773 (the figure obtained from applying the 41% debt to income ratio).

$$\$2,800 - \$350 - \$214 - \$375 - \$210 - \$773 = \$878$$

Robert's residual income is above his required minimum ($823) so he should have no problem qualifying for the loan.

The VA emphasizes that its minimum residual income figures are only guidelines. If the veteran fails to meet the guidelines, it should not mean an automatic rejection of the loan application. The lender should take other factors into consideration, such as the applicant's ability to accumulate a significant net worth, and the number and ages of any dependents.

The VA's 41% income ratio is also flexible. A lender can approve a VA loan even though the applicant's income ratio is above 41% if the application presents other favorable factors, such as an excellent credit reputation, a substantial amount of reserves, a substantial downpayment, or significantly more residual income than the minimum amount required by the VA. Extra residual income is an especially important compensating factor. If the applicant's residual income is at least 20% over the required minimum, the lender can approve the loan even though the income ratio is well over 41% and there are no other compensating factors.

SELLER FINANCING

Institutional lenders such as banks, savings and loans, and mortgage companies are not the only sources of residential financing. In some cases, the home seller may also be a source. When a seller helps a buyer finance the purchase of a home, it's called **seller financing**. Seller financing can take a variety of forms, ranging from the simple to the complex.

HOW SELLER FINANCING WORKS

As you know, institutional lenders require both a promissory note and a security instrument (a mortgage or a deed of trust) when they make a loan. The promissory note is evidence of the debt, and the security instrument makes the property collateral for the loan. In many cases, these same documents are used in seller financing. The home buyer signs a promissory note, promising to pay the seller the amount of the debt, and then signs a mortgage or deed of trust that gives the seller a security interest in the home being purchased. This kind of seller financing arrangement is often called a **purchase money loan** or a carryback loan.

Purchase money loans are quite different from institutional loans. With an institutional loan, the lender gives the borrower cash, which is then given to the seller in return for the deed to the property. With a purchase money loan, the seller simply extends credit to the buyer. Essentially, the buyer is allowed to pay off the purchase price in installments over time, instead of having to pay the total purchase price in cash at closing.

In some instances, the seller may choose to use a land contract instead of the promissory note and mortgage or deed of trust. With a land contract, the buyer takes immediate possession of the land, but does not acquire legal title until the entire purchase price is paid off. A land contract is another way a seller can offer credit to the buyer.

In a seller-financed transaction, the seller usually decides which type of financing documents to use. If your seller is unsure about which type to use, you should recommend that she speak to an attorney. Never advise a seller about the legal consequences of using the various types of documents. And always recommend that an attorney prepare any documents used in a seller-financed transaction. If your seller wishes to prepare the documents herself, strongly recommend that an attorney review them before they are signed by the parties.

WHY USE SELLER FINANCING? Setting up a seller-financed transaction can be complicated. The seller has to decide what kinds of documents to use and, typically, one or more attorneys get involved somewhere along the way. But there are several good reasons to use seller financing. One important reason is to make the property more marketable. This is especially true when market interest rates are high or loans are difficult to obtain. When interest rates are high, mortgage payments are also high. Potential buyers may have a difficult time qualifying for a loan with high mortgage payments, or they may be simply unwilling to take on a long-term loan at such high interest rates. By offering seller financing at a lower-than-market interest rate, a seller can make his home more attractive to potential buyers.

Seller financing can also help a buyer who could not qualify for institutional financing to complete the purchase of a home. With seller financing, the buyer avoids some of the costs of borrowing money from a lender, such as the loan origination fee and any discount points. Also, the seller may agree to a smaller downpayment than an institutional lender would require. Both of these factors mean a buyer can close a seller-financed sale with much less cash than would be required for an institutional loan.

FIG. 10.11 ADVANTAGES OF SELLER FINANCING

WHY USE SELLER FINANCING?

- MAY MAKE PROPERTY MORE MARKETABLE
- SELLER CAN HELP BUYER QUALIFY FOR INSTITUTIONAL LOAN
- BUYER MAY SAVE MONEY ON FINANCING COSTS
- BUYER MAY BE WILLING TO PAY MORE FOR HOME
- POSSIBLE TAX BENEFITS FOR SELLER (INSTALLMENT SALE REPORTING)

Because of the potential advantages that seller financing has for buyers, the seller may be able to get more for her home. For example, if the seller was asking $150,000 cash, a buyer might be willing to pay $157,000 for the property with attractive seller financing terms. In essence, the buyer would pay an additional $7,000 for the property to get the advantages of a low downpayment, fewer closing costs, a favorable interest rate, and lower monthly payments.

Seller financing can also provide the seller with important tax benefits. Because the buyer will be paying the purchase price of the home in installments, over a period of years, the seller can spread out any taxable gain from the sale over that same period. In other words, the seller does not have to report the full taxable profit from the sale on her tax return in the year of sale. Only the amount of profit actually received in a given year is taxed in that year. The seller can spread the tax payments out over a longer period, and may be able to take advantage of a lower tax rate as a result.

Always advise a seller to consult an accountant or attorney about the tax implications of seller financing. There may be some tax disadvantages to a particular transaction that the seller may not be aware of.

CONCERNS OF THE PARTIES. When structuring a seller financing arrangement, it's important to pay close attention to the particular needs of the buyer and the seller. The buyer will be concerned with the cost of the financing, especially the interest rate and the amount of the downpayment. If the seller requires a balloon payment in a few years, the buyer should have some idea where he is going to get the money to make that payment. Will the buyer have the cash to make the balloon payment, or will he have to refinance the transaction? Financing that involves a balloon payment always presents a risk for the buyer. This kind of arrangement often works out fine, but the buyer should make plans about the balloon payment sooner rather than later.

Seller financing raises different concerns for the seller. Obviously, the seller doesn't want to extend financing to a buyer who can't afford the monthly payments. The seller should also be concerned about whether the buyer will be able to make any required balloon payment. But there are other equally important issues for the seller to consider.

First of all, the seller needs to decide whether she can really afford to offer seller financing, or whether she needs to be cashed out. For example, if the seller is purchasing a new home, she may need all of her equity from the old

---

FIG. 10.12   POTENTIAL ISSUES WITH SELLER FINANCING

SELLER FINANCING CONCERNS

- BALLOON PAYMENT: HOW WILL BUYER PAY IT WHEN THE TIME COMES?
- HOW MUCH IMMEDIATE CASH DOES SELLER NEED FROM SALE?
- IS INTEREST RATE CHARGED A GOOD RATE OF RETURN FOR SELLER?
- COULD THE FINANCING TERMS CREATE TAX PROBLEMS FOR SELLER?
- PRIORITY OF SELLER'S LIEN

---

home in cash at closing. And even if the seller does not need all of the equity immediately, will the buyer's anticipated downpayment be enough cash to meet the seller's needs?

Most sellers who offer seller financing do so because they don't need the cash right away and a steady monthly income is attractive. Is the mortgage payment the buyer will pay on the seller financing enough to meet the seller's monthly needs? Is the interest rate charged on the seller financing a good rate of return? If the seller would charge 5% interest on the second mortgage, but could get a 7% return from investing in a mutual fund, the seller may want to rethink the transaction. Also, depending on the rate of interest charged, the seller could be faced with tax penalties based on the "imputed interest" rule. Under the imputed interest rule, if a seller charges an interest rate that is below a specified minimum, the IRS will treat some of the principal received in each installment payment as interest, and thus taxable. If the seller runs afoul of the imputed interest rule, many of the benefits the seller thought he was getting by offering seller financing could be eliminated. Again, it is imperative to advise your sellers to seek competent tax advice before they enter into a seller-financed transaction.

Finally, lien priority is an important consideration for a seller entering into any seller financing arrangement, as we will discuss shortly.

TYPES OF SELLER FINANCING

Seller financing can be used alone, or it can be used in conjunction with institutional financing.

SELLER SECONDS. One of the most common forms of seller financing is the seller second. With a seller second, the buyer pays most of the purchase price with an institutional loan, and the seller finances some of what would normally be the buyer's downpayment with a second mortgage.

> **EXAMPLE:** Schmidt is buying Earnshaw's home for $200,000. She is getting an institutional loan for $170,000. However, she doesn't have enough cash to make a $30,000 downpayment, so Earnshaw agrees to take back a second mortgage in the amount of $15,000. Now Schmidt only has to come up with $15,000 for the downpayment.

There are several advantages to a seller second. As in this example, a seller second allows the buyer to make a smaller downpayment than she might otherwise have to make. A seller second can also help a marginal buyer qualify for an institutional loan. Institutional lenders have certain rules that must be followed when the buyer is going to use secondary financing. The lender should always be consulted to make sure the seller second is acceptable.

As long as the parties stay within the institutional lender's guidelines, they can come up with virtually unlimited ways to structure their financing package.

Lien priority is an important consideration for a seller who offers secondary seller financing. Purchase money mortgages are subject to the same priority rules as institutional mortgages. In the event of foreclosure, the first mortgage must be paid in full from the sale proceeds before any proceeds are allocated to the second mortgage. The seller should keep this in mind when negotiating the amount of a seller second. Is the property worth enough so that the proceeds of a foreclosure sale would be likely to cover both the first and second mortgages? The seller should be especially careful when there is a possibility that property values will decline in the next few years.

PRIMARY SELLER FINANCING. Seller financing may also be used as the main or only source of financing. This is called primary seller financing. Seller financing is at its most flexible when it is the only financing. Lender guidelines for secondary loans no longer have to be followed, and qualifying standards can be virtually ignored if the parties choose to do so.

UNENCUMBERED PROPERTY. Seller financing can be used when the property is either unencumbered or encumbered by a previous mortgage. Property is unencumbered when the seller owns it free and clear of any liens. When the property is unencumbered, seller financing is usually very straightforward. All the buyer and seller have to do is negotiate the sales price and the terms of the financing, and then have the appropriate finance documents prepared.

If the seller financing is the only source of financing, the seller will have first lien position, as long as she properly records the loan documents. However, the seller still has to be prepared to protect her security interest. A first mortgage does not have priority over all other liens. For example, real property tax liens and special assessment liens take priority over mortgages, no matter what the recording date. If the buyer fails to pay the property taxes, the property could be foreclosed on and the seller could take a loss at the foreclosure sale.

Destruction of the premises is another danger. Suppose the buyer fails to keep the property insured and the house burns down. The buyer then defaults on the loan, and the seller has to foreclose. Since the property is now probably worth much less than the amount of the remaining debt, the seller is likely to lose a great deal of money in the foreclosure sale.

The seller can protect her interest in the property by setting up an impound account for taxes and insurance, just as many institutional lenders do. Along with the loan payment, the buyer would make monthly tax and insurance payments, which would be deposited into the impound account. The funds in the impound account would then be used to pay the property taxes and insurance premiums when they become due. Many banks, savings and loans, and mortgage companies are willing to provide and service impound accounts for private parties.

ENCUMBERED PROPERTY. It's relatively uncommon for a seller to own his property free and clear of any other mortgage liens. Typically, the seller used a loan to purchase the property and still owes money on that loan when he decides to sell. When the property is encumbered with a mortgage loan, it is a rare seller who can pay off the first loan with savings or the proceeds of the downpayment alone.

For instance, suppose Brown is selling his home for $600,000. He would prefer to finance the sale and receive payments on an installment basis. However, there's a first mortgage on the property in the amount of $250,000. Brown doesn't have enough cash to pay off a $250,000 loan at closing, and a buyer is unlikely to have that much cash to invest in the home as a downpayment. It's possible that the buyer could assume Brown's existing mortgage, and Brown could then finance the rest of the purchase price with a seller second. But there is another alternative that may be more attractive: wraparound financing.

With a **wraparound loan**, the buyer does not assume the seller's mortgage. Nor does the seller try to pay off this mortgage at closing. Instead, the buyer takes the property "subject to" the existing mortgage. This means the seller remains primarily responsible for making the payments on this mortgage. The seller finances the complete purchase price for the buyer, less the downpayment. The seller then uses part of the monthly payment received from the buyer to make the monthly payment on the existing mortgage (referred to as the **underlying mortgage**) and keeps the remainder.

> **EXAMPLE:** Brown owes $250,000 on his house. The mortgage payment is $2,400. Brown sells his house to Morgan for $600,000. Morgan pays Brown a $70,000 downpayment, and Brown finances the remaining $530,000 purchase price at 7% interest. Morgan's monthly payment is $3,500. Brown uses part of the $3,500 to make the $2,400 payment on the underlying mortgage, then keeps the remaining $1,100 for himself.

Wraparound financing is only possible if the underlying loan does not have a due-on-sale clause. If there's a due-on-sale clause, the lender may call the underlying note, and it will become immediately due and payable.

When there is a due-on-sale clause in the underlying mortgage, it is dangerous to try to get away with a wraparound loan by keeping the lender in the dark about the sale. This is called a "silent" wrap, and it could easily backfire. Real estate agents should never get involved in silent wraps.

With wraparound financing, the buyer typically needs a little extra protection. If the seller fails to make the payments on the underlying loan, the institutional lender could foreclose, and the buyer could lose the property as well as all the monthly payments she has already made.

The best way to protect the buyer is to set up an escrow account for the loan payments. An independent third party in charge of the escrow account uses part of the buyer's payment to make the underlying loan payments and sends the remainder to the seller. Thus, the buyer is assured that the underlying loan payments will always be made in a timely manner. The seller can require the buyer to deposit tax and hazard insurance payments into the same account, thus protecting the seller's security interest in the property as well.

OTHER WAYS SELLERS CAN HELP

In many cases a seller can't afford to offer seller financing to a buyer, usually because the seller can't wait several years to be cashed out. However, there are a number of other ways in which a seller can help a buyer close the transaction. We've already mentioned buydowns and seller contributions to closing costs.

A seller may also help out by agreeing to an **equity exchange**. This means that instead of cash, the seller accepts another asset, such as recreational property, a car, or a boat, as all or part of the downpayment. Again, this kind of transaction enables the buyer to close the sale with significantly less cash.

The other form of seller assistance that we'll mention here is the **lease/option**. Sometimes a prospective buyer may simply not be ready to purchase a home. The buyer may need time to save up for a downpayment, pay off debts, or improve her credit rating. Or perhaps the buyer needs more time to sell a property she already owns. In these circumstances, a lease/option arrangement may help the buyer purchase the seller's home. A lease/option is a combination of a lease and an option to buy. The seller leases the property to a prospective buyer for a specific period of time. At the same time, the seller gives the buyer an option to purchase the property at a certain price during the lease period.

Whenever you're handling a sale that involves seller financing, you should make sure that both parties understand the ramifications of the transaction. While you can't give them legal advice, it's appropriate to raise the concerns we've discussed here, such as the seller's lien priority and the importance of escrow accounts. As a real estate agent, you should never prepare the documents used in a seller-financed transaction, and you should always recommend that both the buyer and the seller get advice from their attorneys or accountants, or both.

CHAPTER SUMMARY

1. The basic features of a residential mortgage loan are the repayment period, amortization, the loan-to-value ratio, secondary financing (in some cases), loan fees, and a fixed or adjustable interest rate.

2. Conventional loans may be 30-year or 15-year, fixed- or adjustable-rate, and fully or partially amortized. Conventional loans with loan-to-value ratios up to 95% are generally available. Private mortgage insurance is required for conventional loans with LTVs over 80%.

3. Lenders charge an origination fee to cover their administrative costs, and may charge discount points to increase the upfront yield on the loan. A seller may pay for a buydown to help the buyer qualify for financing.

4. As a general rule, a conventional loan applicant's debt to income ratio shouldn't exceed 36%. Many lenders also calculate an applicant's housing expense to income ratio, which generally shouldn't exceed 28%.

5. FHA loans are characterized by less stringent qualifying standards, a low downpayment (minimum cash investment) requirement, and mortgage insurance (both a one-time premium and annual premiums).

6. An FHA loan applicant's fixed payment to income ratio should not exceed 43%, and the housing expense to income ratio should not exceed 31%.

7. VA loans generally require no downpayment and no mortgage insurance. VA qualifying standards are lenient. The maximum guaranty for VA loans is adjusted annually. Although the VA does not set a maximum loan amount, most lenders require the guaranty to cover at least 25% of the loan amount.

8. A VA loan applicant's debt to income ratio generally should not exceed 41%, and the applicant must also have residual income that meets VA standards.

9. When a seller helps the buyer finance the transaction, it's called seller financing. The most common form of seller financing is the seller second: the buyer pays most of the purchase price with an institutional loan, and the seller finances some of the buyer's downpayment. Seller financing can also be the only financing in a transaction.

CHAPTER QUIZ

1. A loan that requires monthly payments of both principal and interest, but leaves some of the principal to be paid off in a balloon payment at the end of the loan term, is:

   a. fully amortized

   b. negatively amortized

   c. non-amortized

   d. partially amortized

2. A lender will usually charge a higher interest rate in which of the following situations?

   a. The borrower wants an ARM instead of a fixed-rate mortgage

   b. The seller is offering a buydown

   c. The borrower wants a 5/1 ARM instead of an ARM with a one-year initial rate adjustment period

   d. The borrower wants a 15-year loan instead of a 30-year loan

3. A portfolio loan is a loan that:

   a. the lender plans to keep as an investment

   b. conforms to the rules of Fannie Mae and Freddie Mac

   c. is insured or guaranteed by a government agency

   d. is sold on the secondary market

4. To compensate for the extra risk, a lender making a conventional loan with a high loan-to-value ratio:

   a. might apply stricter qualifying standards

   b. might charge higher loan fees

   c. will require private mortgage insurance

   d. All of the above

5. The Homeowners Protection Act requires:

   a. borrowers to send a written request to their lender in order to cancel private mortgage insurance

   b. all loans closed on or after July 29, 1999, to be covered by private mortgage insurance

   c. lenders to send all borrowers with private mortgage insurance an annual notice concerning their PMI cancellation rights

   d. lenders to automatically cancel the PMI when a loan's principal balance reaches 78% of the home's current appraised value

6. All of the following factors might justify making a loan when the borrower's income ratios exceed the standard benchmarks, except:

   a. substantial net worth

   b. significant energy-efficient features in the home being purchased

   c. a high loan-to-value ratio

   d. education that indicates strong potential for increased earnings

7. With a graduated payment buydown plan, what rate will a lender probably use to qualify the buyer for the loan?

   a. A rate somewhere between the initial rate the borrower will pay and the full note rate

   b. The note rate

   c. A rate 1% or 2% above the note rate

   d. The buydown rate

8. Which of the following can the borrower count as part of the minimum cash investment required for an FHA loan?

   a. Discount points

   b. Closing costs

   c. Prepaid expenses

   d. None of the above

9. Jack, a veteran who wants to buy a house with a VA loan, has full guaranty entitlement. Which of the following is true?

   a. The VA guaranty will cover only a portion of the loan amount

   b. The VA guaranty will cover the entire loan amount

   c. Jack cannot be required to make a downpayment, regardless of the loan amount

   d. Jack is guaranteed a VA loan, so the VA's usual qualifying standards will be waived

10. If a seller wants to help a prospective buyer qualify for a conventional loan, which of the following options may reduce the interest rate used to qualify the buyer for the loan?

    a. Buydown

    b. Lease/option

    c. Silent wrap

    d. Equity exchange

ANSWER KEY

1. d. With a partially amortized loan, not all of the principal is paid off through the monthly payments, and the borrower must make a balloon payment at the end of the loan term.

2. c. With adjustable-rate loans, as a general rule, the longer the initial rate adjustment period, the higher the interest rate. The interest rate on a 5/1 ARM is not adjusted during the first five years, but may be adjusted annually after that.

3. a. If a lender plans to keep a loan as an investment instead of selling it on the secondary market, the lender is keeping the loan "in portfolio."

4. d. For a high-LTV conventional loan, many lenders apply stricter qualifying standards and charge a higher interest rate and loan fees. Private mortgage insurance is generally required on any conventional loan with an LTV over 80%.

5. c. The Homeowners Protection Act requires lenders to send an annual notice to borrowers with PMI, regardless of whether their loans are subject to the other provisions of the act. (PMI must be canceled automatically when the principal balance reaches 78% of the home's original value, not 78% of the current appraised value.)

6. c. If the borrower exceeds the income ratio guidelines, the lender may consider other factors that indicate the borrower will be able to make the monthly payments. A high loan-to-value ratio, however, means the borrower has less invested in the property and is more likely to default.

7. b. Because a buyer with a graduated payment buydown will eventually have to pay interest at the full note rate, the lender wants to make sure the buyer will be able to handle the increased monthly payments. As a result, the lender will qualify the borrower using the note rate.

8. d. Discount points paid by the borrower do not count towards the minimum cash investment, nor do the closing costs or prepaid expenses.

9. a. The VA guaranty covers only a portion of the loan amount. Even veterans who have full guaranty entitlement must meet the VA's qualifying standards in order to obtain a VA-guaranteed loan.

10. a. With a buydown, the seller can lower the interest rate on the buyer's loan, which may allow the buyer to get a loan he might not otherwise qualify for.

CHAPTER 11

CLOSING THE TRANSACTION AND REAL ESTATE MATH

THE CLOSING PROCESS

- Escrow
- Steps in closing a transaction
  - Overview
  - Inspections
  - Financing
  - Appraisal
  - Hazard insurance
  - Title insurance
- Real estate agent's role

CLOSING COSTS

- Costs and credits
- Estimating the buyer's net cost
- Estimating the seller's net proceeds

FEDERAL LAWS THAT AFFECT CLOSING

- Income tax regulations
  - Form 1099-S reporting
  - Form 8300 reporting
  - Foreign Investment in Real Property Tax Act
- Real Estate Settlement Procedures Act

REAL ESTATE MATH

INTRODUCTION

You helped your buyers find an affordable house that suits their needs. They made an offer on the house, and the sellers accepted it. That's not the end of the story, though. The buyers must now order inspections, apply for or finalize their financing, and obtain a preliminary title report. The sellers must pay off the liens against the property, arrange for required repairs, and execute the deed. In other words, the buyers and the sellers must go through the closing process.

As a real estate agent, you will be shepherding your buyers and sellers through closing. Many of your clients will be unfamiliar with the process; you'll need to calm their anxieties and answer their questions. How long will it take to close the sale? What responsibilities does each party have? How much cash will the buyer need to close the sale? How much cash will the seller receive at closing?

In this chapter, we will discuss the closing process, closing costs and which party usually pays them, and how to estimate the buyer's net cost and the seller's net proceeds. We'll also cover some federal laws that affect closing, including the Real Estate Settlement Procedures Act. We'll end the chapter with a quick look at some common math problems you're likely to encounter in your real estate practice.

THE CLOSING PROCESS

The phrase "closing a sale" actually has two meanings in the real estate field. Sometimes it refers to getting a buyer to make an offer. For instance, a seller's agent can "close a sale" by overcoming the buyer's objections and convincing the buyer that it's the right time to make an offer on the house. Here, however, we'll be using "closing the sale" in its other sense, to mean completing all the tasks that have to be taken care of before title can be transferred to the buyer and the purchase price can be disbursed to the seller.

For every sale you handle as a real estate agent, it's part of your job to make sure that all of the closing requirements are met on time. You probably won't be completing all, or even most, of the necessary tasks yourself, but you have to know what needs to be done, who's responsible for doing it, and whether it's being done in a timely manner. If the closing process doesn't go smoothly, it can cause considerable delay and inconvenience, and in some cases the transaction will fall apart altogether.

FIG. 11 .1   CHECKLIST FOR CLOSING

Closing Checklist

Property: _____

Buyer: _____

Seller: _____

Other party's agent: _____

Financing		Inspection 1	
Lender: _____		Company: _____	
Loan application submitted	_____	Inspection ordered	_____
Appraisal ordered	_____	Inspection report issued	_____
Appraisal completed	_____	Approval or disapproval	_____
Loan package submitted	_____	Seller's response	_____
Loan approved	_____	Repairs completed	_____
Loan documents signed	_____	Repairs reinspected	_____
Loan funds disbursed	_____	Reinspection approved	_____

Closing Requirements		Inspection 2	
Earnest money deposited	_____	Company: _____	
Escrow opened	_____	Inspection ordered	_____
Escrow instructions	_____	Inspection report issued	_____
Seller's information	_____	Approval or disapproval	_____
Title search ordered	_____	Seller's response	_____
Preliminary title report	_____	Repairs completed	_____
Demand for payoff	_____	Repairs reinspected	_____
All conditions fulfilled	_____	Reinspection approved	_____
All documents signed	_____		
Buyer deposits funds	_____	**Moving**	
Hazard insurance policy	_____	Seller's belongings out	_____
Documents recorded	_____	Yard cleanup	_____
Title policies issued	_____	Interior cleaning	_____
Settlement statements	_____	Keys for buyer	_____

To help keep track of the steps in the closing process and make sure that everything's getting done, you might want to use a closing checklist, such as the one shown in Figure 11.1. Review the purchase and sale agreement to remind yourself of the basic terms and any unusual provisions; add any special requirements to the checklist. As the days go by, refer to your list on a regular basis, check off what has been accomplished and fill in the date of completion, and note what still needs to be done.

ESCROW

Most transactions in Washington are closed through the escrow process. An **escrow agent** or **closing agent**, who owes fiduciary duties to each party, handles the closing. The escrow agent holds money and documents on behalf of the buyer and seller in accordance with their written **escrow instructions**. The agent will release the money and documents to the appropriate parties only when all of the conditions set forth in the escrow instructions have been fulfilled.

There are two major benefits to closing a transaction through escrow. First, escrow helps ensure that both parties will go through with the transaction as agreed. For example, once a signed deed has been placed in escrow, it's much more difficult for the seller to change his mind at the last moment and refuse to transfer title to the buyer. The escrow agent has legally binding instructions to deliver the deed to the buyer when the buyer pays the purchase price. The seller can't just demand the deed back from the escrow agent. So if the seller changes his mind, a lawsuit may be required to resolve the matter.

The second benefit of escrow is convenience. It isn't necessary for everyone involved in the transaction to be present at the same time for the sale to close.

ESCROW AGENTS. In addition to holding items on behalf of the parties and disbursing them at the proper time, the escrow agent or closing agent is also responsible for seeing that legal documents are prepared and recorded, prorating the settlement costs, preparing the settlement statements, and various other tasks.

LICENSING AND EXEMPTIONS. In Washington, escrow agents must be licensed and registered with the Department of Financial Institutions. However, there are several exemptions from the escrow licensing requirements. Attorneys, title companies, banks, savings and loans, credit unions, insurance companies, federally approved lenders, and those acting under court supervision (such as probate administrators) may provide escrow services without fulfilling the licensing and registration requirements. Real estate agents who provide escrow services for transactions they are handling are also exempt, as long as they don't charge a separate fee for their escrow services.

EXAMPLE: Yamamoto is buying Farley's house. You are the real estate agent representing Farley. You agree to act as the closing agent free of charge.

You may do so, even if you do not have an escrow agent license. But if you charge Yamamoto and Farley an escrow fee in addition to your regular commission, that will violate the escrow licensing law.

Although it's legal for real estate licensees to handle escrow in their own transactions, it isn't necessarily a good idea; the arrangement may create a conflict of interest. A licensee usually represents either the buyer or the seller and owes a duty of loyalty to her client. But a closing agent is supposed to be neutral and act on behalf of both parties.

TERMINOLOGY. Sometimes the term "escrow agent" is reserved for a registered independent escrow company or a licensed escrow officer for such a company, while "closing agent" is used as a general term that refers to any person or entity providing escrow services in a real estate transaction (whether that's a lawyer, a bank, a real estate licensee, or a licensed escrow agent). In other cases, the two terms are used interchangeably to mean any person or entity that is providing escrow services in a real estate transaction, regardless of whether he has an escrow license. Thus, when a lawyer or a real estate licensee is performing the same tasks as an independent escrow company, you may hear the lawyer or the licensee referred to either as the closing agent or as the escrow agent for the transaction.

STEPS IN CLOSING A TRANSACTION

Certain steps must be completed during the closing process in almost every residential transaction. We'll give you an overview of these steps, and then consider some of them in more detail.

OVERVIEW. Our overview will include a brief look at inspections, financing, appraisal, and other key parts of the closing process.

ORDERING INSPECTIONS. If the sale is contingent on one or more inspections—for example, a home inspection and a pest inspection—the inspections should be ordered as soon as possible after the purchase and sale agreement is signed. The orders are usually issued by the buyer or the buyer's real estate agent.

The completed inspection report should be sent to the buyer or the buyer's real estate agent, who in turn may be expected to provide a copy to the buyer's lender. If the report shows that repairs are needed, there may be negotiations between the buyer and the seller about which of them will pay for the repairs (see Chapter 8). For any lender-required repairs, the lender will want proof that the repairs have been completed.

BUYER'S LOAN. Although some buyers pay all cash, many buyers borrow the bulk of the purchase price. If so, the buyer should arrange for financing as soon as possible. The buyer must either apply for a loan or, if he has been preapproved for a loan, fulfill any additional requirements set by the lender. In any case, the lender will order a property appraisal before issuing a final loan commitment.

OPENING ESCROW. Escrow may be opened when the buyer's lender delivers a copy of the purchase and sale agreement to its escrow department. Alternatively, a real estate agent may open escrow by delivering a copy of the agreement to the escrow agent specified by the parties. Either way, the escrow agent uses the purchase and sale agreement as the basis for preparing the escrow instructions for the buyer and seller to sign. The conditions and deadlines in the instructions must match the terms of the agreement.

APPRAISAL. The buyer's lender will require a property appraisal before issuing a final loan commitment. The appraiser sends the appraisal report to the buyer's lender, because the lender is the appraiser's client. With most residential loans, the lender must provide the buyer with a copy of the appraisal report.

TITLE REPORT. The escrow agent orders a preliminary title report if the lender has not already done so. This report, which describes the current condition of the seller's title to the property, is sent to the lender and the buyer for approval. Any unexpected title problems revealed in the report must be addressed.

SELLER'S LOAN PAYOFF. In many transactions, the seller has a mortgage or deed of trust on the property that will be paid off at closing. The closing agent requests a final payoff figure from the seller's lender. A form called a "Demand for Payoff" or a "Request for Beneficiary's Statement" is used to make this request. The closing agent also needs to obtain exact payoff figures for any other liens that must be removed or judgments that must be paid.

BUYER'S LOAN APPROVAL. When the buyer's loan is approved, the lender informs the buyer of the exact terms on which it was approved and the date on which the loan commitment will expire. The lender also gives the buyer an updated good faith estimate of her closing costs. The lender sends all of the new loan documents—the promissory note and the mortgage or deed of trust—to the escrow agent, who arranges for the buyer to review and sign them. Once the loan documents have been signed, they are returned to the lender, who then coordinates loan funding with the escrow agent.

BUYER'S FUNDS. When all of the contingencies listed in the purchase and sale agreement (such as the inspections, the financing arrangements, or the sale of the

FIG. 11.2   STEPS IN THE CLOSING PROCESS

- INSPECTIONS ORDERED BY BUYER OR REAL ESTATE AGENT
- FINANCING APPLIED FOR OR FINALIZED BY BUYER
- APPRAISAL ORDERED BY LENDER
- ESCROW OPENED BY LENDER OR REAL ESTATE AGENT
- ESCROW INSTRUCTIONS PREPARED BY CLOSING AGENT
- PRELIMINARY TITLE REPORT ORDERED BY CLOSING AGENT
- LOAN PAYOFF AMOUNT REQUESTED FROM SELLER'S LENDER BY CLOSING AGENT
- LOAN DOCUMENTS SIGNED BY BUYER
- DOWNPAYMENT AND CLOSING COSTS DEPOSITED BY BUYER
- LOAN FUNDS DEPOSITED BY LENDER
- FUNDS DISBURSED BY CLOSING AGENT
- TITLE POLICY ISSUED BY TITLE COMPANY
- DOCUMENTS FILED FOR RECORDING BY TITLE COMPANY
- HAZARD INSURANCE POLICY ISSUED TO BUYER

buyer's home) have been satisfied, the buyer deposits the downpayment and the closing costs into escrow. Some lenders disburse the loan funds to the escrow agent at this point, but many lenders wait until the title has been transferred and the buyer's deed and mortgage or deed of trust have been recorded.

CLOSING DATE. On the closing date, the escrow agent disburses the funds held in escrow to the seller, the real estate firm(s), and other individuals or entities that are entitled to payment. The title insurance policies are issued, as is the buyer's hazard or homeowner's insurance policy. The deed and the other documents are filed with the county clerk for recording. Once this has all been done, the sale has officially closed.

Next, let's look at certain aspects of the closing process in more detail. We'll discuss property inspections, financing and the appraisal, hazard insurance, and title insurance.

INSPECTIONS. For each inspection required by the parties' agreement or by the lender, an initial inspection must be ordered. The inspection report must then be approved or rejected by the buyer or the lender, repairs must be completed and reinspected, and the parties must be notified about the results of the reinspection. (For more information about the types of addenda and notice forms that can be used for inspection contingencies, see Chapter 8.) It's very important for inspections to be ordered early in the closing process; if repairs are required, they need to be completed early enough so that they don't delay the closing.

TYPES OF INSPECTIONS. There are many different types of real estate inspections. Here are brief descriptions of the inspections most commonly required in residential transactions. The first three on the list may be carried out by a single expert, a licensed home inspector.

- **Structural inspection.** The inspector identifies the materials used in the construction, the type of construction, and the accessibility of the various areas that are to be inspected. In addition, the inspector checks for major and minor problems in the structural systems of the building, including the foundation and the floor, walls, and roof framing.
- **Electrical and plumbing inspection.** The inspector checks the electrical and plumbing systems for capacity, safety, and life expectancy. Plumbing systems are also checked for unsanitary conditions. Upgrades and repairs may be recommended. If the property's water source is a private well, it may also be inspected for water quality and quantity.
- **Interior inspection.** The inspector checks the walls, floors, and ceilings for signs of water damage, settling, fire hazards, or other problems. Ventilation and energy conservation issues are noted. Appliances may also be examined for operational problems.
- **Pest inspection.** A pest inspector checks for damage caused by wood-eating insects such as termites, wood-boring beetles, and carpenter ants.
- **Soil inspection.** A soil inspector or geologist examines the soil conditions to see if there are existing or potential settling or drainage problems.
- **Environmental inspection.** An environmental inspection addresses concerns such as radon, urea formaldehyde, asbestos, lead-based paint, underground storage tanks, or contaminated water. (These problems are discussed in more detail in Chapter 3.)

CHOOSING AN INSPECTOR. For a particular inspection, your buyer may have an inspector in mind, or he may ask you to recommend someone reputable.

When referring home inspectors, you must be sure to follow your brokerage firm's policy on referrals. State law requires every firm to have a written policy on referring home inspectors. This policy must address the buyers' or sellers' right to pick a home inspector of their own choosing and prohibit any collusion between a home inspector and a real estate licensee. Keep in mind that if you refer someone to a home inspector with whom you have (or had) any type of relationship, then full disclosure of the relationship must be provided in writing prior to the buyer or seller using the services of the home inspector.

Many firms require the agent to give the buyer at least three names to choose from. (Ask other agents in your office for suggestions, if necessary.) To help a buyer make the selection, you can suggest that he ask the home inspector the following questions:

1. How long has the firm (or individual inspector) been in business? (A minimum of five years' experience is recommended.)
2. Does the firm belong to the American Society of Home Inspectors? (Membership requires actual experience, passing a written examination, inspection reviews, and continuing education.)
3. Has the firm changed its name recently? If so, why?
4. What type of report does the firm prepare? How long does it take to complete the report and get it back to the client?
5. How many inspectors does the firm have? Are they full-time or part-time?
6. Does the firm engage in other businesses in addition to inspections? (In other words, is home inspection only a sideline?)
7. Does the firm also offer to make any of the repairs recommended by the inspection? (Inspection companies that also make repairs may not give unbiased reports.)
8. Does the firm provide references? If the buyer requests them, an inspector should be willing to give several references.

You must check the state licensing database to make sure any home inspector you recommend is licensed. It is also a good idea to check with the Department of Licensing and the Better Business Bureau to see if any complaints have been lodged against the inspection firm.

INSPECTION REPORTS. After an inspection is completed, the inspector prepares an inspection report. The report should summarize the major points of concern and state which problems need to be repaired or otherwise addressed promptly.

This should include information about substandard workmanship and also about deterioration, such as rotting wood or corroded pipes.

The report should put the property into perspective by comparing it to similar properties. A 15-year-old house can't be expected to be in the same condition as a brand new one.

In addition, the report should project a five-year budget for anticipated repair work and identify potential remodeling problems. For instance, if the buyer were to add rooms onto the house, the entire electrical system might need to be upgraded. Or the septic system might only be adequate for a three-bedroom house and, if another bedroom were added, a new septic tank would be required.

REPAIRS. After an inspection report has been issued, the party who requested it (the buyer or the lender) must either approve or disapprove the report. Depending on the terms of the inspection contingency provision, the buyer may have the right to disapprove the report for any reason and terminate the transaction without giving the seller the opportunity to make repairs. Or the contingency provision may require the buyer to identify which items in the report are unsatisfactory and need to be repaired if the transaction is to continue. (See Chapter 8.) If the buyer's lender ordered the inspection, the repairs may be a condition of loan approval.

Ideally, the parties have already agreed who will pay for any required repairs, but that isn't always the case. The purchase and sale agreement may commit the seller to paying up to a specified amount, but no more than that. If the repair costs significantly exceed that amount, it may be necessary for the seller to negotiate a price adjustment or some other concession to persuade the buyer to go forward.

In many cases, the repairs have to be completed and reinspected—and the buyer or lender has to approve the reinspection report—before the sale can close or the loan can be funded. In some circumstances, however, the closing can take place even though the repairs won't be completed by the closing date.

FINANCING. A home sale can't close unless the buyers have enough money to pay the purchase price. The buyers usually borrow the money they need from a bank or other lender. As explained in Chapter 9, it's now common for buyers to get preapproved for financing. Before choosing a house to buy, the buyers submit a fully completed loan application and the supporting documentation. The lender performs a credit analysis and qualifies the buyers for a certain loan amount at a specified interest rate. If the buyers find a house that can be purchased with that loan amount, and if the property meets the lender's standards, the lender will issue a final loan commitment.

Employees of the buyer's lender are actively involved in closing the transaction. The lender's team orders and evaluates the appraisal, reviews the preliminary title report, and may also order inspections and require repairs. They prepare the financing documents for the buyer to sign, and they are responsible for funding the loan—that is, depositing the loan amount into escrow so that it can be disbursed at closing. As we indicated earlier, in many cases the entire closing is handled by the lender's escrow department.

Because of their role, the loan officer and other employees of the lender can have a big impact on the closing. If they're reputable and competent, they'll make sure that the loan process is completed smoothly and quickly, with a minimum of errors. Find out which lenders have good or bad reputations by asking experienced real estate agents, and pass that information along to your buyers before they choose their lender.

APPRAISAL. The buyer's lender orders the appraisal as part of the loan underwriting process. The property as well as the buyer must be qualified for the requested loan. Regardless of the buyer's financial situation, it's the property that serves as the security for the debt. If the loan is not repaid as agreed, the lender will foreclose on the property to recover the money owed. Before approving the loan, the lender wants assurance that it is lending based on the property's fair market value, so that if the borrower defaults, any loss on the foreclosure sale will be as small as possible. Also, borrowers with little or no equity in the property are much more likely to default, so lenders want borrowers to start out with at least some equity. To ensure that there will be adequate equity, the maximum loan amount for a transaction is tied to the property's appraised value or its sales price, whichever is less (see Chapter 10).

The residential appraisal process has a lot in common with the competitive market analysis that real estate agents use to help price a home (see Chapter 4). In fact, the CMA method is based on the sales comparison approach to appraisal, which is the most important approach for residential appraisals.

You should understand the basic appraisal process well enough to give a brief explanation of the process to the buyer and seller. They are often anxious about the appraisal, since their transaction depends on the appraiser's opinion.

HAZARD INSURANCE. Virtually all lenders require the escrow agent to make sure that the mortgaged property is insured up to the property's replacement cost before the loan funds are disbursed. In most cases the minimum insurance policy is the

HO-3 policy (a broad-coverage homeowner's policy). This type of policy provides coverage against most perils, but does exclude floods and earthquakes, as well as some less common perils (such as war and nuclear hazard).

A buyer who is concerned about floods or earthquakes should consider buying supplemental coverage. However, this type of coverage can be expensive, and it isn't available in all areas or for all properties. For instance, a house may need to have had seismic retrofitting before the buyer can obtain earthquake coverage.

Applying for hazard insurance used to be a part of the closing process that was taken for granted. Buyers rarely had trouble obtaining ordinary coverage. However, because of stricter insurance underwriting standards, it's no longer so unusual for a buyer to be turned down. As a result, some purchase and sale agreement forms now have a hazard insurance contingency provision, which makes the sale contingent on whether the buyer can obtain adequate coverage. The need for hazard insurance may also be met through the financing contingency, since institutional lenders won't fund a loan without proof of insurance. (See Chapter 8.)

TITLE INSURANCE. Title insurance insures the buyer or the buyer's lender against financial losses that could result from as yet undiscovered problems with the seller's title. As we said earlier, the escrow agent or the lender orders a preliminary title report on the property.

The title report should be ordered early in the closing process to allow time for problems to be resolved. For example, if the title report indicates that there is a judgment lien against the property, the seller will have to clear away the lien so that marketable title can be transferred to the buyer at closing. Depending on the circumstances, the seller may simply arrange to pay the lienholder at closing out of the sale proceeds. In other cases, the seller may need to prove to the title company's satisfaction that there is no lien against the property. Perhaps the title searcher overlooked a recorded release, or the lien might be against a completely different person who has the same name as the seller.

TYPES OF TITLE POLICIES. As a condition of the buyer's loan, the lender will require the buyer to purchase a **lender's title insurance policy** for the lender. The lender's policy (sometimes referred to as a mortgagee's policy) protects the lender's security interest.

> **EXAMPLE:** After closing, it comes to light that there's a lien against the property that has higher priority than the lender's deed of trust. That other lien was not discovered by the title searcher and listed in the title report. As a

result, the lien was not paid off before closing. But it also wasn't listed as an exception to coverage in the title policy, so if the lender suffers a financial loss because it doesn't have first lien position, the title company will have to reimburse the lender, up to the face amount of the policy.

The purchase and sale agreement usually requires the seller to purchase an **owner's title insurance policy** for the buyer. This policy will protect the buyer's ownership interest against undiscovered title problems, such as a forged deed or a gap in the chain of title. It will cover the legal fees paid to defend the buyer's title against a covered claim. If the claim is successful despite this defense, the company will compensate the policy holder (the buyer) for the financial loss, up to the face amount of the policy.

It's never wise for a buyer to purchase a home without an owner's title insurance policy. (Keep in mind that the lender's policy offers no protection to the buyer.) The coverage is not particularly expensive, and although title problems are unlikely to surface, they could be very costly if they did.

EXTENT OF COVERAGE. Standard coverage title insurance protects the policy holder against title problems caused by recorded deeds or liens, or other interests (such as a deed that was not signed by all the owners).

Extended coverage protects against all of the same problems that a standard coverage policy does, plus problems that should be discovered in an actual inspection of the property. These include encroachments, adverse possession, construction that may result in a lien that hasn't been recorded yet, and other problems that do not show up in the public record. The title company sends an inspector to the property to look for indications that there may be one of these problems. Lenders require lender's policies to be extended coverage policies.

Homeowner's coverage is the routine choice in transactions involving residential property with up to four units. A homeowner's coverage policy covers most of the same matters as an extended coverage policy, as well as some additional issues such as violations of restrictive covenants. In Washington, most residential purchase agreement forms provide for the seller to purchase this type of policy for the buyer, unless the parties agree on another type.

THE REAL ESTATE AGENT'S ROLE IN THE CLOSING PROCESS

As your sale progresses toward closing, it's important to keep track of the details. Don't assume that everything's going smoothly while you turn your attention to other listings and other buyers.

COMMUNICATION. Throughout the closing process, keep your client up to date on what's happening. Let her know when the appraisal is completed, when the loan is approved, and so on. This will ease her anxieties and reassure her that someone—you—is looking after her interests. Communication is especially important when problems crop up. If there's a delay in getting a preliminary title report or the pest inspection looks bad, tell your client immediately. Explain the problem, suggest what can be done about it, and then work with the client to find a solution.

Communication with the other party's agent is also very important. You need to promote your client's interests, but you should always do your best to get along with the other agent and the other party. Although their interests will sometimes conflict with those of your client, in most cases all of you ultimately want the sale to close. Don't agree to unreasonable demands, but work with the other agent to complete the transaction successfully.

PREVENTING PROBLEMS. Here is a list of questions and suggestions that will help you prevent problems and make the closing process smoother. Of course, what you do in a particular transaction will depend in part on whether you're representing the buyer or the seller.

PREPARING THE PURCHASE AND SALE AGREEMENT. Have the forms used for the buyer's offer and any counteroffers been filled out carefully? Do the parties understand the terms of their agreement? Is the legal description of the property complete and correct? Consider whether the deadlines in the agreement make sense under all of the current conditions. How long will it take to fulfill the contingencies in this market? The contingencies may include inspections, financing, and even the sale of the buyer's current home. When does the buyer need to move? Is it realistic to expect that the seller can be completely moved out by that date?

OPENING ESCROW. Does the escrow agent have a copy of every addendum and amendment as well as a copy of the purchase and sale agreement itself? If the escrow instructions are separate from the purchase agreement form, do they accurately reflect all the terms of the purchase and sale agreement? The parties can sign amended instructions if necessary.

INSPECTIONS. Are you responsible for ordering any inspections? If so, do it right away. And if someone else has that responsibility, make sure they take care of it as soon as possible. Later, check to see whether the inspection report has been delivered to the appropriate parties. Does the report seem thorough and accurate? If the report recommends repairs, do the recommendations seem reasonable? If the transaction is contingent on the results of this inspection, help your client prepare or respond to the inspection notice (see Chapter 8). If repairs are agreed to, they should be ordered and completed as soon as possible. Have arrangements for a timely reinspection been made?

FINANCING. If the buyer is using financing and hasn't been preapproved for a loan, has she gathered all of the personal information that she'll need for the loan application? Has she chosen a competent lender? Check with the lender periodically to find out how the loan process is going.

APPRAISAL. Is the sales price in line with local property values? If the appraisal comes in low, does a request for reconsideration of value seem appropriate? (See Chapter 4.)

SPECIAL PROVISIONS. Are there any special provisions in the purchase and sale agreement that require your attention? Are both parties clear on which personal property items and fixtures are included in the sale, and which the seller is going to take with him?

TITLE INSURANCE. Has a preliminary title report been ordered? When the report becomes available, find out whether there are any title problems that need to be cleared up.

HAZARD INSURANCE. Has the buyer applied for and obtained a new homeowner's insurance policy? Has a copy of the policy been delivered to the escrow agent or the lender?

MOVING OUT. Is the seller packing his belongings and preparing to move out on time? Has he arranged for his mail to be forwarded? Will the seller leave the house reasonably clean and the yard in reasonably good shape? Many sellers will be glad to pay to have junk hauled away, or to have a team of house cleaners go over the house once it's empty. You should be able to recommend junk hauling services and house cleaning services. Ask the other agents in your office which companies they recommend.

MOVING IN. If the buyer wants to move in before closing, or the seller wants to move out after closing, has an interim rental agreement been prepared and signed? (See Chapter 7.) Whenever the buyer moves in, will the seller have all of the house keys ready to turn over to the buyer? If the buyer finds personal property that may have been left behind accidentally, or if there's unforwarded mail for the seller, it's usually more appropriate to contact the seller's agent rather than the seller himself.

LAST-MINUTE PROBLEMS. In the closing process, the risk that the transaction will fall apart is usually greatest before the contingencies have been fulfilled, but something can go wrong at any point, right up through the last few days before closing.

> **EXAMPLE:** The sale of your client's house to the Friedmans has been going well. The seller and the buyers have been taking care of their responsibilities on time, and the financing contingency and inspection contingencies have been satisfied.
>
> But just a week before the date set for closing, you get a call from the seller. He says that there's a problem with the house that he never told you about. There's some dry rot in one of the crawl spaces. He should have listed this in the seller disclosure statement, but he decided not to. The home inspector apparently missed the problem. Now the seller's conscience (and fear of liability) has prompted him to let you know about it. He wants to know what he should do.

How you handle this situation may mean the difference between closing the sale on time and not closing it at all. The problem must be disclosed to the buyers, and they could use it as grounds for canceling the contract. You should do whatever you can to prevent that. For instance, you might go to the house and investigate the extent of the problem, consult with your designated broker or a licensed home inspector, help the seller decide on an appropriate price concession to offer the buyers, and then call the buyers' agent. By dealing with this problem in a straightforward and professional manner, you can make it much more likely that the sale will go through.

To summarize, always stay on top of the closing process. Keep in touch with your client, with the other party's agent, and with the escrow agent. Handle any problems that come up as promptly as you can. Your role in getting the transaction to close can be just as important as your role in negotiating the sale in the first place.

CLOSING COSTS

One of your tasks as a real estate agent is explaining to your clients the various costs associated with closing a real estate transaction. Some examples of closing costs are inspection fees, title insurance fees, recording fees, escrow fees, and loan fees. Some of these are paid by the buyer, some are paid by the seller, and some are split between the two parties.

As a real estate agent, you need to be able to give the buyers and sellers you work with a reasonable estimate of their closing costs. Sellers want to know how much money they'll get from a sale, and buyers want to know how much they'll actually end up paying at closing. They will often ask you about this before they make or accept an offer or counteroffer. An estimate of a seller's **net proceeds** (the amount of cash the seller will walk away with) or a buyer's **net cost** (the amount of cash the buyer must bring to closing) will take into account how the various closing costs are typically allocated.

Some closing costs are **prorated** between the buyer and seller. To prorate an expense is to divide and allocate it proportionately between two or more parties, according to time, interest, or benefit. Figure 11.3 shows the steps involved in proration.

A **settlement statement** (also called a closing statement) sets out all of the financial details of a real estate transaction, including the closing costs each party must pay. In residential transactions, the settlement statement is part of the required closing disclosure form, which we'll discuss later in the chapter. In preparing a settlement statement or closing disclosure form, the lender or closing agent allocates each closing cost to the buyer or the seller (or both) as indicated in the purchase agreement; if the agreement doesn't specify which party is responsible for a particular cost, it is allocated according to local custom. For your estimates, you'll allocate the parties' closing costs the same way.

Many agents use worksheets to help them calculate and explain net costs and net proceeds for their buyers and sellers. A buyer's estimated net cost worksheet is shown later in the chapter, in Figure 11.4. A seller's estimated net proceeds worksheet is shown in Figure 11.5. Your broker may have similar worksheets available for you to use.

The same software that helps you prepare a competitive market analysis may also have a function that lets you prepare a rough estimate of the seller's net proceeds or the buyer's net costs, so it is unlikely you will need to do all of the following steps by hand. It is important to know all of the principles behind estimating these figures, though, so you can assess whether the generated figures seem reasonable, and so you can look for potential errors.

FIG. 11.3   PRORATING AN EXPENSE

STEP 1
Divide the expense by the number of days it covers to find the per diem (daily) rate.
- Divide annual expenses by 365.
- Divide monthly expenses by the number of days in the month in question.

STEP 2
Determine the number of days for which one party is responsible for the expense.

STEP 3
Multiply the number of days by the per diem rate to find that party's share of the expense.

Expense paid in arrears (overdue):
- Seller's share is a debit for the seller.

Expense paid in advance:
- Seller's share is a credit for the seller.

Expense continues after closing:
- Buyer's share is a credit for the buyer if paid in arrears.
- Buyer's share is a debit for the buyer if paid in advance.

COSTS AND CREDITS

On a settlement statement, the costs that a party must pay at closing are referred to as that party's **debits** (the opposite of credits). The buyer's debits increase the amount of money the buyer will have to bring to closing. The seller's debits decrease the seller's net proceeds.

In addition to their debits, each party will usually have some credits that also must be taken into account (and in some cases prorated). Credits are payments that will be made to the buyer or the seller at closing. The buyer's credits decrease the buyer's net cost. The seller's credits increase the seller's net proceeds.

Note that some closing costs are charges that one party owes the other party. At closing, each of these will be treated as a debit for the party that must pay it and as a credit for the other party. For example, the buyer may be required to pay the seller a prorated share of the annual property taxes, because the seller paid the taxes in advance. The prorated amount is a debit for the buyer and a credit for the seller on the settlement statement. On your worksheets, add it to the buyer's net cost, and also add it to the seller's net proceeds.

Other closing costs are charges that one party must pay to a third party. For example, the seller will have to pay the brokerage firm a sales commission. This is a debit for the seller (subtracted from the net proceeds), but it does not affect the buyer.

Also, some of the credits a party receives at closing come from a third party. For example, the seller's lender must refund any unused tax and insurance reserves to the seller at closing. This is a credit for the seller (added to the net proceeds), and it does not affect the buyer.

Residential transactions involve many standard closing costs. Some are allocated according to custom, some are allocated according to the terms of the purchase and sale agreement, and a few are allocated according to law. We'll first go through the process of estimating a buyer's net cost. After that, we'll turn to the seller's net proceeds.

ESTIMATING THE BUYER'S NET COST

Certain costs are the buyer's responsibility in every transaction, or almost every transaction. Responsibility for other costs—whether they'll be paid by the buyer or by the seller, or shared between them—may vary. To estimate a buyer's net cost, add up all of the charges the buyer will have to pay to close the sale and offset them with the credits owed to the buyer.

PURCHASE PRICE. Of course, the purchase price is the major cost for the buyer in every transaction. Use this as the starting point on your buyer's net cost worksheet. The price is offset by the buyer's earnest money deposit and the financing.

EARNEST MONEY. In most transactions, the buyer provides an earnest money deposit. The deposit is applied to the purchase price if the sale closes. Since the buyer has already paid the earnest money, it is treated as a credit for the buyer on the settlement statement. On the net cost worksheet, subtract the amount of the earnest money from the purchase price.

FINANCING. Most buyers pay a large part of the purchase price with borrowed money. Any financing arrangement—a new loan, the assumption of the seller's loan, or seller financing—is treated as a credit for the buyer. On the buyer's worksheet, subtract the loan amount and/or the amount of other financing from the purchase price.

LOAN COSTS. Borrowing money isn't free. In addition to the interest the buyer will have to pay over the life of the loan, she will incur a number of closing costs in the course of obtaining the loan. Unless the seller has agreed to pay some of them, the buyer will pay all of the closing costs associated with the loan. That means you should add these closing costs to the purchase price on your buyer's net cost worksheet.

APPRAISAL. The appraisal is required by the buyer's lender, so the appraisal fee is ordinarily paid by the buyer.

CREDIT REPORT. The buyer's lender charges the buyer for the credit investigation, so this is also a cost for the buyer.

ORIGINATION FEE. This is the lender's one-time charge to the borrower for setting up the loan (see Chapter 10). It's almost always paid by the buyer. If the buyer is assuming the seller's loan, an assumption fee will be charged instead of an origination fee.

DISCOUNT POINTS. Discount points are paid to a lender at closing, in order to get a loan at a lower interest rate than the lender would have charged otherwise. The discount points are paid by the buyer, unless the seller has agreed to pay for a buydown (see Chapter 10). In that case, some or all of the points are paid by the seller.

PREPAID INTEREST. As a general rule, the first payment date of a new loan is not the first day of the month immediately following closing, but rather the first day of the next month after that. For instance, if a sale closes on March 15, the first payment on the new loan is due on May 1 instead of April 1. This gives the buyer a chance to recover a little from the financial strain of closing.

Even though the first loan payment isn't due for an extra month, interest begins accruing on the loan on the closing date. Interest on a real estate loan is almost always paid in arrears. In other words, the interest that accrues during a given month is paid at the end of that month. For instance, a loan payment that is due on September 1 includes the interest that accrued during August. So if the transaction closes on March 15, the first payment will be due on May 1, and that payment will cover the interest accrued in April. However, it won't cover the interest accrued between March 15 and March 31. Instead, the lender will require

FIG. 11.4   BUYER'S ESTIMATED NET COST WORKSHEET

Buyer's Estimated Net Cost

Purchase Price	**$185,000.00**
Earnest money deposit (credit)	− 5,000.00
Financing (credit)	− 166,500.00
Remainder (price less offsets)	**$13,500.00**
Buyer's Closing Costs	
Appraisal fee	+ 275.00
Credit report	+ 40.00
Origination fee	+ 1,665.00
Discount points	+ 4,995.00
Prepaid interest	+ 504.05
Lender's title insurance	+ 600.00
Inspection fees	+ 400.00
Hazard insurance	+ 375.00
Attorney's fees	+ 350.00
Recording fees	+ 50.00
Escrow fee	+ 250.00
Property taxes	+ 960.68
Estimated Net Cost	**$23,964.73**

the buyer to pay the interest for those 17 days in March at closing. This is called **prepaid interest** or **interim interest**. It is almost always paid by the buyer.

> **EXAMPLE:** The buyer is borrowing $166,500 at 6.5% interest to finance the purchase. The annual interest on the loan during the first year will be $10,822.50 ($166,500 × .065 = $10,822.50). The escrow agent divides that annual figure by 365 to determine the per diem interest rate.
>
> $$\$10,822.50 \div 365 = \$29.65 \text{ per diem}$$
>
> There are 17 days between the closing date (March 15) and the first day of the following month, so the lender will expect the buyer to prepay 17 days' worth of interest at closing.
>
> $$\$29.65 \times 17 \text{ days} = \$504.05 \text{ prepaid interest}$$
>
> The escrow agent will enter $504.05 as a debit to the buyer on the settlement statement. When you are preparing your estimated net cost worksheet for the buyer, you can go through the same process to come up with a figure for the prepaid interest. Add it to the buyer's net cost.

The buyer and the seller both owe interest for the closing date (unless the buyer is assuming the seller's loan or the buyer is paying all cash). That's because there are two different loans at issue—one that ends on the closing date and the other that begins on that date. If the buyer is assuming the seller's loan, the parties must agree on who pays the interest for the closing date.

LENDER'S TITLE INSURANCE PREMIUM. As explained earlier, the lender requires the buyer to provide a policy to protect the lender's lien priority. The premium for the lender's policy is paid by the buyer, unless otherwise agreed.

INSPECTION FEES. The cost of an inspection is allocated by agreement between the parties. Customarily, the buyer pays for the inspection fees.

HAZARD INSURANCE. The lender generally requires the buyer to pay for one year of hazard insurance coverage in advance, at closing.

ATTORNEY'S FEES. A buyer who is represented by an attorney in the transaction is responsible for her own attorney's fees. (The same is true for the seller.) In many transactions, the attorney's fees are not handled through escrow. Instead, each lawyer simply bills his or her client directly.

RECORDING FEES. The fees for recording the various documents involved in the transaction are usually charged to the party who benefits from the recording. So the fees for recording the deed and the new mortgage or deed of trust are normally paid by the buyer.

ESCROW FEE. Also called a settlement fee or closing fee, this is the escrow agent's charge for her services. The buyer and the seller commonly agree to split the escrow fee, so that each of them pays half.

PROPERTY TAXES. The seller is responsible for the property taxes up to the day of closing; the buyer is responsible for them thereafter. The parties will agree on (or rely on local custom to settle) which party pays the taxes for the closing date itself; more often than not, the buyer is responsible. If the seller has already paid some or all of the property taxes in advance, he is entitled to a prorated refund from the buyer at closing. The amount of the refund is a debit for the buyer and a credit for the seller.

> **EXAMPLE:** The sale is closing on March 15. This year the property taxes on the house are $1,200.85. The escrow agent determines the per diem rate by dividing that figure by 365, the number of days in the year.

$$\$1,200.85 \div 365 = \$3.29 \text{ per diem}$$

The seller is responsible for the property taxes from January 1 through March 14—in other words, for the first 73 days of the year. The buyer's responsible for them from March 15 to the end of the year.

The seller has already paid the full year's taxes, so at closing he will be entitled to a credit for the share that is the buyer's responsibility. The escrow agent multiplies the number of days for which the seller is responsible by the per diem rate to determine the seller's share of the taxes. The escrow agent subtracts the seller's share from the annual figure to find the buyer's share.

$$73 \text{ days} \times \$3.29 = \$240.17 \text{ (Seller's share)}$$

$$\$1,200.85 - \$240.17 = \$960.68 \text{ (Buyer's share)}$$

This $960.68 will appear on the buyer's settlement statement as a debit and on the seller's statement as a credit. Again, you can do a similar proration for your net cost and net proceeds estimates. Add the buyer's debit to the buyer's net cost, and add the seller's credit to the seller's net proceeds.

ESTIMATED TOTAL COST. When all of the appropriate items on your net cost worksheet have been filled in, the buyer's estimated net cost may be calculated. With the purchase price as a starting point, all of the buyer's credits are subtracted, and all of the buyer's costs are added. The result is the net cost, the amount of money that the buyer will have to pay the escrow agent in order to close the sale.

Be sure your buyer knows what kind of check the escrow agent will accept. A certified check or cashier's check, rather than a personal check, may be required.

ESTIMATING THE SELLER'S NET PROCEEDS

Now let's look at the costs and credits that you should take into consideration when estimating a seller's net proceeds.

SALES PRICE. The largest credit for the seller is, naturally, the sales price. It should be the starting point in your net proceeds calculation. You'll add any other credits that the seller will receive at closing to the price, then you'll subtract the costs that the seller must pay.

REFUNDS. The seller may be entitled to certain refunds at closing. As you've already seen, if the seller has paid the property taxes in advance, the buyer will have to refund the share for which she's responsible to the seller. That will increase the seller's net proceeds. (On the other hand, if the seller hasn't paid the taxes yet, he will have to pay a prorated share of them at closing, which will decrease the net proceeds.)

Another possible credit for the seller is a refund of funds remaining in the reserve account (or impound account) for the seller's loan. A seller often has reserves on deposit with his lender to cover future property taxes and hazard insurance premiums. When the seller's loan is paid off, the unused balance in the reserve account is refunded to the seller by the lender. If your seller will receive this type of refund, add it to the seller's net proceeds. The seller's lender can help you determine how much the refund of reserves will be.

Any other refunds that the seller will receive at closing should be treated in the same way.

TOTAL PROCEEDS. On your net proceeds worksheet, add all of the seller's credits to the sales price to determine the seller's total proceeds. You'll be subtracting the seller's costs from this figure.

SELLER FINANCING OR LOAN ASSUMPTION. We explained earlier that any type of financing is a credit for the buyer. Thus, just like a new loan, seller financing or an assumed loan is subtracted from the buyer's net cost. But unlike a new loan, seller financing or an assumed loan is also subtracted from the seller's net proceeds. That's because either of these financing arrangements will reduce the amount of cash the seller will receive at closing. (Note, however, that if the buyer obtains a new loan from a bank or other third-party lender, the loan amount has no effect on the seller's net proceeds.)

PAYOFF OF SELLER'S LOAN. If, like most sellers, your seller will have to pay off his existing mortgage loan, his net will be reduced by the payoff amount. This is the unpaid principal balance, plus any unpaid interest, as of the closing date. Even if you don't yet know when the closing date will be, you can calculate a good estimate of the payoff amount by asking the seller's lender for the current principal balance.

The actual payoff amount will probably be somewhat less than the estimated payoff (because the principal balance will be less if the seller makes another payment before closing), but you don't need to worry about the difference. Since your estimate of the seller's net proceeds won't match the actual net proceeds exactly, it's better if the estimate turns out to be a little lower than the actual figure, rather than a little higher. That way, the seller will be pleased rather than disappointed at closing. (For the same reason, it's better if the buyer's estimated net cost is a little higher than the actual figure.)

INTEREST ON SELLER'S LOAN. Because interest on a real estate loan is paid in arrears, when a transaction closes in the middle of the payment period, the seller owes his lender some interest after paying off the principal balance.

> **EXAMPLE:** The closing date is March 15. Although the seller made a mortgage payment on his loan on March 1, that payment did not include any of the interest that is accruing during March. The seller owes the lender interest for the period from March 1 through March 15. The escrow agent prorates the interest, charging the seller only for those days, rather than for the whole month.
>
> Suppose the remaining principal balance is $78,000 and the annual interest rate is 7%. First find the per diem amount.
>
> $$\$78,000 \times .07 = \$5,460 \text{ annual interest}$$
>
> $$\$5,460 \div 365 = \$14.96 \text{ per diem interest}$$
>
> $$\$14.96 \times 15 \text{ days} = \$224.40$$

The seller owes the lender $224.40 in interest. Subtract this from the seller's net proceeds.

FIG. 11.5   SELLER'S ESTIMATED NET PROCEEDS WORKSHEET

Seller's Estimated Net Proceeds	
Sales Price	**$185,000.00**
Prorated property taxes (credit)	+ 960.68
Reserve account (credit)	+ 500.32
Total Proceeds to Seller	**+ 186,461.00**
Seller's Closing Costs	
Loan payoff	− 78,000.00
Interest due on loan	− 224.40
Prepayment penalty	− 0.00
Other liens and assessments	− 0.00
Brokerage commission	− 12,950.00
Owner's title insurance	− 725.00
Seller-paid discount points	− 0.00
Excise tax	− 2,960.00
Repairs	− 500.00
Attorney's fees	− 0.00
Recording fees	− 24.00
Escrow fee	− 250.00
Estimated Net Proceeds	**$90,827.60**

Suppose the seller in this example had arranged for the buyer to assume his loan. In that case, the buyer's first payment to the lender would be due April 1, and it would pay all of the interest for March. The seller would be debited for the interest owed up to March 15, and the buyer would be credited for the same amount.

PREPAYMENT PENALTY. This is a charge the seller's lender may impose on the seller for paying the loan off before the end of its term. If the seller must pay a prepayment penalty, contact the lender to determine approximately how much the penalty will be. Subtract the estimated penalty from the seller's net proceeds. Prepayment penalties are prohibited or limited in many types of loans (see Chapter 10).

SALES COMMISSION. The real estate commission is almost always paid by the seller. The amount of the commission is usually determined by multiplying the sales price by the commission rate.

> **EXAMPLE:** Your listing agreement states that the seller will pay a commission of 7% of the sales price. The property sells for $185,000. $185,000 × .07 = $12,950. The amount of the brokerage commission is $12,950.

Since the commission is one of the seller's costs, you should subtract it from the sales price when you're calculating the seller's net proceeds.

OWNER'S TITLE INSURANCE PREMIUM. As explained earlier, the premium for the owner's title insurance policy (which protects the buyer) is customarily paid by the seller.

DISCOUNT POINTS. If the seller has agreed to pay discount points or other costs involved in the buyer's loan, these will be a debit for the seller on the settlement statement. Subtract them from the seller's net proceeds.

EXCISE TAX. An excise tax is imposed on most sales of real property in Washington. The amount of the tax varies depending on the sales price and location of the property. The state's share of the tax ranges from 1.1% of the selling price for lower-priced homes, to 3.0% of the selling price for higher-priced homes. There is an additional percentage owed to the city or county government where the property is located. The excise tax is customarily paid by the seller. (However, if for some reason the tax is not paid at closing, it will become a lien against the property now owned by the buyer.)

REPAIR COSTS. The cost of repairs that the seller agreed to pay for will be deducted from the seller's proceeds at closing, unless the seller has already paid for them.

ATTORNEY'S FEES. The seller will pay his own attorney's fees if he is represented by a lawyer. These will not necessarily be handled through the closing process.

RECORDING FEES. The seller will pay the recording fees for the documents that are recorded for his benefit. For instance, the seller customarily pays the fee for recording a deed of reconveyance to release the property from the lien of the deed of trust he has paid off.

ESCROW FEE. As mentioned earlier, the seller customarily pays half of the escrow fee.

ESTIMATED NET PROCEEDS. When the seller's loan payoff and all of the seller's closing costs are subtracted from the seller's total proceeds, the result is the seller's estimated net proceeds, the amount he can expect to take away from the closing. The escrow agent may offer the seller different options for receiving these funds, such as a cashier's check or direct deposit.

FEDERAL LAWS THAT AFFECT CLOSING

To end our discussion of the closing process, we'll discuss some federal laws that must be complied with in closing a real estate transaction. These include certain income tax laws and the Real Estate Settlement Procedures Act.

INCOME TAX REGULATIONS

There are some income tax requirements connected with closing that you should be familiar with. The escrow agent (or other closing agent) is primarily responsible for ensuring that these requirements are met.

FORM 1099-S REPORTING. The person responsible for closing a real estate sale generally must report the sale to the Internal Revenue Service. IRS Form 1099-S is used to report the seller's name and social security number and the gross proceeds from the sale. In most cases, the gross proceeds figure is the same as the property's sales price.

There are several exemptions to this reporting requirement. Most significantly, the form isn't required in the sale of a principal residence if: 1) the seller certifies in writing that none of the gain is taxable; and 2) the sale is for $250,000 or less ($500,000 or less if the seller is married).

Note that the closing agent is not permitted to charge an extra fee for filling out the 1099-S form.

FORM 8300 REPORTING. To help prevent money laundering and tax evasion, transactions involving large sums of cash must be reported to the federal government. If a closing agent receives more than $10,000 in cash, she must report the cash payment on IRS Form 8300 in order to help detect money laundering. This is true even if the cash isn't received all at once.

EXAMPLE: ABC Escrow is handling the closing for buyer Sam. As part of the process, Sam will bring $12,000 cash to closing. He gives ABC Escrow $8,000 on Thursday, and the remaining $4,000 on Friday. Although the individual amounts are less than $10,000, ABC Escrow will need to submit Form 8300 to the IRS because the transactions are related.

The closing agent must file Form 8300 within 15 days of receiving the cash, and a copy of the form should be kept on file for five years.

FIRPTA. The Foreign Investment in Real Property Tax Act (FIRPTA) helps prevent foreign investors from evading tax liability on income generated from the sale of U.S. real estate. To comply with FIRPTA, the buyer must determine whether the seller is a "foreign person" (someone who is not a U.S. citizen or a resident alien). If the seller is a foreign person, then the buyer must withhold 15% of the amount realized from the sale and forward that amount to the Internal Revenue Service. Usually, the amount realized is simply the sales price. This must occur within 20 days after the transfer date. In most cases, the closing agent handles these requirements on behalf of the buyer.

Many purchase and sale agreement forms have a provision concerning FIRPTA compliance. It requires the closing agent to prepare a certification stating that the seller is not a foreign person under the terms of this law, and the seller agrees to sign the certification. However, if the seller is a foreign person, the closing agent is directed to withhold the required amount and comply with the law, unless the sale is exempt from FIRPTA.

FIRPTA's exemptions cover various types of transactions. Most notably for our purposes, some residential transactions are exempt from the law. For the exemption to apply, the buyer must be purchasing the property for use as her home, and the purchase price must be $300,000 or less. If the amount realized is between $300,000 and $1 million, only 10% needs to be withheld, instead of 15%.

REAL ESTATE SETTLEMENT PROCEDURES ACT

The Real Estate Settlement Procedures Act (RESPA) affects how closing is handled in most residential transactions financed with institutional loans. The law has two main goals:

- to provide borrowers with information about their closing costs; and
- to eliminate kickbacks and referral fees that unnecessarily increase the costs of purchasing a home.

TRANSACTIONS COVERED BY RESPA. RESPA applies to "federally related" loan transactions. A loan is federally related if:

1. it will be secured by a mortgage or deed of trust against:
   - property on which there is (or on which the loan proceeds will be used to build) a dwelling with four or fewer units;
   - a condominium unit or a cooperative apartment; or
   - a lot with (or on which the loan proceeds will be used to place) a mobile home; and
2. the lender is federally regulated, has federally insured accounts, is assisted by the federal government, makes loans in connection with a federal program, sells loans to Fannie Mae, Ginnie Mae, or Freddie Mac, or makes real estate loans that total more than $1,000,000 per year.

In short, the act applies to almost all institutional lenders and to most residential loans.

EXEMPTIONS. RESPA does not apply to the following loan transactions:

- a loan used to purchase 25 acres or more;
- a loan primarily for a business, commercial, or agricultural purpose;
- a loan used to purchase vacant land, unless there will be a one- to four-unit dwelling built on it or a mobile home placed on it;
- temporary financing, such as a construction loan; and
- an assumption for which the lender's approval is neither required nor obtained.

Note that RESPA also does not apply to seller-financed transactions, since the seller is not a federally regulated lender.

RESPA REQUIREMENTS. RESPA has these requirements for federally related loan transactions:

1. If a lender or other settlement service provider requires the borrower to use a particular attorney, appraiser, or other service provider, that requirement must be disclosed to the borrower when the loan application or service agreement is signed.
2. If any settlement service provider refers a borrower to an "affiliated" provider, that joint business relationship must be fully disclosed, along with fee estimates for the services in question and language that the referral is optional.

3. If the borrower will have to make deposits into an impound account (or reserve account) to cover taxes, insurance, and other recurring costs, the lender cannot require excessive deposits (more than necessary to cover the expenses when they come due, plus a two-month cushion).

4. A lender, loan originator, title company, real estate agent, or other settlement service provider may not:
   - pay or accept a **kickback** or referral fee (a payment from one settlement service provider to another provider for referring customers);
   - pay or accept an unearned fee (a charge that one settlement service provider shares with another provider who hasn't actually performed any services in exchange for the payment); or
   - charge a fee for the preparation of an impound account statement or any of the required disclosure forms.

5. The seller may not require the buyer to use a particular title company.

RESPA's prohibition on kickbacks and unearned fees (number 4 above) is intended to prevent practices that were once widespread and that generally benefited real estate agents, lenders, and other settlement service providers at the expense of home buyers. Note that this prohibition doesn't apply to referral fees that one real estate licensee or firm pays to another for referring potential brokerage customers or clients, or to commission sharing agreements between real estate licensees.

CLOSING DISCLOSURE FORM. RESPA and the Truth in Lending Act require lenders to disclose the parties' actual closing costs on a closing disclosure form. (See Figure 11.6.) The escrow agent typically assists the lender in preparing the closing disclosure.

The closing disclosure form includes the seller's closing costs and credits, and any amounts paid by third parties. To present this information clearly, the second and third pages are laid out in a detailed grid that takes the place of a settlement statement.

The buyer must receive the closing disclosure form no later than three business days before closing; the seller must receive one no later than the closing date. The parties should check the closing disclosures closely; errors aren't unusual, especially with long-distance lenders unfamiliar with local practices. (The parties' agents may be able to assist with checking the numbers.)

The law limits how much certain categories of loan costs can increase between the time the buyer receives the estimate form and the closing date. These

FIG. 11.6   SAMPLE CLOSING DISCLOSURE FORM

Closing Disclosure

This form is a statement of final loan terms and closing costs. Compare this document with your Loan Estimate.

Closing Information

Date Issued	4/15/20XX
Closing Date	4/15/20XX
Disbursement Date	4/15/20XX
Settlement Agent	Epsilon Title Co.
File #	12-3456
Property	456 Somewhere Ave
	Anytown, ST 12345
Sale Price	$180,000

Transaction Information

Borrower	Michael Jones and Mary Stone
	123 Anywhere Street
	Anytown, ST 12345
Seller	Steve Cole and Amy Doe
	321 Somewhere Drive
	Anytown, ST 12345
Lender	Ficus Bank

Loan Information

Loan Term	30 years
Purpose	Purchase
Product	Fixed Rate
Loan Type	☒ Conventional ☐ FHA
	☐ VA ☐ _____
Loan ID #	123456789
MIC #	000654321

Loan Terms

		Can this amount increase after closing?
Loan Amount	$162,000	**NO**
Interest Rate	3.875%	**NO**
Monthly Principal & Interest *See Projected Payments below for your Estimated Total Monthly Payment*	$761.78	**NO**
		Does the loan have these features?
Prepayment Penalty		**YES** • As high as **$3,240** if you pay off the loan during the first 2 years
Balloon Payment		**NO**

Projected Payments

Payment Calculation	Years 1-7	Years 8-30
Principal & Interest	$761.78	$761.78
Mortgage Insurance	+ 82.35	+ —
Estimated Escrow *Amount can increase over time*	+ 206.13	+ 206.13
Estimated Total Monthly Payment	**$1,050.26**	**$967.91**

Estimated Taxes, Insurance & Assessments *Amount can increase over time* *See page 4 for details*	$356.13 a month	**This estimate includes**	**In escrow?**
		☒ Property Taxes	YES
		☒ Homeowner's Insurance	YES
		☒ Other: Homeowner's Association Dues	NO
		See Escrow Account on page 4 for details. You must pay for other property costs separately.	

Costs at Closing

Closing Costs	$9,712.10	Includes $4,694.05 in Loan Costs + $5,018.05 in Other Costs – $0 in Lender Credits. *See page 2 for details.*
Cash to Close	$14,147.26	Includes Closing Costs. *See Calculating Cash to Close on page 3 for details.*

CLOSING DISCLOSURE

PAGE 1 OF 5 • LOAN ID # 123456789

Source: Consumer Financial Protection Bureau

Closing Cost Details

Loan Costs		Borrower-Paid		Seller-Paid		Paid by Others
		At Closing	Before Closing	At Closing	Before Closing	
A. Origination Charges		**$1,802.00**				
01 0.25 % of Loan Amount (Points)		$405.00				
02 Application Fee		$300.00				
03 Underwriting Fee		$1,097.00				
04						
05						
06						
07						
08						
B. Services Borrower Did Not Shop For		**$236.55**				
01 Appraisal Fee	to John Smith Appraisers Inc.					$405.00
02 Credit Report Fee	to Information Inc.		$29.80			
03 Flood Determination Fee	to Info Co.	$20.00				
04 Flood Monitoring Fee	to Info Co.	$31.75				
05 Tax Monitoring Fee	to Info Co.	$75.00				
06 Tax Status Research Fee	to Info Co.	$80.00				
07						
08						
09						
10						
C. Services Borrower Did Shop For		**$2,655.50**				
01 Pest Inspection Fee	to Pests Co.	$120.50				
02 Survey Fee	to Surveys Co.	$85.00				
03 Title – Insurance Binder	to Epsilon Title Co.	$650.00				
04 Title – Lender's Title Insurance	to Epsilon Title Co.	$500.00				
05 Title – Settlement Agent Fee	to Epsilon Title Co.	$500.00				
06 Title – Title Search	to Epsilon Title Co.	$800.00				
07						
08						
D. TOTAL LOAN COSTS (Borrower-Paid)		**$4,694.05**				
Loan Costs Subtotals (A + B + C)		$4,664.25	$29.80			

Other Costs						
E. Taxes and Other Government Fees		**$85.00**				
01 Recording Fees	Deed: $40.00 Mortgage: $45.00	$85.00				
02 Transfer Tax	to Any State			$950.00		
F. Prepaids		**$2,120.80**				
01 Homeowner's Insurance Premium (12 mo.) to Insurance Co.		$1,209.96				
02 Mortgage Insurance Premium (mo.)						
03 Prepaid Interest ($17.44 per day from 4/15/13 to 5/1/13)		$279.04				
04 Property Taxes (6 mo.) to Any County USA		$631.80				
05						
G. Initial Escrow Payment at Closing		**$412.25**				
01 Homeowner's Insurance $100.83 per month for 2 mo.		$201.66				
02 Mortgage Insurance per month for mo.						
03 Property Taxes $105.30 per month for 2 mo.		$210.60				
04						
05						
06						
07						
08 Aggregate Adjustment		– 0.01				
H. Other		**$2,400.00**				
01 HOA Capital Contribution	to HOA Acre Inc.	$500.00				
02 HOA Processing Fee	to HOA Acre Inc.	$150.00				
03 Home Inspection Fee	to Engineers Inc.	$750.00			$750.00	
04 Home Warranty Fee	to XYZ Warranty Inc.			$450.00		
05 Real Estate Commission	to Alpha Real Estate Broker			$5,700.00		
06 Real Estate Commission	to Omega Real Estate Broker			$5,700.00		
07 Title – Owner's Title Insurance (optional) to Epsilon Title Co.		$1,000.00				
08						
I. TOTAL OTHER COSTS (Borrower-Paid)		**$5,018.05**				
Other Costs Subtotals (E + F + G + H)		$5,018.05				
J. TOTAL CLOSING COSTS (Borrower-Paid)		**$9,712.10**				
Closing Costs Subtotals (D + I)		$9,682.30	$29.80	$12,800.00	$750.00	$405.00
Lender Credits						

Calculating Cash to Close

Use this table to see what has changed from your Loan Estimate.

	Loan Estimate	Final	Did this change?
Total Closing Costs (J)	$8,054.00	$9,712.10	**YES** • See **Total Loan Costs (D)** and **Total Other Costs (I)**
Closing Costs Paid Before Closing	$0	− $29.80	**YES** • You paid these Closing Costs **before closing**
Closing Costs Financed (Paid from your Loan Amount)	$0	$0	**NO**
Down Payment/Funds from Borrower	$18,000.00	$18,000.00	**NO**
Deposit	− $10,000.00	− $10,000.00	**NO**
Funds for Borrower	$0	$0	**NO**
Seller Credits	$0	− $2,500.00	**YES** • See Seller Credits in **Section L**
Adjustments and Other Credits	$0	− $1,035.04	**YES** • See details in **Sections K and L**
Cash to Close	$16,054.00	$14,147.26	

Summaries of Transactions

Use this table to see a summary of your transaction.

BORROWER'S TRANSACTION

K. Due from Borrower at Closing	$189,762.30
01 Sale Price of Property	$180,000.00
02 Sale Price of Any Personal Property Included in Sale	
03 Closing Costs Paid at Closing (J)	$9,682.30
04	
Adjustments	
05	
06	
07	
Adjustments for Items Paid by Seller in Advance	
08 City/Town Taxes to	
09 County Taxes to	
10 Assessments to	
11 HOA Dues 4/15/13 to 4/30/13	$80.00
12	
13	
14	
15	

L. Paid Already by or on Behalf of Borrower at Closing	$175,615.04
01 Deposit	$10,000.00
02 Loan Amount	$162,000.00
03 Existing Loan(s) Assumed or Taken Subject to	
04	
05 Seller Credit	$2,500.00
Other Credits	
06 Rebate from Epsilon Title Co.	$750.00
07	
Adjustments	
08	
09	
10	
11	
Adjustments for Items Unpaid by Seller	
12 City/Town Taxes 1/1/13 to 4/14/13	$365.04
13 County Taxes to	
14 Assessments to	
15	
16	
17	

CALCULATION	
Total Due from Borrower at Closing (K)	$189,762.30
Total Paid Already by or on Behalf of Borrower at Closing (L)	− $175,615.04
Cash to Close ☒ From ☐ To Borrower	**$14,147.26**

SELLER'S TRANSACTION

M. Due to Seller at Closing	$180,080.00
01 Sale Price of Property	$180,000.00
02 Sale Price of Any Personal Property Included in Sale	
03	
04	
05	
06	
07	
08	
Adjustments for Items Paid by Seller in Advance	
09 City/Town Taxes to	
10 County Taxes to	
11 Assessments to	
12 HOA Dues 4/15/13 to 4/30/13	$80.00
13	
14	
15	
16	

N. Due from Seller at Closing	$115,665.04
01 Excess Deposit	
02 Closing Costs Paid at Closing (J)	$12,800.00
03 Existing Loan(s) Assumed or Taken Subject to	
04 Payoff of First Mortgage Loan	$100,000.00
05 Payoff of Second Mortgage Loan	
06	
07	
08 Seller Credit	$2,500.00
09	
10	
11	
12	
13	
Adjustments for Items Unpaid by Seller	
14 City/Town Taxes 1/1/13 to 4/14/13	$365.04
15 County Taxes to	
16 Assessments to	
17	
18	
19	

CALCULATION	
Total Due to Seller at Closing (M)	$180,080.00
Total Due from Seller at Closing (N)	− $115,665.04
Cash ☐ From ☒ To Seller	**$64,414.96**

Additional Information About This Loan

Loan Disclosures

Assumption
If you sell or transfer this property to another person, your lender
☐ will allow, under certain conditions, this person to assume this loan on the original terms.
☒ will not allow assumption of this loan on the original terms.

Demand Feature
Your loan
☐ has a demand feature, which permits your lender to require early repayment of the loan. You should review your note for details.
☒ does not have a demand feature.

Late Payment
If your payment is more than 15 days late, your lender will charge a late fee of 5% of the monthly principal and interest payment.

Negative Amortization (Increase in Loan Amount)
Under your loan terms, you
☐ are scheduled to make monthly payments that do not pay all of the interest due that month. As a result, your loan amount will increase (negatively amortize), and your loan amount will likely become larger than your original loan amount. Increases in your loan amount lower the equity you have in this property.
☐ may have monthly payments that do not pay all of the interest due that month. If you do, your loan amount will increase (negatively amortize), and, as a result, your loan amount may become larger than your original loan amount. Increases in your loan amount lower the equity you have in this property.
☒ do not have a negative amortization feature.

Partial Payments
Your lender
☒ may accept payments that are less than the full amount due (partial payments) and apply them to your loan.
☐ may hold them in a separate account until you pay the rest of the payment, and then apply the full payment to your loan.
☐ does not accept any partial payments.
If this loan is sold, your new lender may have a different policy.

Security Interest
You are granting a security interest in
456 Somewhere Ave., Anytown, ST 12345

You may lose this property if you do not make your payments or satisfy other obligations for this loan.

Escrow Account
For now, your loan
☒ will have an escrow account (also called an "impound" or "trust" account) to pay the property costs listed below. Without an escrow account, you would pay them directly, possibly in one or two large payments a year. Your lender may be liable for penalties and interest for failing to make a payment.

Escrow		
Escrowed Property Costs over Year 1	$2,473.56	Estimated total amount over year 1 for your escrowed property costs: *Homeowner's Insurance Property Taxes*
Non-Escrowed Property Costs over Year 1	$1,800.00	Estimated total amount over year 1 for your non-escrowed property costs: *Homeowner's Association Dues* You may have other property costs.
Initial Escrow Payment	$412.25	A cushion for the escrow account you pay at closing. See Section G on page 2.
Monthly Escrow Payment	$206.13	The amount included in your total monthly payment.

☐ will not have an escrow account because ☐ you declined it ☐ your lender does not offer one. You must directly pay your property costs, such as taxes and homeowner's insurance. Contact your lender to ask if your loan can have an escrow account.

No Escrow		
Estimated Property Costs over Year 1		Estimated total amount over year 1. You must pay these costs directly, possibly in one or two large payments a year.
Escrow Waiver Fee		

In the future,
Your property costs may change and, as a result, your escrow payment may change. You may be able to cancel your escrow account, but if you do, you must pay your property costs directly. If you fail to pay your property taxes, your state or local government may (1) impose fines and penalties or (2) place a tax lien on this property. If you fail to pay any of your property costs, your lender may (1) add the amounts to your loan balance, (2) add an escrow account to your loan, or (3) require you to pay for property insurance that the lender buys on your behalf, which likely would cost more and provide fewer benefits than what you could buy on your own.

Loan Calculations

Total of Payments. Total you will have paid after you make all payments of principal, interest, mortgage insurance, and loan costs, as scheduled.	$285,803.36
Finance Charge. The dollar amount the loan will cost you.	$118,830.27
Amount Financed. The loan amount available after paying your upfront finance charge.	$162,000.00
Annual Percentage Rate (APR). Your costs over the loan term expressed as a rate. This is not your interest rate.	4.174%
Total Interest Percentage (TIP). The total amount of interest that you will pay over the loan term as a percentage of your loan amount.	69.46%

Questions? If you have questions about the loan terms or costs on this form, use the contact information below. To get more information or make a complaint, contact the Consumer Financial Protection Bureau at **www.consumerfinance.gov/mortgage-closing**

Other Disclosures

Appraisal
If the property was appraised for your loan, your lender is required to give you a copy at no additional cost at least 3 days before closing. If you have not yet received it, please contact your lender at the information listed below.

Contract Details
See your note and security instrument for information about
- what happens if you fail to make your payments,
- what is a default on the loan,
- situations in which your lender can require early repayment of the loan, and
- the rules for making payments before they are due.

Liability after Foreclosure
If your lender forecloses on this property and the foreclosure does not cover the amount of unpaid balance on this loan,

☒ state law may protect you from liability for the unpaid balance. If you refinance or take on any additional debt on this property, you may lose this protection and have to pay any debt remaining even after foreclosure. You may want to consult a lawyer for more information.

☐ state law does not protect you from liability for the unpaid balance.

Refinance
Refinancing this loan will depend on your future financial situation, the property value, and market conditions. You may not be able to refinance this loan.

Tax Deductions
If you borrow more than this property is worth, the interest on the loan amount above this property's fair market value is not deductible from your federal income taxes. You should consult a tax advisor for more information.

Contact Information

	Lender	Mortgage Broker	Real Estate Broker (B)	Real Estate Broker (S)	Settlement Agent
Name	Ficus Bank		Omega Real Estate Broker Inc.	Alpha Real Estate Broker Co.	Epsilon Title Co.
Address	4321 Random Blvd. Somecity, ST 12340		789 Local Lane Sometown, ST 12345	987 Suburb Ct. Someplace, ST 12340	123 Commerce Pl. Somecity, ST 12344
NMLS ID					
ST License ID			Z765416	Z61456	Z61616
Contact	Joe Smith		Samuel Green	Joseph Cain	Sarah Arnold
Contact NMLS ID	12345				
Contact ST License ID			P16415	P51461	PT1234
Email	joesmith@ ficusbank.com		sam@omegare.biz	joe@alphare.biz	sarah@ epsilontitle.com
Phone	123-456-7890		123-555-1717	321-555-7171	987-555-4321

Confirm Receipt

By signing, you are only confirming that you have received this form. You do not have to accept this loan because you have signed or received this form.

_____   _____   _____   _____
Applicant Signature   Date   Co-Applicant Signature   Date

CLOSING DISCLOSURE

limits on increases, referred to as "tolerances," help prevent bait and switch tactics: giving a buyer low estimates when the loan application is submitted, but charging much more than the estimated amounts after the buyer has committed to the lender. If the buyer doesn't have the option of shopping for a particular service (because the lender requires the use of a certain settlement service provider), then a "zero tolerance" rule applies; in other words, the buyer can't be charged any more than the estimate that was given for that service.

A key section of the closing disclosure form is the table at the top of the third page. It directly compares the estimated closing costs that appeared on the buyer's loan estimate form, which was given at the time of the loan application, to the actual charges that the buyer is paying at closing.

Lenders can avoid penalties for excessive increases in their initial cost estimates by providing the buyer with an amended loan estimate form. If a buyer pays an excessive charge, the lender must refund the excess within 60 days after closing.

REAL ESTATE MATH

Real estate agents use math constantly: to determine the square footage of homes they are listing or selling, to prorate closing costs, and so on. Calculators make all of these tasks much easier than they once were, but it is still necessary to have a basic grasp of the math involved. Earlier in this chapter, we showed you how to prorate expenses at closing. In this section, we'll provide step-by-step instructions for solving a variety of real estate math problems.

DECIMALS AND PERCENTAGES

To carry out a calculation, it's easier to work with decimal numbers than with fractions or percentages. So if a problem presents you with fractions or percentages, you'll usually convert them into decimal numbers.

CONVERTING FRACTIONS. To convert a fraction into decimal form, divide the top number of the fraction (the numerator) by the bottom number of the fraction (the denominator).

EXAMPLE: To change ¾ into a decimal, divide 3 (the top number) by 4 (the bottom number): $3 \div 4 = .75$.

CONVERTING PERCENTAGES. To solve a problem involving a percentage, you'll first convert the percentage into a decimal number, then convert the decimal answer back into percentage form.

To convert a percentage to a decimal, remove the percent sign and move the decimal point two places to the left. It may be necessary to add a zero.

EXAMPLE: 5% becomes .05   32.5% becomes .325

To convert a decimal into a percentage, do just the opposite. Move the decimal point two places to the right and add a percent sign.

EXAMPLE: .08 becomes 08% (8.0%)   .095 becomes 09.5% (9.5%)

The percent key on a calculator performs the conversion of a percentage to a decimal number automatically. On most calculators, you can key in the digits and press the percent key, and the calculator will display the percentage in decimal form.

DECIMAL CALCULATIONS. Calculators handle decimal numbers in exactly the same way as whole numbers. If you enter a decimal number into the calculator with the decimal point in the correct place, the calculator will do the rest. But if you're working without a calculator, you'll need to apply the following rules.

To add or subtract decimals, put the numbers in a column with their decimal points lined up.

EXAMPLE: To add 3.755, 679, and 1.9, put the numbers in a column with the decimal points lined up as shown below, then add them together.

```
    3.755
  679.0
+   1.9
  684.655
```

To multiply decimal numbers, first do the multiplication without worrying about the decimal points. Then put a decimal point into the answer in the correct place. The answer should have as many decimal places (that is, numbers to the right of its decimal point) as the total number of decimal places in the numbers that were multiplied. So count the decimal places in the numbers you are multiplying and put the decimal point the same number of places to the left in the answer.

EXAMPLE: Multiply 24.6 times 16.7. The two numbers contain a total of two decimal places.

$$\begin{array}{r} 24.6 \\ \times\ 16.7 \\ \hline 410.82 \end{array}$$

In some cases, it will be necessary to include one or more zeros in the answer to have the correct number of decimal places.

EXAMPLE: Multiply .2 times .4. There is a total of two decimal places.

$$\begin{array}{r} .2 \\ \times\quad .4 \\ \hline .08 \end{array}$$

A zero has to be included in the answer in order to move the decimal point two places left.

To divide by a decimal number, move the decimal point in the denominator (the number you're dividing the other number by) all the way to the right. Then move the decimal point in the numerator (the number that you're dividing) the same number of places to the right. (In some cases it will be necessary to add one or more zeros to the numerator in order to move the decimal point the correct number of places.)

EXAMPLE: Divide 26.145 by 1.5. First move the decimal point in 1.5 all the way to the right (in this case, that's only one place). Then move the decimal point in 26.145 the same number of places to the right.

26.145 ÷ 1.5 becomes 261.45 ÷ 15

Now divide. 261.45 ÷ 15 = 17.43

Remember, these steps are unnecessary if you're using a calculator. If the numbers are keyed in correctly, the calculator will automatically give you an answer with the decimal point in the correct place.

AREA PROBLEMS

A real estate agent often needs to calculate the area of a lot, a building, or a room. Area is usually stated in square feet or square yards. The formula to be used for the calculation depends on the shape of the area in question. It may be a square, a rectangle, a triangle, or some combination of those shapes.

SQUARES AND RECTANGLES. The formula for finding the area of a square or a rectangle is $A = L \times W$.

> **EXAMPLE:** If a rectangular room measures 15 feet along one wall and 12 feet along the adjoining wall, how many square feet of carpet would be required to cover the floor?
>
> $A = L \times W$
>
> $A = 15' \times 12'$
>
> To find A, multiply L times W: $15' \times 12' = 180$ Sq. ft. 180 square feet of carpet is needed to cover the floor.

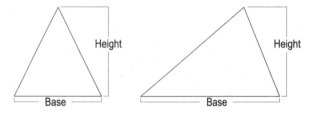

TRIANGLES. The formula for finding the area of a triangle is:

$$\begin{array}{r} \text{Height} \\ \times \tfrac{1}{2}\,\text{Base} \\ \hline \text{Area} \end{array} \quad \text{or} \quad \text{Area} = \tfrac{1}{2}\,\text{Base} \times \text{Height}$$

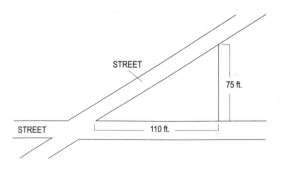

> **EXAMPLE:** If commercial building lots in a certain neighborhood are selling for approximately $5 per square foot, approximately how much should the lot pictured below sell for?

A = ½ B × H
Area = 55′ (½ of 110) × 75′
55′ × 75′ = 4,125 Sq. ft.

The lot contains 4,125 square feet. If similar lots are selling for about $5 per square foot, this lot should sell for about $20,625.

$$
\begin{array}{rl}
4,125 & \text{Square feet} \\
\times \ \$5 & \text{Per square foot} \\
\hline
\$20,625 & \text{Selling price}
\end{array}
$$

ODD SHAPES. The best approach to finding the area of an odd-shaped figure is to divide it up into squares, rectangles, and triangles. Find the areas of those figures and add them all up to arrive at the area of the odd-shaped lot, room, or building in question.

EXAMPLE: If the lot pictured below is leased on a 50-year lease for $3 per square foot per year, with rental payments made monthly, how much would the monthly rent be?

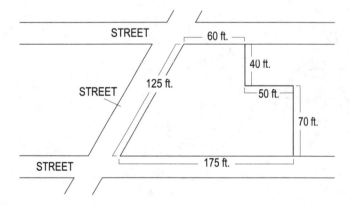

First, divide the lot up into rectangles and triangles.

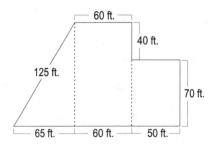

The next step is to find the area of each of the following figures. The height of the triangle is determined by adding together the 70-foot border of the small rectangle and the 40-foot border of the large rectangle.

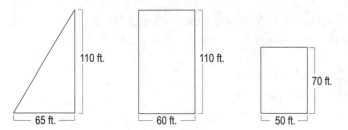

First, find the area of the triangle.

A = ½ Base × Height
A = 32.5′ (½ of 65′) × 110′
32.5′ × 110′ = 3,575 Sq. ft.

Then, find the area of the large rectangle.

A = Length × Width
A = 110′ × 60′
110′ × 60′ = 6,600 Sq. ft.

Next, find the area of the small rectangle.

A = Length × Width
A = 70′ × 50′
70′ × 50′ = 3,500 Sq. ft.

Finally, add the three areas together to find the area of the entire lot: 3,575 + 6,600 + 3,500 = 13,675 Total square feet.

The lot contains 13,675 square feet. At $3 per square foot per year, the annual rent would be $41,025.

13,675	Square feet
× $3	Rent per square foot
$41,025	Annual rent

The monthly rental payment would be one-twelfth of the annual rent: $41,025 ÷ 12 = $3,418.75. Thus, the monthly rental payment for this odd-shaped lot is $3,418.75.

PERCENTAGE PROBLEMS

Many real estate math problems, including problems about mortgage loan interest, involve percentages. To solve percentage problems, you'll usually convert the percentage into a decimal number, calculate, and then convert the answer back into percentage form. As explained earlier, a percentage is converted into a decimal number by removing the percent sign and moving the decimal point two places to the left. If the percentage is a single digit (for example, 7%), it will be necessary to add a zero (.07). To convert a decimal number into a percentage, you reverse those steps: move the decimal point two places to the right and add the percent sign.

In a math problem, whenever something is expressed as a percentage "of" another number, that indicates that you should multiply that other number by the percentage. For instance, what is 75% of $40,000?

<u>Step 1</u>	<u>Step 2</u>
75% becomes .75	$40,000
	$\times$ .75
	$30,000

Basically, percentage problems ask you to find a part of a whole. The whole is a larger figure, such as a property's sales price. The part is a smaller figure, such as a broker's commission. The general formula might be stated thus: A percentage of the whole equals the part. This can be written as an equation: Part = Whole $\times$ Percentage.

EXAMPLE: A house is listed for sale at a price of $172,000, with an agreement to pay a commission of 6% of the sales price. The property sells for $170,000. How much is the commission?

$P = W \times \%$

Change the percentage (6%) into a decimal number (.06) first: $P = $170,000 \times .06$.

$170,000	Sales price
$\times$ .06	Commission rate
$10,200	Commission

The commission is $10,200.

In some percentage problems, the part is given and you're asked to calculate either the whole or the percentage. For those problems, you'll need to rearrange the percentage formula into a division problem. If the whole is the unknown, divide the part by the percentage: Whole = Part ÷ Percentage.

If the percentage is the unknown, divide the part by the whole: Percentage = Part ÷ Whole.

Notice that in either case, you'll be dividing the value of the part by either the whole (to determine the percentage) or by the percentage (to determine the whole).

LOAN PROBLEMS. Loan problems can be solved using the general percentage formula: Part = Whole × Percentage. Here, the part is the amount of the interest, the whole is the loan amount or principal balance, and the percentage is the interest rate.

> **EXAMPLE:** Henry borrows $5,000 for one year and agrees to pay 7% interest. How much interest will he be required to pay?
>
> $P = W \times \%$
> $P = \$5,000 \times .07$
>
> | $5,000 | Loan amount |
> |---|---|
> | × .07 | Interest rate |
> | $350 | Interest |
>
> Henry will pay $350 in interest.

INTEREST RATES. Interest rates are expressed as annual rates—a certain percentage per year. Some problems present you with monthly, quarterly, or semi-annual interest payments instead of the annual amount. In that case, you'll need to multiply the payment amount stated in the problem to determine the annual amount before you substitute the numbers into the formula.

> **EXAMPLE:** If $450 in interest accrues on a $7,200 interest-only loan in six months, what is the annual interest rate?
>
> You're asked to find the annual interest rate, but the interest amount given in the problem ($450) accrued in only six months. The annual interest amount would be double that, or $900.

$$P = W \times \%$$

For the part (the interest amount), be sure to use the annual figure ($900):
$900 = $7,200 × Percentage.

Rearrange the formula to isolate the unknown (in this case, the percentage). The part is divided by the whole to determine the percentage: $900 ÷ $7,200 = .125.

Convert the decimal number back into a percentage: .125 becomes 12.5%. Thus, the annual interest rate is 12½%.

CHAPTER SUMMARY

1. Most real estate transactions in Washington are closed through the escrow process. Money and documents are given to an escrow agent, who holds them until they can be disbursed or delivered to the proper parties. The escrow agent may also handle a variety of other tasks, such as preparing documents for the parties to execute, ordering the preliminary title report, and calculating and prorating closing costs.

2. Some of the most important aspects of the closing process are inspections and repairs, approval of the buyer's loan, the appraisal, and the purchase of hazard insurance and title insurance. As a real estate agent, you should have a checklist of what needs to be done and make sure everything is getting done in time for the closing date. It's part of your job to keep the sale on track.

3. You should be able to provide good estimates of the buyer's net cost and the seller's net proceeds. To do this, you need to be familiar with the standard closing costs and who typically pays them. You must also be able to prorate certain expenses, such as property taxes and hazard insurance.

4. The federal income tax regulations that apply to real estate closings include Form 1099-S and Form 8300 reporting and rules, and the Foreign Investment in Real Property Tax Act. In some transactions, FIRPTA requires the escrow agent to withhold a portion of the seller's proceeds and send the money to the IRS.

5. The Real Estate Settlement Procedures Act, another federal law, helps home buyers and sellers understand their closing costs. RESPA applies to most residential real estate transactions financed with institutional loans. Key provisions include the closing disclosure form requirement and the prohibition on kickbacks and referral fees.

6. Real estate agents should know the mathematical formulas for converting fractions to decimals, percentages to decimals, and decimals to percentages. They should also know the formulas for calculating area, volume, and percentages.

CLOSING THE TRANSACTION AND REAL ESTATE MATH

CHAPTER QUIZ

1. Although the terms are often used interchangeably, the technical difference between an escrow agent and a closing agent is that:

    a. an escrow agent is an independent escrow company or a licensed escrow officer, while a closing agent is anyone providing escrow services

    b. a closing agent represents the interests of only one party to a transaction, while an escrow agent acts on behalf of both parties and is supposed be neutral

    c. the term "closing agent" refers specifically to a real estate licensee who is providing escrow services

    d. None of the above; there is no difference

2. Which of the following is not one of the steps in the inspection process?

    a. Ordering the inspection

    b. Approval or disapproval of the inspection report

    c. Appraisal of the property

    d. Reinspection of any required repairs

3. When choosing a home inspector, a buyer should look for a firm that:

    a. has recently changed its name

    b. will offer to make the repairs recommended by the inspection

    c. belongs to the American Society of Home Inspectors

    d. does other business in addition to inspections

4. An HO-3 hazard insurance policy will cover damages resulting from:

    a. floods

    b. vehicles

    c. earthquakes

    d. encroachments

5. If a home buyer is concerned about title problems that do not show up in the public record, he should:

    a. make sure there are no problems on the preliminary title report

    b. require the seller to purchase a standard coverage title insurance policy

    c. rely on the lender's title insurance policy

    d. get a homeowner's coverage title insurance policy

6. On a settlement statement, the debits represent:

   a. the amount of financing in the transaction
   b. amounts that are owed to a party at closing
   c. costs that a party must pay at closing
   d. costs that the buyer must pay to the seller

7. The earnest money deposit is:

   a. retained by the brokerage firm at closing in lieu of a commission
   b. applied toward the purchase price at closing
   c. a credit for the buyer on the settlement statement
   d. Both b and c

8. Prepaid interest refers to the:

   a. charge that the buyer must pay at closing to cover interest that will accrue on his loan during the last part of the month in which closing occurs
   b. refund to the seller of reserves on deposit in an impound account with her lender
   c. interest owed by the seller at closing after paying off the principal balance of her loan
   d. fact that mortgage interest is usually paid in advance

9. The seller customarily pays the fee for recording the:

   a. deed of reconveyance
   b. deed from the seller to the buyer
   c. new mortgage or deed of trust
   d. None of the above

10. A loan secured by a deed of trust on the home the buyer is purchasing will be considered a "federally related" loan if the:

    a. person responsible for closing must report the sale to the IRS
    b. lender makes real estate loans that total more than $1,000,000 per year
    c. closing agent is required to withhold part of the proceeds under FIRPTA
    d. loan is used to purchase more than 25 acres

ANSWER KEY

1. a. The two terms are often used interchangeably, but technically the term "escrow agent" refers to an independent escrow company or licensed escrow officer. "Closing agent" refers to anyone providing escrow services—a lawyer, an independent escrow company, a real estate licensee, a lender, etc.

2. c. During the closing process, the initial inspection needs to be ordered, and then the inspection report must be approved or rejected by the buyer and/or the lender. If the seller makes repairs, a reinspection will be necessary. (The appraisal is a separate matter, not part of the inspection process.)

3. c. Membership in the American Society of Home Inspectors requires actual experience, passing a written examination, inspection reviews, and continuing education.

4. b. Floods and earthquakes are not covered by a typical hazard insurance policy, although supplemental coverage may be available. (Protection against encroachments would be provided by extended coverage title insurance, not by hazard insurance.)

5. d. A homeowner's title insurance policy protects the buyer against problems that do not appear in the public record, such as an encroachment or adverse possession. It is the default policy in most home purchase transactions.

6. c. Debits are costs that a party must pay at closing, either to the other party or to a third party. The buyer's debits increase the amount of money the buyer will need to pay at closing. The seller's debits decrease the seller's net proceeds.

7. d. The earnest money deposit is applied toward the purchase price at closing; it's part of the buyer's downpayment. Because the buyer has already paid the earnest money, it is treated as a credit for the buyer on his settlement statement.

8. a. The buyer's first payment on a new loan is not due the first day of the month immediately after closing, but the first day of the month after that. To cover the interest that accrues during the remainder of the month in which closing occurs, the buyer must pay prepaid or interim interest at closing.

9. a. The seller would pay the fee for recording a deed of reconveyance to release the property from the lien of a deed of trust. The recording fee for a document is generally paid by the party who benefits most from having that document recorded.

10. b. For RESPA purposes, a loan is federally related if the lender is federally regulated, has federally insured accounts, is assisted by the federal government, makes loans in connection with a federal program, sells loans to Fannie Mae or Freddie Mac, or makes real estate loans that total more than $1,000,000 per year.

GLOSSARY

The definitions given here explain how the listed terms are used in the real estate field. Some of the terms have additional meanings, which can be found in a standard dictionary.

ABSTRACT OF TITLE—*See:* Title, Abstract of.

ACCELERATION CLAUSE—A provision in a promissory note or security instrument allowing the lender to declare the entire debt due immediately if the borrower breaches one or more provisions of the loan agreement. Also referred to as a call provision.

ACCEPTANCE—1. Agreeing to the terms of an offer to enter into a contract, thereby creating a binding contract. 2. Taking delivery of a deed from the grantor.

ACCEPTANCE, QUALIFIED—*See:* Counteroffer.

ACRE—A measure of area for land; one acre is 43,560 square feet.

ADJUSTABLE-RATE MORTGAGE—*See:* Mortgage, Adjustable-Rate.

AD VALOREM—A Latin phrase that means "according to value," used to refer to taxes that are assessed on the value of property.

AFFILIATED LICENSEES—The individual real estate agents licensed under a particular brokerage firm.

AGENCY—A relationship of trust created when one person (the principal) grants another (the agent) authority to represent the principal in dealings with third parties.

AGENCY, APPARENT—When third parties are given the impression that someone who has not been authorized to represent another is that person's agent, or else given the impression that an agent has been authorized to perform acts which are in fact beyond the scope of her authority.

AGENCY, DUAL—When an agent represents both parties to a transaction, as when a real estate agent represents both the buyer and the seller.

AGENCY, EXCLUSIVE—*See:* Listing, Exclusive.

AGENCY COUPLED WITH AN INTEREST—When an agent has a claim against the property that is the subject of the agency, so that the principal cannot revoke the agent's authority.

AGENCY, INADVERTENT DUAL—Providing agency services to one party without disclosing that you already represent the other party; you unintentionally create a dual agency.

AGENCY, NON-—When a licensee limits herself to the role of neutral intermediary in a transaction. Non-agency is typically limited to commercial transactions, but may occur in residential transactions as well.

AGENT—A person authorized to represent another (the principal) in dealings with third parties.

AGENT, DUAL—*See:* Agency, Dual.

AGREEMENT—*See:* Contract.

ALIENATION—The transfer of ownership or an interest in property from one person to another, by any means.

ALIENATION, INVOLUNTARY—Transfer of an interest in property against the will of the owner, or without action by the owner, occurring through operation of law, natural processes, or adverse possession.

ALIENATION, VOLUNTARY—When an owner voluntarily transfers an interest in property to someone else.

ALIENATION CLAUSE—A provision in a security instrument that gives the lender the right to declare the entire loan balance due immediately if the borrower sells or otherwise transfers the security property. Also called a due-on-sale clause.

ALL-INCLUSIVE TRUST DEED—*See:* Mortgage, Wraparound.

AMENITIES—Features of a property that contribute to the pleasure or convenience of owning it, such as a fireplace, a beautiful view, or its proximity to a good school.

AMERICANS WITH DISABILITIES ACT—A federal law requiring facilities that are open to the public to ensure accessibility to disabled persons, even if that accessibility requires making architectural modifications. The ADA also requires employers to make reasonable accommodations for disabled employees.

AMORTIZATION, NEGATIVE—When unpaid interest on a loan is added to the principal balance, increasing the amount owed.

AMORTIZE—To gradually pay off a debt with installment payments that include both principal and interest. *See also:* Loan, Amortized.

ANNUAL PERCENTAGE RATE (APR)—Expresses the relationship between the finance charge (including interest, loan fee, discount points, and mortgage insurance costs) and the amount financed as an annualized percentage.

ANTITRUST LAWS—Laws that prohibit any agreement or unilateral action that has the effect of restraining trade, including conspiracies.

APPRAISAL—An estimate or opinion of the value of a piece of property as of a particular date. Also called valuation.

APPRAISER—One who estimates the value of property, especially an expert qualified to do so by training and experience.

APPRECIATION—An increase in value; the opposite of depreciation.

APR—*See:* Annual Percentage Rate.

AREA—The size of a surface, usually in square units of measure, such as square feet or square miles. The area of a piece of land may also be stated in acres.

ARM—*See:* Mortgage, Adjustable-Rate.

ARM'S LENGTH TRANSACTION—A transaction in which there is no family or business relationship between the parties.

ASBESTOS—A carcinogenic substance that was used in insulation for many years and that should be enclosed or removed if found.

ASSESSMENT—The valuation of property for purposes of taxation.

ASSESSOR—An official who determines the value of property for taxation.

ASSET—Anything of value that a person owns.

ASSETS, LIQUID—Cash and other assets that can be readily liquidated (turned into cash), such as stock.

ASSIGN—To transfer rights (especially contract rights) or interests to another.

ASSIGNEE—One to whom rights or interests have been assigned.

ASSIGNMENT—1. A transfer of contract rights from one person to another. 2. In the case of a lease, when the original tenant transfers her entire leasehold estate to another. *Compare:* Sublease.

ASSIGNOR—One who has assigned his rights or interest to another.

ASSUMPTION—When a buyer takes on personal liability for paying off the seller's existing mortgage or deed of trust.

ASSUMPTION FEE—A fee paid to the lender, usually by the buyer, when a mortgage or deed of trust is assumed.

ATTORNEY IN FACT—Any person authorized to represent another by a power of attorney; not necessarily a lawyer (an attorney at law).

AUTHORITY, ACTUAL—Authority actually given to an agent by the principal, either expressly or by implication.

AUTHORITY, APPARENT—Authority to represent another that someone appears to have and that the principal is estopped from denying, although no actual authority has been granted.

AUTHORITY, IMPLIED—An agent's authority to do everything reasonably necessary to carry out the principal's express orders.

BALLOON PAYMENT—A payment on a loan (usually the final payment) that is significantly larger than the regular installment payments.

BANKRUPTCY—1. When the liabilities of an individual, corporation, or firm exceed the assets. 2. When a court declares an individual, corporation, or firm to be insolvent, so that the assets and debts will be administered under bankruptcy laws.

BENEFICIARY—1. One for whom a trust is created and on whose behalf the trustee administers the trust. 2. The lender in a deed of trust transaction. 3. One entitled to receive real or personal property under a will; a legatee or devisee.

BILL OF SALE—A document used to transfer title to personal property from one person to another.

BLIND AD—An advertisement placed by a real estate licensee that does not include the name of her real estate firm, as licensed.

BLOCKBUSTING—Attempting to induce owners to list or sell their homes by predicting that members of another racial, ethnic, or religious group, or people with a disability, will be moving into the neighborhood; this violates antidiscrimination laws. Also called panic selling.

BOARD OF DIRECTORS—The body responsible for governing a corporation on behalf of the shareholders, which oversees the corporate management.

BONA FIDE—In good faith; genuine; not fraudulent.

BREACH—Violation of an obligation, duty, or law; especially an unexcused failure to perform a contractual obligation.

BRANCH MANAGER—A managing broker who is responsible for the operations of a firm's branch office; the branch manager is authorized to perform branch management duties under the supervision of the firm's designated broker.

BROKER—A licensed individual acting on behalf of a real estate firm to perform real estate brokerage services, under the supervision of a designated and/or managing broker.

BROKER, DESIGNATED—*See:* Designated Broker.

BROKER, MANAGING—*See:* Managing Broker.

BROKERAGE—*See:* Real Estate Brokerage.

BROKERAGE FEE—The commission or other compensation charged for a real estate firm's services.

BROKER PRICE OPINION—A report of property value prepared by a real estate licensee. A CMA is a broker price opinion.

BUMP CLAUSE—A provision in a purchase and sale agreement that allows the seller to keep the property on the market while waiting for a contingency to be fulfilled; if the seller receives another good offer in the meantime, she can require the buyer to either waive the contingency clause or terminate the contract.

BUSINESS OPPORTUNITY—A business that is for sale.

BUYDOWN—When discount points are paid to a lender to reduce (buy down) the interest rate charged to the borrower; especially when a seller pays discount points to help the buyer/borrower qualify for financing.

BUYER REPRESENTATION AGREEMENT—A representation agreement between a prospective property buyer and a real estate firm. The buyer hires the firm to locate a suitable property for the buyer to purchase.

CALL PROVISION—*See:* Acceleration Clause.

CANCELLATION—Termination of a contract without undoing acts that have been already performed under the contract. *Compare:* Rescission.

CAPACITY—The legal ability or competency to perform some act, such as enter into a contract or execute a deed or will.

CAPITAL—Money (or other forms of wealth) available for use in the production of more money.

CAPITALIZATION—A method of appraising real property by converting the anticipated net income from the property into the present value. Also called the income approach to value.

CAPITALIZE—1. To provide with cash, or another form of capital. 2. To determine the present value of an asset using capitalization.

CARRYBACK LOAN—*See:* Loan, Purchase Money.

CARRYOVER CLAUSE—*See:* Extender Clause.

CASH FLOW—The residual income after deducting all operating expenses and debt service from gross income. Also called spendable income.

CERCLA—*See:* Comprehensive Environmental Response, Compensation, and Liability Act.

CERTIFICATE OF ELIGIBILITY—A document issued by the Department of Veterans Affairs as evidence of a veteran's eligibility for a VA-guaranteed loan.

CERTIFICATE OF SALE—The document given to the purchaser at a mortgage foreclosure sale, instead of a deed; replaced with a sheriff's deed only after the redemption period expires.

CHAIN OF TITLE—*See:* Title, Chain of.

CIVIL LAW—The body of law concerned with the rights and liabilities of one individual in relation to another; includes contract law, tort law, and property law. *Compare:* Criminal Law.

CIVIL RIGHTS—Fundamental rights guaranteed to individuals by the law. The term is primarily used in reference to constitutional and statutory protections against discrimination or government interference.

CIVIL SUIT—A lawsuit in which one private party sues another private party (as opposed to a criminal suit, in which an individual is sued—prosecuted—by the government).

CLIENT—One who hires a real estate agent, lawyer, or appraiser. A real estate agent's client can be a seller, a buyer, a landlord, or a tenant.

CLOSING—The final stage in a real estate transaction, when the seller receives the purchase money, the buyer receives the deed, and title is transferred. Also called settlement.

CLOSING COSTS—Expenses incurred in the transfer of real estate in addition to the purchase price; for example, the appraisal fee, title insurance premium, brokerage commission, and excise tax.

CLOSING DATE—The date on which all the terms of a purchase and sale agreement must be met, or the contract is terminated.

CLOSING DISCLOSURE—In a residential transaction subject to RESPA and/or the Truth in Lending Act, a form that the lender must give to the parties before closing, listing the actual closing costs.

CLOSING STATEMENT—*See:* Settlement Statement.

CLOUD ON TITLE—A claim, encumbrance, or apparent defect that makes the title to a property unmarketable. *See also:* Title, Marketable.

CMA—*See*: Competitive Market Analysis.

CO-BORROWER—Someone (usually a family member) who accepts responsibility for the repayment of a mortgage loan along with the primary borrower, to help the borrower qualify for the loan.

CODE OF ETHICS—A body of rules setting forth accepted standards of conduct, reflecting principles of fairness and morality; especially one that the members of an organization are expected to follow.

COLLATERAL—Anything of value used as security for a debt or obligation.

COMMINGLING—Mixing personal or business funds with client funds for any reason. Commingling funds violates the license law.

COMMISSION—1. The compensation paid to a brokerage for services in connection with a real estate transaction (usually a percentage of the sales price). 2. A group of people organized for a particular purpose or function; usually a governmental body, such as the Real Estate Commission.

COMMISSION SPLIT—A compensation arrangement in which listing and selling firms share the commission paid by the seller.

COMMITMENT—In real estate finance, a lender's promise to make a loan. A loan commitment may be "firm" or "conditional"; a conditional commitment is contingent on something, such as a satisfactory credit report on the borrower.

COMMUNITY PROPERTY—In Washington and other community property states, property owned jointly by a married couple, as distinguished from each spouse's separate property; generally, any property acquired through the labor or skill of either spouse during marriage.

COMPARABLE—A recently sold property similar to a subject property, used as a basis for estimating value in the sales comparison approach to appraisal or in a competitive market analysis.

COMPETENT—1. Of sound mind, for the purposes of entering into a contract or executing an instrument. 2. Both of sound mind and having reached the age of majority.

COMPETITIVE MARKET ANALYSIS (CMA)—A comparison of homes that are similar in location, style, and amenities to the subject property, in order to set a realistic listing price. Similar to the sales comparison approach to value.

COMPLIANCE INSPECTION—A building inspection to determine, for the benefit of a lender, whether building codes, specifications, or conditions established after a prior inspection have been met before a loan is made.

COMPREHENSIVE ENVIRONMENTAL RESPONSE, COMPENSATION, AND LIABILITY ACT—A federal law allocating liability for the cost of toxic waste cleanup.

CONDITION—1. A provision in a contract that makes the parties' rights and obligations depend on the occurrence (or non-occurrence) of a particular event. Also called a contingency clause. 2. A provision in a deed that makes title depend on compliance with a particular restriction.

CONDITIONAL COMMITMENT—*See:* Commitment.

CONFORMING LOAN—*See:* Loan, Conforming.

CONSIDERATION—Anything of value (such as money, goods, services, or a promise) given to induce another to enter into a contract. Sometimes called valuable consideration.

CONSPIRACY—An agreement or plan between two or more persons to perform an unlawful act.

CONSTRUCTION LIEN—*See:* Lien, Construction.

CONSUMER FINANCIAL PROTECTION BUREAU—A federal agency that enforces a number of consumer protection laws that affect the real estate business, such as the Truth in Lending Act.

CONTINGENCY CLAUSE—*See:* Condition.

CONTRACT—An agreement between two or more persons to do or not do a certain thing, for consideration.

CONTRACT, BILATERAL—A contract in which each party has made a binding promise to perform (as distinguished from a unilateral contract).

CONTRACT, BROKERAGE AND AFFILIATED LICENSEE—A contract between a brokerage and an affiliated licensee, outlining their mutual obligations.

CONTRACT, CONDITIONAL SALES—*See:* Contract, Land.

CONTRACT, EXECUTED—A contract in which both parties have completely performed their contractual obligations.

CONTRACT, EXECUTORY—A contract in which one or both parties have not yet completed performance of their obligations.

CONTRACT, EXPRESS—A contract that has been put into words, either spoken or written.

CONTRACT, IMPLIED—A contract that has not been put into words, but is implied by the actions of the parties.

CONTRACT, INSTALLMENT SALES—*See:* Contract, Land.

CONTRACT, LAND—A contract for the sale of real property in which the buyer (the vendee) pays in installments; the buyer takes possession of the property immediately, but the seller (the vendor) retains legal title until the full price has been paid. Also called a conditional sales contract, installment sales contract, real estate contract, or contract for deed.

CONTRACT, ORAL—A spoken agreement that has not been written down.

CONTRACT, REAL ESTATE—1. Any contract pertaining to real estate. 2. A land contract.

CONTRACT, SALES—*See:* Purchase and Sale Agreement.

CONTRACT, UNENFORCEABLE—An agreement that a court would refuse to enforce; for example, because its contents can't be proven or the statute of limitations has run out.

CONTRACT, UNILATERAL—A contract that is accepted by performance; the offeror has promised to perform her side of the bargain if the other party performs, but the other party has not promised to perform. *Compare:* Contract, Bilateral.

CONTRACT, VALID—A binding, legally enforceable contract.

CONTRACT, VOID—An agreement that is not a valid contract because it lacks a required element (such as consideration) or has some other fundamental defect.

CONTRACT, VOIDABLE—A contract that one of the parties can disaffirm without liability, because of lack of capacity or a negative factor such as fraud or duress.

CONTRACT FOR DEED—*See:* Contract, Land.

CONTRACT OF SALE—*See:* Purchase and Sale Agreement.

CONVENTIONAL FINANCING—*See:* Loan, Conventional.

CONVERSION—Misappropriating property or funds belonging to another; for example, converting trust funds to one's own use.

CONVEYANCE—The transfer of title to real property from one person to another by means of a written document, especially a deed.

COOPERATIVE SALE—A sale in which the buyer and the seller are brought together by licensees working for different real estate firms.

CORPORATION—An association organized according to certain laws, in which individuals may purchase ownership shares; treated by the law as an artificial person, separate from the individual shareholders. *Compare:* Partnership.

COST—The amount paid for anything in money, goods, or services.

COST, REPLACEMENT—In appraisal, the current cost of constructing a building with the same utility as the subject property using modern materials and construction methods.

COST, REPRODUCTION—In appraisal, the cost of constructing a replica (an exact duplicate) of the subject property, using the same materials and construction methods that were originally used, but at current prices.

COST APPROACH TO VALUE—One of the three main methods of appraisal, in which an estimate of the subject property's value is arrived at by estimating the cost of replacing (or reproducing) the improvements, then deducting the estimated accrued depreciation and adding the estimated market value of the land.

COUNTEROFFER—A response to a contract offer, changing some of the terms of the original offer; it operates as a rejection of the original offer (not as an acceptance). Also called qualified acceptance.

COVENANT—1. A contract. 2. A promise. 3. A guarantee (express or implied) in a document such as a deed or lease. 4. A restrictive covenant.

COVENANT, RESTRICTIVE—A promise to do or not do an act relating to real property, especially a promise that runs with the land; usually an owner's promise not to use the property in a specified manner.

CREDIT—A payment receivable (owed to you), as opposed to a debit, which is a payment due (owed by you).

CREDITOR—One who is owed a debt.

CREDITOR, SECURED—A creditor with a security interest in or a lien against specific property; if the debt is not repaid, the creditor can repossess the property or (in the case of real estate) foreclose on the property and collect the debt from the sale proceeds.

CRIMINAL LAW—The body of law under which the government can prosecute an individual for crimes, wrongs against society. *Compare:* Civil Law.

CUSTOMER—From the point of view of a listing agent, a prospective property buyer.

DAMAGES—In a civil lawsuit, an amount of money the defendant is ordered to pay the plaintiff.

DAMAGES, COMPENSATORY—Damages awarded to a plaintiff as compensation for injuries (personal injuries, property damage, or financial losses) caused by the defendant's act or failure to act.

DAMAGES, LIQUIDATED—A sum that the parties to a contract agree in advance (at the time the contract is made) will serve as full compensation in the event of a breach.

DAMAGES, PUNITIVE—In a civil lawsuit, an award added to compensatory damages, to punish the defendant for outrageous or malicious conduct and discourage others from similar conduct.

DEBIT—A charge payable by a party; for example, in a real estate transaction the loan origination fee is a debit to the buyer and the sales commission is a debit to the seller.

DEBTOR—One who owes money to another.

DEBT SERVICE—The amount of money required to make the periodic payments of principal and interest on an amortized debt, such as a mortgage.

DEBT TO INCOME RATIO—The debt to income ratio measures the relationship between the loan applicant's monthly income and his total monthly debt.

DEED—An instrument which, when properly executed and delivered, conveys title to real property from the grantor to the grantee.

DEED, GENERAL WARRANTY—A deed in which the grantor warrants the title against defects that might have arisen before or during his period of ownership.

DEED, GIFT—A deed that is not supported by valuable consideration; often lists "love and affection" as consideration.

DEED, QUITCLAIM—A deed that conveys any interest in a property that the grantor has at the time the deed is executed, without warranties.

DEED, SHERIFF'S—A deed delivered, on court order, to the holder of a certificate of sale when the redemption period after a mortgage foreclosure has expired.

DEED, TAX—A deed given to a purchaser of property at a tax foreclosure sale.

DEED, TRUST—*See:* Deed of Trust.

DEED, TRUSTEE'S—A deed given to a purchaser of property at a trustee's sale.

DEED, SPECIAL WARRANTY—A deed in which the grantor warrants the title only against defects that might have arisen during his period of ownership (not before).

DEED, WARRANTY—1. A general warranty deed. 2. Any type of deed that carries warranties.

DEED EXECUTED UNDER COURT ORDER—A deed that is the result of a court action, such as judicial foreclosure or partition.

DEED IN LIEU OF FORECLOSURE—A deed given by a borrower to the lender, relinquishing ownership of the security property, to satisfy the debt and avoid foreclosure.

DEED OF RECONVEYANCE—The instrument used to release the security property from the lien created by a deed of trust when the debt has been repaid.

DEED OF TRUST—An instrument that creates a voluntary lien on real property to secure the repayment of a debt, and which includes a power of sale clause permitting nonjudicial foreclosure; the parties are the grantor or trustor (borrower), the beneficiary (the lender), and the trustee (a neutral third party).

DEED RELEASE PROVISION—*See:* Release Clause.

DEED RESTRICTIONS—Provisions in a deed that restrict use of the property, and which may be either covenants or conditions.

DEFAULT—Failure to fulfill an obligation, duty, or promise, as when a borrower fails to make payments, or a tenant fails to pay rent.

DEFENDANT—1. The person being sued in a civil lawsuit. 2. The accused person in a criminal lawsuit.

DEFERRED MAINTENANCE—Maintenance or repairs that were postponed, causing physical deterioration of the building.

DELEGATION AGREEMENT—A written agreement in which a designated broker transfers some of her authority and duties to another managing broker (such as a branch manager). However, the agreement doesn't relieve the designated broker of the ultimate responsibility for the delegated function.

DELIVERY—The legal transfer of a deed from the grantor to the grantee, which results in the transfer of title.

DEPARTMENT OF LICENSING—The state agency in charge of administering the real estate license law in Washington.

DEPOSIT—Money offered as an indication of commitment or as a protection, and which may be refunded under certain circumstances, such as an earnest money deposit or a tenant's security deposit.

DEPOSIT RECEIPT—*See:* Purchase and Sale Agreement.

DEPRECIATION—1. A loss in value. 2. For the purpose of income tax deductions, apportioning the cost of an asset over a period of time.

DESIGNATED BROKER—A managing broker who has a designated broker endorsement added to her license by the Department of Licensing, and who has ultimate responsibility for all of a real estate firm's activities.

DISABILITY—According to the Americans with Disabilities Act and Fair Housing Act, a physical or mental impairment that substantially limits a person in one or more major life activities.

DISBURSEMENTS—Money paid out or expended.

DISCLAIMER—A denial of legal responsibility.

DISCOUNT—1. (verb) To sell a promissory note at less than its face value. 2. (noun) An amount withheld from the loan amount by the lender when the loan is originated; discount points.

DISCOUNT POINTS—A percentage of the principal amount of a loan, collected by the lender at the time a loan is originated, to reduce the interest rate and give the lender an additional upfront yield.

DISCRIMINATION—Treating people unequally because of their race, religion, sex, national origin, age, or some other characteristic.

DISTRESSED HOME—A personal residence that is in danger of foreclosure because the homeowner is delinquent on mortgage or tax payments.

DISTRESSED PROPERTY LAW—A state law intended to help protect financially distressed homeowners from foreclosure scams.

DOWNPAYMENT—The part of the purchase price of property that the buyer is paying in cash; the difference between the purchase price and the financing.

DRAINAGE—A system to draw water off land, either artificially (e.g., with pipes) or naturally (e.g., with a slope).

DUAL AGENCY—*See:* Agency, Dual.

DUE-ON-SALE CLAUSE—*See:* Alienation Clause.

DURESS—Unlawful force or constraint used to compel someone to do something (such as sign a contract) against his will.

EARNEST MONEY—A deposit that a prospective buyer gives the seller as evidence of her good faith intent to complete the transaction.

EARNEST MONEY AGREEMENT—*See:* Purchase and Sale Agreement.

EASEMENT—An irrevocable right to use some part of another person's real property for a particular purpose.

ELEMENTS OF COMPARISON—In the sales comparison approach to appraisal, considerations taken into account in selecting comparables and comparing comparables to the subject property; they include date of sale, location, physical characteristics, and terms of sale.

EMPLOYEE—Someone who works under the direction and control of another. *Compare:* Independent Contractor.

ENCUMBER—To place a lien or other encumbrance against the title to a property.

ENCUMBRANCE—A nonpossessory interest in real property; a right or interest held by someone other than the property owner, which may be a lien, an easement, a profit, or a restrictive covenant.

ENCUMBRANCE, FINANCIAL—A lien.

ENCUMBRANCE, NONFINANCIAL—An easement, a profit, or a restrictive covenant.

ENDANGERED SPECIES ACT—A federal law that limits development in habitats of endangered or threatened species.

EQUITABLE REMEDY—In a civil lawsuit, a judgment granted to the plaintiff that is something other than an award of money (damages); an injunction, rescission, and specific performance are examples.

EQUITY—1. An owner's unencumbered interest in his property; the difference between the value of the property and the liens against it. 2. A judge's power to soften or set aside strict legal rules, to bring about a fair and just result in a particular case.

ESCROW—An arrangement in which something of value (such as money or a deed) is held on behalf of the parties to a transaction by a disinterested third party (an escrow agent) until specified conditions have been fulfilled.

ESTATE—1. An interest in real property that is or may become possessory; either a freehold or a leasehold. 2. The property left by someone who has died.

ESTOPPEL—A legal doctrine that prevents a person from asserting rights or facts that are inconsistent with her earlier actions or statements.

ESTOPPEL CERTIFICATE—A document that prevents a person who signs it from later asserting facts different from those stated in the document. Also called an estoppel letter.

ETHICS—A system of accepted principles or standards of moral conduct. *See also:* Code of Ethics.

EXCLUSIVE LISTING—*See:* Listing, Exclusive.

EXECUTE—1. To sign an instrument and take any other steps (such as acknowledgment) that may be necessary to its validity. 2. To perform or complete. *See also:* Contract, Executed.

EXEMPTION—A provision holding that a law or rule does not apply to a particular person or group; for example, a person entitled to a tax exemption is not required to pay the tax.

EXPRESS—Stated in words, whether spoken or written. *Compare:* Implied.

EXTENDER CLAUSE—A clause in a listing agreement providing that for a specified period after the listing expires, the listing agent will still be entitled to a commission if the property is sold to someone that the agent dealt with during the listing term. Also called a safety clause, protection clause, or carryover clause.

FAILURE OF PURPOSE—When the intended purpose of an agreement or arrangement can no longer be achieved; in most cases, this releases the parties from their obligations.

FAIR HOUSING ACT—A federal law prohibiting discrimination in the sale or lease of residential property on the basis of race, color, religion, sex, national origin, handicap, or familial status.

FANNIE MAE—Popular name for the Federal National Mortgage Association (FNMA).

FED—The Federal Reserve.

FEE SIMPLE—The highest and most complete form of ownership, which is of potentially infinite duration. Also called a fee or a fee simple absolute.

FHA—Federal Housing Administration. *See also:* Loan, FHA.

FIDUCIARY RELATIONSHIP—A relationship of trust and confidence, where one party owes the other (or both parties owe each other) loyalty and a higher standard of good faith than is owed to third parties. For example, an agent is a fiduciary in relation to the principal; husband and wife are fiduciaries in relation to one another.

FINANCE CHARGE—Under the Truth in Lending Act, the sum of all fees charged for a loan, including interest, any discount points paid by the borrower, the loan origination fee, and mortgage insurance costs.

FINANCIAL STATEMENT—A summary of facts showing the financial condition of an individual or a business, including a detailed list of assets and liabilities. Also called a balance sheet.

FINANCING STATEMENT—A brief instrument that is recorded to perfect and give constructive notice of a creditor's security interest in an article of personal property.

FINDER'S FEE—A referral fee paid to someone for directing a buyer or a seller to a real estate agent.

FIRM COMMITMENT—*See:* Commitment.

FIRPTA—The Foreign Investment in Real Property Tax Act; this federal law requires withholding funds from a sale of real property when the seller is not a U.S. citizen or a resident alien, in order to prevent tax evasion.

FIRST LIEN POSITION—The position held by a mortgage or deed of trust that has higher lien priority than any other mortgage or deed of trust against the property.

FIXED-RATE LOAN—*See:* Loan, Fixed-Rate.

FIXED TERM—A period of time that has a definite beginning and ending.

FORECLOSURE—When a lienholder causes property to be sold against the owner's wishes, so that the unpaid lien can be satisfied from the sale proceeds.

FORECLOSURE, JUDICIAL—1. The sale of property pursuant to court order to satisfy a lien. 2. A lawsuit filed by a mortgagee or deed of trust beneficiary to foreclose on the security property when the borrower has defaulted.

FORECLOSURE, NONJUDICIAL—Foreclosure by a trustee under the power of sale clause in a deed of trust.

FOREIGN INVESTMENT IN REAL PROPERTY TAX ACT—*See:* FIRPTA.

FORFEITURE—Loss of a right or something else of value as a result of failure to perform an obligation or fulfill a condition.

FOR SALE BY OWNER—A property that is being sold by the owner without the help of a real estate agent. Also called a FSBO (often pronounced "fizz-bo").

FRANCHISE—A right or privilege granted by a government to conduct a certain business, or a right granted by a private business to use its trade name in conducting business.

FRAUD—An intentional or negligent misrepresentation or concealment of a material fact, which is relied upon by another, who is induced to enter a transaction and harmed as a result.

FRAUD, ACTUAL—Deceit or misrepresentation with the intention of cheating or defrauding another.

FRAUD, CONSTRUCTIVE—A breach of duty that misleads the person the duty was owed to, without an intention to deceive; for example, if a seller gives a buyer inaccurate information about the property without realizing that it is false, that may be constructive fraud.

FREDDIE MAC—Popular name for the Federal Home Loan Mortgage Corporation.

FREE AND CLEAR—Ownership of real property completely free of liens.

FREEHOLD—A possessory interest in real property that has an indeterminable duration; it can be either a fee simple or an estate for life. Someone who has a freehold estate has title to the property (as opposed to someone with a leasehold estate, who is only a tenant).

FRONTAGE—The distance a property extends along a street or a body of water; the distance between the two side boundaries at the front of the lot.

FRONT FOOT—A measurement of property for sale or valuation, with each foot of frontage presumed to extend the entire depth of the lot.

GENERAL WARRANTY DEED—*See*: Deed, General Warranty.

GIFT DEED—*See*: Deed, Gift.

GIFT FUNDS—Money that a relative (or other third party) gives to a buyer who otherwise would not have enough cash to close the transaction.

GINNIE MAE—Popular name for the Government National Mortgage Association (GNMA).

GRANT—To transfer or convey an interest in real property by means of a written instrument.

GRANTEE—One who receives a grant of real property.

GRANTING CLAUSE—Words in a deed that indicate the grantor's intent to transfer an interest in property.

GRANTOR—One who grants an interest in real property to another.

GROUP BOYCOTT—An agreement between two or more real estate agents to exclude other agents from equal participation in real estate activities.

GUARDIAN—A person appointed by a court to administer the affairs of a minor or an incompetent person.

HEIR—Someone entitled to inherit another's property under the laws of intestate succession.

HIGHEST AND BEST USE—The use which, at the time of appraisal, is most likely to produce the greatest net return from the property over a given period of time.

HUD—The U.S. Department of Housing and Urban Development.

IMPLIED—Not expressed in words, but understood from actions or circumstances. *Compare:* Express.

IMPOUND ACCOUNT—A bank account maintained by a lender for payment of property taxes and insurance premiums on the security property; the lender requires the borrower to make regular deposits, and then pays the expenses out of the account when they are due. Also called a reserve account.

IMPROVEMENTS—Man-made additions to real property.

INCOME, DISPOSABLE—Income remaining after income taxes have been paid.

INCOME, EFFECTIVE GROSS—A measure of a rental property's capacity to generate income; calculated by subtracting a vacancy factor from the economic rent (potential gross income).

INCOME, GROSS—A property's total income before making any deductions (for bad debts, vacancies, operating expenses, etc.).

INCOME, NET—The income left over after subtracting the property's operating expenses (fixed expenses, maintenance expenses, and reserves for replacement) from the effective gross income. In the income approach to value, it is capitalized to estimate the subject property's value.

INCOME, POTENTIAL GROSS—A property's economic rent; the income it could earn if it were available for lease in the current market.

INCOME, RESIDUAL—The amount of income that an applicant for a VA loan has left over after taxes, recurring obligations, and the proposed housing expense have been deducted from his gross monthly income.

INCOME, SPENDABLE—The income that remains after deducting operating expenses, debt service, and income taxes from a property's gross income. Also called net spendable income or cash flow.

INCOME APPROACH TO VALUE—One of the three main methods of appraisal, in which an estimate of the subject property's value is based on the net income it produces; also called the capitalization method or investor's method of appraisal.

INCOME PROPERTY—Property that generates rent or other income for the owner, such as an apartment building. In the federal income tax code, it is referred to as property held for the production of income.

INCOME RATIO—A standard used in qualifying a buyer for a loan, to determine whether she has sufficient income; the buyer's debts and proposed housing expense should not exceed a specified percentage of her income.

INCOMPETENT—Not legally competent; not of sound mind.

INDEPENDENT CONTRACTOR—A person who contracts to do a job for another, but retains control over how he will carry out the task, rather than following detailed instructions. *Compare:* Employee.

INDEX—A published statistical report that indicates changes in the cost of money; used as the basis for interest rate adjustments in an ARM.

IN-HOUSE TRANSACTION—A sale in which the buyer and the seller are brought together by licensees working for the same brokerage firm.

INJUNCTION—A court order prohibiting someone from performing an act, or commanding performance of an act.

INSTALLMENT SALE—Under the federal income tax code, a sale in which less than 100% of the sales price is received in the year the sale takes place.

INSTRUMENT—A legal document, usually one that transfers title (such as a deed), creates a lien (such as a mortgage), or establishes a right to payment (such as a promissory note or contract).

INSURANCE, HAZARD—Insurance against damage to real property caused by fire, flood, theft, or other mishap. Also called casualty insurance.

INSURANCE, HOMEOWNER'S—Insurance against damage to a homeowner's real property and personal property.

INSURANCE, MORTGAGE—Insurance that protects a lender against losses resulting from the borrower's default.

INSURANCE, MUTUAL MORTGAGE—The mortgage insurance provided by the FHA to lenders who make loans through FHA programs.

INSURANCE, PRIVATE MORTGAGE (PMI)—Insurance provided by private companies to conventional lenders for loans with loan-to-value ratios over 80%.

INSURANCE, TITLE—Insurance that protects against losses resulting from undiscovered title defects. An owner's policy protects the buyer, while a lender's policy protects the lien position of the buyer's lender.

INSURANCE, TITLE, EXTENDED COVERAGE—Title insurance that covers problems that should be discovered by an inspection of the property (such as encroachments and adverse possession), in addition to the problems covered by standard coverage policies. Sometimes referred to as an ALTA (American Land Title Association) policy.

INSURANCE, TITLE, HOMEOWNER'S COVERAGE—Title insurance that is available only in residential one- to four-unit transactions; covers the same issues as an extended coverage policy, plus some additional issues.

INSURANCE, TITLE, STANDARD COVERAGE—Title insurance that protects against latent title defects (such as forged deeds) and undiscovered recorded encumbrances, but not against problems that would only be discovered by an inspection of the property.

INTEREST—1. A right or share in something (such as a piece of real estate). 2. A charge a borrower pays to a lender for the use of the lender's money.

INTEREST, COMPOUND—Interest computed on both the principal and the interest that has already accrued. *Compare:* Interest, Simple.

INTEREST, INTERIM—*See:* Interest, Prepaid.

INTEREST, PREPAID—Interest on a new loan that must be paid at the time of closing; covers the interest due for the first month of the loan term. Also called interim interest.

INTEREST, SIMPLE—Interest that is computed on the principal amount of the loan only, which is the type of interest charged in connection with real estate loans. *Compare:* Interest, Compound.

INVALID—Not legally binding or legally effective; not valid.

JOINT TENANCY—A form of co-ownership in which the co-owners have unity of time, title, interest, and possession, along with the right of survivorship. *Compare:* Tenancy in Common.

JUDGMENT—1. A court's binding determination of the rights and duties of the parties in a lawsuit. 2. A court order requiring one party to pay the other damages.

JUDGMENT, DEFICIENCY—A personal judgment entered against a borrower in favor of the lender if the proceeds from a foreclosure sale of the security property are not enough to pay off the debt.

JUDGMENT CREDITOR—A person who is owed money as a result of a judgment in a lawsuit.

JUDGMENT DEBTOR—A person who owes money as a result of a judgment in a lawsuit.

JUDGMENT LIEN—*See:* Lien, Judgment.

JUDICIAL FORECLOSURE—*See:* Foreclosure, Judicial.

KICKBACK—A fee paid for a referral (for example, to an appraiser or inspector). The Real Estate Settlement Procedures Act prohibits kickbacks in most residential mortgage loan transactions.

LAND CONTRACT—*See:* Contract, Land.

LANDLORD—A landowner who has leased his property to another (a tenant). Also called a lessor.

LATENT DEFECT—A defect that is not visible or apparent.

LAWFUL OBJECT—An objective or purpose of a contract that does not violate the law or a judicial determination of public policy.

LEASE—A conveyance of a leasehold estate from the fee owner to a tenant; a contract in which one party pays the other rent in exchange for the possession of real estate. Also called a rental agreement.

LEASEBACK—*See:* Sale-Leaseback.

LEGAL DESCRIPTION—A precise description of a parcel of real property that would enable a surveyor to locate its exact boundaries. It may be a lot and block description, a metes and bounds description, or a government survey description.

LENDER, INSTITUTIONAL—A bank, savings and loan, or similar organization that invests other people's funds in loans; as opposed to an individual or private lender, which invests its own funds.

LESSOR—A landlord.

LESSEE—A tenant.

LEVERAGE—The effective use of borrowed money to finance an investment such as real estate.

LEVY—To impose a tax.

LIABILITY—1. A debt or obligation. 2. Legal responsibility.

LIABILITY, JOINT AND SEVERAL—A form of liability in which two or more persons are responsible for a debt both individually and as a group.

LIABILITY, LIMITED—When a business investor is not personally liable for the debts of the business, as in the case of a limited partner or a corporate shareholder.

LIABILITY, VICARIOUS—A legal doctrine holding that a principal can be held liable for harm to third parties resulting from an agent's actions. (This rule usually does not apply to real estate agency relationships in Washington.)

LIABLE—Legally responsible.

LICENSE—1. Official permission to do a particular thing that the law does not allow everyone to do. 2. Revocable, non-assignable permission to use another person's land for a particular purpose. *Compare:* Easement.

LIEN—A nonpossessory interest in real property, giving the lienholder the right to foreclose if the owner doesn't pay a debt owed to the lienholder; a financial encumbrance on the owner's title.

LIEN, ATTACHMENT—A lien intended to prevent transfer of the property pending the outcome of litigation.

LIEN, CONSTRUCTION—A lien on property in favor of someone who provided labor or materials to improve the property. The term encompasses mechanic's liens and materialman's liens.

LIEN, EQUITABLE—A lien arising as a matter of fairness, rather than by agreement or by operation of law.

LIEN, GENERAL—A lien against all the property of a debtor, rather than a particular piece of her property. *Compare:* Lien, Specific.

LIEN, INVOLUNTARY—A lien that arises by operation of law, without the consent of the property owner. Also called a statutory lien.

LIEN, JUDGMENT—A general lien against a judgment debtor's property. The lien is created automatically in the county where the judgment was rendered and may be created in other counties by recording an abstract of judgment.

LIEN, MATERIALMAN'S—A construction lien in favor of someone who supplied materials for a project (as opposed to labor).

LIEN, MECHANIC'S—*See:* Lien, Construction.

LIEN, PROPERTY TAX—A specific lien on property to secure payment of property taxes.

LIEN, SPECIFIC—A lien that attaches only to a particular piece of property. *Compare:* Lien, General.

LIEN, STATUTORY—*See:* Lien, Involuntary.

LIEN, TAX—A lien on property to secure the payment of taxes.

LIEN, VOLUNTARY—A lien placed against property with the consent of the owner; a deed of trust or a mortgage.

LIENHOLDER, JUNIOR—A secured creditor whose lien is lower in priority than another's lien.

LIEN PRIORITY—The order in which liens are paid off out of the proceeds of a foreclosure sale.

LIMITED LIABILITY—*See:* Liability, Limited.

LIQUIDATED DAMAGES—*See:* Damages, Liquidated.

LIQUIDITY—The ability to convert an asset into cash quickly.

LISTING—A written agency contract between a seller and a real estate firm, stipulating that the firm will be paid a commission for finding (or attempting to find) a buyer for the seller's property. Also called a listing agreement.

LISTING AGENT—The agent who takes a listing on behalf of his firm, and thus represents the seller.

LISTING, EXCLUSIVE—Either an exclusive agency listing or an exclusive right to sell listing.

LISTING, EXCLUSIVE AGENCY—A listing agreement that entitles the brokerage firm to a commission if anyone other than the seller finds a buyer for the property during the listing term.

LISTING, EXCLUSIVE RIGHT TO SELL—A listing agreement that entitles the brokerage firm to a commission if anyone—including the seller—finds a buyer for the property during the listing term.

LISTING, MULTIPLE—A listing (usually an exclusive right to sell listing) that includes a provision allowing the brokerage firm to submit the listing to the multiple listing service for dissemination to cooperating licensees.

LISTING, NET—A listing agreement in which the seller sets a net amount he is willing to accept for the property; if the actual selling price exceeds that amount, the real estate firm is entitled to keep the excess as the commission.

LISTING, OPEN—A nonexclusive listing, given by a seller to as many real estate firms as she chooses. If the property is sold, a firm is entitled to a commission only if it was the procuring cause of the sale.

LOAN, AMORTIZED—A loan that requires regular installment payments of both principal and interest (as opposed to an interest-only loan). It is fully amortized if the installment payments will pay off the full amount of the principal and all of the interest by the end of the repayment period. It is partially amortized if the installment payments will cover only part of the principal, so that a balloon payment of the remaining principal balance is required at the end of the repayment period.

LOAN, CALLED—A loan that has been accelerated by the lender. *See:* Acceleration Clause.

LOAN, CARRYBACK—*See:* Loan, Purchase Money.

LOAN, CONFORMING—A loan made in accordance with the standardized underwriting criteria of Fannie Mae and Freddie Mac, and which therefore can be sold to those agencies.

LOAN, CONSTRUCTION—A loan to finance the cost of constructing a building, usually providing that the loan funds will be advanced in installments as the work progresses. Also called an interim loan.

LOAN, CONVENTIONAL—An institutional loan that is not insured or guaranteed by a government agency.

LOAN, FHA—A loan made by an institutional lender and insured by the Federal Housing Administration, so that the FHA will reimburse the lender for losses that result if the borrower defaults.

LOAN, FIXED-RATE—A loan on which the interest rate will remain the same throughout the entire loan term. *Compare:* Mortgage, Adjustable-rate.

LOAN, GUARANTEED—A loan in which a third party has agreed to reimburse the lender for losses that result if the borrower defaults.

LOAN, HOME EQUITY—A loan secured by the borrower's equity in a home that she already owns. *Compare:* Loan, Purchase Money.

LOAN, INTEREST-ONLY—A loan that requires the borrower to pay only the interest during the loan term, with the principal due at the end of the term.

LOAN, INTERIM—*See:* Loan, Construction.

LOAN, JUMBO—A conventional loan that exceeds the conforming loan limit; typically involves higher interest rate and fees and stricter underwriting standards.

LOAN, PARTICIPATION—A loan in which the lender receives some yield on the loan in addition to the interest, such as a percentage of the income generated by the property, or a share in the borrower's equity.

LOAN, PERMANENT—*See:* Loan, Take-out.

LOAN, PURCHASE MONEY—1. When a seller extends credit to a buyer to finance the purchase of the property, accepting a deed of trust or mortgage instead of cash. Sometimes called a carryback loan. 2. In a more general sense, any loan the borrower uses to buy the security property (as opposed to a loan secured by property the borrower already owns).

LOAN, SWING—A loan secured by a buyer's equity in his existing home and used to cover the downpayment and closing costs for the purchase of a new home. It will be paid off out of the proceeds when the old home eventually sells.

LOAN, TAKE-OUT—Long-term financing used to replace a construction loan (an interim loan) when construction has been completed. Also called a permanent loan.

LOAN, VA-GUARANTEED—A home loan made by an institutional lender to an eligible veteran and guaranteed by the Department of Veterans Affairs. The VA will reimburse the lender for losses if the borrower defaults.

LOAN CORRESPONDENT—An intermediary who arranges loans of an investor's money to borrowers, and then services the loans.

LOAN ESTIMATE—In a residential transaction subject to RESPA and/or the Truth in Lending Act, a form that the lender must give to the buyer (the loan applicant), providing detailed information about the loan and estimates of the closing costs.

LOAN FEE—A loan origination fee, an assumption fee, or discount points.

LOAN-LEVEL PRICE ADJUSTMENT (LLPA)—A risk-based loan fee that varies depending on the borrower's credit score and the loan-to-value ratio (or on certain other factors that affect risk); charged on some conventional conforming loans.

LOAN-TO-VALUE RATIO (LTV)—The relationship between the loan amount and either the sales price or the appraised value of the property (whichever is less), expressed as a percentage.

LOAN WORKOUT—An alternative to foreclosure in which a lender agrees to a new payment plan for a loan, or to reduction of the loan's interest rate or principal amount.

LTV—*See:* Loan-to-Value Ratio.

MAJORITY, AGE OF—The age at which a person becomes legally competent; in Washington, 18 years old. *See also:* Minor.

MAKER—The person who signs a promissory note, promising to repay a debt. *Compare:* Payee.

MANAGING BROKER—A licensed individual with at least three years' experience as a broker who has passed the managing broker exam; a managing broker performs brokerage services for a firm, under the supervision of a designated broker.

MARGIN—In an adjustable-rate mortgage, the difference between the index rate and the interest rate charged to the borrower.

MARKETABLE TITLE—*See:* Title, Marketable.

MARKET DATA APPROACH—*See:* Sales Comparison Approach to Value.

MARKET PRICE—1. The current price generally being charged for something in the marketplace. 2. The price actually paid for a property. *Compare:* Value, Market.

MATERIAL FACT—Information that has a substantial negative impact on the value of the property, on a party's ability to perform, or on the purpose of the transaction.

MATURITY DATE—The date by which a loan is supposed to be paid off in full.

MEETING OF MINDS—*See:* Mutual Consent.

MINOR—A person who has not yet reached the age of majority; in Washington, a person under 18.

MIP—Mortgage insurance premium; especially a premium charged in connection with an FHA-insured loan.

MISREPRESENTATION—A false or misleading statement. *See:* Fraud.

MLS—*See:* Multiple Listing Service.

MONOPOLY—When a single entity or group has exclusive control over the production or sale of a product or service.

MORTGAGE—1. An instrument that creates a voluntary lien on real property to secure repayment of a debt, and which (unlike a deed of trust) ordinarily does not include a power of sale, so it can only be foreclosed judicially; the parties are the mortgagor (borrower) and mortgagee (lender). 2. The term is often used more generally, to refer to either a mortgage or a deed of trust—i.e., to any loan secured by real property. *Note: If you do not find the specific term you are looking for here under "Mortgage," check the entries under "Loan."*

MORTGAGE, ADJUSTABLE-RATE (ARM)—A loan in which the interest rate is periodically increased or decreased to reflect changes in the cost of money. *Compare:* Loan, Fixed-Rate.

MORTGAGE, BALLOON—A partially amortized mortgage loan that requires a large balloon payment at the end of the loan term.

MORTGAGE, BLANKET—A mortgage that is a lien against more than one parcel of property.

MORTGAGE, BUDGET—A loan in which the monthly payments include a share of the property taxes and insurance, in addition to principal and interest; the lender places the money for taxes and insurance in an impound account.

MORTGAGE, CLOSED—A loan that cannot be paid off early.

MORTGAGE, DIRECT REDUCTION—A loan that requires a fixed amount of principal to be paid in each payment; the total payment becomes steadily smaller, because the interest portion becomes smaller with each payment as the principal balance decreases.

MORTGAGE, FIRST—The mortgage on a property that has first lien position; the one with higher lien priority than any other mortgage against the property.

Mortgage, Hard Money—A mortgage given to a lender in exchange for cash, as opposed to one given in exchange for credit.

Mortgage, Junior—A mortgage that has lower lien priority than another mortgage against the same property. Sometimes called a secondary mortgage.

Mortgage, Level Payment—An amortized loan with payments that are the same amount each month, although the portion of the payment that is applied to principal steadily increases and the portion of the payment applied to interest steadily decreases. *See:* Loan, Amortized.

Mortgage, Open-End—A loan that permits the borrower to reborrow money he has repaid on the principal, usually up to the original loan amount, without executing a new loan agreement.

Mortgage, Package—A mortgage that is secured by certain items of personal property (such as appliances) in addition to the real property.

Mortgage, Satisfaction of—The document a mortgagee gives the mortgagor when the mortgage debt has been paid in full, acknowledging that the debt has been paid and the mortgage is no longer a lien against the property.

Mortgage, Secondary—*See:* Mortgage, Junior.

Mortgage, Senior—A mortgage that has higher lien priority than another mortgage against the same property; the opposite of a junior mortgage.

Mortgage, Wraparound—A purchase money loan arrangement in which the seller uses part of the buyer's payments to make the payments on an existing loan (called the underlying loan); the buyer takes title subject to the underlying loan, but does not assume it. When the security instrument used for wraparound financing is a deed of trust instead of a mortgage, it may be referred to as an all-inclusive trust deed.

Mortgage Banker—An intermediary who originates real estate loans.

Mortgage Broker—An intermediary who brings real estate lenders and borrowers together and negotiates loan agreements between them.

Mortgage Broker Practices Act—A state law that regulates the mortgage broker business and contains provisions intended to help prevent fraudulent lending practices.

Mortgage Company—A type of real estate lender that originates and services loans on behalf of large investors (acting as a mortgage banker) or for resale on the secondary mortgage market.

Mortgage Loan—Any loan secured by real property, whether the actual security instrument used is a mortgage or a deed of trust.

Mortgagee—A lender who accepts a mortgage as security for repayment of the loan.

Mortgaging Clause—A clause in a mortgage that describes the security interest given to the mortgagee.

Mortgagor—A property owner (usually a borrower) who gives a mortgage to another (usually a lender) as security for payment of an obligation.

Multiple Listing Service (MLS)—An organization of real estate firms and licensees who share their exclusive listings.

Mutual Consent—When all parties freely agree to the terms of a contract, without fraud, undue influence, duress, menace, or mistake. Mutual consent is achieved through offer and acceptance; it is sometimes referred to as a "meeting of the minds."

NAR—National Association of REALTORS.®

National Market—*See:* Secondary Mortgage Market.

National Environmental Policy Act—A federal law requiring federal agencies to provide an environmental impact statement for agency actions that will have a significant effect on the environment.

Negligence—Conduct that falls below the standard of care that a reasonable person would exercise under the circumstances; carelessness or recklessness.

Negotiable Instrument—An instrument containing an unconditional promise to pay a certain sum of money, to order or to bearer, on demand or at a particular time. It can be a check, promissory note, bond, draft, or stock.

NEPA—See: National Environmental Policy Act.

Net Income—*See:* Income, Net.

Net Listing—*See:* Listing, Net.

Net Worth—An individual's financial assets minus her liabilities.

Nominal Interest Rate—The interest rate stated in a promissory note. Also called the note rate or coupon rate. *Compare:* Annual Percentage Rate.

Nonconforming Loan—*See:* Loan, Conforming.

NORMAL MARKET CONDITIONS—A sale taking place in a competitive and open market, with informed parties acting prudently, and at arm's length, without undue stimulus (such as an urgent need to sell the property immediately)

NOTARIZE—To have a document certified by a notary public.

NOTARY PUBLIC—Someone who is officially authorized to witness and certify the acknowledgment made by someone signing a legal document.

NOTE—*See:* Note, Promissory.

NOTE, DEMAND—A promissory note that is due whenever the holder of the note demands payment.

NOTE, INSTALLMENT—A promissory note that calls for regular payments of principal and interest until the debt is fully paid.

NOTE, JOINT—A promissory note signed by two or more persons with equal liability for payment.

NOTE, PROMISSORY—A written promise to repay a debt; it may or may not be a negotiable instrument.

NOTE, STRAIGHT—A promissory note that calls for regular payments of interest only, so that the entire principal amount is due in one lump sum at the end of the loan term.

NOTICE, ACTUAL—Actual knowledge of a fact, as opposed to knowledge imputed by law (constructive notice).

NOTICE, CONSTRUCTIVE—Knowledge of a fact imputed to a person by law. A person is held to have constructive notice of something when she should have known it (because she could have learned it through reasonable diligence or an inspection of the public record), even if she did not actually know it.

NOTICE OF DEFAULT—A notice sent by a secured creditor to the debtor, informing the debtor that he has breached the loan agreement.

NOTICE OF SALE—A notice stating that foreclosure proceedings have been commenced against a property.

NOVATION—1. When one party to a contract withdraws and a new party is substituted, relieving the withdrawing party of liability. 2. The substitution of a new obligation for an old one.

OFFER—When one person (the offeror) proposes a contract to another (the offeree); if the offeree accepts the offer, a binding contract is formed.

OFFER, TENDER—*See:* Tender.

OFFEREE—One to whom a contract offer is made.

OFFEROR—One who makes a contract offer.

OFFICER—In a corporation, an executive authorized by the board of directors to manage the business of the corporation.

OFF-SITE IMPROVEMENTS—Improvements that add to the usefulness of a site but are not located directly on it, such as curbs, street lights, and sidewalks.

ONE-TIME AGENCY AGREEMENT—An agreement entered into by a FSBO seller and a buyer's agent: the seller agrees to compensate the agent for bringing him a particular buyer.

OPEN HOUSE—Showing a listed home to the public for a specified period of time.

OPTION—A contract giving one party the right to do something, without obligating her to do it.

OPTIONEE—The person to whom an option is given.

OPTIONOR—The person who gives an option.

OPTION TO PURCHASE—An option giving the optionee the right to buy property owned by the optionor at an agreed price during a specified period.

ORDINANCE—A law passed by a local legislative body, such as a city or county council. *Compare:* Statute.

ORIENTATION—The placement of a house on its lot, with regard to its exposure to the sun and wind, privacy from the street, and protection from outside noise.

ORIGINATION FEE—A fee that a lender charges a borrower upon making a new loan, to cover the administrative costs of making the loan. Also called a loan fee or points.

"OR MORE"—A provision in a promissory note that allows the borrower to prepay the debt.

OWNERSHIP—Title to property, dominion over property; the rights of possession and control.

OWNERSHIP, CONCURRENT—When two or more individuals share ownership of one piece of property, each owning an undivided interest in the property (as in a tenancy in common or joint tenancy, or with community property). Also called co-ownership or co-tenancy.

OWNERSHIP IN SEVERALTY—Ownership by a single individual.

PANIC SELLING—*See:* Blockbusting.

PARCEL—A lot or piece of real estate, especially a specified part of a larger tract.

PARTIAL RECONVEYANCE—The instrument given to the borrower when part of the security property is released from a blanket deed of trust under a partial release clause.

PARTIAL RELEASE CLAUSE—*See:* Release Clause.

PARTIAL SATISFACTION—The instrument given to the borrower when part of the security property is released from a blanket mortgage under a partial release clause.

PARTNER, GENERAL—A partner who has the authority to manage and contract for a general or limited partnership, and who is personally liable for the partnership's debts.

PARTNER, LIMITED—A partner in a limited partnership who typically is merely an investor and does not participate in the management of the business. A limited partner is not personally liable for the partnership's debts.

PARTNERSHIP—An association of two or more persons to carry on a business for profit. The law regards a partnership as a group of individuals, not as an entity separate from its owners. *Compare:* Corporation.

PARTNERSHIP, GENERAL—A partnership in which each member has an equal right to manage the business and share in the profits, as well as equal responsibility for the partnership's debts.

PARTNERSHIP, LIMITED—A partnership made up of one or more general partners and one or more limited partners.

PARTNERSHIP PROPERTY—All property that partners bring into their business at the outset or later acquire for their business.

PAYEE—In a promissory note, the party who is entitled to be paid; the lender. *Compare:* Maker.

PERSONAL PROPERTY—Any property that is not real property; movable property not affixed to land. Also called chattels or personalty.

PHYSICAL DETERIORATION—Loss in value (depreciation) resulting from wear and tear or deferred maintenance.

PLAINTIFF—The party who brings or starts a civil lawsuit; the one who sues.

PMI—*See:* Insurance, Private Mortgage.

POINT—One percent of the principal amount of a loan.

POINTS—*See:* Discount Points; Origination Fee.

PORTFOLIO—The mix of investments owned by an individual or company.

POSSESSION—1. The holding and enjoyment of property. 2. Actual physical occupation of real property.

POWER OF ATTORNEY—An instrument authorizing one person (the attorney in fact) to act as another's agent, to the extent stated in the instrument.

POWER OF SALE CLAUSE—A clause in a deed of trust giving the trustee the right to foreclose nonjudicially (sell the debtor's property without a court action) if the borrower defaults.

PREAPPROVAL—When a lender determines how large a loan a buyer is qualified for in advance, before the buyer begins looking at specific properties.

PREDATORY LENDING—Deceitful lending practices used by lenders and mortgage brokers to take advantage of unsophisticated borrowers.

PREPAYMENT—Paying off part or all of a loan before payment is due.

PREPAYMENT PENALTY—A penalty charged to a borrower who prepays.

PREPAYMENT PRIVILEGE—A provision in a promissory note allowing the borrower to prepay.

PREVENTIVE MAINTENANCE—A program of regular inspection and care of a property and its fixtures, allowing the prevention of potential problems or their immediate repair.

PRICE FIXING—The cooperative setting of prices by competing firms. Price fixing is an automatic violation of antitrust laws.

PRIMARY MORTGAGE MARKET—The market in which mortgage loans are originated, where lenders make loans to borrowers. *Compare:* Secondary Mortgage Market.

PRINCIPAL—1. One who grants another person (an agent) authority to represent him in dealings with third parties. 2. One of the parties to a transaction (such as a buyer or seller), as opposed to those who are involved as agents or employees (such as a real estate or escrow agent). 3. In regard to a loan, the amount originally borrowed, as opposed to the interest.

Procuring Cause—The real estate agent who is primarily responsible for bringing about a sale; for example, by negotiating the agreement between the buyer and seller.

Profit—A nonpossessory interest; the right to enter another person's land and take something (such as timber or minerals) away from it.

Promisee—Someone who has been promised something; someone who is supposed to receive the benefit of a contractual promise.

Promisor—Someone who has made a contractual promise to another.

Promissory Note—*See:* Note, Promissory.

Property—1. The rights of ownership in a thing, such as the right to use, possess, transfer, or encumber it. 2. Something that is owned.

Property Tax—*See:* Tax, Property.

Proprietorship, Individual or Sole—A business owned and operated by one person.

Proration—The process of dividing or allocating something (especially a sum of money or an expense) proportionately, according to time, interest, or benefit.

Public Record—The official collection of legal documents that individuals have filed with the county recorder in order to make public the information contained in the documents.

Puffing—Statements of exaggerated praise for a property that should not be considered assertions of fact.

Purchase and Sale Agreement—A contract in which a seller promises to convey title to real property to a buyer in exchange for the purchase price. Also called an earnest money agreement, deposit receipt, sales contract, or contract of sale.

Qualifying Standards—The standards a lender requires a loan applicant to meet before a loan will be approved. Also called underwriting standards.

Quitclaim Deed—*See*: Deed, Quitclaim.

Radon—A naturally occurring carcinogenic gas formed in the earth's crust that can enter buildings through cracks in the foundation.

Ratify—To confirm or approve after the fact an act that was not authorized when it was performed.

Real Estate—*See:* Real Property.

REAL ESTATE BROKERAGE FIRM—A business entity that offers real estate brokerage services; it is licensed by the Department of Licensing and must have a designated broker who represent its interests. Also known as a real estate firm.

REAL ESTATE BROKERAGE RELATIONSHIPS ACT—A Washington state law that governs when and how real estate agency relationships are created and terminated, the duties owed by real estate licensees to the parties to a real estate transaction, and when and how agency disclosures are to be made.

REAL ESTATE COMMISSION—A commission appointed by the Governor, consisting of the Director of the Department of Licensing and six commissioners; responsible for preparing and conducting the real estate licensing examinations.

REAL ESTATE CONTRACT—1. A purchase and sale agreement. 2. A land contract. 3. Any contract having to do with real property.

REAL ESTATE FIRM—*See:* Real Estate Brokerage.

REAL ESTATE INVESTMENT SYNDICATE—A group of people or companies who join together to purchase and develop a piece of real estate.

REAL ESTATE INVESTMENT TRUST (REIT)—A real estate investment business with at least 100 investors, organized as a trust and entitled to special tax treatment under IRS rules.

REAL ESTATE SETTLEMENT PROCEDURES ACT—*See:* RESPA.

REAL PROPERTY—Land and everything attached or appurtenant to it. Also called realty or real estate. *Compare:* Personal Property.

REALTOR—A real estate agent who is an active member of a state and local real estate board that is affiliated with the National Association of REALTORS.®

REALTY—*See:* Real Property.

RECONCILIATION—The final step in an appraisal, when the appraiser assembles and interprets the data in order to arrive at a final value estimate.

RECONVEYANCE—Releasing the security property from the lien created by a deed of trust, by recording a deed of reconveyance.

RECORDING—Filing a document at the county recorder's office, so that it will be placed in the public record.

REDEMPTION—1. When a defaulting borrower prevents foreclosure by paying the full amount of the debt, plus costs. 2. When a mortgagor regains the property after foreclosure by paying whatever the foreclosure sale purchaser paid for it, plus interest and expenses.

REDLINING—When a lender refuses to make loans secured by property in a certain neighborhood because of the racial or ethnic composition of the neighborhood.

REFINANCING—When a homeowner takes out a new loan—usually to take advantage of lower interest rates—and uses the loan proceeds to pay off the existing loan.

REDUCTION CERTIFICATE—A signed statement from a lender certifying the present balance on the loan, the rate of interest, and the maturity date. A form of estoppel certificate.

REFORMATION—A legal action to correct a mistake, such as a typographical error, in a deed or other document. The court will order the execution of a correction deed.

REGULATION Z—The federal regulation that implements the Truth in Lending Act.

REINSTATE—To prevent foreclosure by curing the default.

RELEASE—1. To give up a legal right. 2. A document in which a legal right is given up.

RELEASE CLAUSE—1. A clause in a blanket mortgage or deed of trust which allows the borrower to get part of the security property released from the lien when a certain portion of the debt has been paid or other conditions are fulfilled. Often called a partial release clause. 2. A clause in a land contract providing for a deed to a portion of the land to be delivered when a certain portion of the contract price has been paid. Also known as a deed release provision.

RENT—Compensation paid by a tenant to the landlord in exchange for the possession and use of the property.

REPLACEMENT COST—*See:* Cost, Replacement.

REPRODUCTION COST—*See:* Cost, Reproduction.

RESCISSION—When a contract is terminated and each party gives anything acquired under the contract back to the other party. (The verb form is rescind.) *Compare:* Cancellation.

RESERVE ACCOUNT—*See:* Impound Account.

RESERVE REQUIREMENTS—The percentage of deposits commercial banks must keep on reserve with the Federal Reserve Bank.

RESERVES FOR REPLACEMENT—Regular allowances set aside by an investment property owner, a business, or a homeowners association to pay for the replacement of structures and equipment that are expected to wear out.

RESPA—The Real Estate Settlement Procedures Act; a federal law that requires lenders to disclose certain information about closing costs to loan applicants.

RESTITUTION—Restoring something (especially money) of which a person was unjustly deprived.

RESTRICTION—A limitation on the use of real property.

RESTRICTION, DEED—A restrictive covenant in a deed.

RESTRICTION, PRIVATE—A restriction imposed on property by a previous owner, a neighbor, or the subdivision developer; a restrictive covenant or a condition in a deed.

RESTRICTION, PUBLIC—A law or regulation limiting or regulating the use of real property.

RESTRICTIVE COVENANT—*See:* Covenant, Restrictive.

RISK ANALYSIS—*See:* Underwriting.

SAFETY CLAUSE—*See:* Extender Clause.

SALE-LEASEBACK—A form of real estate financing in which the owner of industrial or commercial property sells the property and leases it back from the buyer. In addition to certain tax advantages, the seller/lessee obtains more cash through the sale than would normally be possible by borrowing and mortgaging the property, since lenders will not often lend 100% of the value.

SALES COMPARISON APPROACH TO VALUE—One of the three main methods of appraisal, in which the sales prices of comparable properties are used to estimate the value of the subject property. Also called the market data approach.

SATISFACTION OF MORTGAGE—*See:* Mortgage, Satisfaction of.

SECONDARY FINANCING—Money borrowed to pay part of the required downpayment or closing costs for a first loan, when the second loan is secured by the same property that secures the first loan.

SECONDARY MORTGAGE MARKET—The market in which investors (including Fannie Mae, Freddie Mac, and Ginnie Mae) purchase real estate loans from lenders.

SECRET PROFIT—A financial benefit that an agent takes from a transaction without informing the principal.

SECURITY INSTRUMENT—A document that creates a voluntary lien to secure repayment of a loan; for debts secured by real property, it is either a mortgage or a deed of trust.

Security Interest—The interest a creditor may acquire in the debtor's property to ensure that the debt will be paid.

Security Property—The property against which a borrower gives a lender a voluntary lien, so that the lender can foreclose if the borrower defaults on the loan. It may or may not have been purchased with the loan proceeds.

Selling Agent—The agent responsible for procuring a buyer for real estate; may represent either the seller or the buyer.

SEPA—*See:* State Environmental Policy Act.

Separate Property—Property owned by a married person that is not community property; includes property acquired before marriage or by gift or inheritance after marriage.

Settlement—1. An agreement between the parties to a civil lawsuit, in which the plaintiff agrees to drop the suit in exchange for money or the defendant's promise to do or refrain from doing something. 2. Closing.

Settlement Statement—A document that presents a final, detailed accounting for a real estate transaction, listing each party's debits and credits and the amount each will receive or be required to pay at closing. Also called a closing statement.

Severalty—*See:* Ownership in Severalty.

Shareholder—An individual who holds ownership shares (shares of stock) in a corporation, and has limited liability in regard to the corporation's debts. Also called a stockholder.

Sheriff's Deed—*See*: Deed, Sheriff's.

Sheriff's Sale—A foreclosure sale held after a judicial foreclosure. Sometimes called an execution sale.

Sherman Act—A federal antitrust law prohibiting any agreement that has the effect of an unreasonable restraint of trade, such as price fixing and tie-in arrangements.

Shoreline Management Act—A Washington state law that regulates development within 200 feet of the shoreline of the ocean and larger lakes and rivers.

Short Sale—Selling a home for less than the amount owed, with the lender's consent. The lender receives the sale proceeds and, typically, releases the borrower from the remaining debt.

SPECIAL ASSESSMENT—A tax levied only against the properties that have benefited from a public improvement (such as a sewer or a street light), to cover the cost of the improvement; creates a special assessment lien. Also called an improvement tax.

SPECIAL WARRANTY DEED—*See*: Deed, Special Warranty.

SPECIFIC PERFORMANCE—A legal remedy in which a court orders someone who has breached to actually perform the contract as agreed, rather than simply paying money damages.

STABLE MONTHLY INCOME—A loan applicant's gross monthly income that meets the lender's tests of quality and durability.

STATE ENVIRONMENTAL POLICY ACT—A Washington state law (similar to the federal National Environmental Policy Act) that may require an environmental impact statement for a private development project or for a state or local governmental action.

STATUTE—A law enacted by a state legislature or the U.S. Congress. *Compare:* Ordinance.

STATUTE OF FRAUDS—A law that requires certain types of contracts to be in writing and signed in order to be enforceable.

STATUTE OF LIMITATIONS—A law requiring a particular type of lawsuit to be filed within a specified time after the event giving rise to the suit occurred.

STEERING—Channeling prospective buyers or tenants to or away from particular neighborhoods based on race, religion, national origin, or other protected classes.

STOCKHOLDER—*See:* Shareholder.

SUBCONTRACTOR—A contractor who, at the request of the general contractor, provides a specific service, such as plumbing or drywalling, in connection with the overall construction project.

SUBJECT TO—When a purchaser takes property subject to a trust deed or mortgage, he is not personally liable for paying off the loan; in case of default, however, the property can still be foreclosed on.

SUBLEASE—When a tenant grants someone else the right to possession of the leased property for part of the remainder of the lease term; as opposed to a lease assignment, where the tenant gives up possession for the entire reminder of the lease term. Also called a sandwich lease. *Compare:* Assignment.

SUBORDINATION CLAUSE—A provision in a mortgage or deed of trust that permits a later mortgage or deed of trust to have higher lien priority than the one containing the clause.

SUBPRIME LENDING—Making riskier loans to borrowers who are otherwise unable to qualify for a loan, often charging higher interest rates and fees to make up for the increased risk.

SUBROGATION—The substitution of one person in the place of another with reference to a lawful claim or right. For instance, a title company that pays a claim on behalf of its insured, the property owner, is subrogated to any claim the owner successfully undertakes against the former owner.

SUBSTITUTION OF LIABILITY—A buyer wishing to assume an existing loan may apply for the lender's approval; once approved, the buyer assumes liability for repayment of the loan, and the original borrower (the seller) is released from liability.

SURVEY—The process of precisely measuring the boundaries and determining the area of a parcel of land.

SYNDICATE—An association formed to operate an investment business. A syndicate is not a specific type of recognized legal entity; it can be organized as a corporation, limited liability company, partnership, or trust.

TAX, AD VALOREM—A tax assessed on the value of property.

TAX, EXCISE—A state tax levied on every sale of real estate, to be paid by the seller.

TAX, GENERAL REAL ESTATE—An annual ad valorem tax levied on real property.

TAX, IMPROVEMENT—*See:* Special Assessment.

TAX, PROPERTY—1. The general real estate tax. 2. Any ad valorem tax levied on real or personal property.

TAX DEED—*See:* Deed, Tax.

TAX SALE—Sale of property after foreclosure of a tax lien.

TENANCY IN COMMON—A form of concurrent ownership in which two or more persons each have an undivided interest in the entire property, but no right of survivorship. *Compare:* Joint Tenancy.

TENANT—Someone in lawful possession of real property; especially, someone who has leased the property from the owner (also called a lessee).

TENDER—An unconditional offer by one of the parties to a contract to perform her part of the agreement; made when the offeror believes the other party is breaching, it establishes the offeror's right to sue if the other party doesn't accept it. Also called a tender offer.

TERM—A prescribed period of time; especially, the length of time a borrower has to pay off a loan, or the duration of a lease.

THIRD PARTY—1. A person seeking to deal with a principal through an agent. 2. In a transaction, someone who is not one of the principals.

TIE-IN ARRANGEMENT—An agreement to sell one product, only on the condition that the buyer also purchases a different product. This is an antitrust violation.

TIGHT MONEY MARKET—When loan funds are scarce, leading lenders to charge high interest rates and discount points.

TILA—*See:* Truth in Lending Act.

TIME IS OF THE ESSENCE—A clause in a contract that means performance on the exact dates specified is an essential element of the contract; failure to perform on time is a material breach.

TITLE—Lawful ownership of real property. Also, the deed or other document that is evidence of that ownership.

TITLE, ABSTRACT OF—A brief, chronological summary of the recorded documents affecting title to a particular piece of real property.

TITLE, AFTER-ACQUIRED—A rule applicable to warranty deeds; if the title is defective at the time of transfer, but the grantor later acquires more perfect title, the additional interest passes to the grantee automatically.

TITLE, CHAIN OF—1. The chain of deeds (and other documents) transferring title to a piece of property from one owner to the next, as disclosed in the public record. 2. A listing of all recorded documents affecting title to a particular property; more complete than an abstract.

TITLE, CLEAR—A good title to property, free from encumbrances or defects; marketable title.

TITLE, EQUITABLE—The vendee's interest in property under a land contract. Also called an equitable interest.

TITLE, LEGAL—The vendor's interest in property under a land contract.

TITLE, MARKETABLE—Title free and clear of objectionable liens, encumbrances, or defects, so that a reasonably prudent person with full knowledge of the facts would not hesitate to purchase the property.

TITLE COMPANY—A title insurance company.

TITLE INSURANCE—*See:* Insurance, Title.

TITLE REPORT, PRELIMINARY—A report issued by a title company, disclosing the condition of the title to a specific piece of property, before the actual title insurance policy is issued.

TITLE SEARCH—An inspection of the public record to determine all rights and encumbrances affecting title to a piece of property.

TOPOGRAPHY—The contours of the surface of the land (level, hilly, steep, etc.).

TORT—A breach of a duty imposed by law (as opposed to a duty voluntarily taken on in a contract) that causes harm to another person, giving the injured person the right to sue the one who breached the duty. Also called a civil wrong (in contrast to a criminal wrong, a crime).

TRACT—1. A piece of land of undefined size. 2. In the rectangular survey system, an area made up of 16 townships; 24 miles on each side.

TRUST—A legal arrangement in which title to property (or funds) is vested in one or more trustees, who manage the property on behalf of the trust's beneficiaries, in accordance with instructions set forth in the document establishing the trust.

TRUST ACCOUNT—A bank account maintained by a brokerage for depositing client funds. Most trust accounts must be interest-bearing, with the exception of trust accounts for property management funds.

TRUST DEED—*See:* Deed of Trust.

TRUST FUNDS—Money or things of value received by an agent, not belonging to the agent but being held for the benefit of others.

TRUSTEE—1. A person appointed to manage a trust on behalf of the beneficiaries. 2. A neutral third party appointed in a deed of trust to handle the nonjudicial foreclosure process in case of default.

TRUSTEE IN BANKRUPTCY—An individual appointed by the court to handle the assets of a person in bankruptcy.

TRUSTEE'S DEED—*See*: Deed, Trustee's.

TRUSTEE'S SALE—A nonjudicial foreclosure sale under a deed of trust.

TRUSTOR—The borrower in a deed of trust. Also called the grantor.

TRUTH IN LENDING ACT—A federal law that requires lenders and credit arrangers to make disclosures concerning loan costs to consumer loan applicants.

UNDERWRITING—In real estate lending, the process of evaluating a loan application to determine the probability that the applicant would repay the loan, and matching the risk to an appropriate rate of return. Sometimes called risk analysis.

UNDUE INFLUENCE—Exerting excessive pressure on someone so as to overpower the person's free will and prevent him from making a rational or prudent decision; often involves abusing a relationship of trust.

UNENFORCEABLE—*See:* Contract, Unenforceable.

UNILATERAL CONTRACT—*See:* Contract, Unilateral.

UNJUST ENRICHMENT—An undeserved benefit; a court generally will not allow a remedy (such as forfeiture of a land contract) if it would result in the unjust enrichment of one of the parties.

UREA FORMALDEHYDE—A toxic substance found in adhesives used in pressed wood building products.

USURY—Charging an interest rate that exceeds legal limits.

VA—Department of Veterans Affairs (formerly the Veterans Administration).

VACANCY FACTOR—A percentage deducted from a property's potential gross income to determine the effective gross income, estimating the income that will probably be lost because of vacancies and tenants who don't pay.

VALID—The legal classification of a contract that is binding and enforceable in a court of law.

VALUABLE CONSIDERATION—*See:* Consideration.

VALUATION—*See:* Appraisal.

VALUE—The present worth of future benefits.

VALUE, ASSESSED—The value placed on property by the taxing authority (the county assessor, for example) for the purposes of taxation.

VALUE, FACE—The value of an instrument, such as a promissory note or a security, that is indicated on the face of the instrument itself.

VALUE, MARKET—The most probable price which a property should bring in a competitive and open market under all conditions requisite to a fair sale, the buyer and seller each acting prudently and knowledgeably, and assuming the price is not affected by undue stimulus. (This is the definition used by Fannie Mae and Freddie Mac.) Market value is also called fair market value, value in exchange, or objective value. *Compare:* Market Price.

VALUE, SUBJECTIVE—The value of a property in the eyes of a particular person, as opposed to its market value (objective value).

VALUE, UTILITY—The value of a property to its owner or to a user. (A form of subjective value.) Also called value in use.

VALUE IN EXCHANGE—*See:* Value, Market.

VALUE IN USE—*See:* Value, Utility.

VENDEE—A buyer or purchaser; particularly, someone buying property under a land contract.

VENDOR—A seller; particularly, someone selling property by means of a land contract.

VERIFY—1. To confirm or substantiate. 2. To confirm under oath.

VOID—Having no legal force or effect.

VOIDABLE—*See:* Contract, Voidable.

WAIVER—The voluntary relinquishment or surrender of a right.

WARRANTY, IMPLIED—In a sale or lease of property, a guarantee created by operation of law, whether or not the seller or landlord intended to offer it.

WARRANTY DEED—*See:* Deed, Warranty.

WASHINGTON LAW AGAINST DISCRIMINATION—A state law that is broader than the federal Fair Housing Act; it prohibits discrimination in all real estate transactions (not just residential transactions) on the basis of race, creed, color, national origin, sex, sexual orientation, gender identity, marital status, familial status, mental or physical disability, military or veteran status, or use of a trained guide dog or service animal.

WASTE—Destruction, damage, or material alteration of property by someone in possession who holds less than a fee estate (such as a life tenant or lessee), or by a co-owner.

WRAPAROUND FINANCING—*See:* Mortgage, Wraparound.

YIELD—The return of profit to an investor on an investment, stated as a percentage of the amount invested.

ZONE—An area of land designated for a particular use, such as agricultural, residential, industrial, or commercial.

ZONING—Government regulation of the uses of property within specified areas.

INDEX

*A boldface page number indicates the page on which the form itself appears (or begins), as opposed
to pages on which the form is discussed.*

(continued)